Prabhupāda
Nectar

Prabhupāda Nectar

Anecdotes from the Life
of
His Divine Grace
A.C. Bhaktivedanta Swami
Prabhupāda
Founder-*Ācārya* of the International Society
for Krishna Consciousness

Satsvarūpa dāsa Goswami

GN Press, Inc.

Persons interested in the subject matter of this book are invited to correspond with our secretary, c/o Gītā-nagarī Press, Inc., P.O. Box 445, La Crosse, FL 32658 or visit our web site at www.gnpress.org.

GN Press gratefully acknowledges the BBT for the use of verses and purports from Śrīla Prabhupāda's books.

Library of Congress Cataloging in Publication Data

Gosvāmī, Satsvarūpa dāsa
Prabhupāda Nectar: Anecdotes from the life of His Divine Grace A.C. Bhaktivedanta Swami Prabhupāda/ Satsvarūpa dāsa Goswami.
p. cm.
ISBN 0-912233-62-8
1. A.C. Bhaktivedanta Swami Prabhupāda, 1896–1977—Anecdotes. 2. International Society for Krishna Consciousenss—Anecdotes. I. Title.
BL1285.892.A28G683 1995
294.5'512'092—dc20
[B] 95–23258
CIP

Cover illustration—Original pencil drawing by James Record (1958–1996). James met Śrīla Prabhupāda in 1976. Deeply absorbed in meditation on Śrīla Prabhupāda, he left this unfinished drawing at the time of his passing. We are honored to present James Record's art in this edition of *Prabhupāda Nectar*.

PREFACE TO THE FIRST EDITION

The six-volume biography *Śrīla Prabhupāda-līlāmṛta* did not by any means exhaust the stock of stories, reflections, praises, and quotations that may be usefully gathered and printed about His Divine Grace A. C. Bhaktivedanta Swami Prabhupāda. As one cannot exhaust the glories of the infinite Personality of Godhead, similarly one cannot come to the end of worthy descriptions of His pure devotees. If there is a limit, it is only in the recollective powers of his followers, or in the size of the audience capable of relishing the transcendental topics of Kṛṣṇa and His eternal associates.

In the *Śrīla Prabhupāda-līlāmṛta,* as well as its poetical synopsis, *Remembering Śrīla Prabhupāda,* I mostly confined myself to the chronological sequence of main events in Prabhupāda's life. But there is much more. Let us open the floodgates. The only restrictions now are authenticity of the anecdotes, considerations of etiquette, and the desire to present the stories and meditations in a readable, literary form. Otherwise, all Prabhupāda-*kathā* is beneficial for the hearer, and capable of producing transcendental bliss.

We therefore present the first small volume of *Prabhupāda Nectar* and hope it will be followed frequently with further collections. Our search to gather true Prabhupāda nectar is ongoing and very much dependent on others. The anecdotes and realizations are gathered from disciples and friends of Śrīla Prabhupāda, so we request all readers who know of any unpublished incidents about Prabhupāda to kindly grant us an interview or send us notes of your recollections. Within this poor world there are relatively few reservoirs of Prabhupāda memories, and so we repeatedly request such fortunate persons to be kind upon thousands of readers now and in the future by contributing their memories to *Prabhupāda Nectar.* Even if one is planning to write his own memoirs in his old age, that should not rule out giving an interview for use in this series.

Better it be recorded as soon as possible, before it disappears through time's deterioration.

I have not attempted to compile the *Prabhupāda Nectar* in encyclopedia form by rigidly grouping the entries under numerous categories. In the telling we have chosen to intersperse the different kinds of material, providing more variety for reading, and resembling more the way Prabhupāda distributed his teachings in life. Prabhupāda did not speak all at one time about politics and then all about yoga and then all about the demigods, but he gave some here and some there. To encourage me in this method, Jayādvaita Swami remarked, "In this way it resembles life: a few words here, a few gestures there, or sometimes a whole lot all at once."

In presenting the anecdotes I have not altered any facts, but I have often rewritten them into a narrative form, or sometimes edited or polished what was given to me. For variety, I have created categories like "Prabhupāda Said" (consisting of direct quotes on specific subjects), "Prabhupāda Tells a Story," and "Personal." Future volumes may contain further varieties of talks by and about Prabhupāda.

At the back of the book are Notes. They give a reference for the source of each entry, and there I have also added occasional comments.

For over six years our *Śrīla Prabhupāda-līlāmṛta* staff of interviewers and researchers have been practicing a system of ascertaining whether a Prabhupāda anecdote is authentic, and I have applied the same standards in *Prabhupāda Nectar*. By researching tape recordings of Śrīla Prabhupāda, we try to give accurate quotes of his statements wherever possible. We also always look for several reliable witnesses, in addition to the one who is recalling a particular event. This is done by our interviewer bringing up the same incident in numerous interviews. While we always feel more confident in hearing anecdotes from senior disciples who are leaders and active members of the Kṛṣṇa consciousness movement, we do not absolutely exclude hearing from other disciples, as long as they are favorable and not envious of Śrīla Prabhupāda. In fact, the phenomenon of interviewing a devotee of Śrīla Prabhupāda is itself a remarkable testimony in gauging the authenticity of remembrances of Śrīla Prabhupāda. Experiencing strong emotions, including pains of remembrance, and grief at their distance from Prabhupāda, devotees sometimes cry for the first time in years, and they often later thank us for helping them to remember Prabhupāda. When they are absorbed in such interviews, it seems that the covering of years of forgetfulness is pulled back, at least temporarily, and the devotee obtains again the mercy of Prabhupāda's association through remembrance. A trained interviewer can appreciate these positive symptoms, but he also learns to spot inconsistencies in context when remembrances are inaccurate.

Furthermore, each devotee seems to contain his own repertoire of Prabhupāda stories which he tends to remember again and again. These set remembrances indicate to us that certain Prabhupāda remembrances are permanently etched into the brains of the witnesses. Even if sometimes the same event in Prabhupāda's life is viewed in a variety of ways from person to person, still the remembrances are personal, lasting exchanges between Prabhupāda and the particular persons. Many Prabhupāda stories have already entered into an oral tradition, and are passed down from hearer to hearer in a disciplic succession in which the original source may not always be recalled. These can also be accepted, as well as evaluated for authenticity, by persons familiar with Prabhupāda's life and philosophy. Thus while we have given specific references for the source of each incident in this book, the incidents are usually not dependent on only one person, but are part of a collective tradition. While we cannot claim that our selection system is infallible, we've often refrained from telling an apparently instructive incident because it was weak in authenticity. We are definitely against spinning any concocted yarns about Śrīla Prabhupāda and have done our best to exclude the make-believe.

There are already books in the form of anecdotes like *Anecdotes from Gandhiji's Life, Anecdotes from Abraham Lincoln and Lincoln's Stories,* and anecdote collections about authors, institutions, and countries. Such collections are considered especially memorable because of their ability to capture real-life glimpses of great persons. But *Prabhupāda Nectar* is unique in importance, because Śrīla Prabhupāda was empowered to deliver the highest transcendental science—pure love of Kṛṣṇa, based on the teachings of Lord Caitanya Mahāprabhu—and he delivered it more widely and more effectively than any predecessor. Remarkably, he did so during the era of the greatest faithlessness and strife, known as the age of Kali. Therefore, hearing even small incidents from his life is more beneficial than hearing the greatest public acts of all worldly heroes and benefactors. As it is stated in the *śāstras,* even a moment's association with a pure Vaiṣṇava can grant liberation from the cycle of birth and death. Since even a drop of nectar from the life of Śrīla Prabhupāda can save one from suffering, we are trying to deliver many drops to irrigate this desert-like universe.

—SDG

Prabhupāda Nectar 1

1

It was only after two years of leading ISKCON in America that Śrīla Prabhupāda agreed to be addressed by the proper title Prabhupāda instead of Swamijī. As early as 1960, in his first volume of *Śrīmad-Bhāgavatam,* he had written in a purport, "The pure devotees whose only business is serving are honored by the names Prabhupāda and Viṣṇupāda, which indicates such devotees to be representatives of the lotus feet of the Lord." *(Bhāg.* 1.1.15) Yet although the address Swamijī is common and not very respectful, it was the only name his followers knew and it had become a most endearing term for them. They inquired and prayed to him by that name, and they addressed all their letters, "Dear Swamijī." So it was a bit of a shock when the name changed.

One devotee, on hearing the new name from Śrīla Prabhupāda's secretary, couldn't accept it without personally asking Śrīla Prabhupāda. On the next morning walk he inquired, "Swamijī?"

"Yes?" Prabhupāda replied.

"I understand that you prefer to be called Prabhupāda."

Prabhupāda turned quickly. "Where did you hear this? Who told you this?" Prabhupāda appeared annoyed, and then he became silent. But after a few moments he spoke again. "Actually I do not *prefer*. But it is better."

2

LITTLE DROPS *of* NECTAR

In San Francisco in 1967, Śrīla Prabhupāda only gradually raised the standards of his followers. Most of them were not much more than hippies having a good time eating and singing in the storefront. Right next to the temple was an ice cream shop, and at the end of the street there was a doughnut shop—both frequented by devotees. Unless there was a specific function in the temple, many of the devotees could be found in one of the two food shops. Therefore, when Prabhupāda would come down from his apartment, he would sometimes pass very slowly in front of the ice cream shop to see if any of his followers were there. Then he would go down to the doughnut shop and look in the window there. The "devotees" would even slink down in their seats so as not to be spotted as Śrīla Prabhupāda looked in. More than once in the evening lecture Śrīla Prabhupāda mentioned that devotees don't take part in eating in ice cream shops or eating doughnuts, but they eat only Kṛṣṇa *prasādam*.

From the very beginning of his preaching in America, Prabhupāda used to encourage his devotees to take part in the devotional ecstasy of chanting and dancing. On morning walks he would sometimes ask each devotee, "Were you chanting last night?" referring to the congregational *kīrtana* in the temple.

"I tried to, but there wasn't any room," one devotee replied.

Gargamuni said, "No, because I was afraid I would cry." No doubt these remarks by his disciples contained neophyte emotions, yet Śrīla Prabhupāda replied seriously.

"When you are with ordinary people," he said, "then you should not cry, because they will not understand. But when you are with devotees, you can cry, because the devotees will know that you are crying for Kṛṣṇa."

And Prabhupāda also demonstrated this crying. Once during the Sunday feast program, the devotees enacted the drama of Nārada Muni's rescuing the hunter Mṛgāri. Viṣṇujana dāsa played Nārada, and when he recited verses from "The Prayers to the Spiritual Master," everyone could notice something shining in the corner of Prabhupāda's eye. He had a tear in his eye, but it was particularly shiny, like a diamond. After Prabhupāda left the temple, many devotees were commenting, "Did you see the diamond in Prabhupāda's eye?"

3

Śrīla Prabhupāda's servant was having difficulty controlling his senses and he asked Prabhupāda to give him a special diet. When word got around that Prabhupāda had recommended a special diet, another devotee approached Prabhupāda for similar treatment.

"Prabhupāda, is there anything I could get that would help me control my tongue more? Are there certain things to avoid, like sugar?"

Prabhupāda said, "The method to control the tongue is to chant and to pray."

"Well," the devotee said, "I am chanting and praying, but still I am having difficulty."

Prabhupāda sat back in his seat and laughed. "Yes," he said, "I know. I have a tongue too. It may be difficult, but as much as you can, try to eat simply."

Prabhupāda went on to describe how during World War II there was a bombing of Calcutta—during a time when Prabhupāda was just about to honor *prasādam.* Friends had come running to the house giving warning: "Abhay Charan, come quickly! The air-raid siren is going off! The bombs are coming!" Prabhupāda had responded by saying that he could not go because his wife had just prepared some *kacaurīs.* He told his friends, "You go to the shelter. I will stay here." And so he offered the *kacaurīs,* ate them, and chanted Hare Kṛṣṇa.

4

One evening in Bhaktivedanta Manor in London, Śrīla Prabhupāda was sitting in his room with his disciples and a few guests, including a woman reporter who had come to interview Śrīla Prabhupāda. Despite the chilly English summer weather, the reporter was dressed in a scanty mini skirt. Her first few questions revealed her skeptical and almost cynical attitude toward the Hare Kṛṣṇa movement. As usual, Śrīla Prabhupāda coolly and expertly answered her questions. Somewhat exasperated and in a challenging mood, she brought up the old question, "Why do you people have bald heads?" Śrīla Prabhupāda immediately retorted, "Why do you have bare legs?" She was speechless. Śrīla Prabhupāda then offered, "Better to have warm legs and a cool head." Everyone, including the reporter, laughed with delight. Prabhupāda added, "You must have a cool head to understand this Kṛṣṇa consciousness philosophy."

5

During an early morning walk in Vṛndāvana, devotees were asking Śrīla Prabhupāda about the moon. A pale remainder of the moon could still be seen in the sky and various birds were cooing and calling from the trees. Prabhupāda said the moon is shining and therefore has heat, and yet its effect on the earth is cooling. Viśākhā dāsī was one of the few women who regularly accompanied Śrīla Prabhupāda on his walks because of her assignment as photographer. On this occasion, she stopped taking pictures and walked closer to ask Prabhupāda a question about the moon.

"Prabhupāda, it is stated in your *Bhagavad-gītā* purport that because of the moonlight, vegetables have taste. So why is it that the moon makes the vegetables have flavor?"

Prabhupāda stopped walking to consider her question. His demeanor was mellow and soft, but his look penetrated into her eyes.

"Why don't you ask him?" was his only reply, and then he walked on.

6

PRABHUPĀDA SAID

On Prasādam

"Regarding *prasadam,* leftovers should always be taken if they have not spoiled or if they have not been touched by a diseased person. We should never waste Kṛṣṇa *prasadam.* Best thing is to cook only what is required and then give each person what he wants. That is Vedic system, that the people sit in rows behind their plates and servers pass down the rows and put a very small portion of each foodstuff on each plate, unless there is some objection by a person, then nothing is given. Then if anyone wants more the servers pass up and down the rows continually and give more if anyone requests. In this way nothing is wasted and everyone is satisfied."

—*Letter of November 27, 1971*

In India, Prabhupāda instructed the devotees how a gentleman would eat and how to feed guests who come to the temple. During the meal the host should be very attentive to his guest's needs, supplying them servings of hot *purīs,* fresh water, and more of everything. He should also engage his guest in light, relaxing conversation, and not heavy, anxiety-producing topics.

Prabhupāda said rice was useless unless served hot. He also said reheating rice must never be done, since it causes a poisonous effect.

"So far as offering to Krsna apple cider, this can be done only if it is prepared by the devotees. These food manufacturers do not take proper precautions in cleanliness nor do they have devotion for Krsna in their labors, so it is not a very acceptable offering. If you can make this preparation yourself, then it would be all right."

—*Letter of December 19, 1968*

7

PRABHUPĀDA TELLS A STORY

During Śrīla Prabhupāda's last days in Vṛndāvana he used to be carried up and down the stairs in a palanquin-chair. His habit was to take rest during the day in his bed on the roof. One day, going up the narrow staircase from the first floor to the roof, Śatadhanya Mahārāja carried the rear portion of Prabhupāda's palanquin by its two handles and another man carried the front. Tamāla Kṛṣṇa Goswami led the group, and Upendra dāsa followed, carrying Prabhupāda's drinking *loṭa* and quilt. Suddenly Śrīla Prabhupāda began to laugh uncontrollably. The devotees were amazed because Śrīla Prabhupāda was very ill and had been silent and grave.

"Do you want to hear a funny story?" he asked.

They all answered, "Yes, Prabhupāda!"

"Let us go upstairs. There I can say."

While Upendra rushed to get his tape recorder, the others brought Śrīla Prabhupāda to the roof, placed him on his bed, and sat at his feet. Śrīla Prabhupāda's body was very gaunt from the months of fasting, and he lay back but continued laughing.

"There is a Bengali proverb," he said. "*Garīb manuṣ ca chinga khāi hakta gelo gauḍa jaya.*" Just to say it made Prabhupāda laugh more. The devotees remained mystified, and expectant.

"Now I'll explain," said Śrīla Prabhupāda. "*Garīb manuṣ. Garīb* means 'poor' and *manuṣ* means 'man.'" Again Śrīla Prabhupāda broke into laughter, his thin body shaking and his whole face smiling. "*Ca chinga khāi*," he continued. "*Ca chinga* means 'grasshopper.' *Khāi*, 'eats.' So this poor man has nothing to eat except he is finding some grasshoppers and eating them. *Garīb manuṣ ca chinga khāi hakta gelo.* But when he goes to pass stool—*gauḍa jaya,* he rides on a big white horse." Prabhupāda laughed loudly, and all the devotees sat by in amazement. Then Prabhupāda turned to Upendra and said, "You understand?" Upendra's face became red in nonunderstanding. Śatadhanya Mahārāja was thinking, "I hope Prabhupāda does not ask me." Śatadhanya turned to Tamāla Kṛṣṇa Mahārāja and whispered, "Tamāla, do you understand?" Tamāla Kṛṣṇa Mahārāja gave an unsure nod and said, "Yes," but he remained silent.

Prabhupāda said, "Just see. *Garīb manuṣ.* He is a poor man eating only grasshoppers. But when he goes to pass stool, he rides a big white horse." When Prabhupāda saw that they could not understand, he explained further. "Similarly, I am a *sannyāsī.* So a *sannyāsī* is a beggar, a poor man. I am a poor man, and yet when I have to go to sleep, then four men must carry me in a palanquin." In this way, they all laughed and enjoyed Prabhupāda's story, but not quite as much as did Prabhupāda himself.

8
PERSONAL

His Height

In height he was maybe 5′5″. A nondevotee would say, "a small man." Most of his disciples stood taller than he. But we didn't think like that, that he was a little man. If we saw reporters describe him as a little man, it didn't make sense. That was obviously the defective vision of the nondevotee. (His servant once said, "For someone who is supposed to be small, it takes all your energy to cover his back to massage it. I can't understand it!) His shoe size was 8, his sweater size around 36″. The palms of his hands were soft and boldly lined, with long, firm life lines.

There was something protective that came out of his disciples in the fact that Prabhupāda's height was shorter. We wanted to be sure to protect him because he was so great, so valuable, our spiritual master. In the company of *karmīs* or in the company of devotees, he was regal as he walked with his cane, not at all like a "small" or "old" man. Any person, regardless of his physical stature, would approach Prabhupāda respectfully, deferring to him. Prabhupāda was elderly and a gentleman and was almost always treated in that way, very respectfully. Because when he spoke he was very refined and proper, he himself proclaimed his spiritual mission by his every action, and people could see that for themselves.

Usually accompanying him were his Western disciples, who were very worshipful of Prabhupāda; that was also impressive. He was not alone, but with his servants; if he looked small, still he controlled others who were tall; therefore he was taller than they. He had strength; he would say his mind was strong. His face was not small, nor was his aristocratic nose and full mouth; his eyes were large. Again, these contradicted the "small man" idea. He was saint, *sādhu,* not small. He didn't sit small. His voice was deep, could be gruff, loud, commanding—not small. His control of big men like Brahmānanda, Jayapatāka, Bhavānanda was complete. His word, the raising of his eyebrows, or the turn of his mouth could humiliate them utterly or drive them running into action. And he wrote so many books. He was not small. But if he chose, he could be like a child and you had to care for him completely; that was his love.

9

In India, Śrīla Prabhupāda was often invited to attend programs in people's homes. Sometimes these people were very pious and became devotees by such contact with Śrīla Prabhupāda. In some cases they mainly wanted material blessings—health and prosperity—in return for hosting a *sādhu* and his followers. On one occasion, Śrīla Prabhupāda, along with twenty of his devotees, was sitting in a man's living room while the man introduced each member of his family.

"This is my wife," said the man, and the wife came forward, bowing slightly and folding her palms. "And this is my older son, and this is my daughter, and this is my younger son"—each came forward and said his name while Prabhupāda nodded genially. "This is the husband of my daughter," the man continued, "and these are their children." Each both quickly appeared and exited. Finally, all the members had been introduced and had departed, momentarily leaving Śrīla Prabhupāda alone in the room with his devotees. In a confidential aside, Prabhupāda spoke quietly to his disciples, "This is my sex life."

10

Śrīla Prabhupāda once said that whenever a manuscript of his was printed and published as a book he felt as if he had just conquered an empire, so for his disciples, it was also an opportunity for intimate association to be able to prepare his books for printing and to bring him an advance copy fresh from the printer.

When Canto 7, Part 2, of the *Śrīmad-Bhāgavatam* was printed, Śrīla Prabhupāda was staying at the New York City ISKCON center. Rāmeśvara Swami and Rādhā-vallabha had gone to the airport and received the first two copies by special freight. It was about 2 A.M. when they returned to the temple. Eager to present the book to Prabhupāda, they took the elevator up to his rooms on the eleventh floor. The light was on in his sitting room. Quietly opening his door, they found that he was not there. They went again into the hall and saw the light on in the bathroom. With child-like glee, barely controlling their laughter, they each hid a book behind their backs and waited, smiling, to present it to Prabhupāda. When Prabhupāda came out, he saw them and said, "Oh, you are here?" He noticed they were holding something behind their backs and trying to control their smiling. "You have something for me?" he said, perfectly reciprocating their mood. He then walked ahead into the sitting room, looking playfully over his shoulder, and invited them, "Come on!"

When they handed Śrīla Prabhupāda the books, he exclaimed, "Aaah!" and immediately took one and touched it to his head. He looked at the cover and then turned the book and looked at the back cover. He opened up the front page and read aloud the selected epithet verse. He went through the front matter page by page and then carefully looked at all the pictures. Then Śrīla Prabhupāda started reading the book aloud, from "Prahlāda Pacifies the Lord with Prayers."

The joyful presentation party merged into the ecstasy of a *Bhāgavatam* reading by Śrīla Prabhupāda. He read on for about forty minutes, seemingly oblivious to everything else.

11

There were many inconveniences Prabhupāda had to face due to old age and disease, but he was never affected in his pure Kṛṣṇa consciousness. Even externally, he often refused to bow to the dictates of his maladies, variously diagnosed as diabetes, poor digestion, and many others. He or his followers would call for doctors periodically, but Śrīla Prabhupāda rarely took their prescriptions or followed their diet regimes. He was not what you would call a good patient.

When in New York an Indian allopathic doctor visited and gave Prabhupāda medicine and antibiotics, Prabhupāda was polite and agreeable, but his servant, Hari Śauri, was doubtful.

"Will you take your medicine?" he asked.

Prabhupāda patted the little pills on his desk and said, noncommittally, "We shall see." He never took them. Some of the devotees thought that Śrīla Prabhupāda was seeing doctors just to engage them in devotional service.

He rebelled against strictures on his diet even when he was quite ill. A *kavirāja* in India ordered that Prabhupāda couldn't eat rice, potatoes, sugar, and certain fruits. When he called in his cook, Daiviśakti, in Vṛndāvana and asked her to make *panjāb bolī,* a hot potato *sabjī,* she dutifully reminded him, "But Prabhupāda, you can't eat potatoes." He endured it for few days and then overthrew the order. He called for his old lunch of rice, *dāl, capātīs,* and *sabjī.* At that time another of his well-meaning servants, Upendra, intervened and tried to restrain him. "But Prabhupāda, the doctor told you not to take all these things. You're going to get sick."

Prabhupāda replied, "We are not *doctor* dāsa, we are *Kṛṣṇa* dāsa." From then on he resumed his normal diet.

In Māyāpur, his cook Pālikā dāsī, attempted an even stricter discipline based on the instructions of a famous *kavirāja* from Calcutta. In this case, Prabhupāda was to follow an intricate schedule by which he would take pills and eat and drink only at certain hours. This was in 1977, when Prabhupāda was so sick that he was rarely coming down to the temple to give classes or to go on morning walks. One afternoon, a devotee named Ānakadundubhi, unaware of the tight schedule of Prabhupāda's drinking and eating, brought Prabhupāda a fresh coconut *dob* to drink, as usual. Although Prabhupāda knew very well that he was not supposed to take anything at this time, he quietly accepted the *dob* and poured it into his cup. Just as he started to drink it Pālikā came by and admonished him, "Śrīla Prabhupāda, you're not supposed to take anything."

Prabhupāda became defiant. "Who said?" he challenged, and immediately drank down the whole cup of juice, although it was usually his custom to sip it slowly. "All my life," he said, "I have done whatever I wanted!"

12

A disciple, Satya-nārāyaṇa dāsa, had been advised by other devotees that serious study of Āyur-veda would be important. Satya-nārāyaṇa was living in Florida, but he planned to go to India to take up the medical study. He had written to a *kavirāja* in Calcutta, one whom Prabhupāda also sometimes saw, and the *kavirāja* had written back agreeing to accept Satya-nārāyaṇa as his student.

Arriving in Māyāpur, Satya-nārāyaṇa went to see Śrīla Prabhupāda, who at that moment was receiving a massage on the roof of the building. At his disciple's first attempts to explain the Āyur-veda project, Śrīla Prabhupāda put up his hand and said, "Oh, I am very tired now." It seemed that he was not only tired but not particularly inclined to hear.

Within a day or two, Satya-nārāyaṇa managed to get another interview. This time he entered Śrīla Prabhupāda's room, offered his *daṇḍavats,* and explained things a little further. "I can stay as a *pūjārī* here in Calcutta. It's only a mile away to the doctor, and I can study under him. I have permission from my GBC man."

Prabhupāda interrupted him. "No, this is not very important." Then he just looked away. Satya-nārāyaṇa couldn't believe that he was just supposed to accept it with no further comment. He wanted an answer and a reason, so he sat silently looking at Prabhupāda. Prabhupāda kindly turned to him. "We are not interested in studying these different sciences. Whatever medicines work, you use it. Actually Western medicine is very advanced, so there is no reason to study this. We want to become *brāhmaṇas.*" Prabhupāda pointed to the *Kṛṣṇa* book on his desk and said, "You simply read my books. That is what you should do!"

Satya-nārāyaṇa felt satisfied and said, "Thank you, Prabhupāda."

Prabhupāda replied strongly, "Hare Kṛṣṇa!" And that was the end of Satya-nārāyaṇa's career in Āyur-veda.

13

PRABHUPĀDA SAID

On Raising Children

"I discussed the contents of your letter with His Divine Grace Srila Prabhupada. Srila Prabhupada stated that our *grhasthas* should simply chant fifty rounds before conceiving a child. Prabhupāda said, 'We do not want all these rituals. Chanting Hare Krsna is our only business. According to the *Manu-samhita* you are all *mlecchas* and *yavanas.* You cannot touch the *Manu-samhita*, what to speak of translating it. So if you try to follow the *Manu-samhita* then you will become a *mleccha* and *yavana* and your career is finished.'"

—*Letter of May 19, 1977*

"I understand you are now expecting a nice child for raising in Krsna consciousness. In this connection you should avoid any spicy foods, so long the child is within the womb. So far natural childbirth is concerned, natural delivery is possible if we keep ourselves naturally. And so far I know, a pregnant woman should not even eat pungent foodstuffs, she should not move in cars, she should not sit idly. She should move and do some physical work. These are the general rules and regulations I have seen in India. They have natural delivery. But so far your country is concerned, especially the situation of women there, that is a different thing. I cannot say definitely what is to be done. And under the circumstances, the best thing is to consult a doctor as they usually do. And after all, Krsna is the ultimate Master, so if you keep the natural habits and depend on Krsna, then everything will be done nicely without any difficulty."

—*Letter of March 24, 1969*

"You ask if the children should be taken to ordinary medical doctors. Why not? Of course, we can't always trust that these doctors may be doing the right thing, but what can be done? The governing principle for our activity should be to do what is favorable for pleasing Krsna. So if your child requires medical attention to be fit for serving Krsna, then it is only practical she should get it. The same thing—the government is giving you money, why not use it for Krsna? The only thing you must avoid cheating them while falsely claiming something to get money. Then we are risking our very high reputation as pious people. But if they are willing to give us money and food, then of course we should accept."

—*Letter of November 27, 1971*

"Regarding the child problem: [in class] I may inform you that our children born of Krsna conscious parents are all welcome, and Krsna conscious parents are all welcome, and I want hundreds of children like that, because in the future we expect to change the face of the whole world, because the child is the father of the man. Anyway, I have seen M. is nursing her child so nicely that she attended my meeting every day and the child was playing not crying. Similarly L.'s child also never cries or disturbs the meeting. L. was always present with her child, so it depends on the mother. How to keep the child comfortable, so that he will not cry. The child cries only when it feels uncomfortable. The child's comfort and discomfort depends on the mother's attention. So the best solution is we train all our small babies in such a way that they are always satisfied, and there will be no disturbance in the meeting. Then there will be no complaint. But there cannot be any hard and fast rules that only children who are grown up, seven or eight years old, can be admitted and no other children can be admitted. That is not possible, and I am not going to sanction any such rule. Rather, I shall welcome the baby from the very beginning, so that the transcendental vibration may enter into its ear, and from the very beginning of its life, it becomes purified. But of course children cannot be allowed to disturb in the meeting by crying, and it is the mother's responsibility to keep them comfortable and not disturb the meeting.

—*Letter of August 26, 1968*

"Why should the parents not feel attachment for their children, that is natural. But our affection is not simply sentimental, we offer our children the highest opportunity to become trained up in Krsna consciousness very early so as to assure their success in this life to go back to Godhead for sure. That is real affection, to make sure my child gets back to Godhead, that is my real responsibility as a parent. And I have seen that *gurukula* offers this opportunity more than any other place anywhere. So I think that you are an intelligent girl, and you can explain it to the others in this way."

—*Letter of March 23, 1973*

14

PRABHUPĀDA TELLS A STORY

When Śyāmasundara dāsa was in charge of ISKCON England, he bought very expensive crystal chandeliers. They cost three thousand pounds, and the devotees had to take them back because they couldn't afford them. On this occasion, Prabhupāda was talking about the crystal chandeliers. He said, "This reminds me of a story of a *nawāb. Nawāb* means 'rich one.' He has so much money he doesn't know what to do with it all. One *nawāb* had one servant cleaning a big, big crystal chandelier. So as the servant was cleaning the chandelier, a crystal fell, and as it crashed onto the marble floor it made an unusual tinkling sound, which the *nawāb* heard from his room. The *nawāb* came running out and asked, 'What was that sound?'

"The servant was petrified and asked forgiveness. 'I'm sorry,' he said. 'When I was cleaning the chandelier, one of the precious crystals fell and shattered on the floor. I am very sorry.'

"The *nawāb* said, 'Oh, this is a very nice sound. Throw one more down.'

"So the servant smashed another onto the floor. 'Very nice sound,' said the *nawāb*. 'Throw another one down.' And so, in this way, every single crystal of the chandelier was thrown and smashed on the ground. Because the *nawāb* had so much money at his disposal, he could do anything he liked.

"Similarly," said Prabhupāda, "Śyāmasundara thinks he's got so much money he can just throw it . . . "

15

PERSONAL

His Preaching Spirit

In the evening he wanted to see guests. We suggested he not see people who would waste his time, and he agreed, but then he would become angry with us if we kept people from seeing him because he existed for preaching to them. It was his duty to preach, he felt. Prabhupāda was self-satisfied and never restless or bored, yet if the place was really quiet with no preaching there, he seemed to want to go where there was some action. This was also a manifestation of his desire to accomplish as much as possible. Prabhupāda was already accomplished in terms of self-realization and love of Kṛṣṇa; therefore his travel was only for the benefit of others.

He felt he had to travel and he kept on the move. When he arrived in a new place, he was immediately ready to see the local people. The room would fill up and he would preach for hours. This feature of Prabhupāda's behavior was astounding. Day and night people would come into his room —sometimes a few, sometimes many. Prabhupāda would always speak to them about Kṛṣṇa; he would speak on the basis of *Bhagavad-gītā,* calling for verses to be cited, answering questions, preaching much as in his classes. The informal talks were more unusual. Many of his talks in later years were recorded. He would preach, preach, preach. He kept going, hours on end, preaching the basic philosophy, holding the room full of people, then taking a little *prasādam* and distributing it.

When he would travel to certain places, as in Europe, where he could speak to many people and bring them to devotional service, he would be especially enlivened to preach. Preaching included encouraging the local ISKCON disciples wherever he visited, and preaching also meant his book writing. It also meant his spirit of maintaining and expanding ISKCON in all its activities. We cannot describe the full glories of his preaching spirit. His enthusiasm was unlimited and even today is nourishing all the preachers of ISKCON.

When he was ill and feeling inconvenience, when the people he was speaking to were low-class or disinterested, when his body was very old, and when in order to preach he had to interrupt his schedule, when there was difficulty going on within his ISKCON—still his preaching would go on. Sitting at his low desk talking, his eyes sometimes widening, hands sometimes gesturing, taking water to drink, chanting almost soundless *japa* when not talking, focusing in on special guests to develop a whole argument with them, Prabhupāda was intent on his preaching points, although he had made the same points millions of times. Thus he was not just a scholar, but a pure devotee attempting to convince everyone that they had to change—the whole world had to change—*or else.*

16

It didn't happen very often, but sometimes Śrīla Prabhupāda was overcome by ecstatic emotions while lecturing. It happened, for example, in the San Francisco storefront when Prabhupāda was describing Lord Caitanya's mood of separation from Kṛṣṇa. It also happened in Gorakhpur, India, while Prabhupāda was seated before the Deities of Rādhā-Mādhava discussing Kṛṣṇa's pastimes. Again it happened in Los Angeles during a lecture. He said that his disciples were young and had much opportunity to preach, whereas his life had no value because "I am an old man who may die at any moment." As soon as he uttered these words, Prabhupāda was suddenly unable to talk and a very perceivable change in his consciousness took place. It seemed to some of the devotees who witnessed these states that the spiritual world had suddenly opened up directly before Prabhupāda's vision and Kṛṣṇa was communicating with him in a way that made him unable to speak.

One time after the same thing happened before a large gathering of devotees in Māyāpur, the devotees inquired from Śrīla Prabhupāda about their own behavior on such occasions. In Māyāpur, when Śrīla Prabhupāda became stunned, the whole congregation became breathlessly silent, waiting for a cue from their spiritual master. But suddenly one of the *sannyāsīs* broke the mood and began singing, "*nama oṁ viṣṇu-pādāya* . . ." At first no one followed his singing, but when he persisted, others gradually joined and then Prabhupāda broke out of his meditative trance. Afterwards, there was a strong disagreement among the devotees over the *sannyāsī's* behavior. Some said it was offensive. Finally the issue came to Prabhupāda's secretary, Brahmānanda Swami, who was asked to settle the matter by asking Prabhupāda.

Brahmānanda Swami asked Prabhupāda if he remembered how during the lecture that morning he had gone into a deep silence. Śrīla Prabhupāda replied shyly, almost embarrassed, and said, "I do not do that very often."

"But when it does happen," Brahmānanda Swami asked, "what should we do? Should we be silent or should we chant *japa?*"

Prabhupāda said, "Yes, just chant. Just chant Hare Kṛṣṇa. That's all right."

Brahmānanda then asked if what the *sannyāsī* disciple had done that morning was all right, by chanting.

"Yes," said Prabhupāda, "that was all right." Prabhupāda treated the whole occasion as rather insignificant and thus gave his devotees the hint that they should not get involved in speculation. Of course, they could not forget what they had seen, but they should not make a big thing about Prabhupāda's going into ecstasies. It had occurred, but it was not his main method of precept or example. And to chant Hare Kṛṣṇa at such a time was all right.

17

Mahābuddhi dāsa tells of the first time he met Śrīla Prabhupāda. His name at that time was Randy, and he had long blond hair. He was a football player at San Diego State University, a leader in student government, and a son of wealthy parents. He had been taking part in the congregational *kīrtana* in the Los Angeles temple when Prabhupāda's secretary invited him to come upstairs to Prabhupāda's room. Randy like the idea, but when he entered Prabhupāda's quarters, he found himself the only guest in the small room.

Śrīla Prabhupāda was seated at his desk, surrounded by *sannyāsīs* and GBC disciples, none of whom knew Randy. While Randy was trying to gather his wits about the situation, Prabhupāda began to preach, looking straight at him, saying, "Why be a *kṛpaṇa?*"

"What's a *kṛpaṇa?*" thought Randy, and Śrīla Prabhupāda replied, "*Kṛpaṇa* means 'miser.'" Randy thought of his family's wealth and how he and his parents had their own plans for using it. Prabhupāda continued speaking about the *kṛpaṇa* mentality, and by now Randy had the direct impression that Prabhupāda was speaking to his mind and defeating each of his defiant thoughts. It was like a conversation between Randy's rebellious thoughts and Śrīla Prabhupāda's smashing, spoken replies.

"Because you have been given some ability, wealth, and opulence by Kṛṣṇa," said Prabhupāda, looking to Randy, who sat against the wall, "therefore you should use it in Kṛṣṇa's service. If you use it only for your personal sense gratification, that's simply miserly. If you do not take to Kṛṣṇa consciousness, you will ruin your human form of life."

Śrīla Prabhupāda continued explaining the process of devotional service and Randy managed to resume some of his pride and defensiveness. He began to feel insulted that Prabhupāda had called him a miser. Randy admitted to himself that Prabhupāda seemed to have read his mind, but if Prabhupāda were actually perfect, that he should know the future. In this way, Randy began to feel the return of his usual pride. As if in response to these thoughts, Prabhupāda suddenly called for a copy of the Twelfth Canto of the *Śrīmad-Bhāgavatam* and began reading aloud the predictions for degraded humanity in the coming age, the age of Kali.

"Men will consider that to have long hair means they are beautiful," said Śrīla Prabhupāda. When Randy heard that he began to shake. He felt stunned. He thought to himself, "He has completely defeated me."

18

LITTLE DROPS *of* NECTAR

When Śrīla Prabhupāda flew on planes, his servants carried his silver plates and served him full meals. His disciples usually cooked much more for his travels than he would eat. One time Śrīla Prabhupāda asked to eat just before the plane was to take off. The stewardesses were making preparations for departure, but Śrīla Prabhupāda's servant brought him his *prasādam,* which had been recently cooked at the temple. Prabhupāda sat alone, undisturbed, as the other passengers looked at him, buckled their seat belts, and put their trays and seats in the upright position. Somehow the stewardesses didn't insist on Prabhupāda's conforming, so he continued calmly eating as the jet sped down the runway. His servant anxiously held on to the drinking cups while Prabhupāda ate his meal with no notice or care for his surroundings. Only when the plane was high in the air did Prabhupāda finish. Turning to his servant, he said, "All right, you can take these away now."

At one of the ISKCON international festivals in Vṛndāvana, Prabhupāda rejected the singing of one of his disciples. The devotee had previously been a singer in a band, and his *kīrtanas* were much appreciated by some devotees, especially those from his home temple. But when, with showy professionalism, he began leading the *guru-pūjā* in Prabhupāda's presence, making the tune sound like a rock 'n' roll ballad, Prabhupāda didn't like it. He shook his head and indicated that someone else lead. The "great" *kīrtana* singer was devastated by the rejection, another form of Prabhupāda's mercy.

For a time in Māyāpur, two Bengali ladies were cooking a large feast of about twenty-five preparations and sending it over to Śrīla Prabhupāda at his mealtime. But he was eating very little of it. "I'm eating with my eyes," he laughed. He then described how in the old days in Bengal aristocratic people would invite one another for meals. One would prepare a huge, sumptuous feast, and another would come and appreciate how it was cooked and arranged so nicely. The guest would merely look at the feast and say, "Oh, very nicely done." Then all the servants would actually eat it.

19

Śrīla Prabhupāda was very good at imitating the sounds of men, animals, and machines. He did not do it by any gross oral manipulations as some modern comedians do, but by the use of onomatopoeic sounds and even Sanskrit derivations. He always did it to prove a Kṛṣṇa conscious point.

One time in Beverly Hills, Prabhupāda gave a whole *tour de force* of imitative sounds. Prabhupāda had been alone writing when his servant went into his room. Prabhupāda began speaking, "There are so many material sounds. Just now I was listening and I could hear the freeway." Prabhupāda then imitated the cars. The sound he made for the cars might be written down as "*whooo-whooo,*" but it is not possible to capture the actual sound in print, or even by imitating the sound. It gave an exact impression of what cars sound like on the freeway. Prabhupāda's car sound even included a criticism of the foolish endeavors of the highway-rushing *karmīs.*

"And in the alley," said Prabhupāda, "the garbage truck is coming." He then made another perfect imitation. "I also hear these birds," said Prabhupāda. "Someone nearby has roosters." Prabhupāda then gave a Sanskrit version of cockadoodledoo, which was also perfect.

"But some day . . . " said Prabhupāda, and then he became completely quiet. This whole conversation had been taking place in the early morning in Prabhupāda's room, and therefore when he became silent, it seemed liked the whole world was silent. He repeated, "And then some day . . . " Suddenly Prabhupāda imitated an exploding bomb. "The atom bomb will go off, and it will all be finished."

20

Once in Vṛndāvana, Prabhupāda noticed that some of his men disciples were letting their hair grow. Different men had their reasons for growing hair, so Prabhupāda had not said anything, but one day in the presence of his servant, Hari Śauri, and Bhāgavata dāsa, Prabhupāda expressed his displeasure. Turning to Bhāgavata dāsa, he said, "You look very beautiful by keeping hairs. What is your explanation?"

"Oh, I was advised," said Bhāgavata, "that because I was going to the European countries it would be required to keep this hair."

"But they have won victory in the court by keeping a shaven head," said Prabhupāda, referring to a recent New York court case.

"I asked their advice," said Bhāgavata, "whether I should shave or keep the hair." Bhāgavata was about to say more, but Prabhupāda interrupted him.

"What is that nonsense advice? Who is that rascal advice? By keeping hair, you become beautiful. This is without advice, this mentality of growing thick hair. We are known as shaven-headed, the whole society."

Hari Śauri attempted to explain his own case, saying, "It is about three weeks since I—" but Prabhupāda interrupted him.

"Every fortnight at least," said Śrīla Prabhupāda, and then again he turned to Bhāgavata. "Before going to Europe six years ago, you were keeping hairs like that. 'Oh, I have to go to Europe.' That I have seen. You *like* to keep hairs. That hippie mentality is going on."

21

Śrīla Prabhupāda regularly gave out cookies from the *vyāsāsana,* but on a visit to New Vrindaban he once gave out an entire meal of *prasādam* right off the Deities' plate. Rādhānātha dāsa had a strong desire to approach Śrīla Prabhupāda with the Deities' plate immediately after offering it to Rādhā-Vṛndāvanacandra, so he rather boldly approached Śrīla Prabhupāda on the *vyāsāsana.* At first he had been stopped by Śrīla Prabhupāda's secretary, Puṣṭa Kṛṣṇa, who asked, "Where are the cookies?" Rādhānātha said they had none, only this full Deity plate.

"Forget it," said Puṣṭa Kṛṣṇa. "You can't give out that kind of stuff." But Rādhānātha managed to approach Prabhupāda from a different direction. When Śrīla Prabhupāda saw the plate, he smiled, took it up, and began sampling each preparation with a spoon. He took a spoonful of sweet rice, tasted it, and then began handing out spoonfuls. Over a hundred devotees were present and they rushed forward, unlike their usual, formal lines for receiving a cookie. Prabhupāda went from preparation to preparation, eating a few spoonfuls of *sabjī* and then distributing it to the urgent, outstretched hands of the surrounding devotees. After finishing each preparation, he also gave away the silver bowl. Finally, all that was left were two large *gulābjamūns.*

Children began to cry out, "Prabhupāda, give it to me!" Śrīla Prabhupāda took his time, and at last he shook his head no. He took the *gulābjamūn* up himself and bit into it. At the first bite, the *gulābjamūn* juice squirted out, wetting several nearby devotees, who began dancing and shouting. After two bites, Śrīla Prabhupāda gave out the remnants of the *gulābjamūn.* His first bite of the second *gulābjamūn* also produced a stream of juice, and by now the whole temple room was turned into a state of happy pandemonium. The whole episode lasted about fifteen minutes and Śrīla Prabhupāda was obviously feeling great enjoyment, laughing and watching everyone trying to get the *mahā-prasādam* from his hand.

22

PRABHUPĀDA SAID

On Kīrtana and Music

"The harmonium may be played during *bhajana* if there is someone who can play melodiously. But it is not for *kirtana* and *arati.*"

—*Letter of January 11, 1976*

Prabhupāda was present during a *kīrtana* performed by his disciples in the Brooklyn temple. For the devotees, it was the perfection of their singing and playing, to do it for Prabhupāda's personal pleasure. The *mṛdaṅga* player had been practicing to learn complicated beats and he was demonstrating his rapid and intricate abilities in the *kīrtana.* But Prabhupāda stopped the music and said to the drummer, a devotee named Dhīra Kṛṣṇa, that he should follow the leader. Then he started the *kīrtana* again, but it happened again and again Prabhupāda stopped the *kīrtana* and asked the drummer to follow the leader. On another occasion Prabhupāda said, "The drum should not be louder than the voice."

In 1966 in New York City, a boy came by with a record of a famous Indian musician playing a sitar. As soon as the music began, Śrīla Prabhupāda started to smile. The boy asked, "Do you like this music?" Śrīla Prabhupāda said, "This is sense gratification music." The boy was hurt and said, "What do you mean? They play this in the temples in India." So Prabhupāda insisted, "No, this is sense gratification music and this musician is just a businessman." The boy then replied, "Well, you used to be a businessman." Prabhupāda laughed and said, "Because I went naked then, I should go naked now?"

"Well, what if this musician wanted to become a devotee?" asked the boy.

"Oh, that would be very nice," said Prabhupāda, "if he can come. But this is sense gratification music."

23

PRABHUPĀDA TELLS A STORY

In India Śrīla Prabhupāda once gave Tejās dāsa advice on how to elicit the help of big men. He told him to use the rabbit-and-lion philosophy.

Once a group of rabbits were being eaten by a lion, so they made an agreement and met with the lion, pleading with him to limit his killing. They said, "We are all terrified, and you also are not getting to eat everyday. Why don't we make this agreement that every day one of us will come to you and you can eat us? In that way, we will not be so terrified and you will at least get one rabbit a day." The lion agreed to the proposal. But one day, one of the more intelligent rabbits thought, "What is this? Why am I rushing into death? Today is my last day. Let me enjoy on the way." So in a very leisurely way, stopping sometimes beside a river and then a well, the rabbit finally arrived, late, before the lion. The lion was very angry and roared, "Why have you come late?" The rabbit replied, "It is not my fault, because on the way another lion said he was going to eat me. It was all that I could do to get away from him."

The lion said, "Who is challenging my authority? Let me find him." So the rabbit led him to the edge of a well and said, "He's in there." The lion looked inside and saw the shadow of a lion. When he roared, the reflection lion roared back, so the lion jumped into the well to attack. In this way, the rabbit finished the lion.

Prabhupāda told Tejās that he could also do that. If a high-level man says something favorable, then you can go back to him and complain on his behalf. Tell him that you have told one of his clerks or ministers that the top-level man says they must give permission but the clerks are not caring for his word. Then the top minister will say, "Oh? Then I will go and finish him." In this way, Prabhupāda advised how to get a top minister to help obtain permission.

24

PERSONAL

His Silence

He could take a morning walk in silence and then break it. Even more striking was his silent response to something you said. A disciple could ask a question and receive a long silence. A strange-minded woman from Cleveland once went into Prabhupāda's room with some of her relatives and sat in his presence for a long time while no one spoke at all. Later, she said that they all thought Prabhupāda was doing something mystical, that they weren't supposed to talk, and that he was reciprocating by sitting there and not speaking, although considerable time went by.

With his servants he could travel long distances without talking. Once on a long flight from Germany to Australia he was silent and said only a few things. (When the plane landed in Australia, Prabhupāda said that here in Australia it was green and there in Germany it was green, so how can they say there is no life on the moon and other planets?)

Some of his comments were surrounded by long silences. Sometimes he would chastise or question us by his silences, which became so intense that we could not bear them. And you could not penetrate his silence. The quality of gravity is defined as follows in *The Nectar of Devotion:* "A person who doesn't express his mind to everyone or whose mental activity and plan of action are very difficult to understand is called grave."

And he liked quiet in his room. He wouldn't tolerate noises. He would wake his servants to chase dogs when they were howling outside, especially when he was trying to translate in the early morning, and he would send his servants out to track out any odd noises in the building or thereabouts. During his lectures and classes he would detect the slightest noise and ask that it be stopped. A slamming door broke his heart, he said—and sirens in New York, garbage trucks, dogs, in India the tap-tapping of the building construction—but he *could* tolerate it all.

For Prabhupāda, however, real silence was the fact that he never spoke any nonsense. He could talk unendingly about Kṛṣṇa. Sometimes a foolish guest would speak some mundane nonsense and Prabhupāda would tolerantly be silent, but it was unnatural to see Prabhupāda silent in the presence of another person because Prabhupāda was the one who should be speaking. He had absolute knowledge and all others should have been silent to let him speak if he desired to speak. He complied with Kṛṣṇa's wishes and with our wishes that he talk. He spoke from duty, from love, from the preaching spirit.

25

When Śrīla Prabhupāda first went back to India with his American disciples, he sometimes took them on tours of holy places in Vṛndāvana and Māyāpur. One day Prabhupāda was to go with a few disciples in an old American Dodge automobile to visit Devnagar, the birthplace of Bhaktivinoda Ṭhākura. Prabhupāda rode in the front seat with the driver, Śyāmasundara dāsa, and about four other devotees squeezed into the back seat.

They soon discovered, unfortunately, that the old Dodge didn't have a horn. Driving in India without a horn is almost impossible, and the journey was an anticipated two hours. Śrīla Prabhupāda was therefore concerned how they would be able to make it. Soon after they had started, however, Prabhupāda devised a "horn" of his own making. He found a metal plate in the car. Then he had the car stop and the boys got him a stick off the ground. As they rode along, Śrīla Prabhupāda would hold the plate outside the car window and bang on it with a stick whenever there was need of a horn for passing cars and for shooing people and animals from the road. The devotees were amazed and overjoyed at the simple display of Prabhupāda's horn, which he continued to operate from the front seat during the whole journey.

"This will be copied by the Indians," said Śrīla Prabhupāda. "They will think that it is a new American invention. They will also get plates and sticks and use them instead of the horn."

26

When his Godbrothers saw that Tejās dāsa and his wife were sometimes quarreling, they suggested that he should ask Prabhupāda to allow him to take *sannyāsa.* They said it would better enable him to preach. Tejās admittedly thought that his marriage was difficult, and so he resolved to ask Śrīla Prabhupāda at the next opportunity. In those days in India, it was not at all difficult for the devotees to approach Śrīla Prabhupāda in the privacy of his room and ask him such personal questions.

Finding Prabhupāda alone one evening, Tejās approached him.

"So, what do you want?" asked Prabhupāda in his typically direct manner.

"I want to take *sannyāsa,* Prabhupāda," said Tejās.

Just at that moment, before Prabhupāda gave an answer, his servant brought him his evening *prasādam,* some vegetables and fruits.

"Take some *prasādam,"* said Prabhupāda, and he put a piece into Tejās's hand. Then Prabhupāda gave him more and more, until it was falling out of his disciple's hand. Tejās put out his other hand and Prabhupāda filled that one up also. While Tejās became preoccupied in balancing all the *prasādam* in his two hands, Prabhupāda asked, "Why do you want to take *sannyāsa*?"

"For preaching, Prabhupāda."

"But that you're already doing," he said.

"Prabhupāda," Tejās said, "having family life is full of hindrances."

"But your wife is a very nice wife," Prabhupāda objected. "She is cooperative. She is expert at Deity worship, she plays *mṛdaṅga* nicely, and harmonium. She is a nice girl. Why do you want to take *sannyāsa?"*

Tejās replied, "Prabhupāda, because married life is very dangerous."

Prabhupāda replied, "Married life dangerous? I don't see any danger. You tell me what is the danger."

Tejās could see the drift of Prabhupāda's instruction. He thought, "If the spiritual master says there is no danger . . ." Tejās no longer felt up to arguing, and Prabhupāda changed the subject to the practical preaching matters in India.

27

Starting in the 1970s, India became more and more Śrīla Prabhupāda's home base, and his travels to the West became like tours away from home. While traveling to America in the winter of 1973, Śrīla Prabhupāda caught a cold and tried to get rid of it by moving from Los Angeles to Dallas, which he had heard was sunny and warm. But Dallas was also overcast. Prabhupāda began talking of returning to Māyāpur as the only place where he could be at ease and get well. It would be a long trip back, so he had made no definite decision. But one night, about 1 A.M., he walked into the room adjoining his and woke his servant and his secretary.

"Let's go back home, back to Godhead," Prabhupāda said to them while standing in the darkness of the unlit room. His disciples awoke and offered their obeisances at Prabhupāda's feet, wondering what he meant.

"Prabhupāda?" they asked.

"Yes," he repeated. "I want to go back to Godhead. I want to go to Māyāpur."

So they returned to Māyāpur as soon as possible. Once in Māyāpur, Śrīla Prabhupāda's health recovered. There he was most informal and pleased. In those early years, there was not much building development and the devotees were undergoing austerities just to live there. Śrīla Prabhupāda mixed with them freely and in a friendly way. They would walk into his room and sometimes he would walk into theirs. Sometimes even his own servants didn't know exactly where he was at different times of the day. He might be on the roof alone or sometimes he would walk unaccompanied out to the front road. The devotees at Māyāpur couldn't help but appreciate that Prabhupāda was special when he was living in the *dhāma*. They felt it was like the informality of Kṛṣṇa in Goloka as contrasted to Kṛṣṇa's opulence in Dvārakā. Śrīla Prabhupāda in Māyāpur was special and informal in that way.

28

LITTLE DROPS *of* NECTAR

Madhudviṣa dāsa had been the president in Bombay ISKCON, but to Prabhupāda he expressed his dissatisfaction, particularly in working with the Indians. He wanted another preaching field. He said that he considered the Indians to be very sneaky and tricky and that he didn't like dealing with them.

Prabhupāda said, "I am an Indian. Do you think I am very tricky?"

"No, not you, Śrīla Prabhupāda," said Madhudviṣa.

"Actually, I am tricky," said Śrīla Prabhupāda, "because I have tricked all of you into surrendering to Kṛṣṇa, and now you are caught and you cannot get away."

Pañcadraviḍa Swami endured a serious bout of boils in India. The doctor said that he had come close to dying and he had had to perform surgery on his back. When Pañcadraviḍa described his diseased condition to Śrīla Prabhupāda, Prabhupāda looked at him and said, "These diseases are simply imaginary."

"No, Śrīla Prabhupāda, I really have them," said Pañcadraviḍa. He thought that Prabhupāda was saying that the boils were all in his mind. He therefore showed Prabhupāda a big scar that he had on his back from the surgery. Prabhupāda touched the scar with his finger and said nothing further.

Soon after that, in *Bhāgavatam* class, Śrīla Prabhupāda was describing how the sufferings of all living entities are imaginary, created by identification with the material body. Hearing this, Pañcadraviḍa realized the import of Śrīla Prabhupāda's previous words. Yes, in the absolute sense, even the attack of boils was imaginary.

Śrīla Prabhupāda sometimes traveled throughout India by train, accompanied by his disciples. On one occasion, the train stopped in a field full of purple flowers. One of the devotees climbed down, ran into the field, picked some flowers, and ran back to Prabhupāda's car just as the train started to leave. Then the devotees brought Prabhupāda a bouquet of purple flowers as an offering of devotion. Prabhupāda calmly accepted them but said, "Lord Śiva wears these flowers." The devotees were worried that they had made some *guru-aparādha,* but Prabhupāda smiled and stuck one flower behind each of his ears. He widened his eyes and made a large grin, "See?" playing as if he were Lord Śiva with the purple flowers in his hair.

29

PRABHUPĀDA SAID

On Book Production and Distribution

Some of Prabhupāda's well-known maxims stress the value of his books and the necessity to print them with the greatest care.

1. "If there are any mistakes in my books, then the books will not be taken seriously."

2. "Every word in these books is like a document." (And therefore the editors shouldn't be careless or speculate.)
3. "These purports are my devotional ecstasies."

Prabhupāda's first books were printed by devotees at ISKCON Press, but they weren't expertly done. When Prabhupāda received the first copy of one paperback edition of a *Bhāgavatam* chapter, he opened it and the binding fell apart in his hands. To the devotees who saw this he asked, "What will it take for my disciples to learn how to print these books so that they will not fall apart?"

Brahmānanda replied, "Sincerity, Prabhupāda. If we were more sincere, then we could do it."

Śrīla Prabhupāda looked down at the broken book in his hand and said, "No."

The assembled devotees were surprised. One of them asked, "Not sincerity?"

"Sincerity, yes," said Prabhupāda, "plus intelligence."

"Here at Mayapur my Guru Maharaja was printing one paper. It was selling for only a few paisa. Sometimes whenever one *brahmacari* would go to Navadvipa and sell even a few copies, I would see my Guru Maharaja become very much pleased . . . So I am always emphasizing book distribution. It is the better *kīrtana.* It is better than chanting. Of course chanting should not stop, but book distribution is the best *kīrtana.*"

—*Letter of October 24, 1974*

Once, on speaking to a gathering of book distributors, Śrīla Prabhupāda explained to them how Bhaktivinoda Ṭhākura had wanted a temple built in Māyāpur. "You will be the cornerstones," said Prabhupāda to his book distributors. He said that by their distributing books, the temple would be built.

30

PRABHUPĀDA TELLS A STORY

When Śrīla Prabhupāda's edition of *Caitanya-caritāmṛta, Madhya-līlā,* Volume 1, was first published, devotees were surprised and pleased to read about the humorous joking between Lord Nityānanda and Advaita Ācārya during the taking of *prasādam* at Advaita Ācārya's house. One morning, during a car ride with Śrīla Prabhupāda, one of the devotees expressed his appreciation for the new volume.

"There is such nice humor in the *Caitanya-caritāmṛta,* Śrīla Prabhupāda."

"Yes," said Śrīla Prabhupāda, "spiritual life is humor also." Then he began to tell a story. "Kṛṣṇa said to one old lady, 'You are so ugly, you should marry a monkey.'

"'No,' said the old lady, 'I have given up all material desires. I will marry You, Kṛṣṇa!'

"'Yes! Yes! Yes!' All the *gopīs* and boys clapped and laughed."

While Prabhupāda said this, his eyes lit up and he became animated, laughing at the humorous pastimes of Kṛṣṇa. "So Kṛṣṇa was defeated," said Prabhupāda, "by that laughing of the *gopīs.*"

31

PRABHUPĀDA TELLS ANOTHER STORY

In a lecture, Prabhupāda remarked that foolish people often criticize devotees as do-nothings and weaklings, but such people do not understand the intelligence of a devotee. Therefore, a devotee does not have to heed such people. To illustrate the point, Śrīla Prabhupāda told a story.

Some laborers were criticizing the minister of the king, claiming that he only sat around and did no work. The king reminded them that it took intelligence to become a minister. He said he would give everyone a test, including the minister. Whoever could pass the test could become the next minister. The king said, "Take this big elephant, weigh him, and let me know the exact weight."

The ordinary men were baffled. Where was there a scale for weighing an elephant? They could not do anything. They came back to the king with no information. Then the king turned to his minister and asked, "Will you kindly weigh this elephant?" In six minutes he came back and reported, "It is twenty mounds (1,930 lbs)." The other men were standing open-mouthed in surprise. "How is that?" they asked. "Within six minutes he came back and he gave the exact weight!"

The king asked, "How did you weigh him? Did you get some very big scale?"

"No, sir," replied the minister. "It is not possible to weigh the elephant on a scale. It is very difficult."

"Then how did you weigh it?"

"I took it on a boat. When I got him on the boat then I saw the watermark and I marked it. Then, after getting the elephant off the boat, I added weight onto the boat, and when it came to the same watermark, then I understood."

So the king addressed the laborers and questioned them. "Now you see the difference?" They agreed, "Yes."

After telling this story, Prabhupāda quoted from the scripture. "*Buddhir yasya baliṁ tasya-nirbuddhes tu kuto balaṁ:* one who has got intelligence, he has strength, and one who has no intelligence, a rascal, has no strength." Prabhupāda concluded, "Scientists, atheists, and different critics of devotees are like that—rascal, fools. We don't take advice from them. We take advice from Kṛṣṇa or His representative."

32

PERSONAL

Evening Massage

Evening massage was not as thorough as his pre-noon one—just massage his legs, squeeze them, up and down from the knee down to the feet, then the feet and toes also. He taught the technique. He said it gave some relief. At these times he was prone to sweet reflections. Was he sleeping? Sometimes. Or he would speak something. The servant might have to stay up a considerable while. Usually it was in a darkened room. In Australia, at the end of the day, after he and the devotees had marched a great distance in the Ratha-yātrā parade, Prabhupāda complimented his servant on his dancing so nicely in the parade. It was also during a night massage that he told another servant the story of how he got a special pair of shoes as a child from England, a gift from his father. Also, he would bring up the philosophy and the inability of *mūḍhas* to take to it.

To us, Prabhupāda was a mystical ocean. His utterances were not coming by our dictation. Yet we were also as close as possible, right by his side, touching his body, connected by speech, so he was tangibly with us. And yet he was like a mystical ocean, and his purity created an aloofness for those who were still impure. One didn't even dare to think, "What is Prabhupāda thinking?"

In the dark room during the evening massage, his servant used to want to take rest. Now, he may consider what a fool he was. If he had another chance, would he be the same fool? No one likes to be the servant; we want to be the master, but Prabhupāda kept us in check. He made us devotees.

33

One morning in Berkeley, Śrīla Prabhupāda was walking on the university campus. *Sannyāsī* disciples and others were there, and also Kṛṣṇa dāsa Adhikārī. Kṛṣṇa dāsa had left the movement and grown long hair, but he had recently shown a revival of interest and was now walking with Prabhupāda. His questions were full of his various doubts. At the very end of the walk, somehow the topic of feeling separation from the spiritual master came up. Kṛṣṇa dāsa asked, "You must always be feeling separation from your spiritual master." He was hoping to prompt Śrīla Prabhupāda to talk about his feelings of separation from Śrīla Bhaktisiddhānta Sarasvatī Ṭhākura. Śrīla Prabhupāda was silent, Kṛṣṇa dāsa asked the question again: "I suppose you must always be feeling separation from your spiritual master." Prabhupāda then answered, "That you do not require." (In other words, "That's none of your business to ask.") Then he got in his car and left.

34

When Śrīla Prabhupāda visited Hawaii, he had to deal with controversial persons who claimed to be his followers and yet denounced the International Society for Krishna Consciousness. Prabhupāda wanted to encourage everyone to go on chanting Hare Kṛṣṇa, yet at the same time he wanted to clearly establish that his sincere follower works within ISKCON. The questions and answers after his lectures in Hawaii often dealt with these matters.

"What is ISKCON?" asked a long-haired beach boy wearing a *japa* beadbag.

"ISKCON?" Śrīla Prabhupāda replied. "It is a simple thing. You do not know?" Then he described what each letter in the acronym ISKCON stood for. "We have a worldwide society, so we say international."

"Well, are *you* ISKCON?" the boy asked. This was a loaded question. The devotees had been preaching that Śrīla Prabhupāda was ISKCON because one cannot refuse service to ISKCON and yet claim to serve Śrīla Prabhupāda. But the anti-ISKCON party had argued that Śrīla Prabhupāda and ISKCON were different. Prabhupāda was pure and transcendental; ISKCON was corrupt, a mere organization.

Śrīla Prabhupāda started to laugh. "I am not ISKCON," he said. "I am a member of ISKCON." Then he looked at his disciple who was the GBC secretary for Hawaii. Prabhupāda pointed at him and said, "And he is a member of ISKCON." Then he pointed to the ISKCON Hawaii temple president. "And he is a member of ISKCON. We are all members of ISKCON, the International Society for Krishna Consciousness." Almost everyone present cried out, "*Jaya*!" Then Śrīla Prabhupāda looked back, smiling. There was no further challenge to his perfect, humble reply.

35

In Bombay, devotees were able to freely see Śrīla Prabhupāda and ask their questions, but Pañcadraviḍa Swami sensed that as the movement grew he might not be able to maintain such an intimate relationship with his spiritual master. One day he entered Śrīla Prabhupāda's apartment and revealed his doubt.

"I don't understand," Pañcadraviḍa said. "ISKCON is such a big society. How can I understand that I have a personal relationship with you? If I am somewhere halfway around the world and I am, for instance, sweeping or washing a floor in a temple, how can I know that I am serving you personally?"

"Yes, ISKCON is so big," Prabhupāda answered simply, "But I am so small." Pañcadraviḍa immediately felt satisfied, but Śrīla Prabhupāda explained it further.

"You speak of serving in the temple somewhere," said Prabhupāda, "but actually you don't have to do anything. I am responsible directly. I have to maintain all the temples, see that the floors are swept, the pots washed, and that everything is clean in all the ISKCON temples all over the world. But I cannot do it all by myself. It is like an *ārati* ceremony. I may be offering the *ārati*, but I ask you, 'Please hand me the fan,' so that I can offer it to Rādhā-Kṛṣṇa. In the same way, I am asking you to help me in the temple by preaching or sweeping the floor. Do you understand?"

36

LITTLE DROPS *of* NECTAR

In Hyderabad, after a *paṇḍāl* lecture program, a teenaged Indian boy spent the night with the devotees. The next morning he entered Śrīla Prabhupāda's room along with the initiated devotees and sat down close to Prabhupāda. As soon as Prabhupāda saw the boy, he pointed to the door without saying a word. The boy also said nothing, but got up and left. Śrīla Prabhupāda then turned to one of the *sannyāsīs* and said, "First he must wash all the pots." He explained that Bhaktisiddhānta Sarasvatī Ṭhākura had always first tested the sincerity of someone who wanted to join by asking him to wash pots.

In Japan, Śrīla Prabhupāda rode the monorail. At first the seat in front of him was empty, and Bhūrijana dāsa invited Prabhupāda to put his feet up there, since the seats were uncomfortably cramped. The empty seat was actually reserved for one of Prabhupāda's disciples, Bhānu dāsa, and the monorail authorities finally insisted that everyone must sit in his own seat. Bhūrijana then again turned to Śrīla Prabhupāda, this time with trepidation.

"Śrīla Prabhupāda, one of the devotees has to sit down. Will you remove your lotus feet?"

"Yes," Śrīla Prabhupāda replied, "I will move my feet so that the lotus-like devotee can sit down."

Śatadhanya Mahārāja was talking with Śrīla Prabhupāda in his room in Māyāpur when he discovered that ants were crawling over Prabhupāda's desk. Śatadhanya stood and began pushing away the ants with light, brushing motions of his cloth. Peacefully sitting back against the bolster pillows, Prabhupāda watched and commented, "Before you would have killed them, but now you are purified."

37

PRABHUPĀDA SAID

On Money

One time on a walk, Prabhupāda was explaining how the paper currency is a cheating process. He said that the government encourages people to work hard in the factories to develop the economy of the nation, and yet they pay them only pieces of paper. When the government doesn't have enough pieces of paper, they print up more, and thus the whole economy is based on cheating. Prabhupāda said that the Vedic economy is based on the bartering system. If the bartering system is not possible, then at least the gold standard should be used because the gold has some value and the quantity of gold is limited. After hearing Prabhupāda describe the ideal economy based on the Vedic civilization, one devotee asked, "But if all transactions are done in gold, it would be very difficult to make large deals, because to carry the gold and exchange it would be very cumbersome."

"That's very good," replied Prabhupāda. "Why should there be big transactions? Big transactions means that people are accumulating more than they require. We don't want big transactions. We want each person to have what they require."

Prabhupāda told a proverb about money. One man asked another, "Are you intelligent?" The second man started to look in his pockets. The first man asked, "Why are you looking in your pockets?" The second man said, "Well, if there is any money there, that means I'm intelligent." Prabhupāda explained, "Actually, in our movement everything is going on by my intelligence and your cooperation. So you are preaching very intelligently, but if there is not money, then where is the intelligence?"

Prabhupāda instructed that fifty percent of income should go to the Book Fund and fifty percent should go to construction or other projects. He said that the Kṛṣṇa consciousness movement was, in one sense, just like a business, and so it should be run in that way. In other words, it was on the basis of his books that the movement was getting its collections, whether by life membership or book sales. Therefore, just as in any business, the capital assets had to be invested in. "You must therefore give fifty percent of your money to the Book Fund."

"We should live on a paltry income, whatever we receive by selling our magazines, but in dire necessity when there is no other way, we may accept some service temporarily. But on principle, we should go on *sankirtana,* not work. So whatever Krsna gives us, we should accept on that principle. You are a senior member of the society; you should have known all these things. Anyway, send them back on *sankirtana.* All the Amsterdam devotees should be engaged in *sankirtana,* not in a cigarette factory."

—*Letter of August 17, 1971*

Prabhupāda approved of his disciples making ambitious plans for spreading Kṛṣṇa consciousness. "But Prabhupāda," one devotee asked, "how are we going to get the money to do all this?" Prabhupāda said, "You make the plans, Kṛṣṇa will provide the money."

"Concerning Ganesa worship, it is not actually necessary for us. But, if someone has the sentiment for getting the blessing of Ganesa to get large amounts of money for Krsna's service, then it is all right. But anyone who takes up this kind of worship must send me at least one hundred thousand dollars monthly—not less. If he cannot send this amount, he cannot do Ganesa worship."

—*Letter of December 28, 1974*

Śrīla Prabhupāda was not keen on banking money. "As soon as there will be money in the bank," he said, "there will be headache. This tax, that tax."

Prabhupāda said, "We have no problems, although we have so much money. If we were to lose that money, still we would not be hampered in our mission. *Ahaituky apratihatā*—without being checked. Kṛṣṇa consciousness is prosecuted in pure devotion."

"Yes," one of the devotees agreed, "even if we had to write the books out by hand and distribute them."

38

PRABHUPĀDA TELLS SHORT STORIES

In Australia, Śrīla Prabhupāda was waiting in an airport terminal for a delayed flight. He asked Amogha dāsa to go to the desk to find out the departure time. The desk clerk answered that the new boarding time would be in fifteen minutes. Śrīla Prabhupāda heard this, but after twenty minutes, when there was no call, he asked the devotees to check again. Again, the report was fifteen minutes. Śrīla Prabhupāda kept looking at his watch every fifteen minutes and asking the devotees to find out more information.

After some time, Prabhupāda told a story. He said that a man once testified in a court case that he had been fifty years old for the last fifteen years, and he claimed that due to honesty, he had not wished to change his statement. "So," Śrīla Prabhupāda said, "still they say fifteen minutes to boarding time. That is honesty. It is one hour and fifteen minutes, and still they do not change their word—'fifteen minutes.'"

One of Prabhupāda's Bengali stories was about a doctor visiting a house to diagnose two patients, a rich housewife and her maidservant. The doctor said, "The maidservant's fever is 105°, so there is some anxiety. I will give her some medicine. But the landlady of the house has practically no fever, 99°, so there is no anxiety for her." When she heard this, the landlady became angry and said, "This doctor is useless. I'm the landlady. I've only got 99° and my maidservant has 105°. The maidservant should have 98°, I should have 110°!"

Prabhupāda compared this to the modern civilization, which is inclined to increase the degree of its fever up to 110°. As in the human body there is death as soon as the temperature reaches 107°, so Prabhupāda said that by the nuclear weapons, modern civilization will come to the point of 107° and over. But devotees want to decrease the fever, by living the highest, ideal life and decreasing the demands of the body.

39

MORE SHORT STORIES

Śrīla Prabhupāda said that many of his Godbrothers were envious of his success in preaching. He did not like to point it out, but he wanted his disciples to be aware of the nature of the criticisms his Godbrothers would make to belittle the work of ISKCON. "They cannot do anything themselves," said Śrīla Prabhupāda, "and if somebody does something they will be envious. That is the nature of a third-class man."

To illustrate, Prabhupāda told a story he had heard from his spiritual master. One man informed another that a man known to them had become the high court judge.

"Oh no," said the second man. "No—that cannot be right."

"Yes, he is now a judge," said the first friend. "I have seen him sitting on the bench."

The second man replied, "Maybe, but I don't think he is getting any salary."

Prabhupāda said such envious men will find out some fault anywhere. Even if there is no fault actually, they will manufacture some fault. That is their business. Prabhupāda said that many persons were envious of his Guru Mahārāja, but Bhaktisiddhānta Sarasvatī did not care for them.

For years in India, Śrīla Prabhupāda had traveled in dilapidated autos, and he often had to borrow cars. But as his movement grew, he felt it was not right. "We are spending crores of rupees to finish this Bombay construction," he said, "but whenever I arrive at the airport, I am picked up in a borrowed car. What kind of impression is it to the life members that we always have to approach them to borrow their car?"

For years, the car was discussed and contemplated, but it never appeared. Later, Prabhupāda received a letter from a disciple in Europe who said that he would purchase a Mercedes for Prabhupāda in Germany and drive it to India. Prabhupāda sent him a telegram, "Yes, purchase Mercedes." At that time, the devotees with Prabhupāda in India said that they had heard the devotee was going to purchase the car with money from Prabhupāda's Book Fund. Prabhupāda said this was like a famous story. A guru went to his disciple's home and was greeted very elaborately. When he inquired how it was possible for his disciple to afford such nice arrangements, the disciple told him, "Gurudeva, everything belongs to you." Later the guru saw that he had no money left in his own bank account and he could understand that the disciple had spent all of his guru's money.

Prabhupāda ordered that his disciples should not purchase a car for him with money from the Book Fund and then claim, "Prabhupāda, everything belongs to you."

40

MORE SHORT STORIES

In Bengali there is a saying, "If you can walk on your hands, do it, but whatever you do, change." Prabhupāda told this to illustrate his dislike for whimsical changes. He was especially anxious that after his departure his followers might take a free hand with his books or the Deity worship and make unnecessary, unauthorized changes.

There was the story about the expert craftsmanship of a plasterer who worked on the construction of the Taj Mahal. One of the top directors of the construction was inspecting the building in progress and noticed for three days in a row a certain plasterer who was sitting in the same place mixing plaster. On the third day the inspector became angry and said, "Why are you still simply sitting and mixing this plaster? You are so lazy!" The man who was mixing the plaster also became very angry, and he threw a handful of his plaster at the inspector. The plaster missed the inspector but landed on a wall. The plaster was so well mixed, however, so solid and hard, that no one could get it off the wall, and it is still there today.

Prabhupāda told this story to stress the importance of good craftsmanship and of doing everything nicely in Kṛṣṇa's service.

One of Prabhupāda's disciple-secretaries knew some Hindi and wrote out a letter that Prabhupāda had dictated. But the devotee apologized, "My handwriting is not very good."

"It doesn't matter," said Śrīla Prabhupāda. "No one can write Hindi nicely." Then Prabhupāda told a joke.

Someone wrote a letter to a friend in Hindi. The man replied, "Next time you write a letter in Hindi, please send train fare to go to your place."

The friend wrote back, "Why is that?"

The other friend replied, "Because I have to go to you to decipher your letters."

41

PERSONAL

Drinking Water

Once after silently demonstrating his technique of drinking water, Prabhupāda said to a boy who was present, "You cannot do that." One reason for drinking in that manner was cleanliness; one's lip or mouth doesn't touch the edge of the drinking vessel. Prabhupāda would pour the water down, swallowing, and then tilting the chalice upright, stop the flow of water without spilling a drop.

In India, the water would be kept cool in big clay jugs. In the West, water was served with ice sometimes. Once when Prabhupāda asked for water, his servant asked, "Do you want cold water?" Prabhupāda replied, "Water *means* cold water."

And water must be covered. In India, to leave a clay jug of water uncovered is, he said, "signing your death warrant." In the West, the pitcher also should be covered.

He could appreciate different tastes of water. We would make efforts to get him the best water from special sources, like Bhagatjī's well in Vṛndāvana.

He would drink quite a bit of water for health and digestion. He would make comments about it as we sat with him in his room watching him drink water. But don't draw his water from a bathroom! Pradyumna dāsa asked how it is actually different if the water comes from the bathroom, provided one doesn't know where the water comes from. Prabhupāda replied that it would affect the mind, even if you didn't know where the water came from, because the bathroom is a contaminated place.

Only a disciple could know how sweet it was to talk about these apparently mundane things. To confer with Prabhupāda about his needs or to talk about water was relief from greater problems. One thought, "Let me stay here and supply Prabhupāda water so he can preach and write books; nothing else is as important as his water, his health, his daily *Bhāgavatam* work, his being pleased. Nothing is as nice to see as his drinking, as the water falls from the cup to his mouth."

42

When Śrīla Prabhupāda was about to leave Los Angeles for a world tour in 1976, he called some of the devotees to his room. "Open my *almirā*," he said to Rāmeśvara Swami, who opened the metal locker containing Śrīla Prabhupāda's clothes.

"Do you see those *kūrtas*?" said Prabhupāda. "Pick one." Rāmeśvara Swami picked out a bright orange one.

"You like that one?" Prabhupāda asked.

"Yes."

"All right. That is for you." Rāmeśvara was overwhelmed to receive the treasure of a remnant of Prabhupāda's clothes. Other devotees also received clothes and gifts from Prabhupāda's hand. Then it was almost time for him to go to the airport. With graceful artistry, Prabhupāda sat at his desk and applied the Vaiṣṇava *tilaka* to his forehead. Rāmeśvara Swami thought to himself that everything about Prabhupāda, the way he sat or walked, the way he dressed, and the way he put on his *tilaka,* was all majestic and opulent. As Prabhupāda stood to leave the room, Rāmeśvara voiced his appreciation.

"Prabhupāda, you appear to us to be just like a king."

"I am much more than any king," said Prabhupāda, and then he walked downstairs. There he was met by a hundred devotees who accompanied him to the airport as he began another world tour.

43

A few months before Śrīla Prabhupāda's first visit to ISKCON Dallas, a strong windstorm hit the area, felling trees. A tall, valuable shade tree in the courtyard of the temple also fell over and remained leaning against an adjoining building, the children's *prasādam* hall. The tree still had its roots in the ground, but its heavy weight, with dangling branches, now lay in a sharp angle right across the walkway, leaving barely enough room to walk under it. Satsvarūpa dāsa, the temple president, took no immediate action, but different devotees approached him and said that the tree had to be removed right away or it might cause collapse of the building it was leaning against. Satsvarūpa agreed, and one of the devotees climbed the tall tree with a power saw and gradually dismantled the upper branches and trunk, until nothing remained but the lower ten feet of tilted trunk.

And thus the tree appeared when Śrīla Prabhupāda came there in September 1972. As soon as he walked into the courtyard, accompanied by temple leaders and trailed by the whole assembly of *gurukula* children and teachers, Prabhupāda saw the remains of the big tree, and his face expressed trouble. He walked off the cement path and went up to the tree, and so did everyone else behind him.

"Who has done this?" he demanded. Satsvarūpa admitted responsibility and explained the reason the tree had been destroyed. Prabhupāda shook his head angrily. "That was no reason to kill it," he said. Satsvarūpa tried to explain the dangerous condition and pointed to the dent in the roof of the building. He also said that the fallen tree would probably have soon died.

"No, it is not dead," Prabhupāda challenged. "Look. There is a green twig growing out of it." Prabhupāda walked away, disgusted, and the devotees remained shocked at what they now saw as a brutal, unnecessary act. In his room, Prabhupāda continued to criticize the killing of the tree. He said this was the typical American attitude—when something is wrong, immediately cut it down and destroy it, with no understanding or compassion for the presence of the soul.

Later, feeling repentant, Satsvarūpa asked if he had committed an offense.

"Not offense," said Śrīla Prabhupāda. "You are ignorant."

44

In an attempt to make Śrīla Prabhupāda's quarters in Los Angeles attractive and pleasing for him, the women used to change his vases daily, putting in abundant fresh flowers.

One day, Śrīla Prabhupāda entered from his morning walk and noticed that the flower vases were missing.

"Where are the vases?" he asked.

The servant replied that the women had probably taken them to put in fresh flowers.

"The flowers in it were fine," he said. Then he began complaining. "Why do they change these flowers every day? Why are they so wasteful? Who is doing this? Tell them to change them only when they go bad. Where is the vase? Go find it immediately."

Prabhupāda's servant went down to the kitchen and found the girls changing the flowers. "You'd better stop changing these flowers every day," he said. "Prabhupāda doesn't want it. Make sure the vase is never out of his room." When his servant returned to the room with the vases of flowers, Prabhupāda continued on the same theme.

"Just do it when it is necessary," he said. "You shouldn't waste so much on flowers. This is your custom in America, simply wasting. If you have some extra cloth, you cannot fold it, you cut it off and throw it away. Whatever goes wrong, you solve it with money and it appears good. You make some accident and you cover it quickly with money. It is not that you are very capable, but with money you can cover your deficiencies."

45

Girirāja dāsa had been serving Śrīla Prabhupāda in Bombay for quite a few years when he finally returned for a visit to the United States to recover his health and to see his parents in Chicago. When he returned again to Bombay, Prabhupāda inquired about his health and his visit to his parents' home.

Girirāja described how during the two-day visit with his family, his father had invited a friend, who was a psychologist, to have a talk with Girirāja. The psychologist, a woman, had begun asking Girirāja whether he felt that in his childhood there was any lack in his relationship with his parents. Girirāja had replied on the basis of *Bhagavad-gītā,* that actually each of us had passed through many bodies in many different lifetimes, and in each lifetime we had different parents, but our real father is Kṛṣṇa. The psychologist had kept trying to speak to him on the psychological level, but Girirāja had kept replying to her on the spiritual platform, so it was very difficult for her to make progress in her analysis. After she left the room, Girirāja had overheard her speaking to his parents in the hallway, saying that as far as she could see, there was nothing more she could do.

"Yes," Prabhupāda replied, "they called her so that she could try to cure you, but actually your disease is incurable. You can never go back." Hearing these words from his spiritual master, Girirāja became engladdened.

46

An elderly Indian gentleman who visited Prabhupāda in his room became gradually critical of Śrīla Prabhupāda's preaching.

"Swamijī," the man said, "you should not criticize so many persons. You should see everyone equally. The *Bhagavad-gītā* says, *paṇḍitāḥ sama-darśinaḥ:* you should see everybody equally."

Prabhupāda replied, "That is a higher stage. I am not on that stage. I distinguish. On the higher stage you don't distinguish between pious activity and sinful activity. But I distinguish. I say, 'You are sinning and you should stop.'"

As the discussion continued, Prabhupāda kept referring to the previous *ācāryas* in order to support his viewpoint. "I have my *Bhagavad-gītā,*" said Prabhupāda. "I have my *ācāryas.* I stand on their authority."

Pursuing the argument, Prabhupāda's visitor said, "What have you done beyond that? You are just repeating what they've done. What have you done?"

Prabhupāda replied, "I've not done anything. I'm simply repeating. So my contribution is that I have made this knowledge available to people all over the world. Without discrimination, I have given Kṛṣṇa consciousness to everyone. That is my contribution and that is my version of *paṇḍitāḥ sama-darśinah.*" Prabhupāda concluded the interview with those words, and the man expressed gratefulness.

Later in the hall, while leaving, the man was remarking out loud to himself, "Very interesting . . . He sees everyone equally . . . "

47

LITTLE DROPS *of* NECTAR

Bhavānanda Goswami had been a professional decorator before meeting Śrīla Prabhupāda, so Prabhupāda engaged him in that propensity by asking him to decorate the altar for the first Rādhā-Kṛṣṇa Deities in America. Bhavānanda had just completed his work and was bowing down before the forms of Rādhā and Kṛṣṇa when Śrīla Prabhupāda entered the room.

"Oh, very nice," Prabhupāda said. "Who has done this?"

"I have, Śrīla Prabhupāda," Bhavānanda replied.

"Yes," said Śrīla Prabhupāda, "you can decorate the naked dancing club and go to hell, or you can decorate the temple and go back to Vaikuṇṭha."

When Śrīla Prabhupāda stayed in Los Angeles, a two-year-old boy named Bhakta Viśvaretā became very attached to him, and Prabhupāda showed him special mercy. Bhakta

Viśvaretā used to crawl up the stairs and into Prabhupāda's room without knocking. He would sit with his back straight before Prabhupāda, and when Prabhupāda gave him some *prasādam,* he would not eat it until Prabhupāda asked him to do so. Prabhupāda was very pleased that at such a young age, the boy could chant *japa,* recite verses, and sing and dance in *kīrtana.* When Bhakta Viśvaretā was five years old, Prabhupāda asked his parents to send him to the *gurukula* in Dallas. Then one time when Prabhupāda visited Dallas, he again met with Bhakta Viśvaretā, and it was like the reunion of two old friends.

Yet this time, Bhakta Viśvaretā was extremely shy. He wouldn't bow down or say or do anything in Prabhupāda's presence. He just stood there looking down. Prabhupāda began to pinch him in several places and tugged at his *śikhā,* but the boy wouldn't respond. Then Prabhupāda finally asked him whether he would like a sweetball. Bhakta Viśvaretā nodded his head yes. Prabhupāda had his servant get one, and they gave it to him. When he took it and immediately ate it, Prabhupāda smiled and said, "Ah, he is a devotee of *prasādam.*"

48

PRABHUPĀDA SAID

On the Origin of the Living Entity

"The next question is about the living entity falling down in this material world and not from the impersonal Brahman. Existence in the impersonal Brahman is also within the category of non-Krsna consciousness. Those who are in the Brahman effulgence are also in a fallen condition, so there is no question of falling down from a fallen condition. When fall takes place, it means falling down from the non-fallen condition.

"The non-fallen condition is Krsna consciousness. So long as one can maintain pure Krsna consciousness, he is not fallen. As soon as he is out of Krsna consciousness, he is fallen down. It does not matter where a living entity stays. In the material world also there are different stages of living conditions, and to remain in the Brahman effulgence is also another phase of that fallen condition. Just like in the *Bhagavad-gita* it is stated that conditioned souls by their pious activities are elevated to the higher planetary systems, but as soon as their stock of pious activities is finished they again come down on the earthly planet. Similarly, those who are elevated beyond the planetary systems to the Brahman effulgence, they are also prone to fall down as much as the living entity from a higher planetary system."

—*Letter of June 13, 1970*

49

PERSONAL

His wearing a hat and other striking, casual poses and attitudes

Sometimes Śrīla Prabhupāda would wear a "swami" hat at a comical angle, with the flaps sticking out on either side of his head. Sometimes he would lie with his body draped across his sitting place, feet and legs hanging over the bolster pillows, completely relaxed. Sometimes he would transcendentally doze in a sitting position in his room. Of course, he did not behave so casually when guests were there.

His walk with his cane was aristocratic, as was the tilt of his head. Everyone received him as a refined gentleman. He was usually seen in public with a large entourage. Often when he was alone or at least in smaller groups, the casual and graceful poses of his body, sitting or walking, his movements in holding a chalice of water, the pinky extended (a *mudrā* signifying perfection), the silk cuff of his sleeve showing under his sweater, and then the soft, smooth-lined palms of his hands displayed while talking—all these charmed and pacified the heart.

Sometimes Prabhupāda would be preaching at length and then suddenly stand up and walk out of the room while everyone waited for his return. On his exit and on his re-entry, everyone would bow down. These small, pleasurable aspects of his presence were a background to the serious business of life with Śrīla Prabhupāda. Prabhupāda was stern and grave, always talking about immediate plans, heavy surrenders that he asked of his disciples. And yet the steady joy of being with Prabhupāda was always there. Both were there—the joys of being near his person, and the heaviness of his orders. And in his presence, Kṛṣṇa's protection was always there.

50

SERVICE IN SEPARATION

"Our meeting and separation in the material world is like the flowing tide of the river. During the flowing tide of the river, so many different floating articles meet together, and with the flowing, they again become separated by the movement of the waves. That is exactly the way of material life. But our separation, although it resembles exactly the material way, is completely different. In the spiritual world, separation is more relishable than meeting. In other words, in spiritual life there is no separation. Separation is eternal, and meeting is also eternal. Separation is simply another feature of meeting."

—*Letter of April 3, 1969*

The fact that Prabhupāda had the potency to empower young boys and girls to go all over the world and establish this movement is a transcendental reality. That was his glory. And the people who were not physically with Prabhupāda, they were having just as intense, and sometimes more intense, experiences. Prabhupāda was sometimes more intensely present in those places.

The reality of Prabhupāda's appearance on the earth is even today expanding. It's not that he is a material person—that's the whole point. Prabhupāda was not a human being confined only to wherever he was personally present. His personal presence was special; and those were special pastimes. But practically Prabhupāda was like the sun—he expanded his potency everywhere. And he is still doing so. Prabhupāda is the *jagat-guru* who expands himself all over the world and is continuing to expand himself into the hearts of everyone.

That is stated in the *Bhāgavatam,* in the case of Sūta Gosvāmī: *taṁ sarva-bhūta-hṛdayaṁ munim ānato 'smi.* Sūta said about his guru, Śuka, "I offer my obeisances to my spiritual master, who enters into the heart of everyone." And similarly, Vyāsadeva glorified his guru, Nārada, by saying: *tvaṁ paryaṭann arka iva tri-lokīm antaś-caro vāyur ivātma-sākṣī.* "You are just like the sun. You go everywhere, exactly like the sun, all over the universe." So Vyāsadeva said, *antaś-cara:* you actually enter within everything. And *vāyur iva:* you are just like the wind. "Just as the air goes inside your body and also outside your body," so he said, "my spiritual master can go inside and outside of everything." So it should be understood that Prabhupāda actually was and is expanding himself all over the whole universe.

—*Hṛdayānanda Goswami*

Someone who takes the Bhaktivedanta Book Trust very seriously, they consider that to be their relationship with Prabhupāda. I consider that I was his personal servant for helping to manifest his books as quickly as possible. My relationship with Prabhupāda has always been in that way, by reading his books, making his books, and distributing his books on *saṅkīrtana,* and I've never felt lack of association. When I was editing his books I felt completely fulfilled just handing in those chapters every week. It was all I wanted in life.

—*Devāmṛta Swami*

I know that as long as we try to please Prabhupāda by preaching within ISKCON, then we cannot go wrong. So my shelter, when Prabhupāda left the planet, was to stay in his society, with the devotees and the preaching that is going on. I know that Prabhupāda will bless anyone who stays in this society, especially his disciples.

—*Jaya Mādhava dāsa*

I know how Prabhupāda felt about different aspects of the Māyāpur project. One day I was walking up the road when all of a sudden it just flashed into my mind that this road is so sacred because Prabhupāda used to take his morning walk here. Feelings like that give you stronger affection and motivation in devotional service, in your project. You see a spigot and it's dripping water, and you know how Prabhupāda reacted to that—that Prabhupāda consciousness is there.

—*Ānakadundubhi dāsa*

Devotees come here to Prabhupāda's house in Vṛndāvana, and they become completely absorbed in the mood of service here. Many of them just come and sit here alone and remember Prabhupāda while chanting. There were so many intimate experiences here for many of Prabhupāda's devotees, just in these few rooms. So I realize that Prabhupāda's house is a special place for so many of Prabhupāda's loving disciples who had many personal exchanges with Prabhupāda here. If the place is not being taken care of nicely, that's an offense to them as well, because it means that Prabhupāda's memory isn't being maintained nicely.

—*Daiviśakti-devī dāsī*

I have probably read the books about four or five times since Prabhupāda left the planet, and one thing I can say is that I have begun to feel that I am actually with Prabhupāda when I read his books. I think, "Now is the time to sit down with Prabhupāda." Just as if Prabhupāda were coming to your temple, if you could get away and listen to him speaking, you certainly should. When the guru is speaking, the disciple should come as soon as possible. So in that way, I try to give time every day to reading Prabhupāda's books.

—*Rohiṇīnandana dāsa*

I think my relationship with Prabhupāda to a large extent revolves around duty. He gave me my service, and I think that a devotee should not ask for any different service. He should have his service given him by his spiritual master until he is asked to do something else, even if that means he does it all his life. It took me about ten years to come to this point. Before this, there would always be doubts coming in that "Maybe something else . . . Maybe I'm not so suited to this and should do something else." But I think that in most cases it is *māyā*. A devotee is given a certain service, and just like in any army, you have to do your duty even if you are going to be killed. This is for me a very strong principle in my consciousness of Prabhupāda, that I cannot give up the duty of pushing on Kṛṣṇa consciousness in my area.

—*Bahūdak dāsa*

"Thank you very much and all the devotees for offering me a garland daily as you were doing when I was physically present. If a disciple is constantly engaged in carrying out the instructions of his spiritual master, he is supposed to be constantly in company with his spiritual master. This is called *vani-seva*. So there are two kinds of service to the spiritual master. One is called *vani-seva* and the other is called *vapuh-seva*. *Vani-seva* means 'executing the instruction,' and *vapuh-seva* means 'physically personally rendering service.' So in the absence of physical presentation of the spiritual master, the *vani-seva* is more important."

—*Letter of August 22, 1970*

Prabhupāda
Nectar 2

"Although we are unable to glorify you adequately, we nonetheless have a transcendental taste to glorify your activities. We shall try to glorify your activities. We shall try to glorify you according to the instructions received from authoritative sages and scholars. Whatever we speak, however, is always inadequate and very insignificant."

—*Śrīmad-Bhāgavatam* 4.16.3
Praise of King Pṛthu
by the Professional Reciters

1

Although Śrīla Prabhupāda taught by constantly giving encouragement to his disciples, he could also teach by humiliating them and thus very quickly bringing them to a better self-awareness. Many devotees give testimonies of these sometimes brief but powerful moments with Prabhupāda.

Once on a walk along Juhu Beach with Śrīla Prabhupāda, Girirāja dāsa was describing the preaching he had done to newspaper men.

"Yes, you are a very good public relations man," said Śrīla Prabhupāda, which made Girirāja feel highly elated. A little later the discussion turned to humility. Girirāja said that sometimes he felt he wasn't really doing anything for Kṛṣṇa and the Kṛṣṇa consciousness movement.

"That is good," said Prabhupāda. "That feeling is humbleness."

"But sometimes," said Girirāja, "that feeling is turned into *māyā*."

Śrīla Prabhupāda stopped walking and looked abruptly at his disciple. "Being *turned* into *māyā*?" said Prabhupāda. "You are *always* in *māyā*!" These words hit Girirāja so strongly that he immediately offered obeisances before Śrīla Prabhupāda. He had suddenly realized his actually position and had gained a glimpse of Śrīla Prabhupāda's position as his spiritual master.

Another time, Nava-yogendra dāsa got a dose of the same medicine. He was chanting in a room with Śrīla Prabhupāda, who pointed out that Nava-yogendra's beadbag was on the floor.

"No, Prabhupāda, it's on my *cādar,*" said Nava-yogendra.

"But you walk on that *cādar,*" Prabhupāda said. "You have no respect for your beadbag?" Nava-yogendra accepted the criticism, but took heart and began chanting loudly. Then Prabhupāda remarked, "Don't chant so loudly." So Nava-yogendra began to chant quietly. But Prabhupāda said, "If you are chanting, you should not disturb the spiritual master."

On a morning walk into the fields near Bhaktivedanta Manor in England, Rohiṇīnandana dāsa—in his first face-to-face exchange with Śrīla Prabhupāda—got a similar treatment. Prabhupāda and the devotees were walking down the narrow, winding country road when they came upon a sign that said, "Horticultural Show." Prabhupāda pointed to the sign with his cane and said, "What is 'horticultural?'" The devotees stopped walking, but no one said anything until Rohiṇīnandana spoke from the back of the group.

"Śrīla Prabhupāda," he said, "I think it means fruits and flowers and vegetables growing." Prabhupāda turned quickly and looked back at Rohiṇīnandana. "*You think*! You do not know? You think?" Rohiṇīnandana bashfully hung his head and became speechless, while everyone else gathered around, looking from Rohiṇīnandana to Śrīla Prabhupāda. Prabhupāda banged his cane on the ground and repeated, "*You think*? You do not know?" Rohiṇīnandana did not take the reprimand lightly; he felt that a whole lifetime's pride of "*I think*" had been smashed to pieces by Prabhupāda.

2

Many devotees saw Śrīla Prabhupāda drive away small and large dogs by raising his cane and crying out, "Hut!" When Nanda-kumāra was traveling with Prabhupāda, he saw Prabhupāda do this in a dangerous situation and later he had the opportunity to try the technique himself.

While Prabhupāda and the devotees were walking on the beach in California, a large Doberman pinscher approached them, snarling and baring his teeth. Prabhupāda continued walking peacefully, but Nanda-kumāra stopped and tensely faced the dog. This challenge only provoked the dog into more threatening and growling until Nanda-kumāra turned and ran to catch up to Prabhupāda. As soon as he ran, the Doberman pinscher pursued him, barking and threatening to attack. Before the dog reached them, however, Prabhupāda suddenly turned. He crouched with his feet somewhat apart, raised his cane high over his head, gave a loud "Hut!"—and made a growling sound at the dog. At this display from Prabhupāda, the dog turned and retreated quickly back to its house.

Months later, Nanda-kumāra recalled Śrīla Prabhupāda's method and tried it on a large monkey in Jaipur. While Śrīla Prabhupāda was staying at the Rādhā-Govinda temple in Jaipur, he and his party were being harassed by the monkeys there, who stole food and clothes. While the devotees were cooking, these monkeys would drop from the trees and steal *capātīs* off the stove. Prabhupāda had advised the devotees to take a neutral attitude toward the monkeys' mischief, but one time, while with the devotees in Prabhupāda's room, Nanda-kumāra heard a monkey rattling the kitchen door. He suddenly remembered the technique Prabhupāda had used on the beach with the large Doberman pinscher and he decided to try it with the thieving monkey. Quietly excusing himself from the room, he picked up a club outside Prabhupāda's door and walked toward a large monkey, who was just opening the kitchen door. Nanda-kumāra raised the club over his head, crouched, and growled. The monkey, who had noticeably big biceps, growled back, bared his teeth, and advanced toward him. Nanda-kumāra turned and ran back into Prabhupāda's room, slamming the door behind him. Prabhupāda had seen the whole incident through the window and burst out laughing. "You do not know the process."

Nanda-kumāra sat down in embarrassment. His imitation had failed.

"Prabhupāda," said Nanda-kumāra, "you have a special potency."

3

In 1971, when the ISKCON Māyāpur project was in its beginning stages, Prabhupāda met with a group of devotee-planners to design the first buildings. Included in the plans was a residential building for Śrīla Prabhupāda, which the devotees took a special pleasure in discussing; it would be a wonderful home for their spiritual master. Śrīla Prabhupāda had also agreed that the spiritual master's residence should be built even before the construction of the magnificent temple for Rādhā-Kṛṣṇa. But one time when the devotees went before Prabhupāda to discuss his residence, they were surprised to find that he was not interested.

"I don't require a house," said Prabhupāda.

The devotees were baffled. "But this has been part of the planning all along."

He repeated, "I do not want a house."

"But you will have to live somewhere."

"I will live in a simple hut."

The planners went away from this conversation confused about how to construct the Māyāpur city without a place for Śrīla Prabhupāda, but after conferring among themselves, they realized the defect was in their presenting the idea to Prabhupāda. So they went back and tried again.

"Śrīla Prabhupāda, Māyāpur is the central place for our movement, and people must learn to worship the guru there. So we would like to show you the plans for your residential building. In this way, by making a nice place, the whole Vaiṣṇava *sampradāya* will be honored."

"Yes, that's true." Prabhupāda now agreed, and discussions about his residence continued in a positive way. As long as the discussions had been whether or not Prabhupāda would like to have a big house, he had not shown enthusiasm, but when the plan was presented as service to Kṛṣṇa, Prabhupāda's interest was strong.

4

Śrīla Prabhupāda noted symptoms of *prākṛta-sahajiyā*—the tendency to take devotional service cheaply and to imitate the realizations of highly advanced devotees—in one of his artist-disciples, and he gave him early warnings of danger.

One time in Vṛndāvana, the artist brought a sketch before Śrīla Prabhupāda for his approval before beginning a serious painting.

Śrīla Prabhupāda's first remark was, "Is this Śiva and Pārvatī?"

"No, Śrīla Prabhupāda, it is Rādhā-Kṛṣṇa."

"They look too old," said Śrīla Prabhupāda. "They should look no more than sixteen years old—very fresh youth."

The artist went back to work and redid the sketch, but when Prabhupāda saw it the second time, he again said the couple looked too old. He then showed his disciple a picture on his desk of the ISKCON Calcutta Deities, Rādhā-Govinda, and he said, "They should be painted like this. Kṛṣṇa is a young, sweet boy."

For the third time the artist did the sketch and showed it to Śrīla Prabhupāda. Śrīla Prabhupāda was still unenthusiastic, but since he did not specifically forbid the work, the artist took this as his permission and began work on a large canvas. After weeks of work, he brought his opus before Śrīla Prabhupāda. The painting showed Rādhā and Kṛṣṇa on a swing. Kṛṣṇa was lifting Rādhārāṇī's veil and looking into Her face in a very intimate, conjugal way. The more traditional elements of Rādhā and Kṛṣṇa standing together, appearing in the artist's preliminary sketches, had evolved into a scene more imagined by the artist.

"It is concoction," said Śrīla Prabhupāda. Despite all the effort put into it by the artist, Śrīla Prabhupāda couldn't spare feelings on such an important, responsible matter as the depiction of Rādhā and Kṛṣṇa. In a mood of hurt pride, the artist took back the painting and did not inquire further about what was wrong or what he should do to rectify it.

On another occasion in Māyāpur, Prabhupāda alerted the same artist that his spontaneous expression was unauthorized. While painting large portraits from the *Caitanya-caritāmṛta* on the boundary wall to ISKCON Māyāpur, the artist had created his own original Bengali verse and painted it in large script. When Śrīla Prabhupāda first noticed it while on a morning walk, he became disturbed.

"You should not have dared," he said. The verse employed a metaphor praising Lord Caitanya and Lord Nityānanda. Prabhupāda said the sentiment wasn't bad, although the Bengali wasn't perfect—but the main objection was that his disciple had dared to put his own verse on the wall rather than one provided by the previous *ācāryas,* such as Narottama dāsa Ṭhākura. Śrīla Prabhupāda even mentioned the incident in that morning's *Bhāgavatam* class. "Don't concoct," he said. "The *sahajiyā* tendency is to take everything cheaply. Don't do this," said Prabhupāda, "or you will become a *sahajiyā* and everything will be ruined."

5

LITTLE DROPS *of* NECTAR

While Prabhupāda was living in Los Angeles in 1969, he got a letter from one of his relatives stating that one of his brothers had died. Prabhupāda received this information in the presence of some of the devotees and he informed them, "I have just received this letter saying that my brother died. Previously my other brother died. These two brothers were very nice. They wanted to live long, healthy lives, but they didn't care so much for Kṛṣṇa consciousness. But my sister and I," Prabhupāda laughed softly, "we didn't want to live long, healthy lives. We only wanted to do some service, and when

Kṛṣṇa wanted to, He would take us. Now I see that my two brothers are both dead, and my sister and I are living long, happy lives."

Śrīla Prabhupāda was very fond of Mr. Panilal Pithi, a friend from Hyderabad. One time Mr. Pithi came to Bombay and dropped in unexpectedly to visit Prabhupāda. Prabhupāda had just begun his lunch. He was glad to see his friend, however, and asked him to sit down and have lunch with him. Prabhupāda told his cook, Pālikā, to make up a plate for Mr. Pithi. She stared back silently at Prabhupāda because she had hardly any extra food for serving another person. But Prabhupāda looked back steadily at her and again asked her to make the extra plate. Pālikā came in with a plate, as best she could arrange, for Mr. Pithi. Mr. Pithi then got up to go to another room to wash his hands. As soon as Mr. Pithi left the room, Śrīla Prabhupāda, with the demeanor of a surreptitious child, took the bowl of yogurt from his plate and quickly put it onto Mr. Pithi's plate before he could come back and see.

Prabhupāda's disciple Subhaga dāsa tells of his first meeting with Prabhupāda. Prabhupāda noticed him in the temple room and asked him his name. Subhaga answered with a few words in Bengali.

"Oh, you are a Bengali?" said Prabhupāda. "Come to my room."

Subhaga followed as Śrīla Prabhupāda entered his room. There, Prabhupāda began changing his clothes. Keeping his body always covered with cloth, he removed the *dhotī* while putting on his *gamchā* in preparation for his massage. Prabhupāda continued talking affectionately, asking Subhaga about his life. Subhaga began to feel that he was talking with a near and dear family relative, an affectionate, respected grandfather. It was as if he had known Śrīla Prabhupāda a long time, although he had been in Prabhupāda's association for only a moment. While Prabhupāda's servant knelt beside Prabhupāda and began massaging his head, Prabhupāda began to explain Kṛṣṇa consciousness to the newcomer.

6

ŚRĪLA PRABHUPĀDA SAID

On Management

Prabhupāda advised that those who are leaders in ISKCON have to know how to bend men without breaking them or making them angry. After all, he said, it is all voluntary service.

George Harrison once said, "In the future, ISKCON will be so large it will require executive management."

Prabhupāda replied, "I have divided the world into zones and representatives. As long as they keep to the spiritual principles, Kṛṣṇa will help them."

A disciple with managerial responsibility approached Prabhupāda and expressed a desire to leave India. Prabhupāda asked him to stay on, but the devotee was determined to leave, and ultimately Prabhupāda conceded. But at one point Prabhupāda said, "You can renounce management, but I cannot. I have to stay and manage."

Once on a visit to Boston, Śrīla Prabhupāda had a meeting with his ISKCON Press workers. Satsvarūpa dāsa complained to Prabhupāda that he had so many duties in the temple that he was distracted in trying to do all of them and at the same time also do press work. Prabhupāda said, "Real management means to delegate it to others. You have so many responsible devotees there, so you can delegate it to them."

While walking up the stairs in Māyāpur one morning, Prabhupāda began complimenting Bhavānanda Goswami.

"You are a good manager because you keep things clean. If you can keep everything clean, then you are a good manager. That's all there is to it." As they walked up the stairs, Prabhupāda could see that everything was shiny and clean—the walls, the pictures on the walls, the marble floors—everything was clean. When they went to the roof, however, Śrīla Prabhupāda found a scrap of paper and dust in a corner, and he began to criticize everyone for neglect.

Once, in India, Prabhupāda was joined in his room by his senior disciples Bhagavān, Brahmānanda, and Girirāja.

"You are the future and hope of the world," said Śrīla Prabhupāda, and he began to instruct them about the importance of attentive management.

"Just like your American Express corporation," he said. "What have they done? They have simply taken pieces of paper, and for those pieces of paper you pay good money. But what have they done? Actually they have done nothing. It is simply management. You pay them some money and they give you a piece of paper, and if you lose that piece of paper, they say, 'All right, we will give you another piece of paper.' It is organization. Simply from that management they have made millions of dollars."

In Calcutta, when Abhirāma dāsa was the temple president, he went one day to tell Śrīla Prabhupāda that he was having difficulty with his marriage. Prabhupāda asked him what was the difficulty.

"She wants that I should be engaged in more *pūjārī* work and chanting rather than management."

Śrīla Prabhupāda replied, "She is less intelligent. Management is spiritual activity. Just like Arjuna was fighting."

"There is no difference between chanting Hare Krsna or *sankirtana* and doing one's assigned work in Krsna consciousness. Sometimes we have to do so much managerial or office work, but Lord Caitanya promises us that because in the Kali-yuga this is required for carrying out the preaching mission, He gives assurance that we will not become entangled by such work. When the work has to be done, do it first, then chant. But you must fulfill at least 16 rounds daily. So if necessary, sleep less, but you have to finish your minimum number of rounds."

—*Letter of January 2, 1972*

7

ŚRĪLA PRABHUPĀDA TELLS A STORY

Śrīla Prabhupāda would speak from a large repertoire of traditional stories and apply them in different ways. His use of the story about the *brāhmaṇa* who lost his caste illustrates this nicely.

In India there is a custom that Hindus never take their meals in the house of a Mohammedan or Christian, or anyone other than a Hindu *brāhmaṇa,* but one *brāhmaṇa* was very hungry, and he went to a little-known acquaintance and asked for some food. The man supplied the *brāhmaṇa* with a little foodstuff, but still his hunger was not satisfied. When the *brāhmaṇa* asked the man for more food, the man said that he was sorry but he had no more.

"Oh," said the *brāhmaṇa,* disappointed. Then he asked, "Sir, which caste do you belong to?"

"I am Mohammedan," the man replied.

Then the hungry man lamented, "Oh, I have lost my caste and still I am hungry!"

Śrīla Prabhupāda told this story on one occasion to a devotee-artist. She had suggested to Prabhupāda that she should improve her artistic craftsmanship by painting and selling nondevotional pictures, and then after becoming talented and famous, she could better paint for Kṛṣṇa. Śrīla Prabhupāda replied that to come to the point of being a reputed artist would take a long time, but a devotee's time is short—and is only for serving Kṛṣṇa. As for fame, Prabhupāda said, according to *Caitanya-caritāmṛta* a man is famous who is known as a great devotee of Kṛṣṇa. If she insisted on becoming a great artist, she would be like the *brāhmaṇa* who lost his caste but his belly remained unfilled.

Another time Prabhupāda applied the same story when a devotee, at Prabhupāda's suggestion, tried to get Prabhupāda a teaching position on a college faculty. The salary they offered him was very low, so Prabhupāda rejected it. The devotee then thought that he had insulted Prabhupāda by even asking such a thing. Prabhupāda wrote back assuring the disciple that there was no offense, but that the offer was useless. He related the story about the caste *brāhmaṇa,* then commented, "The idea is that if we have to ask some service, there must be proper remuneration. So I thought that since I required some money for my book fund, I might gather some money in this way, but this does not satisfy my hunger. So forget this incident."

8

PERSONAL

His personal remnants

Once, after a servant shaved his hair, Prabhupāda noticed that he was saving little bits of gray hair. "What are you doing with that?" The servant replied that he was saving it as remnants. Prabhupāda said, "It is *muci.* Hair is *muci.*"

When the servant insisted that the disciples worship it, Prabhupāda laughed and said, "All right."

When he received extra sweaters as gifts, he would carry them for a while in the suitcase and then personally give them away. He gave away gold rings, once giving one each to his servant and his servant's wife on the occasion of their marriage. He carried watches and beadbags and gave them all away. He gave everything away bit by bit, and always he received more. What we gave him transformed into his charity to others, while the personal effects he kept were very few.

His remnants of food

He liked to give *prasādam* from his hand and everyone liked to receive it. It was not just food, but the blessings of *bhakti,* the essence of devotional service. Śrīla Prabhupāda gave out *prasādam* happily, calmly, and without discrimination. When he gave to children, they liked the sweet taste of it, in the form of a cookie or sweetmeat, yet also they liked it as a special treat from Prabhupāda, who sat on the *vyāsāsana* leaning forward to them. Women liked it because they got a rare chance to come forward and extend their hands before Prabhupāda. They felt satisfied and chaste. And stalwart men came forward like expectant children, sometimes pushing one another just to get the mercy from Prabhupāda. To Prabhupāda it was serious and important, and he would personally supervise to make sure that a big plate was always ready for him to distribute. He wrote in *Śrīmad-Bhāgavatam,* "No Vedic sacrifice is complete without distribution of *prasādam.*" Although now *prasādam* distribution in the Kṛṣṇa consciousness movement is done on a huge scale, as Prabhupāda desired, it all started from his own hand, as he gave it out one-to-one.

"Come," he would say, "take *prasāda.*" The fortunate receiver would extend his arm, right hand, palm up, and Prabhupāda touched him or her with a small amount of foodstuffs. It fully satisfied the mind, body, and soul. With his deft hands and shapely fingers selecting pieces from the plate, he gave it out. He knew that the urchins in Bombay and Bhubaneswar were coming mainly because their bellies were hungry, and he also arranged to give out thousands of full plates of *kitchri* in Māyāpur. In the U.S.A. he introduced delicious vegetarian "love feasts," teaching Westerners the art of cooking and eating. So all *prasādam* distribution goes back to the simple act initiated by Prabhupāda—his offering his remnants. No guest could leave his room without it, even a hostile onlooker. "Come, please take."

9

One time while traveling on a train in India, Prabhupāda asked for *samosās* and the devotees purchased a bagful. Then one of the women began arranging to offer the food as *prasādam* for Prabhupāda and the devotees. In the presence of Prabhupāda, she stood up and began to make a place for an offering. She put down a cloth and placed Kṛṣṇa's picture there, got a plate, and proceeded to prepare an offering. Prabhupāda was watching, but before she had placed the plate down on the improvised altar he stopped her.

"This is not the way to offer," he said, "in front of all these people."

Prabhupāda quoted a Sanskrit verse, beginning *dravya-mūlena śudhyati:* when a thing is purchased, even if its source is not pure, it can be offered to Kṛṣṇa. He also stated that sometimes in awkward circumstances a devotee may have to offer food to Kṛṣṇa mentally, as long as it is not forbidden food.

One time in Tehran, Iran, Prabhupāda showed a similar flexibility to time and place. Prabhupāda's secretary had noticed that the devotees were keeping frozen vegetables in the freezer. The secretary told the devotees that they should immediately throw them all out. He said that it was offensive to the guru to offer him vegetables that were not fresh and that they did not understand Prabhupāda's instructions.

"You don't know how angry he would get," said the secretary, "if he saw those frozen vegetables. And you are even feeding them to him!"

Nandarāṇī, who was living in Tehran with her husband, Dayānanda, became distressed since she was using the frozen vegetables in her cooking for guests in their preaching dinners three nights a week. She went to Prabhupāda to ask what to do. By this time Prabhupāda had already been informed by his secretary about the frozen vegetables.

"Why are you using frozen vegetables?" he asked.

"Because we have dinner parties," she replied. "We have to feed them something. These dinner parties are our only preaching here. If we can't feed them *prasādam,* then practically we are finished."

"That's all right," said Śrīla Prabhupāda. "You cannot get other vegetables?"

"No, Śrīla Prabhupāda, nothing is available here. Maybe we can feed them some potatoes."

"That's all right," Prabhupāda said. "Use frozen vegetables. It is part of our *saṅkīrtana.*"

10

According to the *Bhāgavatam* verse, even the briefest association with a pure devotee can bring one to the perfection of human life. Śrīla Prabhupāda delivered many conditioned souls from illusion, sometimes just by his merciful glance. For the person receiving his benediction, such moments were experienced in a very personal individual way; yet Śrīla Prabhupāda was able to give his blessings even while tending to many persons at once.

Jaya Mādhava dāsa was standing in a crowd of devotees while Prabhupāda was getting into a car. As Prabhupāda looked from the back seat at the devotees, Jaya Mādhava felt Prabhupāda's glance fall on him. It was as if Prabhupāda was saying, "What are you doing here? Why are you wasting your time in the material world?" This reciprocation was a deeply sobering experience.

Another devotee, Raṇacora dāsa, had been practicing Kṛṣṇa consciousness for a number of years under Śrīla Prabhupāda's direction, but on one particular visit by Śrīla Prabhupāda to London, Raṇacora received the unforgettable boost through a brief but deep, personal exchange with his spiritual master. It was in the crowded temple room. At the end of the lecture, Raṇacora asked Prabhupāda question. "When you become initiated by the spiritual master, does he take all of your karma, even if you might perform sinful activities —does he take the suffering you might have received?"

Prabhupāda replied heavily, "You must simply become ruled by your spiritual master." Those words by Śrīla Prabhupāda entered the heart of his disciple, and his glance cut through all impersonalism.

Many devotees experienced the same thing—a moment or occasion with Śrīla Prabhupāda in which they realized their eternal relationship with him and in which they rejoiced to know it.

Once on a morning walk in the fields near Bhaktivedanta Manor, Prabhupāda was talking to a group of his disciples. Sākṣī Gopāla dāsa was also there and received a special realization. Prabhupāda was explaining how each humble creature in the universe is empowered by Kṛṣṇa with a small degree of His own mystical power, *acintya-śakti.* Prabhupāda explained that the frogs can breathe underground, the trees can eat through their feet, and the grass can tolerate trampling that humans could not endure. Then Prabhupāda started criticizing and laughing at the material scientists and their limited vision. By his infectious laughing, the devotees also began laughing. For a moment Prabhupāda looked directly at Sākṣī Gopāla, to whom it seemed the whole universe was laughing with Prabhupāda at the foolishness of the puffed-up materialists. In this way, another disciple suddenly met Prabhupāda as if for the first time and felt unforgettably grateful and convinced. This happened not only to one or two, but almost every disciple knew it and realized it in different ways.

Through his instructions, his books, his mission, and through other devotees, Śrīla Prabhupāda constantly brought awareness of a disciple's eternal relationship with guru and Kṛṣṇa. After Prabhupāda's disappearance, his association is obtainable in the same way, provided the follower is submissive. As Prabhupāda replied to one devotee when asked whether the spiritual master was in the heart of the disciple, "Yes, if you let me enter."

11

While Śrīla Prabhupāda lived in Māyāpur, his routine was punctuated by visits and news from the various fronts in his worldwide campaign against *māyā.* Particularly welcome moments occurred when Prabhupāda received advance copies of his books. However, when he received a copy of *Śrīmad-Bhāgavatam,* Canto 6, Volume 3, with its cover portrait of Lord Śeṣa receiving the worship from Citraketu and the four Kumāras, Prabhupāda looked at it only briefly and then went on with his routine. He went to the roof, where he sat on a straw mat in the sunshine. There his servant massaged him with mustard oil, and then Prabhupāda bathed, took *prasādam,* and rested for an hour in his upstairs room. According to his regular habit, he came down from his room on the roof at about four o'clock in the afternoon and received guests in his main sitting room on the second floor.

Ānakadundubhi dāsa had a small part to play in Śrīla Prabhupāda's daily routine, as each afternoon he brought Prabhupāda a fresh afternoon garland of flowers and applied *candana* paste to Prabhupāda's forehead. On the day that the Sixth Canto of the *Bhāgavatam* arrived, Prabhupāda took it up again when he came down to his room. While his disciple stood by waiting with the garland and *candana* paste, Prabhupāda began to peruse the book in his usual manner, looking first at the illustrations. Prabhupāda suddenly noticed Ānakadundubhi and signified with a glance that he could go ahead and put on the garland and the paste. Then Prabhupāda continued to look through the book.

"Who has painted this?" asked Prabhupāda as he looked at the painting of Lord Śeṣa.

"That was done by Parīkṣit," said Ānakadundubhi, who stood looking over Prabhupāda's shoulder at the open book in Prabhupāda's hands. Prabhupāda then turned the page to a plate reproduction of Mahā-Viṣṇu lying in the Causal Ocean, manifesting all the universes from His gigantic form.

"Who has painted this one?" asked Prabhupāda.

"That's by Raṇacora dāsa," said Ānakadundubhi. Prabhupāda then began quoting from the *Brahma-saṁhitā.*

yasyaika-niśvasita-kālam athāvalambya
jīvanti loma-vilajā jagad-aṇḍa-nāthāḥ
viṣṇur mahān sa iha yasya kalā-viśeṣo
govindam ādi-puruṣaṁ tam ahaṁ bhajāmi

Prabhupāda was just about to turn to the next page, when suddenly a drop of the wet *candana* paste fell from Prabhupāda's forehead onto the page. Ānakadundubhi became frightened, expecting Prabhupāda to reprimand him for making the paste so runny that it had dripped onto the book. But Prabhupāda only touched it with his thumbnail and asked, "What is this?" Ānakadundubhi explained what it was, but Prabhupāda said nothing. Ordinarily the runny paste might have been enough to draw a word of disapproval from Śrīla

Prabhupāda, but he was drawn so much into the *Bhāgavatam* that he continued his study of the book, overlooking the spot of sandalwood paste that now adorned the page.

12

While Hṛdayānanda Goswami was Prabhupāda's secretary in Māyāpur, he was pleased to see how Prabhupāda liked to hear his own singing of *bhajanas* on the tape recorder. Even while working, Prabhupāda played a tape, and when the recording stopped, he asked that the other side be played again. One day, in a very jolly mood while listening to his own singing of *haraye namaḥ kṛṣṇa,* which had full harmonium, drum, and *karatāla* accompaniment and a strong rhythm, Prabhupāda began to speak.

"Just go everywhere and play this tape and dance." He motioned with his hands to show how the devotees should dance. "Go all around the world performing like this and people will be so much attracted that you will make a million dollars!"

As the GBC secretary responsible for all of South America, Hṛdayānanda Goswami usually served Śrīla Prabhupāda in a mood of separation as he worked and traveled constantly on Prabhupāda's behalf. He often enhanced his remembrance of Śrīla Prabhupāda, however, by playing his tapes wherever he went. Serving in separation, he felt intensely close to Śrīla Prabhupāda, as much as when he was personally with him, if not more so. Yet late at night after the demands of traveling, preaching, and managing, Hṛdayānanda Goswami would put on a tape of Prabhupāda singing and playing harmonium, and as the transcendental sound of Prabhupāda entered his ears, Hṛdayānanda felt even more increased feelings of loving reciprocation for Śrīla Prabhupāda. Thus *vāṇī* (service to the order of Śrīla Prabhupāda) enhanced *vapuḥ* (service to the personal form of the spiritual master). And conversely, *vapuḥ* enhanced *vāṇī.*

13

LITTLE DROPS *of* NECTAR

When Śrīla Prabhupāda was planning the layout of the temple room in Māyāpur, his disciples were also taking part.

"Where can we build a *vyāsāsana*?" one devotee asked. "Should we put it at the other end of the temple facing the Deities?"

But another devotee objected, "Isn't that too far for you, Śrīla Prabhupāda? Will you be able to see the Deities from such a distance?"

Śrīla Prabhupāda replied strongly, "There's no question of separation of distance between me and Kṛṣṇa." So the *vyāsāsana* was placed at the opposite end from Śrī-Śrī-Rādhā-Mādhava and Prabhupāda could see Them very nicely.

On a departure from Australia, Śrīla Prabhupāda was waiting for his plane. Devotees had brought him a simple chair and he sat in an outdoor garden, just outside the entrance to the airport. Watching while hundreds of people walked in and out of the terminal, Prabhupāda sometimes inquired about their appearance and their clothing styles. When he asked about the elevated shoes he saw men wearing, devotees explained that they were called "stacks."

"Some of them are elevated five or six inches high," said Amogha dāsa. "People even twist their ankles trying to walk in them."

Śrīla Prabhupāda laughed lightly. "There is a Bengali proverb," he said. "'Do something new.' That is Western civilization. And they think that God is very old. Not new."

The devotees were feeling awkward and apologetic that Prabhupāda had to sit in such a crowded public place. One of them remarked, "Some day, Prabhupāda, we shall have our own airport."

"It is our airport," he said. "Everything belongs to Kṛṣṇa, so it is already ours."

14

PRABHUPĀDA SAID

On Preaching

One day in Vṛndāvana, Śrīla Prabhupāda allowed a morning *darśana* in his room, but some of the important devotees were absent. When he asked where they were, he was told that some of the devotees were cleaning the temple.

Prabhupāda was surprised. "Cleaning the temple? We can employ people to clean the temple, but one thing you cannot employ people to do is to preach. So they should hear from me when I am speaking, or how will they preach?"

"If you feel at all indebted to me, then you should preach vigorously like me. That is the proper way to repay me. Of course, no one can repay the debt to the spiritual master, but the spiritual master is very much pleased by such an attitude by the disciple."

—*Letter of August 14, 1976*

"Yes, preaching is more important than management. Just because you are preaching nicely and distributing so much *prasadam*, management will follow like a shadow and Krsna will send you unlimited help."

—*Letter of November 21, 1971*

One time in Hawaii Prabhupāda was discussing how he was able to defeat the nondevotees' arguments. "I know the art, like karate, " he said, "of pushing on a person's weak spot until he dies. I find their weak point and push until they die."

15

ŚRĪLA PRABHUPĀDA TELLS STORIES

About Lazy Men

Prabhupāda was annoyed when devotees in Vṛndāvana repeatedly walked in and out of his room and left the door open behind them, letting in flies.

"Why are you leaving the door open?" he yelled. "It is a contagious disease." And then he told a story.

An employer advertised for an opening in his firm and received many applications. Based on these, he selected two men and asked them to come for an interview. The employer then observed each man carefully during the interview. When the first man entered the room, he left the door open behind him. The employer spoke with him for about fifteen minutes and then asked him to wait outside. When the second applicant entered, he shut the door behind him. After speaking with him, the employer asked him to also wait outside and then he called his secretary.

"That first man I spoke to," he said, "has all the qualifications, but I have decided to give the job to the second man."

"Why is that?"

"Because the first man left the door open. It appears he is a lazy fellow. The other man shut the door, so while he may not be so qualified, he will learn quickly."

In Hrsikesh in 1977, Śrīla Prabhupāda was staying with about eight of his disciples in a house on the bank of the Ganges. One day Prabhupāda entered the kitchen and was astonished to see that the devotees had cut up a huge amount of vegetables in preparation for lunch. Prabhupāda said they had cut enough vegetables to feed fifty people. Commenting that his disciples had no common sense, Prabhupāda then sat in a chair and began directing them in all the details of the cooking. He watched the rice boiling and tested it for softness. Then he personally cooked the *capātīs.* At this time, Prabhupāda commented that only a lazy man cannot cook, and he told the story of some lazy men.

There was a king who announced that all lazy men in his kingdom could come to the charity house and be fed. Hundreds of people came and they all said, "I am a lazy man." The king then told his minister to set fire to the charity house. Everyone inside, except two men, immediately ran out of the burning building. Of the two remaining, one man said to the other, "My back is becoming very hot from the fire." The other man advised, "Just turn over to the other side." Seeing these two, the king said, "They are actually lazy men. Feed them."

16

PERSONAL GLIMPSES

Prabhupāda and His Photo

He like the photo of himself on the back of the first Hare Kṛṣṇa "Happening" album. In that photo his hair seems to be standing on end and his visage is grave, penetrating, mystical. He said of that photo, "A swami should look philosophical."

A disciple named Dīneśa told Śrīla Prabhupāda that he wanted a picture of him with his *mṛdaṅga* for a second record album, *"Vande 'ham."* Prabhupāda said, "I am not a professional musician that I should pose with a *mṛdaṅga."* He suggested instead more formal pictures, like those of his own Guru Mahārāja.

The guru is in his picture. "There is no difference between me and my picture," he wrote in a letter. "Therefore we should honor and keep pictures in that spirit. If we throw pictures this way and that way, that is offense. The name and the picture are as good as the person in the spiritual world. In the material world, either picture or person, everything is illusion."

His Sense of Personal Worth

Once he explained the importance of the philosopher in human society by a story. "In England," he said, "a philosopher was once invited to meet with a famous theater actor. The philosopher replied, 'I cannot meet with a dancing dog!'" Prabhupāda thought of himself very humbly, as a servant of the servant, delivering the message of Kṛṣṇa consciousness, but because the gift of Kṛṣṇa consciousness was very important, therefore he was important, and he was empowered by his spiritual master to deliver it. He taught the same to us: devotees who are serving the Lord are important.

Dancing

You can see his motion on films. Don't expect to see much big, athletic jumping up and down. He would mostly start from the waist and shoulders, moving up and down in rhythm with *kīrtana,* and then jump. Dancing for Prabhupāda always meant upraised arms and extended fingers, like the depiction of Gaura and Nitāi. That was how he introduced dancing in his room at 26 Second Avenue, leading us around in a circle, showing how you put your left foot to the right side and how you sway back and forth with the arms always upraised. Kīrtanānanda called it "the Swami step." Once in Chicago he admonished boys who were twisting, disco style. Emphatically from the *vyāsāsana* he raised up his arms. He did it once, and when the dancers did not heed, he did it again: "Like this!"

It would come upon him at different memorable times, walking-dancing with ecstatic *kīrtana* at Ratha-yātrās in London and Australia or in temple rooms packed with devotees or before thousands at outdoor *paṇḍāls* in India. Suddenly creating waves of excitement—all devotees rising with him—he would dance, and we would dance. He danced, and we are dancing.

17

Śrīla Prabhupāda managed to encourage every one of his disciples. He made them feel they had worth, that he loved them, and he showed that he knew their particular problems.

Some were problem cases who could not work well with others, and some were always unsteady. One devotee with problems once came before Śrīla Prabhupāda and pleaded for some relief.

"Śrīla Prabhupāda, I would like to apologize for being so fallen and wretched. I never seem to be able to do anything right. I try to give some advice to people, but it's no use, because even if I think I'm right, they tell me I'm wrong. I just want your forgiveness because I'm so confused."

Śrīla Prabhupāda replied, "They criticized Lord Caitanya and Kṛṣṇa."

The dejected devotee was astounded to hear this, but he thought maybe Prabhupāda did not understand what he meant.

"Śrīla Prabhupāda, I am not trying to criticize Lord Caitanya and Kṛṣṇa. I'm just trying to apologize. I'm sorry that I'm so fallen, that I'm not better than I am."

Prabhupāda repeated, "They criticized Lord Caitanya and Kṛṣṇa. Even when Lord Kṛṣṇa was here, they did not accept. Only a few hundred people accepted that He was God. Everyone else was criticizing. And when Lord Caitanya was here, they even threw a pot at Lord Nityānanda. They did not like to accept Him. So what to speak of you and I?"

The dejected disciple then became overwhelmed to understand that Śrīla Prabhupāda had indeed understood him, understood him better than he knew himself.

"Then what is to be done?" asked the disciple. "Just go on trying?"

"Yes," said Śrīla Prabhupāda.

There was a similar incident with a devotee photographer. He had trouble rising early and in controlling his tongue from overeating. He was not very regulated or prone to the philosophy, but he liked taking pictures for Śrīla Prabhupāda's books, at which he was very good. One day after following Śrīla Prabhupāda to different places in his travels, the photographer asked Prabhupāda's permission so that he could return to his home temple. Aware of his precarious, weak situation in spiritual life, he submitted himself before Śrīla Prabhupāda saying, "Prabhupāda, I'm such a rascal."

"That is good," said Prabhupāda. "You remain a rascal your whole life." This statement confused the disciple. What to make of it? Was Prabhupāda delivering a curse, to "remain a rascal?" Then Śrīla Prabhupāda explained. "Lord Caitanya was also called a rascal. Do you know the story of Lord Caitanya and His spiritual master?" Prabhupāda's photographer suddenly felt that his mind and tongue were being controlled because without even thinking he began to tell the story of how Lord Caitanya was instructed by His spiritual master that He was too foolish to understand Vedānta and that He should just chant Hare Kṛṣṇa. Prabhupāda smiled and said no more. In this way, another dejected disciple became pacified, realizing his lack of intelligence and the fact that his only hope was the holy name of Kṛṣṇa.

Śrīla Prabhupāda's ability in these and many other cases prove that he was a great psychologist. Even when no one else could, Śrīla Prabhupāda knew the ways and means to give a fallen servant some renewed hope and strength. Neither did he do it by resorting to the mundane techniques of personnel managers, who are often cynical and manipulative. Yet on behalf of Kṛṣṇa, Śrīla Prabhupāda was expert with people.

18

One day in Vṛndāvana, Prabhupāda's servant Śrutakīrti heard him yelling from his room on the roof. Running into the room, Śrutakirti was greeted by a shout from Prabhupāda: "Rascals!" Prabhupāda picked up a block of clay on his desk and threw it at the doorway.

"What's the matter?"

"The monkey has stolen my shoes!" said Śrīla Prabhupāda, and he got up and went out the door.

"Get some *perā* and get my cane," said Prabhupāda. Śrutakīrti went off and returned with the cane and a piece of sweet, while Śrīla Prabhupāda found the monkey, who was keeping just out of reach on the small concrete roof above Prabhupāda's room. With his cane in hand, Prabhupāda jumped and tried striking the monkey, but it kept out of reach, scampering back and forth and waving the slipper in provocation.

"These monkeys are such rascals," said Prabhupāda, appearing serious and intent. Knowing well the monkey's game, Prabhupāda asked his servant to extend the sweet as a trade for the slipper. As soon as the sweet was offered, the monkey came forward and extended the slipper. He came closer and closer but then snatched the sweet and kept the slipper. Three times they tried the same thing and the monkey cheated and won each time. Triumphantly the monkey sat back out of reach, growling and making grinning faces. Finally, he placed the slipper in his mouth and began chewing. Prabhupāda had been keenly involved in trying to get the slipper back, but now he said, "He's ruined the shoe." The monkey had ripped out the heel and the inner sole stuffing. Prabhupāda went back to his room, and after trying a few more moves, his servant also walked away. The monkey then dropped the shoe and ran off.

Later, a devotee climbed on the roof and brought Prabhupāda the chewed slipper. Prabhupāda decided to keep it and use it, even though it was ripped and teeth marks were visible. He continued to wear it for a year after the incident.

The devotees asked Prabhupāda if it were true that the present-day monkeys in Vṛndāvana were very special—were sages from past lives who had fallen down from spiritual life and who would be liberated in their next life. Prabhupāda said, "Yes." Although the monkeys are mischievous and steal food, he said, still, in Goloka Vṛndāvana Kṛṣṇa allows them to take butter, and He Himself distributes it. Exactly who this monkey was or what was his relationship with Prabhupāda, no one could say for sure. The only thing certain was that Prabhupāda considered him a mischievous rascal, and that this incident took place in inconceivable Vṛndāvana-dhāma.

19

During a winter visit to Japan, Prabhupāda stayed in a cottage where the walls were made of paper. The landlord supplied a kerosene heater, but it only warmed a small area. Prabhupāda wrapped himself in his gray wool *cādar* and went on translating the *Bhāgavatam* through the cold early morning hours, but he remarked that it was very uncomfortable. When devotees went to the landlord and asked for a second heater, the landlord's wife objected. The landlord finally found a spare second heater, but the kerosene fumes made the room too stuffy. In addition, the house was filled with a bad odor. In that neighborhood there was an open sewage system: a truck was supposed to come by with a vacuum cleaner and suck out the contents of the stool pits, but the truck hadn't been there in over a week. In anxiety that their spiritual master was suffering much inconvenience, the devotees went to the landlord and pleaded with him to do something about the stench. The man was humble and accommodating, and he respected Prabhupāda as a spiritual leader. He agreed to clean out the pits himself, using hand buckets. But the landlord's wife again objected that her husband should make such an extraordinary, humiliating effort to accommodate Śrīla Prabhupāda. The man did it anyway, and the bad odor disappeared.

On Prabhupāda's last evening in the paper cottage, he gave a public lecture. The house had one floor plus a stage-like mezzanine. The speaker's dais was set on the stage, along with a microphone. The little dwelling was filled with guests, and Śrīla Prabhupāda led *kīrtana* and then began lecturing in English, which at least some of his audience could understand. In the midst of his talk, the landlord's wife, a small, middle-aged Japanese lady, entered the house and began screaming in anger. A few devotees moved forward to stop her, but she evaded them. She walked up onto the stage beside Śrīla Prabhupāda, making angry gestures and completely disrupting the meeting. Prabhupāda asked a guest who she was and what was the matter with her, and he heard that the lady was the landlady and that she was angry that Prabhupāda had made her husband clean out the stool pits. When he understood, Prabhupāda broke into a grin. He leaned forward and spoke into the microphone, as if making an announcement. "Japanese landlady," he said, and the audience and devotees relaxed and laughed. It was as if, by two words, Prabhupāda had made a philosophical statement, explaining the universal phenomenon of landladies and how they had to be tolerated. After a pause, Prabhupāda continued his lecture, and the landlady, who had become disarmed by Prabhupāda's smiling words, went down the stairs and left the cottage.

20

Śrīla Prabhupāda was very strong in his denunciation of materialists. He would denounce even big industrialists as thieves. Everything belongs to Kṛṣṇa, he said, and the capitalists (or communists) have taken far more than their God-given quota. Sometimes when disciples heard Prabhupāda's criticisms, they wondered how they could repeat such things to the nondevotees. Prabhupāda himself spoke with businessmen, and on those occasions, devotees would see his successful method of explaining to self-centered men the concept of *īśāvāsya,* a God-centered society.

On a morning walk around White Rock Lake, devotees pointed out to Śrīla Prabhupāda the mansion of one of the world's richest oil men. The white building on the spacious property was barely visible in the distance beyond the lake. Prabhupāda didn't take much note of it as he walked along the shore, which was bordered on the waterside with tall palm grass, while the road before them was littered with paper and beer cans. A devotee described how he had tried to approach the oil billionaire to give him a *Bhagavad-gītā,* but he had been successful only in giving a copy to one of the friendly entrance guards.

"What would you have said," asked Prabhupāda, "if you were actually able to see him?" About ten devotees walked with him, and one spoke out. "I would tell him that we have a school here in Dallas and that actually we are model citizens."

"What else would you say?" Prabhupāda asked. One devotee replied that she would invite him to visit the temple, and another said he would bring him *prasādam.*

"No," said Prabhupāda, "you should say to him, 'You are a big thief. You have taken for yourself so much oil which all belongs to God. So now you will have to be punished.'" Prabhupāda's followers felt embarrassed that they had not given Prabhupāda such a strong answer, and they were also surprised. As the quiet morning walk continued, Prabhupāda went on to say that one day the lord of death would come for the oil billionaire and no entrance guards could stop him. At that time, no matter what the richest man in the world might say, death would take him away to face his karma.

Not long after Prabhupāda's visit to Dallas, the Texas billionaire died. Some of the devotees remembered Prabhupāda's words and how they never were able to approach the man. One of the devotees present on the walk was Dayānanda dāsa, who vividly recalled this whole incident years later, when he witnessed Prabhupāda in the presence of a wealthy industrialist.

The scene was Māyāpur and Prabhupāda was taking his morning walk on the roof of the residential building. Jayapatāka Swami introduced Prabhupāda to a prominent businessman who had come to visit from Calcutta.

Speaking in English, Prabhupāda greeted him pleasantly.

"I am pleased to see you," said Prabhupāda. "Thank you for coming to Māyāpur. So, what is your factory?"

The businessman from Calcutta, a heavy-set man in an immaculate white *dhoti, kūrta,* and vest, spoke in a loud voice.

"I manufacture glass," he said.

"Hmm," Prabhupāda reflected. "So where does the glass come from?"

The man was now walking beside Prabhupāda, along with other devotees and friends, as they circumambulated the roof, talking and viewing the surrounding flatlands of Māyāpur.

"It is from silicon," the man replied. "It is from sand."

"Yes," said Prabhupāda, "but who owns the sand?"

The Calcutta man was not only an intelligent businessman, but he was pious and could understand what Bhaktivedanta Swami, as guru, was driving at. He said, "Oh, the sand comes from Bhagavān."

Prabhupāda replied quickly, "Oh, you are stealing from Bhagavān?"

Prabhupāda's retort made everyone laugh—even the industrialist could not help but join in the laughter. After the quick exchange, the Calcutta businessman dropped toward the back of the group, and others came forward to ask Prabhupāda their philosophical questions. Prabhupāda's morning walks were often this way, fragmented conversations with different guests and devotees who would come forward and ask Prabhupāda some query. He would answer one after another, sometimes developing different themes or going from one theme to another. After walking for about half an hour, the industrialist again moved to the front for another round of questions with Prabhupāda. He had been considering what Prabhupāda had said and he felt a little guilty.

"Swamijī," the man offered, "although I may be taking from Bhagavān, but I am giving in charity also."

Prabhupāda smiled and replied, "Oh, you are just a little thief." Again everyone on the walk laughed at Prabhupāda's last word on the subject. Thus Śrīla Prabhupāda showed the practical application of the theoretical advice he had given in Dallas.

21

A young Californian man, David Shapiro, became attracted to Prabhupāda through his books and through the devotees' association. He then moved to the Los Angeles temple at a time when Prabhupāda was visiting, but unfortunately, David's mother was outraged that her grown-up son had chosen to become a Kṛṣṇa conscious devotee. A journalist, she went on a letter-writing campaign against the Kṛṣṇa consciousness movement. She wrote letters to the newspapers and also to government departments, complaining that her son was practicing too much renunciation in Kṛṣṇa consciousness and she felt this was a mistreatment. David tried to pacify her, but he was not very good at it. Most of the time he was washing pots in the temple kitchen or going out on chanting parties downtown, and he didn't remember or bother to phone his mother. The devotees in the temple didn't help much when they sometimes forgot to pass on messages from his mother. As part of her letter-writing campaign, David's mother also wrote letters to Prabhupāda. Śrīla Prabhupāda replied to one of her letters, but she was not interested in any dialogue or consideration of her son's spiritual benefit as described by Prabhupāda. She just wanted her son to return.

Sensing that the Los Angeles temple could get into trouble through this woman, the temple president asked David to leave the temple. Although David was a submissive devotee, he refused to leave and began to cry. He said, "I'm not initiated. I've been in this movement for a year, but I'm not initiated, so I don't have a link to my spiritual master. How can I leave the temple without a link? I may never come back!" Both the temple president and David were bewildered. Prabhupāda was then informed how the boy had refused to leave and he called him to his room.

David came into Prabhupāda's quarters and bowed down before him while Prabhupāda was taking *prasādam.*

Prabhupāda spoke mildly: "So you have been having some difficulty with your mother?"

"Yes, Śrīla Prabhupāda."

"That's all right," said Prabhupāda. "I've decided to initiate you." Right on the spot, without any of the usual, formal ceremony, Prabhupāda gave David his new, spiritual name.

"Your name is now Nṛsiṁhānanda dāsa. Is that all right?"

"Yeah, that—" David could hardly speak.

Prabhupāda continued, "I'm giving you this name, Nṛsiṁhānanda because through this name you will always be protected from your parents." Prabhupāda then offered some *prasādam* from his plate to Nṛsiṁhānanda and said, "Now you can go home and stay there for some time. That will be all right. I think you can make vegetarian *prasādam* there?"

"Yes," said Nṛsiṁhānanda.

"So you can go for some time, and also come back," said Prabhupāda.

Nṛsiṁhānanda understood Prabhupāda's desire, and he had faith that it would work. "Thank you, Śrīla Prabhupāda," he said and left.

David Shapiro, now Nṛsiṁhānanda dāsa Brahmacārī, returned to his mother's home. Ten months later, when both son and mother had gained a more mature outlook about Kṛṣṇa consciousness, Nṛsiṁhānanda rejoined Prabhupāda's movement, this time to stay.

22

LITTLE DROPS *of* NECTAR

Śrīla Prabhupāda wanted devotees and guests to be attentive while he spoke on the *Bhagavad-gītā* and *Śrīmad-Bhāgavatam*. One time when Prabhupāda objected to a baby's crying, a person in the audience challenged, "If you are a guru, why are you disturbed?" Prabhupāda replied that it was the audience who was disturbed from attentive hearing and that was why he had asked the baby's noises be stopped. Even when Prabhupāda spoke Hindi, which most of his disciples could not understand, he expected them to stay and be quiet. He said that even if they couldn't understand the language, the sound vibration would purify them.

One time in New Delhi, while Prabhupāda was speaking to a government minister and other guests in his room, two of his disciples created a disturbance. Brahmānanda Swami was ill and needed the address of a doctor, so he entered the room to catch Tejās's attention. At first Tejās didn't want to speak at all, but Brahmānanda insisted and poked him in the side. Tejās turned and gave the doctor's address, but Brahmānanda requested more information, and the two of them began to argue. In response to the disturbance, Prabhupāda stopped speaking. When the devotees looked at him, he was staring at the spot on the ceiling just above where they were sitting. Prabhupāda then lowered his vision from the ceiling and looked straight and steady at the two offending disciples. "It is very annoying to me," said Prabhupāda. He shook his head with displeasure and added, "It is very disconcerting." These last words were spoken in a soft tone, but with anger. The atmosphere of the room became very tense. The distinguished guests were looking at the boys and Prabhupāda, and the boys were devastated. Prabhupāda's displeasure continued unrelieved, until suddenly another devotee entered the room and announced, "Prabhupāda, the car is ready." Only by Prabhupāda's rising to exit for another engagement did he release his disciples from his instructive displeasure.

In 1969, when Prabhupāda stayed at John Lennon's estate, he liked to walk in the misty morning through the gardens and groves. It was there that Prabhupāda met the head gardener, an old English gentleman who used to wear a tweed suit jacket even when digging in the earth. The gardener had shown no interest in the philosophy or the devotees, but when Prabhupāda came he was interested to meet him. On Prabhupāda's first morning walk the head gardener presented himself. Prabhupāda was also dressed in a gentlemanly way, wearing a long black coat, black hat, and Wellington boots.

"I am the head gardener here," said the man. Prabhupāda said he was glad to meet him and asked him, "What are you growing?" The gardener eagerly showed Prabhupāda some of the plants and fruits he was raising in the greenhouse, including watermelons and varieties of flowers. He also pulled out trays from underneath a greenhouse table and showed Prabhupāda his mushrooms.

"Oh, we do not eat this," said Prabhupāda. "This is fungus." The man admitted that it was a fungus. Prabhupāda explained that mushrooms do not have a good taste, and because they grow in a dark damp place, they are considered food in the mode of ignorance. Śrīla Prabhupāda then suggested that the gardener should try to grow ladyfingers, but the man didn't know what Prabhupāda meant. Prabhupāda pointed to his own fingers. "You should grow these ladyfingers." He gave the Hindi word, *bhiṇḍī,* which the man also couldn't understand. Finally the gardener understood that Prabhupāda was talking about okra. Prabhupāda asked if the man could grow mangos, but he said he couldn't, not even in the greenhouse.

"What is your age?" asked Prabhupāda. The gardener replied that he was sixty-six.

Prabhupāda said, "Do you still have all your teeth?"

The gardener seemed to be a little embarrassed, but replied, "No, I don't. I have all false teeth."

"My age is seventy-two," said Prabhupāda, "but I have all my teeth." Prabhupāda opened his mouth and showed.

The gardener replied, "I've lost all my teeth because I like sweet things too much."

"I also like sweets," said Prabhupāda. "I eat many sweets myself—*rasagullā, gulābjamūns.* But I am eating the right kind of sweets. You should also eat these sweets."

After that, when taking his morning walk, Prabhupāda regularly greeted the gardener with a few words, or at least, whenever the gardener was working at a distance, they exchanged a wave of hands.

23

LITTLE DROPS *of* NECTAR

Calcutta was Prabhupāda's hometown, and even in the 1970s when he had ISKCON centers in major cities all over the world, his visits to ISKCON Calcutta brought old friends and acquaintances to see him. One evening he was sitting in his room with old family friends from the Mahatma Gandhi Road neighborhood where he had grown up. They insisted that he come and visit the Rādhā-Govinda temple. Although it was almost 10:00 P.M., Prabhupāda suddenly decided to go, so he traveled by car, along with some of his Western disciples. As he passed his old neighborhood, he pointed out the house where he was raised as a child and the spot where he used to purchase kites. At the Govindajī temple, relatives came forward, embracing him and touching his feet. Old and young surrounded him, smiling and chatting in Bengali. Prabhupāda then went before the Deity of Govinda, whom he had worshiped from the beginning of his life. "Practically everything I have done," he explained to his disciples, "is by the grace of Rādhā-Govinda." He recalled his original Ratha-yātrās up and down Mahatma Gandhi Road and how his father paid for the festival. Prabhupāda said that the same spirit he had imbibed here he was now carrying on throughout the world in Ratha-yātrās and by establishing many Rādhā-Govindajīs all over the world.

In India, when out walking or traveling, Prabhupāda would often deal directly with merchants and laborers rather than allow his Western disciples to be cheated. One day, on leaving the temple grounds in Māyāpur, accompanied by a few devotees, Prabhupāda approached a *ricksha-walla* and asked him how much he wanted for a ride to Navadvīpa-ghāṭa. The *ricksha-walla* said two rupees and Prabhupāda told him it was much too high. "Why are you asking so much?" Prabhupāda argued. "We are coming to preach. We have brought devotees from all over the world." But the *ricksha-walla* said that two rupees was the final price. Prabhupāda held his head high, turned to his disciples, and said, "We shall walk." The contemplated walk was several miles, but Prabhupāda began to walk steadfastly and his disciples joined behind him. His walking pace continued strong and fast for a few minutes until the same *ricksha-walla* drove up, pulled in front of Prabhupāda, and stopped. Without speaking or even turning sideways, Prabhupāda stepped up onto the *ricksha* and went off victoriously at the one-rupee price.

24

ŚRĪLA PRABHUPĀDA SAID

On Deity Worship

"There is no question of using paper or plastic fruits and flowers for worshiping the Deities. If no fresh fruits or flowers are available, then you can decorate with some fresh leaves. You have seen our temples; nowhere do we use such things. You are experienced devotee. Why you propose like that? We are not after decoration; we are after devotional service for pleasing Krsna's senses. Decoration must be there, of course, to make the temple as opulent as possible for pleasing Krsna. Outside the temple, you can use the plastic ornaments. But not for worship. For daily worship there must be fresh fruits, flowers, and leaves."

—*Letter of December 26, 1971*

"Who is in charge of the Deity room? It must be secured at night, every window and door must be locked, and you must personally see to this. You have had sufficient experience at Bury Place that the Deity was attacked. You have already experienced that, so you should not be negligent in this matter. Please see that adequate security is given to the temple, especially to the Deities, so that They will not be exposed to any attack."

—*Letter of January 1, 1974*

"Regarding your questions, it is not very good to put "statues" of Radha and Krsna on a shelf. If They are not worshiped as Deities, what is the use of such display? Visitors will get the wrong idea that They are merely decorative figures or idols, that we do not take Them very seriously. Why you do not worship Them on the altar?"

—*Letter of December 8, 1971*

"The proper method of dressing Jagannatha is as a *ksatriya* king, and there is no limit to the opulence you can give Him."

—*Letter of February 19, 1973*

For a few years Prabhupāda traveled with small Deities of Rādhā-Kṛṣṇa. His personal servant and secretary were responsible for making arrangements for the Rādhā-Kṛṣṇa Deities as Prabhupāda moved from one location to another. On one occasion in India when Prabhupāda made a temporary stop, his servant did not unpack the Deities. Prabhupāda became angry and asked why the devotee had not unpacked.

"I didn't think it would be very rational," replied his servant, "to unpack the Deities in these conditions." Prabhupāda replied with a shout, "You are unpacked, and you are very comfortable!"

25

PRABHUPĀDA TELLS SHORT STORIES

Prabhupāda wanted his devotee-scientists to form the Bhaktivedanta Institute. By writing books and giving lectures, they should destroy the theories that life comes from matter and that there is no supreme being. The atheistic scientists will be very stubborn, he warned them. To illustrate the stubbornness of the materialists, Prabhupāda told the story of "scissors philosophy."

Two men were arguing about which cutting instrument should be used, a knife or scissors. "Knife!" said one. "No, scissors!" said the other. Their talk became a heated fight.

"If you don't agree," said the man who advocated the knife, "I will throw you in the river."

"No, I'll never change my mind. It's scissors!" So the knife advocate threw the other into the swift river. He swam for a while but became exhausted and began to sink. But he was so stubborn about holding his point of view, that even after he was sinking under the water to his death, he held up his arm and crossed his fingers back and forth like a pair of scissors cutting.

"The scientists will be like that," said Prabhupāda. "Even after defeating them with all logic, still they will say, 'Life comes from matter.'" But more sane and innocent people would be convinced by Vedic presentation, that life comes from life.

Śrīla Prabhupāda did not like his disciples to perform artificial austerities. When one devotee appeared bare-chested in the cold at a Kumbha-melā, Prabhupāda reprimanded him. On another occasion, in America, he teased his disciple Nara-Nārāyaṇa, who came into the cold temple room wearing only a light T-shirt.

"Nara-Nārāyaṇa," said Prabhupāda from the *vyāsāsana*, "you must be eating chickens." The other devotees turned and stared.

"Yes," said Prabhupāda, "this is how the Mohammedans keep warm. Are you eating chickens, Nara-Nārāyaṇa?"

"No, Śrīla Prabhupāda."

Prabhupāda then began telling a story how the Mohammedans keep warm. The system is that a man tries to eat one hundred chickens by eating a single chicken. A farmer will take a hundred chickens and then feed one of them to the ninety-nine. He then feeds another one to the remaining ninety-eight, and another one to the remaining ninety-seven. Finally, when there are only two chickens left, he feeds one chicken to the other. Then that chicken is fed to the emperor. In that way, it is considered that he is eating one hundred chickens.

26

MORE SHORT STORIES

In order to push his disciples to work harder, Prabhupāda sometimes used sarcasm. He was tired of delays by the workers in constructing a Māyāpur residential building and he blamed it on his devotees. When one of the leading managers among his disciples made an excuse, Prabhupāda retorted by quoting a humorous verse:

"Big, big monkey,
Big, big belly,
Ceylon jumping,
Melancholy."

Everyone laughed with Prabhupāda, without at first catching the meaning. He explained that his managers were like the monkeys who, unlike Hanumān, could not jump to Ceylon. Despite having big muscles and big bellies, when asked to do something heroic, they could not.

One of Prabhupāda's disciples had a chronic disease that the doctors couldn't diagnose, although the doctors said she was incurable. Prabhupāda said that these doctors were like a group of men who formed a conspiracy against a man named Bhagavat.

Bhagavat's friends wanted to play a trick on him, so about ten of them conspired. Then when Bhagavat went to visit one of his friends, the man gasped and cried, "Oh, you have become a ghost!" Bhagavat, in amused disbelief, replied,

"No, I haven't become a ghost. What's the matter with you?" But the friend repeated, in a horrified voice: "You've become a ghost!" Bhagavat didn't take it seriously, but when he saw his next friend, the man acted in the same frightened way. After this happened ten times, Bhagavat himself became horrified: "Yes, I've become a ghost! I've become a ghost!" Prabhupāda indicated that sometimes by conspiracy and *māyā* we think that we are sicker than we really are.

One time, while Prabhupāda was eating jackfruit, he joked about the taste of jackfruit. A man in a foreign land tried to describe jackfruit to a friend, but he confessed that there was no way to describe it unless you tasted it. When the friend insisted on some verbal description, the man replied that if you were to drink sugarcane juice through a Muslim's beard, then you might understand the taste of the jackfruit. Prabhupāda said that attempts to understand the *rāsa* dance of Kṛṣṇa by unrealized persons are like that.

27

PERSONAL

Prabhupāda and the Deity

He was so kind to bring the accessible Kṛṣṇa *mūrti.* What did we know? How could we succeed? But he did it, starting with Lord Jagannātha, then little Rādhā-Kṛṣṇa in New York City. Prabhupāda crouched down before Them, ordered simple service, kept Them in his room, and explained to us that They are not idols. The Deity is Kṛṣṇa.

He advised us, "If you think of Swamijī and Lord Jagannātha all the day, then at night you will dream of them." Dancing before the forms of the Deity, he taught us. Otherwise, no one could introduce the Deity to the Westerners. Now that They are here in so many temples, future religious historians may think They came by another means or that any devotee could have called Them, but *Prabhupāda was the one empowered to call the Deity.*

In the beginning he asked Him to please take care of Himself if the *mlecchas*-turned-devotees made offenses. But it was also Prabhupāda who later saw that the worship was going on nicely, and he approved that Kṛṣṇa was being worshiped in grand style. Like the *brāhmaṇa* who called the Deity to witness, Prabhupāda asked the Lord, and He agreed to come. On Prabhupāda's invitation, along with the sound of *kīrtana,* Kṛṣṇa was received in simple settings—in converted rooms, *pūjā* began for the Lord in rented houses in places such as Boston, St. Louis, Buffalo, and then in grand temples. Great *ācāryas* of the past installed one Deity, their beloved Rādhā-Kṛṣṇa, but Prabhupāda worshiped dozens of Rādhā-Kṛṣṇas, and he traveled to see Them. He was the champion of Rādhā-Kṛṣṇa, installing and distributing Rādhā-Kṛṣṇa on every continent, again and again bathing, chanting, dressing, performing the installation.

Śrīla Prabhupāda crouched before the Lord and sometimes he cried joyful tears at the *darśana* of the glowing Rādhā-Kṛṣṇa. He noticed how They were being served and dressed, and he made a stern point, that we should never change things whimsically after he had left. It was transcendental and matter-of-fact to Śrīla Prabhupāda that we must worship the Deity of Kṛṣṇa. Of course we must do it, or how will we remain purified? And of course He is Kṛṣṇa, with flute and three-curved form, with Rādhā beside Him. And of course we have to give Them our devotion! It was a matter of devotional fact: He will come when there are devotees and they will worship Him. Yet, is it not a great miracle? Prabhupāda has brought Kṛṣṇa—Kṛṣṇa has agreed and the ex-*mlecchas* have agreed to accept Him, and they pray, "O Lord of the universe, by Prabhupāda's grace, kindly be visible unto me."

28

Prabhupāda was sitting on a straw mat on the sunny balcony of the Calcutta temple about to receive a massage from his servant when a new disciple, Pañcadraviḍa dāsa, approached to ask a few questions.

"Prabhupāda, I used to be a musician," said Pañcadraviḍa, "so could I be a musician again and just play music for Kṛṣṇa?"

"Yes," said Prabhupāda, "you can do that." Prabhupāda spoke calmly, relaxing under the hands of his massaging servant. "But then there will still be some karma you will have to accept."

"Well, maybe that's not what I should do then," said Pañcadraviḍa. "But it's just that *brahmacārī* life is a little difficult for me. In the life of a *brahmacārī* you have to live under very institutional conditions." A few other devotees had gathered around, watching Prabhupāda and listening to his words. The sound of birds and street noises filled the air.

"You can be a *brahmacārī* and live outside the temple," said Prabhupāda.

"Really?" Pañcadraviḍa was surprised to hear such liberal concessions, but again Śrīla Prabhupāda qualified it.

"Yes, you can live outside, follow the four principles, and be a *brahmacārī*, but of course if you did that, you wouldn't be part of our movement."

"Oh." Pañcadraviḍa sounded disappointed. "Well, maybe, Prabhupāda," he continued, "maybe I can get married."

"Yes," said Prabhupāda in a leisurely, tolerant manner, "you could do that if you like." Pañcadraviḍa decided to ask no more questions, and he excused himself from Prabhupāda's presence.

Later, some of the senior devotees told Pañcadraviḍa that they had never heard Śrīla Prabhupāda speak quite like that, sanctioning whatever his disciple had asked for. Pañcadraviḍa wasn't satisfied.

The following day he happened to be outside Prabhupāda's room just as Śrīla Prabhupāda was looping his brahminical thread around his ear as he prepared to enter the bathroom. Seeing his spiritual master, Pañcadraviḍa spoke his mind again.

"Śrīla Prabhupāda, you know yesterday I asked you all those questions and you said I could do so many things, play music, live as a *brahmacārī* outside the temple, or get married? So I'm a little confused. I was wondering, if I do these things, will I have your blessings?"

Prabhupāda cast a penetrating glance into his disciple's eyes and replied, "Why are you asking so many stupid questions? If you do not know what the spiritual master wants, how do you expect to have his blessings?" Śrīla Prabhupāda then walked away and entered his bathroom. Pañcadraviḍa was left with his first lesson of spiritual life: do what the spiritual master wants. And he also better appreciated, by the way Śrīla Prabhupāda was dealing with him, that Prabhupāda was transcendental, not an ordinary being of this world.

29

A few months after his questions to Prabhupāda in Calcutta, Pañcadraviḍa approached him in Bombay and handed him a piece of paper, saying, "I wrote this song."

"All right," said Prabhupāda, "just leave it here and I'll look at it later." Pañcadraviḍa thanked Śrīla Prabhupāda and started to leave the room when suddenly Prabhupāda spoke again. "Here, let me see that."

Prabhupāda then looked at the words to Pañcadraviḍa's song and said, "So, can you sing this?"

"Yes, Śrīla Prabhupāda," said Pañcadraviḍa. "I have a guitar."

Prabhupāda then asked Pañcadraviḍa to get the guitar and sing along with Prabhupāda and his servant. Prabhupāda took the *mṛdaṅga* on his lap, his servant played *karatālas,* and Pañcadraviḍa began strumming chords to accompany his own singing of his original devotional song.

"Five thousand years ago on this very day
a small blue boy made His way
into this dark and troubled land,
into this dark and troubled world.

"The men rushed by on their charging steeds
looking for the child who will one day
kill the king,
looking for the child who will one day
kill the king.

"Nanda Mahārāja, I can find thirty-two auspicious
symptoms
on the body of your son. I am wondering
how this child could have taken His birth in the family
of cowherd men.
how this child could have taken His birth in the family
of cowherd men."

Prabhupāda smiled and enjoyed the song along with his disciples. Outside Prabhupāda's room, one of the devotees told Pañcadraviḍa that he should consider this the perfection of his guitar-playing career, and that he could now forget about the guitar. Pañcadraviḍa held on to his guitar for another month or so, however, although it wasn't much appreciated by the other *brahmacārīs.* Then one day he decided to give it up. Although it was a two hundred-dollar guitar, he accepted five dollars for the guitar and case and sold it to another devotee musician. The same guitar then became part of further interaction with Śrīla Prabhupāda in Māyāpur.

The new owner of the guitar, an American disciple, had been causing considerable trouble for the devotee community because of his violent temper and almost all the devotees were apprehensive of his presence. Prabhupāda heard different complaints and one day called the devotee before him.

"You sing so nicely," said Śrīla Prabhupāda. "Why don't you and your wife just travel all over the world, singing to attract people to Kṛṣṇa consciousness?"

Greatly encouraged, the devotee soon left Māyāpur. On the authority of Śrīla Prabhupāda, he walked off singing with his guitar. Although the *śāstras* say that no one can know the mind of the *ācārya,* and although Prabhupāda never said that he had sent away a troublesome devotee by suggesting that he travel and sing, nevertheless most of the devotees in Māyāpur could not help but appreciate how Prabhupāda was masterfully solving problems.

30

It was Prabhupāda's custom while visiting the ISKCON temple on Henry Street in Brooklyn to receive the ISKCON artists and review their latest paintings for his books. But when one of the veteran painters, Jadurāṇī-devī dāsī, showed Prabhupāda a recent picture of Kṛṣṇa in Vṛndāvana, she got an unusual response. The picture showed youthful Lord Kṛṣṇa, sitting in the bushes of Vṛndāvana. His head was tilted, and with His hand to His forehead, He was in a dejected mood. Beyond the bushes some of the *gopīs* were searching for Kṛṣṇa.

"What is this?" asked Prabhupāda. It was as if he did not know what to make of it.

"Is something wrong?" asked Jadurāṇī. "This is Kṛṣṇa lamenting because Rādhārāṇī has left Him."

"No," said Prabhupāda.

"Yes," said Jaduraṇī. "It's right there in *The Teachings of Lord Caitanya.* Kṛṣṇa is lamenting because Rādhārāṇī went off, and so He went into the bushes and was lamenting."

"No," said Prabhupāda. "Kṛṣṇa's not like that."

Jaduraṇī insisted that it was in the book, but Prabhupāda objected. "Kṛṣṇa does not lament like that," he said. Prabhupāda did not say exactly what was wrong, but the devotees became distressed, especially the artist. Everyone felt uncomfortable until Śrīla Prabhupāda found a solution.

"You can use this painting for another idea," he said. "This can be the picture where Kṛṣṇa has a headache." Prabhupāda leaned back satisfied and repeated, "Yes, Kṛṣṇa has a headache."

Everyone sighed in relief as Prabhupāda found another way to appreciate a devotee's service.

31

On another visit to the Brooklyn temple, while Śrīla Prabhupāda was seeing the latest paintings of his artist disciples, he suddenly asked that a tape be brought of his singing the *bhajana, jīva jago.*

Within a few minutes the tape was found and Prabhupāda sat back silently listening along with the roomful of devotees. He became so absorbed in listening to the singing that to the devotees, it appeared he had entered a spiritual trance. Even when he looked up and glanced around the room, they felt that Prabhupāda's spiritual mood was deep and unapproachable. When the tape was over, Prabhupāda still could not speak, so it appeared that the meeting was over. The devotees began to reluctantly rise and leave, but one of them came forward with another painting.

"Prabhupāda, we forgot to show you. Here's one more painting."

"Yes," said Prabhupāda, still in a very thoughtful mood. "Yes, it is good." He then looked around at the assembled devotees in the room and began shaking his head appreciatively.

"Actually, all of you are good," he said. "You are all good, and in your association, even I am good. Otherwise, I am very bad." Now the meeting was over, as no one was able to reply to Prabhupāda's humble statement.

32

LITTLE DROPS *of* NECTAR

Some of Prabhupāda's disciples were in the midst of famous or infamous careers just before they joined him to take up full-time spiritual life. Jagattāriṇī-devī dāsī had been a leading movie actress in Australia and had just made a film with Mick Jagger before deciding to surrender to Śrīla Prabhupāda. One time while Prabhupāda was visiting in Australia, a reporter picked up on the story that the former actress had now become a renounced devotee. They ran two pictures in the newspaper showing Jagattāriṇī first as a movie actress with make-up and fashionable attire, and then in a *sārī*, washing a pot. When the newspaper came out, the devotees were amused and wanted to bring it to Prabhupāda, although Jagattāriṇī was frightened that he would be displeased. When Prabhupāda saw the photos, he laughed.

"In this picture as a movie actress, she looks morose and she is not very beautiful," said Prabhupāda. Then he pointed to the picture of his disciple in a *sārī*. "But in this picture she looks very lively and very beautiful. But to the materialist, he will see it the other way."

That evening in the temple, when Jagattāriṇī approached Prabhupāda's *vyāsāsana* to receive a piece of *prasādam,* he said to her, "You are very fortunate because Kṛṣṇa saved you from all that nonsense."

A newlywed disciple once approached Śrīla Prabhupāda for advice about marriage and got a puzzling reply.

Śrīla Prabhupāda had himself performed a fire *yajña* ceremony for the young man and woman in his London temple, and the next morning the newlyweds managed to accompany Śrīla Prabhupāda alone on his morning walk. The husband walked next to Prabhupāda and the wife walked three paces behind.

"Prabhupāda, what does it mean to be married in Kṛṣṇa consciousness?"

Prabhupāda was silent for a moment and then said, "To be married in Kṛṣṇa consciousness means that before you eat your *prasādam,* you go out in the street and you call three times loudly, 'Does anyone want to take *prasādam*? Does anyone want to take *prasādam*? Does anyone want to take *prasādam*?' If no one comes, then you take your *prasādam."*

The husband felt somewhat bewildered, because he was hoping to hear direction about the position of a married couple and how they should deal intimately in relating with each other. The young man thought that perhaps Prabhupāda had not understood him, so near the end of the walk he again asked the same question.

"Prabhupāda, what does it mean to be married in Kṛṣṇa consciousness?"

Prabhupāda steadily repeated his answer, "To be married in Kṛṣṇa consciousness means that before you take *prasādam,* you go out into the street and you call loudly three times, 'Does anyone want to take *prasādam*?' If no one comes, then you take *prasādam."*

33

In Australia Prabhupāda was talking to a roomful of guests. He spoke of misused intelligence. He said that people in the human form of life have the opportunity for spiritual realization, and yet they are simply misusing their intelligence. Śrīla Prabhupāda's talk was being recorded by several tape recorders, and microphones were propped up on the desk before him. The mood was serious, just as in a formal lecture, and Prabhupāda was intent on his deliverance of Kṛṣṇa consciousness to the people.

In the midst of the talk, a newly-initiated *brahmacārī* disciple was sent forward to give Prabhupāda a goblet of water. The goblet was a fancy one with a small base and a large opening. It had been placed upside down on the silver tray along with a pitcher of ice water. The *brahmacārī* nervously placed the tray on Prabhupāda's table while everyone watched him and waited. Not perceiving that the glass was upside down, the boy somehow thought that the base was actually a funnel in which he should pour the water. But as he started pouring, the water splashed off the base of the goblet and onto the desk.

"What is that?" said Prabhupāda.

"It is water, Prabhupāda," said the *brahmacārī* disciple.

By now several people in the audience rose to help the situation. No one was laughing. Rather, there was pained embarrassment that such a strange thing had happened in Prabhupāda's presence. Finally the boy sat down again and Śrīla Prabhupāda recommenced his lecture.

"Misused intelligence," said Prabhupāda, and the audience laughed with him, appreciating his wit and his ability to relieve the awkward moment.

34

One time while Prabhupāda was in Māyāpur, a disciple of his came from Africa with the intention of performing extreme austerities in the holy *dhāma.* Instead of living in the residential building, the devotee stayed in a small hut near a field of banana trees. Reportedly, he was chanting 120 rounds of *japa* a day, sleeping two hours a day, and only taking a small bit of *prasādam.*

Śrīla Prabhupāda knew of the boy's presence in the *dhāma,* but at first he said nothing publicly. Then one morning while Prabhupāda was walking around the pond, one of the devotees mentioned the latest austere practices of the devotee from Africa. Some of the devotees had been impressed, since they knew how difficult it was to chant so many rounds and to sleep and eat so little.

"Śrīla Prabhupāda," said one of the devotees, "he is now increasing his chanting and he's not associating with anyone so that he won't engage in any idle talk."

"Yes," said Prabhupāda noncommittally, "he wanted to live on the river."

"Śrīla Prabhupāda, now he wants to live in a tree."

Then Prabhupāda revealed his mind. "All nonsense," he said. And he waved his hand, dismissing the whole endeavor. "As soon as you say, 'I want,' it is all sense gratification, all nonsense."

35

LITTLE DROPS *of* NECTAR

In Māyāpur, especially at the time of the international festivals, different disciples would take the service to guard Śrīla Prabhupāda's door. Their function was mostly to screen potential visitors so that Śrīla Prabhupāda was not constantly interrupted. The guard would also go and fetch anything that Śrīla Prabhupāda wanted.

One time, while Mahābuddhi dāsa was guarding Prabhupāda's door, Śrīla Prabhupāda called him in and asked for the juice of a fresh *dob,* but even while Prabhupāda was talking, his sister, Bhavātariṇī, suddenly entered his room. Prabhupāda's sister, known as Piśimā (or "aunt") to Prabhupāda's disciples, had free entrance to see Prabhupāda whenever she wanted. Besides, no one could really restrain her if she wanted to see Prabhupāda, to talk with him, or to cook for him.

As Piśimā sat down in the room, Mahābuddhi got up to carry out Prabhupāda's desire for the fresh *dob,* but Prabhupāda spoke sternly, "Sit down." Mahābuddhi sat down again.

Śrīla Prabhupāda spoke with his sister in Bengali, for about twenty minutes while Mahābuddhi waited, chanting silently on his beads. The talk between Prabhupāda and his sister was enthusiastic until towards the end when Prabhupāda became somewhat reprimanding. Finally Bhavātariṇī offered her respects to her exalted brother and left the room. Prabhupāda stood up, and Mahābuddhi started to leave to carry out his interrupted errand.

As if to explain his action, Prabhupāda quoted a verse:

mātrā svasrā duhitrā vā
nāviviktāsano bhavet
balavān indriya-grāmo
vidvāṁsam api karṣati

"Never stay alone with a woman," said Prabhupāda.

Spreading Kṛṣṇa consciousness in India often meant that Prabhupāda went with his disciples to honor *prasādam* at people's homes. Thus, eating became a form of service to Kṛṣṇa.

When Girirāja dāsa first arrived in India, he was used to strict training as a *brahmacārī,* and his personal habit was to be particularly reserved about accepting any sweets. On one occasion, however, Prabhupāda saw that his disciple's austerity was causing discomfort to their host.

The father of the man who had invited Prabhupāda to eat had repeatedly tried to give Girirāja a second *rasagullā,* but Girirāja kept refusing. Since Girirāja was sitting quite close to Prabhupāda, he did not want Prabhupāda to think that he was a sense enjoyer, so for that reason also he staunchly refused to accept the *rasagullā* from the elderly father of the host. Finally, when the man came around again to coax Girirāja, Śrīla Prabhupāda glanced lovingly at Girirāja and said, "You can take a sweet to make an old man happy." Girirāja accepted another sweet.

36

ŚRĪLA PRABHUPĀDA SAID

On Health and Sickness

"Regarding your physical malady, you should do whatever is required to treat it properly—whatever is most practical."

—*Letter of May 7, 1975*

"First of all there is no question of a devotee becoming ostracized because he has become ill, nor do I think this is being widely practiced. Who has been ostracized? One of the symptoms of a devotee is that he is kind, so if our Godbrother becomes ill, it is our duty to help him get the proper medicine and treatment so that he can recover."

—*Letter of April 5, 1974*

"Regarding Bhumata-devi dasi's affliction, she should simply take the proper treatment. Make the best out of a bad bargain. This material body is a bad bargain because it is always miserable. So to make the best out of this bad bargain means to render devotional service in any circumstance. The dust from the lotus feet of the spiritual master is never to be used for material benefit. That is a great misconception. The best thing is that the girl tries her best to chant sixteen rounds daily and to follow all the rules and regulations even if she is afflicted with something, and in this way she will fully understand the mercy of Krsna and the spiritual master."

—*Letter of April 8, 1975*

"Doctors give medicine and they speak surety, but there is no surety, and where there is no surety why should we break our four basic principles? I don't think there is guarantee of surety by taking this medicine with animal products. But if there is surety, you can take. But it is very doubtful."

—*Letter of February 12, 1972*

"There are many examples in history of persons who have been very much disabled physically but who still have executed Krsna consciousness. Still, up-to-date in places like Vrndavana, India, there are many persons who are blind, crippled, lame, deformed, etc., but they are determined to practice Krsna consciousness to their best ability. Simply be determined to practice the process of *bhakti-yoga* with whatever abilities you have. If you are really sincere, then Krsna will give you help. If you require any medical help, you take as much as is needed."

—*Letter of June 3, 1975*

"So you have done your duty at the last moments of your wife's life so that she could hear the chanting. As to where she has gone, that depends on what she was thinking of at the time of her passing away. That is stated in the *Bhagavad-gita:*

anta-kale ca mam eva
smaran muktva kalevaram
yah prayati smad-bhavam
yati nasty atra samsayah

'And whoever at the time of death quits his body remembering Me alone, at once attains My nature. Of this there is no doubt.' To remember Krsna requires practice, and this is mostly to be done by chanting Hare Krsna mantra."

—*Letter of November 6, 1974*

"Regarding the auto accident, just hold a condolence meeting for Raghava dasa Brahmacari and pray for his soul to Krsna for giving him a good chance for advancement in Krsna consciousness. Certainly Krsna will give him a good place to take birth where he can again begin in Krsna consciousness activities. That is sure. But we offer our condolences to a departed soul separated from the Vaiṣṇavas. Do you know that there must be *prasadam* distributed? Three days after the demise of a Vaisnava a function should be held for offering the departed soul and all others *prasadam*. This is the system."

—*Letter of November 14, 1973*

37

PRABHUPĀDA TELLS A STORY

Prabhupāda introduced his disciples to the stories of the jester Gopāla Bhan, who was famous in Bengal for his intelligence, wit, and quick thinking in the court of Kṛṣṇacandra. Prabhupāda said that no one, not even an emperor, can always be serious without any relief. But since everyone had to treat the king very respectfully, there would be one person allowed to spoof with the king. The king would also be able to joke with him, because if the king were to do that with his prime minister, the prime minister's prestige would be reduced. So King Kṛṣṇacandra was always engaged in a battle of wits with his joker, Gopāla.

One time Gopāla walked into the king's court and the king said, "Gopāla, you are an ass."

"My lord," said Gopāla, "I am not an ass. There's a difference between me and an ass."

Then Gopāla measured out the distance between himself and the king and said, "Six feet."

When Prabhupāda laughingly told this story, his devotees were not only amused but amazed that Prabhupāda was inviting them to hear and laugh at the wit of Gopāla Bhan.

Then Prabhupāda told another story. Gopāla was building a new house, and according to the Vedic custom, before you open a house you have to have a sacrifice called a *gṛha-praveśana.* This means there is a *yajña* so that the house is pure and offered to God. No one is allowed to pass any stool in the house or it will be considered contaminated. Nothing is used by anyone until the *brāhmaṇas* enter with *saṅkīrtana-yajña,* reciting mantras and sprinkling Ganges water. Thus in the Vedic culture everything, including building a house and conceiving a child, is regulated so that at every point one is conscious of Kṛṣṇa. But, Prabhupāda explained, the king wanted to defeat Gopāla, so he offered a large reward of gold coins if anyone could outsmart Gopāla and pass stool in his newly constructed house.

One day Gopāla was inspecting his house when a man sent by the king came up and pretended to be suffering from an urgent call of nature.

"Gopāla," he said, "I have to immediately pass stool. Please show me your bathroom. I cannot contain myself."

"All right," said Gopāla. "Come on." He took him over to the bathroom of the newly constructed house and allowed the man to squat down inside. But when he tried to close the door for privacy, Gopāla stood there by the open door.

"Gopāla, why are you standing there and not allowing me to close the door? Why are you holding that big stick in your hand?"

Gopāla said, "No, you can pass stool in my bathroom, but if you pass one drop of urine, then I'm going to smash your head." Then the man laughed and confessed, "You are very clever," and he ran off, defeated.

Prabhupāda laughed after this story also, although the devotees were a little puzzled. Prabhupāda admitted that the Vedic humor was somewhat subtle. He said that the humor was connected inseparably with the culture and if one did not know the culture, he might not understand the humor. But in Vedic culture, religion, humor, art, music—everything was connected.

38

PRABHUPĀDA TELLS A STORY

One day, the king's wife gave birth to a male child and the king was rejoicing. At that moment, Gopāla came into the room and the king said, "Gopāla, on this very, very happy occasion, please tell me, what do you have to say? Tell me exactly how you feel at this moment."

Gopāla replied, "Frankly, at this moment, I feel very happy after passing stool."

"Gopāla! How could you say such a thing?" The king was mortified. "On this auspicious moment, that's all you have to say? I am completely disgusted. It's not funny and I don't appreciate your humor at all."

After that, the relations between the king and Gopāla were strained for some time. One day, Gopāla was rowing the king down the river when the king suddenly had an urgent call of nature. Gopāla said, "On this side there is a very heavy jungle area. It's not very suitable. Let us go a little further down and we'll find a better place."

The king said, "Go over to the side!"

Gopāla said, "Not here. There is danger. Some thieves and dacoits. Your life may be endangered. There's a place ahead."

The king said, "Gopāla, I cannot wait any longer. Immediately go over!" Gopāla had to go over and the king jumped out. He could hardly contain himself. When the king returned, Gopāla asked him, "How are you feeling?"

The king replied, "I am feeling very happy after passing stool."

Then Gopāla said, "Don't you remember? This was exactly the situation I was in after your child was born. When you asked me at that moment what exactly I was feeling, I was in the same situation as you are now. I told you how I was feeling, but you thought I was insulting your son and you never appreciated it. Now do you understand?"

39

PERSONAL

His Regular Schedule

Prabhupāda followed his own schedule and only occasionally departed from it. He was supposed to take massage at about eleven or eleven-thirty in the morning, but if he had guests and was preaching, he would not stop for the schedule. Or at night, he would keep talking, especially with some life member or solicitor in Bombay. But he was never whimsical about time or about where to be for Kṛṣṇa's service.

Once, after walking along Juhu beach for half an hour, Dr. Patel, one of his friends who joined us to walk, suggested that we turn back. Prabhupāda looked at his watch and said that it was too early, the Deity of Rādhā-Rāsabihārī would not give *darśana* for another hour. Dr. Patel said, "If you come back early, since you are a pure devotee, Kṛṣṇa can give *darśana* early." Prabhupāda said that was out of the question: we cannot change the Deities' schedule to suit our own.

He never went off alone without devotees accompanying him. It was unheard of that he would say, "I am leaving for a few days," or "I am going on some private business," or "I am going on a vacation."

Everything was done at the right Kṛṣṇa conscious moment —even his solitude (one could overhear it) as he produced the *Bhāgavatam* or when he was chanting Hare Kṛṣṇa mantra on beads. The silence of his pure consciousness we could not try to understand, but there were glimpses of it when he would sometimes tell us of a dream he had or he would reveal something he had been thinking of alone.

In New York City, in 1968, after staying up very late at night, Prabhupāda rose and traveled early in the morning to Boston. He then wrote back to his temple president in New York City, who had not been able to rise on the morning of Prabhupāda's departure to Boston. "Don't just praise me," Prabhupāda wrote, "but do as I do." Prabhupāda followed his schedule with considerable strictness. Events would crash down on him. News of a demon's attack might make him grave, yet he would go off gravely to his bath or take *prasādam*—unless it became too much. Then, out of anxiety, he would not attend to his eating. Once he stayed up all night worrying when a leading disciple showed signs of serious deviancy. One time when shown color photos of the first Ratha-yātrā in Los Angeles, he stared in transcendental pleasure for hours and did not take his massage. Promptness was the steady factor, punctuated by these departures which showed us something beyond the schedule. Usually, however, everything was taken care of, absorbed into his routine.

He did not fit the stereotype of an Indian who was always two hours late for every meeting. Prabhupāda regularly glanced at his watch, and sometimes when his servants were not ready to leave, he would walk out his room and head for a waiting car, prepared to leave them behind. Yet he did not appear like a *karmī,* bound hand and foot to following an imposed schedule that gave him no freedom.

The *Bhagavad-gītā* describes the "regulated principles of freedom." Prabhupāda was liberated, but both to show us and to live in the most effective way to accomplish his service, he organized the twenty-four hours of the day and night. There was a best time—when the air was cool and the neighborhood quiet for taking a morning walk. There was a best time to greet the Deities—according to Their time. There was a best time for devotees to gather, a suitable time to eat for health, and a reasonable time to answer letters. To regulate his men so they would rise early, he rose early. He preached to his guests at times convenient for their schedules. Thus he scheduled his transcendental acts, not for the rule's sake, but for performing constant, optimum service to Kṛṣṇa for spreading and solidifying his ISKCON movement in this world.

40

One of Prabhupāda's artist-disciples, Bharadvāja dāsa, had his own ideas of how he should preach until Prabhupāda impressed him with his own desire and definition of preaching.

At the time of receiving his *gāyatrī-mantra,* Bharadvāja asked, "Prabhupāda, may I ask you a question?" Prabhupāda nodded and Bharadvāja pursued it: "I would like to go and preach." He was about to speak further, but Prabhupāda cut him off.

"What do you know about preaching?" Prabhupāda challenged. His disciple became speechless.

"Preaching means to describe Kṛṣṇa," said Prabhupāda. "So you are doing it by your painting." Prabhupāda leaned forward across the table and looked into Bharadvāja's eyes. "Please try to understand," said Prabhupāda. "If you don't do this important service, who will do it? Go on painting."

Bharadvāja left the room, contemplating what Prabhupāda had said. He thought how he had wanted to tell Prabhupāda, "I want to go to Russia." Maybe if he had said that, it would have made a difference. But then Prabhupāda's own words reverberated in his mind, and finally he began to understand them. He began to realize that just knowing another language was no great qualification for preaching, but by painting a picture of Kṛṣṇa's name, fame, and pastimes, he could preach anywhere and very straightforwardly in the universal language that requires no translation. The more he thought about it, the happier he became to follow Prabhupāda's order.

The next day Prabhupāda again met with the ISKCON artists. Bharadvāja was eager to show Prabhupāda that he had understood his teachings. Prabhupāda was explaining the meaning of *sannyāsa*, which he said was to preach, by serving Kṛṣṇa with body, mind, and words. Service with the mind, said Prabhupāda, means the intelligence; the artists' special task was to serve Kṛṣṇa with their intelligence. They should serve with their intelligence and not become diverted by many things. Thinking that he had finally understood the point clearly, Bharadvāja spoke up.

"Prabhupāda," he said, "the other day you said preaching is to describe Kṛṣṇa."

"Yes," said Śrīla Prabhupāda, "one should offer the words to Kṛṣṇa through speaking." Bharadvāja became bewildered again, and his former desire to preach by traveling and speaking words and not painting came to his mind. He thought he had understood Prabhupāda, but now as Prabhupāda enlarged his explanation, Bharadvāja wondered.

"The artist can also preach in the temple to the devotees," Prabhupāda said. But mostly he continued to stress that the artists sit and paint as their best preaching. Seeing Bharadvāja's confusion, Prabhupāda turned to him.

"So, Bharadvāja. Where do you want to go?"

Bharadvāja felt himself falling into a trap, but he could not resist it. "Russia," he said.

Prabhupāda moved his head back in surprise. "Russia!" he said, and he laughed. On that note, Prabhupāda ended his conversation with the artists.

"I have now been a fool twice in front of Prabhupāda," thought Bharadvāja, and he resolved never to again bring up his restlessness in front of Prabhupāda. "When will I learn?" he thought. "Prabhupāda wants me to paint."

41

Śrīla Prabhupāda said that one had to first become acquainted with Kṛṣṇa in order to love Him. As the representative of Kṛṣṇa, Prabhupāda attached his devotees to himself and then he attached them to Kṛṣṇa's service. So it is stated in the Vedic *śāstras* that the infinite Personality of Godhead reveals Himself to the tiny spirit soul through the agency of the spiritual master. Śrīla Prabhupāda attracted devotees through his books, through his lectures, through the *mahā-mantra,* and by many other direct methods of *bhakti-yoga.* He also developed individual relationships with his disciples, sometimes based on seemingly ordinary matters. Of course, the main relationship he had with each disciple was through their regular service, but sometimes he would exchange with them over little things. If he had met a devotee's parents, he might regularly ask the devotee about the well-being of his mother and father, or he would accept a gift of a daily mango, or a twig for brushing his teeth, or he would call on a particular devotee to become an antagonist in mock debates. With Prabhupāda's disciple Candanācārya dāsa, Śrīla Prabhupāda developed an ongoing acquaintance based on their mutual dealings over an Omega watch.

When Candanācārya was given *hari-nāma* initiation by Śrīla Prabhupāda in Boston, he gave Śrīla Prabhupāda an Omega watch as a gesture of *guru-dakṣiṇā.*

"You do not need this watch?" asked Śrīla Prabhupāda.

"Well, you have given something very dear to you to me, so I am giving the most dear thing I have." The watch had been given to Candana by his father, and Candana considered it his most treasured possession. Prabhupāda was pleased by the gift and explained to Candana that giving and accepting gifts was one of the six kinds of loving exchanges in Kṛṣṇa consciousness. The watch then became the basis of a series of conversations that took place over a year between Śrīla Prabhupāda and his new disciple.

Since the watch was running a little slowly, Candana asked Prabhupāda if he could first have it adjusted and cleaned before giving it to Prabhupāda. Prabhupāda agreed, but was disturbed to hear later that Candanācārya had left the watch at the jewelers without asking for a receipt.

Months later, when Śrīla Prabhupāda was in New Vrindaban, Candana traveled along with hundreds of others to see his spiritual master and Śrīla Prabhupāda received him affectionately.

Prabhupāda was wearing the Omega watch, and on seeing Candana, he said, "This is a very nice watch. Do you have a watch?" Prabhupāda instructed his servant to give his old watch to Candanācārya. Prabhupāda said that he had replaced the original Omega wrist band with a spring-type metal wrist band "because it is much easier to take on and off." Candana was pleased to receive the old wrist band from Prabhupāda, which now smelled sweetly of sandalwood oil from being worn on Prabhupāda's body. He put his old band onto a new, expensive watch that Prabhupāda gave him. As they sat together in Prabhupāda's small room above the New Vrindaban temple room, Prabhupāda admired his Omega watch. "The only difference with this watch," said Prabhupāda, "is that it does not tell me the day or the date. That old watch did."

"Prabhupāda, I can get you a little calendar," said Candana, "which will fit on the wrist band and that can be changed every month." Prabhupāda said that would be good, and in the following weeks there were further exchanges as Candana mailed Prabhupāda the wrist calendars and Prabhupāda wrote back thanking him.

Months later they met again in New York and talked more about watches. "How is your watch?" asked Prabhupāda.

"It's good, Śrīla Prabhupāda. How's yours?"

"It's slow," said Prabhupāda. "Why are they cheating like this? This is such an expensive watch, and you took it to be fixed, and it is a slow a minute or two every day."

"This watch," said Candana, raising his wrist and showing the watch he had been given by Prabhupāda, "is fast about five minutes every day."

"Well, at least it has a good qualification," said Prabhupāda, "that it's fast."

Candana and the other devotees present laughed with Prabhupāda about the cheating defects of the watches. Kīrtanānanda Mahārāja was also present and brought Prabhupāda a plate of *prasādam.* Prabhupāda took a single bite and then distributed the rest to everyone.

"Śrīla Prabhupāda," said Kīrtanānanda Mahārāja, "I just tried to make the *sandeśa* the way you told me, but it never comes out the way you make it. I did everything you showed me."

Prabhupāda turned his head to the side and said, "Craftsmanship."

Thus in as many different ways as there were different disciples, Prabhupāda exchanged with them and brought them into a loving bondage with Kṛṣṇa, even while talking of watches and cooking.

42

LITTLE DROPS *of* NECTAR

When in January 1974 devotees saw Kohoutek's Comet and told Śrīla Prabhupāda, he called the comet a bad omen. "In our childhood," he said, "we saw a comet, and the First World War was declared." The witnesses of the Kohoutek Comet told Prabhupāda that it had filled up the sky near their airplane with flashes of light.

"And they say the tail is three million miles long. It's going very fast, so it is emitting a tail of gasses."

"So who is supplying the gasses?" asked Prabhupāda. "The Arabians?"

He said the comet was like a policeman who all of a sudden comes before us. By his presence, we can understand that some criminal is present and the policeman is searching. He said disasters would follow.

The anti-cult crusade in American was only beginning its campaign during Śrīla Prabhupāda's very last years, but Prabhupāda gave good advice how the devotees could combat it and how they could realize they were protected by Kṛṣṇa.

Rāmeśvara Swami was once explaining to Śrīla Prabhupāda about these activities during a visit with Prabhupāda in India.

"We're actually getting much free exposure on the radio and television," said Rāmeśvara Swami, "and each time we come off sounding very intelligent, religious, and nice, and the deprogrammers come off sounding like fanatics and bigots. So people are getting a good impression of us because of the publicity on radio and television."

"Yes," said Prabhupāda. "Just like Sītā was put into the fire and she came out unburned. Sītā was blasphemed. They said, 'This woman was kidnapped by Rāvaṇa, and Rāmacandra is so henpecked that He has again picked her up and is living with her.' So Rāmacandra put her in the fire, and she came out unharmed."

43

LITTLE DROPS *of* NECTAR

Prabhupāda was talking with an Indian guest and well-wisher. The topic turned to the publication of *Back to Godhead* magazine in various languages. Prabhupāda was saying that the Indians would gladly read an English magazine, but Prabhupāda's guest said that it would be much more popular if they could publish in Hindi, Gujarati, Marathi, and Bengali.

"That is not possible," said Prabhupāda. "That is for you Indians to do. But you have not time. You are busy with your daughter's marriage and you simply advise."

"I am busy?" replied the man with surprise.

"Yes, everyone," said Prabhupāda. "Every Indian is busy with his own affairs. He'll come and advise, that's all. Advice *gratis*. But he will not do himself."

The man protested, "No, but—"

But Prabhupāda knew better. "No, this is going on," he said. "I have got full experience that Indians, they will come and give some advice and go away for daughter's marriage. That's all."

"Well," the man tried to hold his ground, "there are various types of Indians, you know."

"That type," said Prabhupāda, "is ninety-nine percent. You'll advise, but you'll never do it. This is going on."

On different occasions, Prabhupāda explained how the British empire had done great damage to India's culture. Once he explained the Home Bill, which had ordered India's gold to London. Even the Mohammedans made their expenditures within India, but the British took away India's wealth. Then he described how the British sent Indian laborers all over the world.

"First of all it was conquered by Indian soldiers," said Prabhupāda, "then when it was to be organized, Indian coolies, Indian laborers. Because they have got Indian men and money, so they expanded the empire. So I am doing the same business—American money and American men." Prabhupāda laughed to think of it. "I am already a great politician."

"Home Bill," quipped one of the devotees.

"Yes," said Prabhupāda, "but I am not for home. I am for the whole world."

44

PRABHUPĀDA SAID

On a Balanced Temple Program

In a letter of June 12, 1974, to Śrī Govinda dāsa in Chicago, Śrīla Prabhupāda stressed book distribution and stated that other programs should be minimized. After this letter had been distributed to various temples, several devotees wrote to Prabhupāda asking whether they should actually cut back on other existing programs, like Deity worship and other kinds of outside preaching. Prabhupāda's replies stressed the absolute nature of any Kṛṣṇa consciousness service.

"The thing is we should have a little common sense in all activities. The example can be given that women by nature do not forget to dress very nicely although always engaged in household affairs. Deity worship or lecturing in the colleges is just as important as book distribution. So these things must be done very nicely, and at the same time, book distribution should be done. Not that we should do one thing at the sacrifice of another. That requires a little common sense. Factually, we should be engaged twenty-four hours in Krsna's service and everything should be done very nicely and perfectly."

—Letter of January 2, 1975

"Regarding your question about the controversial talks going on, this kind of talk is not befitting my advanced students. This is childish. In Krsna's service, there is no inferior and superior. Deity worship is just as important as book distribution. It is not material. . . . You should understand the importance of each and every item of devotional service. Do not make any misunderstanding by devaluating any of the spiritual activities. . . . One who distinguishes a particular type of service as inferior or superior, he does not know the value of devotional service. It is all transcendental. Whatever item is suitable, that is accepted as very elevated. Just like Maharaja Pariksit. He simply listened to Sukadeva Gosvami. That is *sravanam*. . . . So any devotee executing any one of the nine items is transcendentally glorious. One devotee may be proud that his process of service is best. That is not inglorious. Everyone should feel proud of his particular type of devotional service. But that does not mean that other types of service are inferior. Everyone should feel proud of becoming a sincere servant of Krsna, but the pure devotee never minimizes the importance of other devotees. Krsna is the enjoyer of varieties of service. It is not stuck up with any particular type of service."

—Letter of January 19, 1975

On Instructions from Outside Institutions

"Regarding the books from other Maths being circulated there, who is distributing? Who is sending these books? These Maths do not sell our books; why should we sell their books? Who has introduced these books? Let me know. These books should not at all be circulated in our society. You say that you would read only one book if that was all that I had written, so you teach others to do like that. You have very good determination."

—*Letter of November 14, 1973*

"I understand that in the past you were visiting L. and that you may also be planning to continue to visit him when you return to India. This is not approved by me, and I request you not to go see him anymore. He holds a grudge against my Guru Maharaja, and even if it is transcendental, it will gradually appear mundane in your eyes. Whatever is to be learned of the teachings of Srila Bhaktivinoda Thakura can be learned from our books. There is no need whatsoever for any outside instructions."

—*Letter of December 25, 1973*

45

PRABHUPĀDA SAID

Preaching Methods

"If our men are trained, one man can run a place. One experienced man can sit down in a hut and simply talk about Krsna and organize the local people. That is how I started in the beginning at 26 Second Avenue in New York City. If there is genuine preaching, they will be attracted, so long as the preacher has no self-motivation but simply chants and preaches."

—*Letter of April 8, 1974*

"There is no question of bigness or smallness of the center as far as pleasing me is concerned. It is the sincerity of the attempt that is the important thing. Of course, as Krsna sees the sincerity of our hearts He supplies the facility. Just like I came to your country with only 40 rupees and now we have this huge institution. So you can be sure that Krsna will supply you according to your capacity. I think that if you continue working sincerely, you will get all facilities that you require for your purposes."

—Letter of September 12, 1974

"Brahmananda Swami seemed to think that you need more men there. His telegram reads, 'Trivikrama alone, more men required urgently.' I do not understand what he means by alone. What is this alone? Vaisnava is never alone. When I first came to the United States, I was seemingly alone for one year. But I never felt alone. I always felt the presence of my Guru Maharaja. Myself, I was cooking, I was printing books, I was selling books, everything seemingly alone. But I did not lose my determination. Actually you should know this, you are never alone. So local men are coming daily. By good association, good preaching, nice *prasadam,* etc., they can become devotees."

—Letter of December 27, 1974

"Regarding sending men to Bangkok, let us see who is a spare man or who is having visa problems. But our policy as you know is not to import devotees but to make devotees out of the local men there. That is better."

—Letter of January 4, 1975

"One copy of our book *Lord Caitanya in Five Features* should be handed over to Swami Chinmayananda as our humble presentation. If somebody, or yourself sees him personally, give him thanks for his letter recommending our admission in the temples and present this book to him. That will be nice. As far as possible, all big Mayavadi *sannyasis* should be presented with this book."

—*Letter of February 4, 1975*

46

PRABHUPĀDA TELLS A STORY

One of Śrīla Prabhupāda's *sannyāsī* disciples had gradually drifted away, stopped strictly following the principles, allowed his hair to grow back, and stopped wearing a *dhotī*. Despite these changes, the devotee still fancied that he could be a spiritual leader. When he came to visit Śrīla Prabhupāda in Melbourne, Australia, however, Prabhupāda told him he would never succeed unless he followed the standard practice. To illustrate this, Prabhupāda told a story.

A servant of a very rich man came before his master one day and told him of an interesting *yogī* he had seen in the river. The servant said that this *yogī* claimed he could stay in the cold water of the river all night in the middle of winter without any outside heat. The *yogī* was willing to wager with anyone to prove that he could do it. When the rich man heard this, he decided to wager against the *yogī*. So the bet was made to see whether the *yogī* could stay in the water all night.

The *yogī* went into the water, and the rich man and his servant went home. The next day the word came that the *yogī* had successfully stayed in the water all night. The rich man went out to see the *yogī*, and indeed he was still standing in the water. Therefore, by all rights, the rich man had lost the wager. Then a friend of the rich man said, "Wait! See that light?" He pointed to a small flame far away in the tower of a temple.

The rich man's friend said, "By his mystic power, this *yogī* has been using the heat of that light to keep warm in the water. So he shouldn't be paid, because the bet was that he would stay in the water without taking any heat."

Taking advantage of this word jugglery, the rich man said, "Yes, I'm not going to pay you. You've tricked me."

Then the rich man and his servant went back to their house. The rich man asked his servant to quickly cook him a nice breakfast, but after waiting for some time, the servant had not produced anything. The rich man expressed his impatience, but the servant replied, "Please wait, I'm cooking." The rich man waited, but it got later and later and no food was brought. When he demanded from the servant, the servant only replied, "I'm cooking. It's going to be ready soon." Finally the rich man became angry and walked into the kitchen. "What is this cooking?" he demanded, and there he saw that the servant had a very strange arrangement for cooking. He had a very small fire on the ground and a tall bamboo tripod to hold the pot he was supposed to heat high by the ceiling. Obviously, the small flame would never be able to reach the pot to heat it.

"What do you think you're doing?" demanded the rich man.

"Well," said the servant, "if you claim that the *yogī* was keeping warm in the water by that light, then I am also cooking." The man could understand that his servant was dissatisfied with the outcome of his wager with the *yogī* so he went and paid the *yogī* the wager.

When Prabhupāda told this story, the devotees kept waiting for a punch line or further conclusion. It didn't seem very obvious. Then Prabhupāda explained it.

"If you want to cook, then you have to cook according to the method. You may have a pot and you may have a flame, but if you don't cook according to the method, then you'll never get the food. It will never work. So he may be chanting Hare Kṛṣṇa," and now Prabhupāda looked to his fallen *sannyāsī* disciple, "but if you're not following the process, then what good is your chanting? If you want to get the result, you have to follow the method."

47

PRABHUPĀDA TELLS SHORT STORIES

Prabhupāda said that when his spiritual master was in Burma opening a Kṛṣṇa conscious center, he used to cook very nice *purīs* in ghee, but all the tenants in the building would come out covering their noses with their cloths. They complained, "What are you cooking? What an obnoxious smell!" Yet these same inhabitants had a favorite preparation called *nakil.* At every door they would keep a big covered pot, and whatever animals died in that vicinity—cats, dogs, rats, whatever—they would put them in the big pot. After two or three years, the bodies would decompose, leaving a liquid substance. This liquid would then be strained, kept in a bottle, and a little bit of it would be used on foodstuffs during festive occasions. Whenever anyone opened one of these pots, the whole neighborhood would be filled with the most obnoxious smell for days, and yet they preferred this to the smell of pure ghee.

"Just see," said Prabhupāda, "how the nature is working. Nature grabs them by the ear and punishes them. They are not allowed to eat nice foods. Nature's dictating, 'You eat all nasty things like hog.' Such persons cannot eat palatable foods like *rasagullā* and *sandeśa.* They prefer stool."

Śrīla Prabhupāda said that a woman's only protection is shyness. In the modern age, women are giving up that shyness and therefore they are creating devastation in society. Śrīla Prabhupāda remembered a personal experience in which a chaste girl defended her modesty against the mocking of another girl.

In the year 1945, Prabhupāda witnessed this scene while traveling on a train. A young girl riding on the train was traveling for the first time to her husband's house. Her face was covered with a veil, as she was observing the ceremony that after puberty and after engagement the girl goes to her husband's house carrying presentations from her mother and father. Another modernized girl mocked the village girl and reached over and pulled at her veil. The city girl did this once and then did it again. When she tried a third time, however, the village girl slapped her in the face. "Yes, you have done right," said Prabhupāda, who was seated nearby in the same train car.

Years later while telling the story, Prabhupāda explained, "The city girl was thinking, 'What is this nonsense?' and she wanted to criticize, but when the other girl gave her a good slap, the whole train laughed. Shyness is the only protection for them. But now there is no modesty left. That is a woman's beauty, but we are breaking that, so there is no beauty, no attraction."

48

PRABHUPĀDA TELLS SHORT STORIES

In Washington D.C., devotees showed Śrīla Prabhupāda news photos of the planet Mars taken recently by a space craft that had supposedly gone near the planet. The news article described how the Martian landscape was similar to the Grand Canyon in Arizona. Prabhupāda laughed to hear this and related a story from Bengal.

A man was in his room at night when he suddenly heard a noise. Starting up in bed, he called out, "Who is there?"

"Oh!" came a voice in reply. "I am not stealing!"

Prabhupāda said, "This is the psychology. No one asked if he was stealing, but because that was his business, he revealed himself without being asked. Similarly, no one has asked the scientist to compare Mars to Arizona, but they have done so because actually that is where their business is. They have never been near Mars with their spaceship; their real business is in Arizona."

When one of Prabhupāda's disciples left Hong Kong, his area of preaching, without authorization, Śrīla Prabhupāda was displeased. Meeting up with him in another country, Prabhupāda reprimanded him. "But why did you leave, rascal?" Then he told a story, as given by the poet Kālidāsa.

A man was sitting on the end of a tree branch sawing on the portion of the limb between himself and the tree trunk. Seeing the danger, a passerby called out, "If you keep on sawing, you are going to fall."

"Go away, " said the man on the limb, "I don't want anything to do with you. I don't want to listen." The man continued sawing until the branch broke and he fell to the ground. He then hurried after the man who had warned him. "You must be an astrologer—you can predict the future."

Prabhupāda said, "That's the definition of a rascal. Someone who is going, but he doesn't know where he is going. So that is like you," he said to the disciple. "You left Hong Kong, but you didn't know what you were going to do next."

To illustrate the foolishness of becoming a blind follower, Prabhupāda told a story about the death of Sargal Singh.

Sargal Singh was very much loved by a merchant, so when Sargal Singh died, the man shaved his head and wore dark clothes. When another man came into the merchant's shop, he asked who had died.

"Sargal Singh has died," said the merchant. The visitor did not want to seem ignorant, so he did not ask who Sargal

Singh was, but he also shaved his head and wore dark clothes. Other people in town began to follow, not wanting to appear ignorant. When anyone asked who had died, they replied, "Sargal Singh has died."

When a minister of the king saw so many citizens in mourning he also wore dark clothes and shaved his head, but when the king saw this, he inquired, "Why are you mourning and for whom?"

"Sargal Singh," the minister replied. The king asked, "Who is that?" When the minister couldn't answer the king told him to find out. The minister then inquired and inquired and finally reached the merchant.

"Who is Sargal Singh?"

The merchant replied, "Sargal Singh was my donkey, whom I loved very much."

49

PERSONAL

Śrīla Prabhupāda Demanded Loyalty

Śrīla Prabhupāda himself was loyal. He always wore the *sannyāsī* saffron *dhotī*, shaved head, and behaved as a perfect Vaiṣṇava wherever he went. He was the most loyal son of his Guru Mahārāja; therefore he carried out the instructions of Bhaktisiddhānta Sarasvatī to go to the West. When Śrīla Prabhupāda first came to New York City, he was advised by Indian swamis there to give up his strict vegetarianism and *sannyāsa* observances, but Śrīla Prabhupāda was loyal. And in his Bhaktivedanta purports, he is always loyal to the conclusion of the previous *ācāryas*.

At least when one became his disciple, then Prabhupāda asked for complete loyalty. Kṛṣṇa conscious knowledge is exclusive; one has to understand that Kṛṣṇa in Goloka Vṛndāvana is the Supreme Truth. Loyalty to Śrīla Prabhupāda means not to follow other versions of the Absolute. If other versions are to be read at all, he said, it is only to know their philosophy. Even Vaiṣṇava heritage should be received through him. Once a disciple said to Prabhupāda that Bhaktivinoda Ṭhākura was his favorite writer. Śrīla Prabhupāda corrected his disciple and said, "Your second favorite writer."

Prabhupāda also asked for loyalty for our own benefit because his Godbrothers were antagonistic. They did not appreciate what Śrīla Prabhupāda had done in going to the West to preach.

Not being loyal to Prabhupāda means to create a very serious erosion in the most crucial place—dedication to the guru. Prabhupāda once said that if you lose faith in the guru, it is like a crack at the very foundation of your Kṛṣṇa consciousness.

His demand for loyalty was not something that he regularly asked for; it was love between him and his disciples, and it was expected. He would refer to "our men" and "the Hare Kṛṣṇa people," meaning all his followers, yet although he asked for their attachment and affection, it was without any false prestige.

Śrīla Prabhupāda humbly accepted that he was the authorized person to prosecute the worldwide Kṛṣṇa consciousness movement. In the purports to his books he expresses that it is not right when so-called Vaiṣṇavas do not respect an empowered Vaiṣṇava who is spreading Kṛṣṇa consciousness all over the world. Therefore, for the followers of Śrīla Prabhupāda, a person's real spiritual advancement can be tested to the degree that he accepts Śrīla Prabhupāda. Ecumenical good manners and sincere participation in dialogue with other religious sects is part of spreading Kṛṣṇa consciousness, but ultimately, a Prabhupāda follower has to appreciate that Prabhupāda is topmost. The reasons he is topmost are within the very conclusions of the *Bhagavad-gītā* and the *Śrīmad-Bhāgavatam*. Śrīla Prabhupāda always said that we should not disparage other religions or other God conscious teachers, yet to recognize and to be loyal to the topmost truth in its fullest manifestation, as Rādhā and Kṛṣṇa worship, was the precious gift Śrīla Prabhupāda gave to his followers. We cannot follow Rādhā-Kṛṣṇa without following Śrīla Prabhupāda.

Exclusive affection and loyalty to Śrīla Prabhupāda is expressed in different ways. It is expressed when a follower stays in the place where Prabhupāda sent him and performs the service that Prabhupāda gave him. Out of personal loyalty to Śrīla Prabhupāda, one refuses to break the regulative principles because a disciple promises Prabhupāda that he will always follow them.

When a devotee complained how hard it was to work with a troublesome devotee, Prabhupāda said, "That is your austerity." Determination to continue working with Godbrothers is another expression of loyalty to Śrīla Prabhupāda.

Being loyal to the International Society for Krishna Consciousness is another expression. Loyalty to Śrīla Prabhupāda without loyalty to ISKCON is impossible. Loyalty is not only theoretical, it is practically expressed according to one's degree of surrender: I will "do the needful" as a faithful son.

Loyalty is expressed in living, personal qualities. Because of our attachment, we do not forget Śrīla Prabhupāda and we take to practices that help us remember him. Loyalty also means that we feel a great distaste and guilt if, in any context, we find ourselves accepting someone else as our guru. During Śrīla Prabhupāda's presence, when his *gurukula* teachers began to seriously follow the teachings of Mary Montessori, Kīrtanānanda remarked, "They have taken a new guru." That was the worst pronouncement and a sign that the *gurukula* teachers had to immediately adjust their priorities and decide who was their guru.

The more we can retain habits we have learned from him —the style of eating, a way of dressing—then the more we can keep remembrance of him a loyal reality, provided we do these things in an intelligent way.

A disciple of Śrīla Prabhupāda is loyal to his philosophy, even in the face of opposition. Śrīla Prabhupāda said that life comes from life and that the scientist cannot create life. He also said that they have not gone to the moon, and they cannot. The demigods and God Himself are all real persons. One has to read Śrīla Prabhupāda's books regularly (this itself is another item of loyalty), without modifying or changing his conclusions. Maintaining what he has given us, living in a society of devotees, always chanting the *mahā-mantra*—these are loyal responses. This very concept of being loyal to Śrīla Prabhupāda is itself another of Prabhupāda's matchless gifts. He gave us ample reasons and inspiration to be loyal.

50

REALIZATIONS

One morning we were walking with Śrīla Prabhupāda in Battery Park in New York City. On this particular morning Śrīla Prabhupāda wasn't talking, and he told us, "Chant Hare Kṛṣṇa." He wanted us to chant *japa* and he was also chanting *japa.* By a stroke of good fortune my *japa* was coming out nicely that day. I was chanting my *japa* very enthusiastically and Prabhupāda appreciated it. He was encouraging me by his glances. It was an intimate, confidential thing. I was feeling ecstatic, and Prabhupāda was glancing at me, acknowledging my ecstasy. As my spiritual master he was encouraging me, and I was also looking to him with great gratitude and reverence in understanding that all of my ecstasy was actually coming from his lotus feet.

Then as we were walking in the park, I suddenly realized we were in Vṛndāvana. By Prabhupāda's mercy, the whole park had been transformed into the spiritual world. I felt I was in Vṛndāvana. As I was walking and chanting more enthusiastically, I realized that Prabhupāda, by his causeless mercy upon me, had manifested the spiritual world within that park in Brooklyn. I became more ecstatic realizing that somehow or other Rādhā and Kṛṣṇa and Lord Balarāma and the cowherd boys and everyone were somehow in that park. As I was realizing this, Prabhupāda glanced at me, and I realized that he was giving me his special mercy. I was somehow getting this wonderful insight, looking at him with gratitude as he glanced his approval because I was chanting enthusiastically. Of course, my realization was completely insignificant compared to Prabhupāda's understanding, but still, I was like his child, and he was encouraging me in my ecstasy.

—*Hṛdayānanda Goswami*

"Prabhupāda is here! Prabhupāda is here!" Everyone was running outside the temple, so I joined. The car had just pulled up and the door opened and out came Prabhupāda. As soon as I saw him for the first time, then and there I said, "I want to surrender." I saw the person who was everything that I had been looking for. He had perfect taste, perfect bearing—everything about him was perfect. I'd always been seeking that perfection. I thought I would find it in the Duke of Windsor. When I met him, he didn't have it. I thought I would find it in John F. Kennedy. He was killed. Then it turned out that he was not so perfect. I thought I would find it in Martin Luther King. I was getting involved in that movement, and then he was killed. I thought I would find it in Bobby Kennedy. He was killed. All these people I thought had the answer kept getting killed. It was very discouraging. I always thought either this movie star or that actor or writer or social leader, one of these heroes would measure up. But none of them did. Yet as soon as I saw Prabhupāda as he came out of that car—the way he was dressed, the way he walked on down the sidewalk and into the temple holding his hand out in a special way, it was completely aristocratic. I knew that he was the person to whom I could surrender.

—*Bhavānanda Goswami*

I was talking with Śrīla Prabhupāda when another devotee brought in a tall glass of tea. I accepted it, but Prabhupāda said, "Why are you drinking this tea?" He used a semi-reprimanding tone. I replied that I was taking it because a devotee had offered it to me. Prabhupāda said that tea is for taking if you have a cold; it is not to be taken otherwise. I was holding the glass of tea in my hand, and instead of just putting it down I looked at Prabhupāda and said, "Then I shouldn't take it?" I was thinking it really wasn't so serious and that unless Prabhupāda really insisted, I could go ahead and take it anyway. When Prabhupāda understood my mood, that I wasn't really taking the whole thing very seriously, he chose to be lenient and said that I could take it this time but not again. I didn't want to sit there and drink it slowly in front of Prabhupāda, so I drank the whole glass down very quickly. Then I began to feel guilty.

Then after drinking the tea, while I was talking to Prabhupāda, my face began to perspire profusely and I felt embarrassed for that also. Prabhupāda appeared to flow along with everything, and I had a strong sense that he was just tolerating me. I knew that he was never compromising in his principles, yet I felt that it was very wonderful that he was willing to experience new, different things in different people and that he was a very lenient and flexible person. I considered this part of his greatness, and I think it's mainly because I knew that he actually, inwardly, was not making any compromises at all. But we all felt very grateful and enlivened with the way Prabhupāda was interacting with us and relating with us."

—*Mukunda Goswami*

My strongest observation was that Prabhupāda's whole life was preaching. Every inch of his body and every bit of his thought was dedicated to preaching Kṛṣṇa consciousness. Before going to bed he would be preaching, and then he would rest thinking about preaching. As soon as he woke in the early morning, he would have some transcendental idea about preaching. His whole life was preaching. And by his burning desire for spreading Kṛṣṇa consciousness, Prabhupāda had manifested a perfect personality, because a preacher has to be very careful.

—*Yaśomatīnandana dāsa*

I don't know how I ever cooked under such austere conditions for Śrīla Prabhupāda. In Bhubhaneswar and different places I would cook in a little shack in the fields. I was covered with black from the wood smoke, and I was full of smoke. My eyes would be bloodshot red, constantly tearing, and I couldn't open the door because all sorts of Indians were constantly coming. If I opened the door, they would just stand there and watch me cook, and I couldn't do that. It was Prabhupāda's offering. Every once in a while, I'd suddenly get up. I would hardly be able to breathe. All of a sudden you'd hear me because I'd just crash out of the door. The door would fly open and I'd stand out there and pant, pant. I would try to get air, just enough to go back in and cook. Kṛṣṇa empowered me to do that at that time because I could never do such a thing again and I don't know how I ever did it.

I would just go to any place where Prabhupāda was, even if there were no facilities, and I would set up and cook for him. It is Prabhupāda's association. It does something that is completely beyond this material world. And I didn't mind it, I loved it the whole time. I would go on like this cooking for him all morning long. When it came time for me to serve him, my white *sārī* would be black. My face would have soot over it. My eyes would be bloodshot, puffy, and swollen from crying. But when I went into Prabhupāda's room with his plate, he wouldn't even blink an eyelash. It didn't faze him. It was just as though I were there in the best of silk *sārīs* or something. It didn't matter what things would go on, Prabhupāda would be in his transcendental position, equipoised.

—*Pālikā-devī dāsī*

Prabhupāda Nectar 3

"Although we are unable to offer prayers to the Lord in an adequate fashion, our duty is to make the attempt to purify ourselves. It is not that we should stop our glorification because demigods like Lord Brahmā and Lord Śiva cannot adequately glorify the Lord. Rather, as stated by Prahlāda Mahārāja, everyone should glorify the Lord according to his own ability. If we are serious and sincere devotees, the Lord will give us the intelligence to offer prayers properly."

—purport by Śrīla Prabhupāda 4.16.2.

1

One day while Śrīla Prabhupāda was in Bombay, he simultaneously had visitors from Vṛndāvana and Māyāpur. This was during a period when temple construction was going on in both places. Prabhupāda expected his disciples in those places to come and ask him for money. The disciples knew that Prabhupāda would be expecting and demanding results from them on these important construction projects.

When these disciples visited from distant places, however, Prabhupāda always first welcomed them according to Vaiṣṇava etiquette. Prabhupāda had said that his mission was like a war on *māyā,* so he received his soldiers from the field by first offering them sweet words and relief. He asked them if they had taken *prasādam* and he suggested that they might want to rest. At least for a few minutes, the immediate, pressing problems were put aside, as Prabhupāda's disciples basked in the sweetness of his *darśana* and his kind welcome.

When, however, Śrīla Prabhupāda did ask Gargamuni and Jayapatāka Swami the reason for their visit, they said that they needed 150,000 rupees to continue construction on their respective projects.

"I just gave you!" said Prabhupāda. "All the time you are asking for money, but when it is going to be finished?" The disciples remained silent while Prabhupāda inquired and criticized their demands. Surabhi Swami became anxious and thought, "If they can't even get Rs150,000 for Māyāpur, then what will Prabhupāda say when he hears me ask for Rs250,000?"

Prabhupāda argued that in neither Vṛndāvana nor Māyāpur was sufficient collection going on, but they were simply coming regularly to him as the money supplier. After speaking for some time, Prabhupāda agreed to give the Māyāpur men 70,000 rupees, which they accepted gratefully.

"So, Surabhi Prabhu," said Prabhupāda, "what can I do for you?"

Surabhi had a more systematic presentation, listing all the needs for construction to continue in Vṛndāvana.

Hearing attentively, Prabhupāda then asked, "This adds up to how much?"

"Two and a half lakhs, Śrīla Prabhupāda."

Prabhupāda then turned to his secretary and asked that a check be made out for two and a half lakhs (approximately $25,000). Two checks were made out and presented to the devotees. Surabhi was about to leave the room when Prabhupāda called him back.

"How much does it cost to take a *ricksha* from our temple in Vṛndāvana to the Punjab Bank and then back?" Surabhi replied that it was about Rs1.25.

Then Prabhupāda asked his secretary, "Brahmānanda , how much does it cost to send a registered letter from Bombay to Vṛndāvana?" The answer was seventy-five paisa. Śrīla Prabhupāda then took back the check from Surabhi and said, "We will send the check by mail."

Just to save fifty paisa out of a sum of two and a half lakhs of rupees, Prabhupāda preferred to mail the check to his bank account rather than have Surabhi carry it by hand. Śrīla Prabhupāda was ultimately willing to spend whatever was required to build his important temples in India, yet he nevertheless instructed his disciples that as far as possible, they should save every paisa.

2

When Śrīla Prabhupāda visited the ISKCON temple in Amsterdam in July 1972, he agreed to the devotees' request to install deities of Lord Jagannātha. Due to the temple leaders' mismanagement, however, the event turned into a fiasco. TV cameramen were present, as well as reporters from the biggest newspapers in the city, and the temple room was crowded with guests, but when Prabhupāda came into the temple room and sat to perform the *yajña*, he saw many discrepancies.

"Where are the fruits and grains?" he asked. The temple president replied that the fruits had all been used in the fruit salad. Prabhupāda became angry.

"Where are the flowers?" he asked. The reply was, "We forgot."

"Who is responsible for this?" Prabhupāda demanded. In his transcendental anger, Prabhupāda was not the least bit intimidated by the presence of the TV, press, and guests. He was more concerned about Lord Jagannātha and the installation—and his disciples' incompetence.

"Well, Prabhupāda," stammered the temple president, "they didn't follow my instructions."

"What instructions?" said Prabhupāda loudly. "Who's responsible for this? Which rascal!" The devotees present were all frightened by Prabhupāda's anger. His eyes widened and the devotees felt it was like the wrath of Lord Nṛsiṁhadeva.

Despite the mistakes, Prabhupāda proceeded with the ceremony, but when it came time to actually place the deities on the altar, major miscalculations became evident. The devotees suddenly discovered that the altar they had built was too small. The deities could not fit. The *pūjārī* closed the curtains, while half a dozen devotees rushed behind the altar to make emergency alterations. As Śrīla Prabhupāda, the media people, and the large crowd waited, sounds of banging and chopping emitted from behind the closed curtain. The whole throne had to be taken apart and carried to a corner of the hall. Finally, the curtain opened and the deities were placed on the altar.

The deities were dressed and decorated very plainly, and Prabhupāda's visage remained displeased. But after his initial, fiery expressions, his anger abated. He proceeded with the ceremony, chanting the mantras and delivering a full Kṛṣṇa conscious lecture. At this time he also awarded the *sannyāsa* order to the Amsterdam temple president. Due to the density of the crowd and the heat and smoke from the fire, the unventilated room became uncomfortable for everyone. By now, Śrīla Prabhupāda was beyond such discomforts. In fact, he also seemed undisturbed as smoke filled the room and the ceremony continued for installing Lord Jagannātha in His Amsterdam temple.

3

LITTLE DROPS *of* NECTAR

In Los Angeles Śrīla Prabhupāda liked to have impromptu recording sessions in his room. When the recording technician, Kṛṣṇakānti dāsa, tried to schedule a special session, Prabhupāda often postponed it. But on an impromptu basis, either in the morning, afternoon, or evening, whenever Prabhupāda would say, "Let's record," the devotees would try to immediately respond. If they said that they didn't have the right microphones or equipment ready, Prabhupāda would reply, "Then record with whatever you have." He did not seem overly concerned about the exact technical arrangements, and he did not want to spend much time with it either.

When he was in the mood, Prabhupāda would call for different devotees to play the *karatālas* and *mṛdaṅga* and begin the recording. He liked to set up everything quickly and start at once, and he did not want to be stopped in the middle. One time, the devotees delayed in setting up the tape recorder and microphone, and when Prabhupāda finally began to sing, they asked him twice to please stop because of a technical difficulty in the recording process. At the end of that particular session, the devotees discovered that the machine was defective and had not recorded at all.

"This machine is worthless," said Prabhupāda. He then looked over to the devotee-technician and added, "You are worthless also."

In the days when there was no Ratha-yātrā held in Los Angeles, the devotees used to travel *en masse* to San Francisco to attend the Ratha-yātrā there. One morning, when Prabhupāda came down to the temple at his usual time, there were only a handful of devotees remaining, since most of them had already gone to San Francisco. (Śrīla Prabhupāda was to leave later that day by plane.) Earlier that morning someone had thrown a pipe bomb into the temple room through the back door. The bomb had exploded, shaken the building, and a few devotees had been cut with small pieces of shrapnel.

Prabhupāda sat on the *vyāsāsana* and said he was now going to teach them a new mantra. He then taught the devotees the Nṛsiṁhadeva mantras, beginning with the words *namas te narasiṁhāya*. He went over the words with them several times and then they sang it together.

Prabhupāda remarked on this occasion that as his movement was now growing, the demons were becoming more envious. He said that as the Kṛṣṇa consciousness movement grew, there would be attacks, but the devotees should not be afraid and should not stop from pushing on. They should chant these mantras to Lord Nṛsiṁhadeva. "Lord Nṛsiṁhadeva will always protect us," said Prabhupāda. Prabhupāda also approved that these mantras be sent out to all his ISKCON centers for the devotees to chant.

4

In September 1976 a circus magician visited the Krishna-Balaram Mandir in Vṛndāvana and showed Prabhupāda and the devotees his repertoire of tricks. Hearing that Prabhupāda had agreed to see the magician, Prabhupāda's friend Bhagatjī hurried to the *gurukula* to gather all the students and teachers. Within minutes, most of the temple leaders, teachers, and *gurukula* boys gathered in Prabhupāda's room to see the fun. Prabhupāda sat pleasantly behind his desk and asked the magician what he could do. The magician placed a coin in Śrīla Prabhupāda's hand. When the magician commanded "Go," the coin somehow slipped out of Prabhupāda's hand.

"Can you make the money come?" Prabhupāda joked.

"No," the magician replied.

"You can only make the money go," said Śrīla Prabhupāda. The magician then produced boxes in which different colors suddenly appeared in different slots. He also had games with feathers. He would take a white feather, rub it, pull it with his fingers, and it would turn into many different colors. Several times he asked Śrīla Prabhupāda to help him with the tricks. Coins appeared from Prabhupāda's ears and Prabhupāda laughed at the illusion, but some of the devotees felt uneasy that their spiritual master was being made the object of the mystification and tricks. Śrīla Prabhupāda seemed to enjoy it, but after a while he deliberately changed the mood.

"What about the miseries of life?" Prabhupāda asked the magician. "Can you make these disappear? Birth, death, disease, and old age?"

The magician replied submissively, "No, that I cannot." At these words the magician sat down and Śrīla Prabhupāda took the superior position.

"But I can make these things disappear," said Śrīla Prabhupāda. "That is the real magic." The magic show ended and Śrīla Prabhupāda spoke his realized, transcendental wisdom to the magician and all the assembled devotees. Śrīla Prabhupāda then gave the magician a garland and distributed sweets to everyone in the room.

5

On Distributing Books

"Distribution of my books is the most important thing. These other things such as selling incense and records, etc., are not so much important as this. I want that my books be distributed in huge quantities, thus we will be able to thoroughly convince the majority of the population especially there in America. But finances are also needed. Therefore for further direction you please contact the GBC men and they will give you consultation."

—*Letter of December 19, 1974*

"In the evening, Tamāla Kṛṣṇa Mahārāja came in and discussed with Śrīla Prabhupāda about organizing book sales in India. He reported to Śrīla Prabhupāda that actually, if they organized correctly, they could probably sell at least a hundred thousand books a month, and with the five lakhs that Śrīla Prabhupāda had promised, they would spend two and a half lakhs each on Hindi and Bengali publications. Śrīla Prabhupāda was very pleased and told him, 'Yes, organize this. You have got experience. Now show them how to do it. Make arrangements with your good brain. This is good business. Sell books, print more with profit, and support the temple.' Prabhupāda then told a story how one man wanted to go from Bengal to the Ratha-yātrā in Jagannātha Purī, but he wanted to make money at the same time. So he took some bananas, sat on the roadside where the Ratha-yātrā cart was due to pass, saw the *ratha*, and sold all his bananas. 'In this way,' said Śrīla Prabhupāda, 'he combined business with pleasure. We should also do.' "

—*Hari Śauri dāsa*
Diary entry, February 16, 1977

"That is my opinion. Instead of spending so much money for films, you should spend money for propagation of book distribution. Any advertisement is good, it never goes in vain, but the film advertisement is very expensive. In comparison to the money expended, the success is little. Just like I, in the beginning, I advertised my books in *The New York Times*. They charged me $63 for a small space. So there was inquiry, not order, but three inquiries. I have got this experience. For me, at that time, $63 was too much. So I did not get any response. I got three inquiries, but not even one order. *The New York Times* has millions of customers and millions of readers, but I got only three inquiries."

—*Morning walk, Tehran*
August 10, 1976

"There is no hindrance of your being a householder so far as distributing books is concerned. Lord Caitanya Mahaprabhu had many householder disciples who would preach Krsna consciousness. I understand recently in Toronto the entire temple distributed many *Isopanisads* and other books. So you can engage yourself in spare hours in this book distribution without any hindrance. Side by side you can also paint pictures for Krsna. In this way, fully engage yourself in Krsna's service."

—*Letter of November 22, 1974*

6

PRABHUPĀDA TELLS A STORY

There was once a factory in India where all the workers were Hindus and mostly Vaiṣṇavas. The Vaiṣṇavas had freedom, therefore, to wear their Vaiṣṇava *tilaka* to work, and they also displayed other Vaiṣṇava paraphernalia. After some time, however, the factory went to new management and the new proprietor was a Muslim. On taking over the business, the Muslim owner declared that he would no longer allow the workers to come to work wearing Vaiṣṇava *tilaka*. Most of the workers obeyed, and on the given date announced by the owner, they appeared at the factory without their *tilaka*. One employee, however, thought that he would take his chances and depend on Kṛṣṇa, so he went to work wearing very clear, white Vaiṣṇava *tilaka*. After seeing all the workers assembled, the new Muslim proprietor said, "This one devotee who has worn Vaiṣṇava *tilaka* is very courageous. He may be permitted to continue wearing the *tilaka* to work, but all others are forbidden to wear it any more."

In this way, Prabhupāda encouraged the devotees to not unnecessarily abandon the markings of a Vaiṣṇava. Where situations forbid it, Prabhupāda said that it was not absolutely necessary to wear *tilaka*, although a devotee should at least put water *tilaka* on his body in the morning and consecrate his body with the names of Viṣṇu. But if the paraphernalia is permitted, then a devotee should not unnecessarily do away with the dress or beads of a Vaiṣṇava.

7

PERSONAL

His Response in Difficult Times

Śrīla Prabhupāda endured difficulties. Difficult years occurred, especially during his household life, with the war and the days of Hindu-Muslim riots. It was also difficult for Prabhupāda when his family members gave him no cooperation in his attempt to preach, but rather tried to dissuade him. Then during the 1950s, when Prabhupāda was alone with no money or support trying to preach in places like the streets of New Delhi, he endured. In the first years in America, and even later as his movement grew, he experienced serious illnesses. Furthermore, he had to carry the great burden of his worldwide movement, especially in times when leaders he depended on fell down from the principles of Kṛṣṇa consciousness or deserted him. He had to carry all the responsibility to preach, to manage, and to settle the quarrels.

Despite the difficulties, Prabhupāda never showed signs of weakening or of giving up the saintly qualities for which he was so well known and so dear to the devotees. He never abandoned duty during difficult times. During his household years he accepted the responsibility of maintaining his family, even though it was a great struggle. Typically, during illnesses, he chose opportunities for preaching over those for recuperation. In 1973 he rose almost immediately from serious dysentery in Calcutta to attend the Ratha-yātrā in London. In 1976, Prabhupāda gave up an extended stay at his Pennsylvania farm, because he said he wanted the opportunity, like Arjuna, to always fight for Kṛṣṇa, by traveling and preaching. His example to his followers was that they should never abandon their posts; they should rather die on the battlefield as Kṛṣṇa conscious preachers.

Not only did Prabhupāda accept his duty, but he endured difficulties with all his composure intact. He was not afraid; he trusted Kṛṣṇa. During the 1971 wartime blackout in New Delhi when Prabhupāda was being interviewed by a nervous reporter, the reporter remarked that here was the ugly reality. Prabhupāda reminded him that we are always in the midst of the ugly reality. In New York City he said to a similar inquirer that we are always at war. "If you go out into the street during winter in New York City without a coat," said Prabhupāda, "you will die. Is it not war?"

Śrīla Prabhupāda was always a true *sādhu*. He once defined *sādhu* by saying that he's not a person who complains, "I cannot see you today because I am not feeling well." A *sādhu* tolerates; therefore he is know as *titikṣavaḥ kāruṇikāḥ*—tolerant and merciful. During Prabhupāda's difficult times he remained calm, in control of his senses, and preached continually.

One of Prabhupāda's noticeable responses to difficulties was that he would become especially serious and grave. This gave his followers an understanding of real spiritual life. His gravity was more instructive and revealing than the unswerving smiles of pseudo swamis. Śrīla Prabhupāda was always in touch with Kṛṣṇa, the reservoir of pleasure, and yet the gravity Prabhupāda showed in the face of the material nature was a personal response that gave his followers strength. When, for preaching purposes, he entered the East Village Theater and saw an amateur rock group dancing "like monkeys" onstage, Prabhupāda became grave, although later when he recalled it in his room, he laughed heartily.

Prabhupāda's gravity also meant that he did not reveal when he was in difficulty. During a 1967 TV show, Śrīla Prabhupāda experienced discomfort under the hot lights, yet he mentioned it only later. A week after that, his health broke down and he experienced heart palpitations and partial paralysis.

One time in India, when one of Prabhupāda's disciples went several times to discuss the symptoms of his jaundice with Prabhupāda, Prabhupāda said that he should not bother so much about his material situation. A Vaiṣṇava "neglects" his own health, Prabhupāda said, since he is not attached to the body.

When Prabhupāda experienced physical difficulty, he took it as a time to accept service from his disciples. He allowed them to massage him and care for him, but he warned them that if they had done this during a normal situation, it would have been too familiar. Therefore, when Prabhupāda experienced trouble, he provided a means for his disciples to serve the guru intently. During times of illness he allowed disciples to give him constant massages, and they regularly guarded him and stayed up with him. They also discussed problems in his spiritual movement with him and learned firsthand how to give all their energy for Kṛṣṇa—how to accept difficulties for spreading Kṛṣṇa consciousness. If a disciple thought that by his assistance he was giving his spiritual master life, however, Prabhupāda said that that was offensive. The guru gives service, but the disciple should not think that by his care he is maintaining his spiritual master.

Sometimes Śrīla Prabhupāda made light of his difficulties. When one time in his last years he was offered a plate of *prasādam* in a room with professors in Toronto, he replied softly, "I have no teeth and no appetite." He joked that his disciples were getting good service out of him since he could not eat or sleep, but still he worked.

Śrīla Prabhupāda always met his difficulties as one protected by Kṛṣṇa. He showed he was transcendental to any situation—and that his disciples should be also.

8

SERVICE IN SEPARATION

The greatest part of Prabhupāda's *līlā* is how devotees are serving him in separation. In fact, most devotees grew up in Kṛṣṇa consciousness, came into Kṛṣṇa consciousness, and are maintained in separation. And now that's still going on.

Prabhupāda's *līlā* is spiritual and eternal. We all have our different perspectives from which we understand Prabhupāda. As the representative of Kṛṣṇa he's almost unlimited. Just as in the *rāsa* dance, Kṛṣṇa could dance with so many of the *gopīs* simultaneously, so Prabhupāda gave orders to all his disciples simultaneously. Each one is unique.

Every one of us has a unique relationship with Prabhupāda. With me, I felt closer to Prabhupāda when I was preaching in the political campaign. I've been in the same room as Prabhupāda and not felt anywhere near him. That's obvious even in material dealings sometimes. A man and wife, for example, can be married and can be total strangers because they don't like each other any more. The same with Prabhupāda. You could be in the same room, but if you weren't pleasing him, you might as well be a million miles away. So that's where we're really close, by rendering pleasing services, and that's how we can get even closer.

Even if someone had never been personally in the room with Prabhupāda or been on a walk with him, it didn't matter. He could also know Prabhupāda through serving him. By service, disciples have direct spiritual realization; they have direct spiritual experience. When someone goes on *saṅkīrtana* and distributes books, he experiences a higher taste from the book distribution and that's Prabhupāda's presence. Otherwise, he couldn't go out. It is not just another activity like any other in the material world. No, he is experiencing something, and that experience goes beyond the bodily coverings into the spirit soul. The spirit soul tastes that relationship. By distributing Prabhupāda's books or rendering any service personally he is tasting his relationship with Prabhupāda.

—*Balavanta dāsa Adhikārī*

9

While serving in the beginning of Śrīla Prabhupāda's project in Bombay, Pañcadraviḍa dāsa traveled to visit him in Vṛndāvana in October of 1972.

Pañcadraviḍa was thinking of asking Śrīla Prabhupāda if he would permit him to take the *sannyāsa* order, but before he could even ask, almost immediately on greeting, Śrīla Prabhupāda said, "Yes, now you can take *sannyāsa*. Now you are qualified."

Ecstatically happy, Pañcadraviḍa began to praise Kṛṣṇa conscious preaching activities, and he mentioned Prahlāda Mahārāja and Dhruva Mahārāja, who were young boys and yet knew Kṛṣṇa conscious philosophy so nicely.

"Yes," said Śrīla Prabhupāda, turning to others in the room. "This boy, Pañcadraviḍa, is very intelligent."

Hearing these words, Pañcadraviḍa became even happier, and a little proud also.

"So how is everything in Bombay?" asked Prabhupāda.

"Well," said Pañcadraviḍa, "not so good, Śrīla Prabhupāda."

"Not so good?" Prabhupāda replied in a challenging way. "Oh, why is that?"

"There are so many rats, Śrīla Prabhupāda. It's a disturbance."

"That means you are not clean," Prabhupāda replied sternly. "This is the habit of you Americans. You take a plate of *prasādam*, you eat half of it, and then you stick it in the corner for six months. *Isn't* it! *Isn't* it!" Prabhupāda had shouted the last words, and Pañcadraviḍa became confused, but Prabhupāda continued with his hammering criticism.

"This means you are not clean," said Śrīla Prabhupāda. "Therefore you are not chanting your rounds."

Pañcadraviḍa replied in mood of confused protest. "As far as I know, Śrīla Prabhupāda, the devotees are all chanting their rounds."

Śrīla Prabhupāda looked back at his disciple with annoyance and said, "So you are suggesting that there is some defect in Lord Caitanya's process?"

"No, Śrīla Prabhupāda."

"Well, then," replied Śrīla Prabhupāda, "Lord Caitanya says *ceto darpaṇa-mārjanam*. Chanting cleanses the heart. So how is it possible that if the heart is clean, the outside will be dirty?" By now Pañcadraviḍa was on the point of tears before Prabhupāda's anger. Pañcadraviḍa said no more. He began to think that Śrīla Prabhupāda was seeing some of his defects. He decided that he had been too proud, and in criticizing Prabhupāda's Bombay project, he seemed almost to be putting himself on the same level as Prabhupāda.

After about ten minutes, Pañcadraviḍa offered his crestfallen obeisances before his spiritual master and moved to leave, but as he was leaving Prabhupāda said, "That's all right. The spiritual master only sees the service that you offer and not your faults."

10

During the 1977 Māyāpur festival, a government minister visited Śrīla Prabhupāda and gave a lecture as part of the opening-night festivities.

Before going to the outdoor stage, Śrīla Prabhupāda and the minister went to see the photo display of ISKCON temples. Walking down the long hallway and viewing pictures of preaching activities in almost every country of the world,

Śrīla Prabhupāda was himself impressed at the vast scope of ISKCON. At one point he shook his head, turned to the accompanying devotees, and said, "It is inconceivable."

In his introductory speech, the minister surprised the audience as he began glorifying Vivekananda as one who helped humanity, just like the incarnations of God, Rāma, Kṛṣṇa, and Viṣṇu. Giving faint praise to Lord Caitanya, the minister said, "Of course, we don't know whether Caitanya was an incarnation, but certainly He did great good." At the end of the minister's lecture, he gave his appreciation for Prabhupāda's movement, stating that it was spreading by "moral strength," and that he hoped it would do good to humanity at large.

Śrīla Prabhupāda had been prepared to lecture on *Śrīmad-Bhāgavatam*. He had brought his volume of the *Bhāgavatam* and reading glasses. After he heard the minister's speech, however, Prabhupāda spoke very strongly in response. The speech was in Bengali, so most of the devotees could not understand it, but they could appreciate that Prabhupāda was countering the speculations of the official guest.

Later that night in his room, Prabhupāda laughed as he discussed the minister's speech. He had his servant bring the tape recorder and Prabhupāda again heard his own lecture. At one point, when he heard himself stating that Vivekananda had never made a single disciple despite his propaganda, Śrīla Prabhupāda grimaced and slapped the palm of his left hand with the palm of his right. Looking up to the devotees in the room he said, "I have smashed him."

11

LITTLE DROPS *of* NECTAR

Prabhupāda's Vṛndāvana acquaintance, Bhagatjī, once entered Prabhupāda's room and found him sitting silent and motionless. Bhagatjī sat for a long time beside Prabhupāda before Prabhupāda actually moved and then realized that Bhagatjī was in the room.

"Prabhupāda," said Bhagatjī, "you were in deep meditation."

"Yes," said Prabhupāda. "I was studying these mosquitoes. I was looking at how wonderfully Kṛṣṇa has created these things. Every mosquito looks the same, so I was looking at the legs and wings . . . "

In January 1977, Prabhupāda was returning to his temple in Bhubhaneswar from a preaching program. As the driver sped along, Śrīla Prabhupāda closed his eyes and rested in the front seat of the car. The devotees who remained awake suddenly observed a ghastly sight. First they saw a group of people holding a woman who was crying, screaming, and foaming at the mouth. About two hundred yards further, they saw what was left of a man who must have been her husband. The body was lying in the middle of the road on its side. All the clothes had been ripped off, and the head, one arm, and one leg had been smashed flat by a truck. The devotees gasped in horror, but said nothing, not wanting to disturb Śrīla Prabhupāda.

Later that morning in his room in Bhubhaneswar, Prabhupāda was speaking with his servant, Hari Śauri. Prabhupāda said that people are suffering in *māyā* because they identify with the body. Hari Śauri mentioned the incident of the dead body on the road, and he told Prabhupāda what they had seen and how the man had been killed just a minute before they passed by in their car. On hearing this, Śrīla Prabhupāda opened his eyes wide in surprise and said, "*Acchā.*" Then he commented, "But still, the sight of such a dead body is really not any different from any other lump of matter. Simply because we identify the living being with that matter, then it becomes a shock to see it all squashed."

12

A VISIT TO A HILL STATION

Śrīla Prabhupāda and several disciples flew to a city near a hill station in South India. They were met at the airport, only a small shack, by Mr. H., his brother, and family. The brother was wearing long saffron robes and so was his wife. They received Prabhupāda's party cordially and drove them to their home, where they had breakfast before starting for the hill station.

Mr. H. had a large house, but he was not as cultured as the more traditional Hindu families. At meals everyone sat at a table together. The food was brought in large bowls and put in the center of the table. The system was that everyone should simply dip into the bowls and help themselves as the food was passed around. After eating, they sat in the courtyard next to the swimming pool. Mr. H.'s brother came out, sat next to Prabhupāda, and began asking him a few questions.

Prabhupāda asked him what his philosophy was and why he and his wife were wearing saffron robes. The man explained that his guru had given him and his wife neo-*sannyāsa*. Prabhupāda shook his head and described to Mr. H.'s brother the real method of *sannyāsa*. He described the four stages, *kuṭīcaka, bahūdaka, parivrājakācārya,* and *paramahaṁsa*. Śrīla Prabhupāda gave a short explanation of the four sections of the *sannyāsa* order and explained to him that there could not be anything such as neo-*sannyāsa. Sannyāsa* had already been established as part of the *varṇāśrama* system, and one cannot concoct. Gradually, as they spoke, the man brought out all of his impersonal misunderstandings and Śrīla Prabhupāda defeated them one after another, explaining to him the genuine process of self-realization. In the beginning the man challenged, but soon he sat listening to Śrīla Prabhupāda.

Prabhupāda's party and the H. family all got into cars, and Śrīla Prabhupāda continued to speak to this man on the drive to the hill station. After a short time, however, everyone lapsed into silence. The narrow road twisted up the steep hills for three hours. Prabhupāda did not like the bends in the road and said that he felt physically upset.

The weather on the hill was pleasant, with soft breezes, and Prabhupāda wanted to stay there for three days or more. Mr. H.'s whole family, except for the brother, soon left for the nearby town to do shopping. Alone with no engagement, Prabhupāda called the brother into his room and they resumed their talk. Prabhupāda began explaining the whole process of Kṛṣṇa consciousness from the beginning, describing how the spirit soul is not the body and what is the soul's position in relation to the supreme whole. The man objected that there are many paths and different questions and questioners. Prabhupāda replied that still there is only one answer. The man responded with different Māyāvāda explanations—how everyone has his own path in life. For almost an hour Prabhupāda carefully and patiently explained everything to him, indirectly indicating that the man's guru was incorrect. Śrīla Prabhupāda emphasized that one must approach a genuine spiritual master for real knowledge, and not a cheater. Gradually the man understood and listened carefully to everything that Prabhupāda had to say.

When the family returned, after light conversation they gathered to eat a heavy meal in the same style as before, with everyone reaching into a common bowl.

When they were all situated in their rooms for a night's rest, however, Śrīla Prabhupāda called in his devotees. He said that they should now plan to leave this place as soon as there was light in the morning. Prabhupāda said that he had difficulty digesting the food and he did not like to stay here and associate so closely.

The next morning Śrīla Prabhupāda rang his bell at 5 A.M. and found his disciples still sleeping. Only his servant, Hari

Śauri, woke and went into Śrīla Prabhupāda's room. Śrīla Prabhupāda was sitting on the edge of his bed with a table and dictating machine in front of him.

"So you have become infected like this," Śrīla Prabhupāda said to his servant, indicating the loud snoring noise coming from the bedroom of the H. family. Hari Śauri replied, "Well, I don't think we are as infected as that." But Prabhupāda said, "I mean to say that you should have risen at four and had *maṅgala-ārati* and bathed. But due to only one evening's association, you are already infected."

As planned, Prabhupāda made a quick departure and drove by car four hours back to Bombay. Along the way Prabhupāda became sick from the constant twists and turns of the road. When he finally returned to his Bombay quarters, he remarked that Kṛṣṇa had quickly punished them for eating the *karmīs'* food.

13

PRABHUPĀDA SAID

On Health

You accept these principles of life, no meat-eating, no intoxication, no illicit sex, and there will be no cancer. Those who are strictly on this line, they never suffer from cancer or any such disease. Now take for example me. I've come here in this country for the last eight years. How many times have I gone to the doctor? That one heart attack. That is serious, that is another thing. Otherwise, generally how many times have I gone? I don't pay any bill of doctor.

So if we live a very hygienic life, regulated life, there is no question of cancer or any disease. The disease is created by violating nature's law. One of the causes of cancer disease is this contraceptive method. You can make research on it. So they are on one side discovering contraceptive method, contraceptive chemicals, and on the other side researching for cancer disease. And they say also smoking is one of the causes. So why not give up smoking and illicit sex, contraceptive method?

—*Morning walk, Los Angeles*
May 4, 1973

Prabhupāda: "They foolishly say 'struggle for existence,' 'survival of the fittest,' but who is fit? He does not know. Fittest means one who does not get next a material body. He is fit. Because as soon as you get a material body, *nūnaṁ pramattaḥ kurute vikarma . . .*"

—*Morning walk, Hyderabad*
August 23, 1976

"So far your health is concerned, Hawaii is very good climate. You can take bath in the sea, and that will keep your health. Take *dal,* especially *urad,* a little cheese, peanuts, green vegetables, especially squash leaf."

—*Letter of December 10, 1973*

"I am sorry to learn that your health is not very good at the present time. The best thing is that you rest for some time until you are feeling stronger. When J. was feeling very weak, I advised her to take complete rest until she was stronger and then I advised her to go out on *sankirtana* party. So you may follow the same procedure of taking as much rest as you feel you require, and then when you feel it is all right, you resume your activities."

—*Letter of July 23, 1969*

"For your toothache trouble you can brush your teeth with the following mixture: common salt, one part, and pure mustard oil, quite sufficient to make it a suitable paste. With this paste brush your teeth, especially the painful part very nicely. Gargle in hot water, and keep always some cloves in your mouth. I think that will cure your troubles. It doesn't require to extract any teeth."

—*Letter of February 14, 1969*

"Regarding your fasting, if you are sick, then fasting is the best medicine. For disease and unwanted guests, if you do not give them food, they will go away."

—*Letter of January 16, 1975*

14

ŚRĪLA PRABHUPĀDA TELLS A STORY

On a morning walk on Venice Beach in May 1973, Śrīla Prabhupāda presented a number of analogies exposing false logic.

Prabhupāda had been explaining to Svarūpa Dāmodara, Brahmānanda Swami, and others that each living creature lives in a certain environment suited for it. Therefore, we never find a frog in the ocean. This living habit of the frog is the basis of the example known as "the frog in the well."

"This example is available in the *Bhāgavata,* Prabhupāda?" asked Svarūpa Dāmodara.

"Yes," said Śrīla Prabhupāda. "In *nyāya-śāstra* it is said, *kūpa-maṇḍūka-nyāya. Kūpa* means 'well' and *maṇḍūka* means 'frog.' The frog in the well. Dr. Frog is never visible in the ocean. He has never seen what is the ocean; therefore all these scientists are compared to frogs. They have never seen what is the kingdom of God."

Śrīla Prabhupāda then explained another logic, known as *bakāṇḍa-nyāya. "Baka* means 'duck,' and *aṇḍa* means 'testicles of the bull.' The bull is going, and his testicle is hanging, and the duck is following after that. He is thinking, 'Here is a fish.' You will find the ducks always going and wondering when the 'fish' will drop. It will never drop, but he is going after it. And neither is it a fish. The *bakāṇḍa* is comparable to any materialist in illusion, who chases after *māyā*."

Then Prabhupāda explained *aja-gala-stana*. "You have seen in the goats, in the necks—it is just like nipples," said Prabhupāda. "So if one is expecting milk from that nipple, he is also a fool. It is not a nipple, but it looks like one. These are illusions. *Aja-gala-stana* applies to those rascals who think that from matter, life is coming. Exactly the same, they are thinking that here is a nipple and some milk will come. 'Let us milk here. Maybe in the future.'

"Another is *nagna-mātṛkā*. This means someone says, 'Mother, when you were a child you were naked; why do you put on clothes now?' The mother was naked when she was a child. Therefore the logic is that she should remain naked still. If someone was not very important, and now he has become important, the logic is, 'How has this man become important?' Because the mother was naked in childhood, therefore she should not put on any garments? We change according to the circumstances. You cannot say that this must remain like this. So when one comes to Kṛṣṇa consciousness, that is perfect." (And one cannot say that he is disqualified by a lower birth or bad behavior in a previous life.)

"In Sanskrit logic," said Śrīla Prabhupāda, "all these examples are there from nature's study."

15

ŚRĪLA PRABHUPĀDA TELLS SHORT STORIES

There was a professional dancer who used to hold performances in many different places, including outdoor sites. After one scheduled performance a friend asked the dancer, "So did you perform last night?"

"No," the dancer replied. "I could not."

His friend was surprised and asked why not, and the dancer replied, "There was a hill." In other words, due to the non-ideal situation, the dancer did not perform. Prabhupāda said that this is not a real dancer. A real dancer would have danced even if the hill was offered as the site for dancing. Even if the dancing performance was not up to standard, a real dancer would have danced under any circumstances. Similarly, a dedicated disciple will perform his or her duty even if facilities are lacking.

Śrīla Prabhupāda related the story of a rat who became liberated by offering service to Viṣṇu. The rat was running on the altar of the Deity, just at a time when one of the ghee lamps was about to go out. The rat thought that the flame might be some foodstuffs, so he stuck his whiskers in it. The dying flame caught on to the rat's whiskers and the fire flared up, catching on to the unused portion of the wick. In this way, by the rat's foolish sacrifice, the flame on Viṣṇu's altar continued to burn nicely. And for his service to Kṛṣṇa, the rat went to Vaikuṇṭha. This is the potency of devotional service to Kṛṣṇa, even performed unknowingly.

16

PERSONAL

His Innocence

Śrīla Prabhupāda sometimes said that innocence was almost like ignorance. To be innocent of knowledge of God, for example, was not at all admirable. An "innocent" victim of a bogus guru is also not praiseworthy. Yet if we consider innocence as freshness and purity, as freedom from nastiness, it is a notable characteristic of Prabhupāda.

When Śrīla Prabhupāda told a group of devotees how he first saw snow in New York City and thought the buildings had been whitewashed, some of the disciples could hardly believe that Prabhupāda was actually so innocent. But by his mercy we came to see this innocence as his non-deceptive, Kṛṣṇa conscious beauty. Prabhupāda's innocence was not only *what* he said, it was his freshness of expression, his outlook, such as when he wrote of his Guru Mahārāja, "The line of service as drawn by you is pleasing and healthy like morning dew."

Prabhupāda said that if one were to ask a heavy sense-indulger, one who has give his whole life in trying to please his senses, if he had actually attained happiness, the sense gratifier would have to say, "No, my life was hellish." Śrīla Prabhupāda was the opposite of this jaded outlook; he had no worldly weariness. His outlook was like a spring day, and this came from his transcendental consciousness. Therefore he could respond with wonder to the world. As Prabhodhānanda Sarasvatī says, describing a devotee in spiritual consciousness, "He sees the whole material world as Vaikuṇṭha."

One time on a morning walk through the pleasant English countryside, a devotee asked Prabhupāda if this countryside was something like the kingdom of God. Prabhupāda said, "*This is* the kingdom of God." Thus Prabhupāda's devotees were able to see through his eyes how even this world is Vaikuṇṭha for one who sees Kṛṣṇa everywhere.

Freedom from sex desire in the material world is another kind of innocence, which is a strength of the transcendentalist. Although with sense enjoyers there is always an undercurrent of sexual meaning, Prabhupāda was free of this. As a learned sage he was well aware that people were captivated by sex desire at every turn; yet he was not, and anyone who was with Prabhupāda felt the possibilities of being free from sexual implications. Young men who were previously corrupt in taking drugs and in the illicit ways of sex became clean under his guidance. They themselves became bright-faced—"happies, not hippies."

Prabhupāda's goodness was not a too-sweet, saccharine, goody-ness however. It was not in the mode of material goodness. Indeed, Prabhupāda's viewpoint of the material world was pessimistic, and he often expressed it with salty words. He did not speak sweet talk when describing the material world as it is.

Under Kṛṣṇa's protection, Śrīla Prabhupāda lived in the material world in a simple way and was never corrupted or tainted by it. He often appeared to be like an innocent young boy. He once asked his disciples Nandarāṇī and Dayānanda if they could adopt him as their son as a strategy to get permanent residency in the U.S.A. If we consider innocent to mean "not guilty," then Śrīla Prabhupāda was certainly innocent of any material entanglement. Unlike most people, he lived in the world without implication by karmic reaction.

Prabhupāda also felt compassion for the innocent creatures of this world, like the cows, bulls, and calves, and also the women. He saw how women are victimized by others, although they themselves are innocent. Prabhupāda felt that as they could easily be corrupted, they should rather be protected. He also referred to all his devotees as innocent boys and girls. Prabhupāda once used this phrase, "innocent boys," during a public lecture in Tompkins Square Park. Allen Ginsberg was present with some of his friends, and he laughed sarcastically at Prabhupāda's remark. Ginsberg was so decadent that the concept of "innocent boys" was something beyond him. For a person like Ginsberg, "innocent boy" often implies victims for one's sense gratification. Prabhupāda's disciples, however, were innocent of sinful life by chanting Hare Kṛṣṇa under Prabhupāda's protection. Therefore, it is not impossible that innocence can prevail in this world. When one becomes a devotee, he can remain innocent of further guilt and sinfulness, and he will not be corrupted.

Śrīla Prabhupāda trained his devotees to be shrewd so that they would not become corrupted by the material world. They could retain their innocence and still be well aware of the dangers of *māyā*. They could then be prepared to deal with those dangers. As Prabhupāda traveled and preached in cities all over the world, he saw and heard more and more of the horrors of Kali-yuga, yet he always remained innocent of the atrocities. He worked to save mankind and to convert the viciously guilty into saintly human beings.

17

PERSONAL

His Special Use of Language

Śrīla Prabhupāda sometimes used the English language in special ways. His disciples didn't consider his usage awkward or mistaken, but they appreciated it in a transcendental way.

Hṛdayānanda dāsa Goswami writes as follows:

"Śrīla Prabhupāda was completely Kṛṣṇa conscious. And from the material point of view, he was very brilliant. He was trained in British schools, so his English was brilliant. He would say so many humorous things, like 'stalwart demon.' The British are very expert in the use of language, and Prabhupāda was trained in the English system, so he had a very good English vocabulary. Anyone who reads his books will be struck by his brilliant use of English."

Śrīla Prabhupāda's main English editor was his disciple, Jayādvaita Swami. He writes:

"In regard to Prabhupāda's unique use of words, he would sometimes use words in very unusual ways. Often he would use words very precisely, although in an unusual way that was not consistent with the usual, current usage. Sometimes I would look in a dictionary to find an appropriate synonym, but upon looking up the word Prabhupāda used, I would find that because of its etymology, it was actually the perfect word to convey the meaning that Prabhupāda intended. Another thing that Prabhupāda would do would be to pronounce words in such a way as to give them a special meaning. For example, Prabhupāda would say *ignorance* as *ignorance,* and it would seem to give special meaning to the word, because our ignorance was due to ignoring Kṛṣṇa. Other times Prabhupāda would just pronounce words in a way that was logical but not according to correct usage. The most famous example is probably *infinite-simal.* He would say *infinite* and *infinite-simal,* and devotees always took special pleasure in these peculiarities of Prabhupāda's speech, even to the point of adopting them in their own lectures. And, of course, devotees have universally adopted Prabhupāda's pronunciation of "de*vo*´tees" rather than "dev´o *tees*." When Prabhupāda would say something, the impression would be very memorable, so the devotees would try to reproduce or convey that spiritual potency by sometimes using Śrīla Prabhupāda's language exactly as he used it.

Some examples follow.

Prabhupāda's disciple, Gargamuni, was the first treasurer of ISKCON, and he was inclined to business and money-making. Prabhupāda used to call him "Garga-money." Seeing Kīrtanānanda's efficiency in cooking, Śrīla Prabhupāda called him "Kitchen-ānanda."

Sometimes Prabhupāda invented his own words. To describe the pastimes of Kṛṣṇa, he sometimes said "pastimious activities of the Lord."

In his first apartment in San Francisco, Prabhupāda once observed a bread truck passing on the street below. "SIMPLY DELICIOUS" was painted in large letters on the bread truck. Śrīla Prabhupāda laughed and said, "Simply dangerous . . . Death is always standing behind us and waiting."

"Mystic means misty," he said. "Our concept of Kṛṣṇa is not misty. It is very clear. Kṛṣṇa comes and delivers

Bhagavad-gītā, and He says, 'This is the way I am.' So we must understand properly, like Arjuna understood."

One time while visiting Germany, Śrīla Prabhupāda had a long talk with his disciples Hayagrīva, who was an English professor, and Śivānanda. They discussed different uses of the English language. Prabhupāda especially liked the word *sin.* They looked up the word in a dictionary and saw that *sin* comes the German word *apsunder,* which means "to be broken away from." The word *sind* is the German word for *sin.* It is a derivative of the word *apsunder.* Prabhupāda liked that definition, that the ultimate sin is to be broken away from God.

In Hawaii, when he saw surfers riding waves, he said that they would take birth as fish in their next lives because they were becoming so absorbed in thinking how to swim and play in the waves. In his morning class, Prabhupāda referred to the surfers as "sea-sufferers."

"Kṛṣṇa consciousness is autocracy," he said. "There is no democracy. I call it 'demon-crazy.' Actually demon-crazy. A bunch of demons get together, what good can they do?"

When Śrīla Prabhupāda's disciples drove him to different places in the U.S.A., he often remarked what a foolish civilization we were living in. Commenting on the cars whizzing up and down the highway, Prabhupāda laughed and referred to it as neck-break civilization.

In 1975 in Berkeley, Prabhupāda was shown Parīkṣit dāsa's new painting of baby Kṛṣṇa carrying Nanda Mahārāja's shoes on His head. Prabhupāda liked the painting very much. "Just see how Kṛṣṇa is serving His devotee just like a little child," Prabhupāda said. He also pointed out that Parīkṣit had not spoiled the painting by putting "big,

big hairs," whereas "Jadurāṇī always puts big, big hairs. Woman is very fond of big, big hairs." One of the devotees then took a copy of *Teachings of Lord Caitanya* from the bookshelf. Showing Prabhupāda the cover painting of the Pañca-tattva, the devotee said, "Śrīla Prabhupāda, what about Śrī Caitanya Mahāprabhu? Generally we paint Him with long hair." Śrīla Prabhupāda began to joke. "Yes," he replied, "Caitanya Mahāprabhu—He was a hippy. Therefore He has come to save you." The devotees began to laugh at Prabhupāda's humor, but because Śrīla Prabhupāda's Bengali inflection added a slight "sh" to *save,* no one was positive whether Prabhupāda was saying *save* or *shave.* Śrīla Prabhupāda immediately noticed this. He was chuckling and repeated, "Yes, He has come to save you and shave you. Caitanya Mahāprabhu has come to save you and shave you."

More Prabhupāda-isms

When Prabhupāda's cook served him an unusually heavy breakfast, including *rasagullā* and *sandeśa,* Prabhupāda remarked, "This is breakfast? No, this is break-head."

When Prabhupāda first came to Chicago's O'Hare Airport, he quipped, "Just add the Kṛṣṇa there. Then it will be O'Har'e Kṛṣṇa Airport. Ask them to change it."

In a lecture, Prabhupāda was describing alcoholics. "Just like in New York, you have seen on Bowery Street the drunkard—what is called? Alcoholic bumpers? What is the name?"

"Bums," suggested a devotee from the audience.

"Yes," said Prabhupāda, "the bums."

When Prabhupāda found someone's beads dangling near the floor or hanging from a doorknob, he sometimes would say, "Whose beads are crying here?"

Referring to a short afternoon rest, Prabhupāda called it a "snap" rather than a nap.

18

REALIZATIONS

There are so many ways you can glorify Prabhupāda. There are so many ways you can speak about Prabhupāda. There are so many things you can say, because Prabhupāda was unlimited. Prabhupāda is unlimited. Everything he ever did was unlimited. No one could understand the depths of Prabhupāda's actions or his words. They're inconceivable. Sometimes I hear devotees tell me, "Oh, you are so lucky. You associated personally with Śrīla Prabhupāda so much." And sometimes I might say, "Oh, yes," because I don't want to make an argument. It's not that I'm trying to say I wasn't lucky. I felt very fortunate. But I don't feel like I ever associated with Śrīla Prabhupāda personally. It may be hard to understand how you can be with somebody so much yet not associate with him personally. Because I could never understand Śrīla Prabhupāda, therefore I could not even begin to conceive of how to associate with him personally.

I often became very jealous. I became very much jealous often of Hari Śauri dāsa because I could sit in front of Śrīla Prabhupāda and him, and Śrīla Prabhupāda would talk with him like an old friend. I used to be envious like anything because Śrīla Prabhupāda never spoke to me like that. Tamāla Kṛṣṇa Mahārāja would sit in front of Śrīla Prabhupāda and they would discuss all kinds of things, and I would be envious because Śrīla Prabhupāda never spoke to me like that. And Bhavānanda Mahārāja would come to Śrīla Prabhupāda, and Prabhupāda would be so nice with him all the time, and all he ever did was hit me on the head. I'm envious because they all have such a deep relationship with

Śrīla Prabhupāda, yet in my case, I don't even understand that relationship very well. All I know is that every time I wanted to be close with Śrīla Prabhupāda, he would end up taking out his club and just cracking my head. This went on consistently.

It's very difficult to understand, because when I was secretary, I tried to imitate former secretaries, and all I did was get smashed to pieces. When I was servant, I tried to imitate former servants, and it never worked. When I was GBC and I came to visit, I tried to imitate other GBCs who came to visit, and it didn't work. When Prabhupāda was going to leave the planet, I couldn't even be part of that. I was not part of that. I was not part of Prabhupāda's appearance pastime in the Western world. I was not part of Prabhupāda's disappearance pastime in the manifested universe.

I always lamented why I was so stupid, wasting my time in the university in 1969 doing nothing, when Śrīla Prabhupāda was downstairs in my dormitory, sitting there. I walked right through the room. Didn't even know it. Didn't see him. Didn't see the devotees. Didn't see anything. Just walked right through. Didn't see him. Didn't see anybody. Never heard of it. Until four years later, the person I was living with said, "Do you remember that Swami who was in our dormitory that day?" I said, "What Swami?" Later on I told this to Śrīla Prabhupāda. He just laughed. I then asked, "Why didn't I see you then? I always wanted to be part of this. First days." He just shook his head. "You were not ready." I hung my head on the floor.

Then I remember when Śrīla Prabhupāda was departing, I wanted to be there. There were so many things—huge court cases. Prabhupāda was happy if I gave him some books, so I wanted to make so many books. I was running around going to printers. I had just gotten another batch of books ready to bring to Śrīla Prabhupāda and then he disappeared. I wasn't part of Prabhupāda's pastimes, and I don't feel that I ever really personally associated with him. And on his disappearance days I don't feel a part. Yet I was trying to understand why. Then I understood just listening to everybody today for the first time. This has been very instructive.

In 1976, in January, Prabhupāda sent me away. He sent me away and he gave me the instruction that was to be the instruction by which I was always to remember him. He always used to chastise me on this one point: why I always insist on being with him personally, and why I don't understand his instructions. "Why are you always so attached to this so-called personal association? Don't you understand that the *vāṇī* is more important than the *vapuḥ*? Don't you understand that I want you to do something?"

Then I was always trying to again come back to Śrīla Prabhupāda, even after he had sent me away to perform his services. I understand now. That was the final sending away at that time. I was not going to have that personal relationship that I always had. I was just sent away. Menial servant.

One time I tried to forcibly put myself back into Prabhupāda's association. After about three days of being Prabhupāda's secretary in 1976 in August, when he was in New Māyāpur, France, Prabhupāda asked me to write a letter and I spelled every other word wrong. I'm a horrible speller. He wanted to get rid of me then and there after three days because I was such a terrible speller, and why didn't I use a dictionary? Actually, I had to take a devotee as my editor. He had to edit the whole letter because I was so hopeless. I said to Śrīla Prabhupāda, "But your other secretaries can't spell either! I've seen! Why are you chastising me for not being able to spell, and now kicking me away?" And then he was very insistent. He was chastising me for everything I did. I was getting more and more upset, and I was holding on more and more. "No, I won't go. I refuse." It became a huge battle. "Go away." "No. I won't." And then more and more beating and beating and beating and beating. Finally, at the end of all this beating here in Vṛndāvana, I came and I said, "I quit! I can't take it any more." He said, "You can't quit. I FIRE YOU." Even to the last, "Get out. Go. Serve."

I said, "I don't want to go back. There's so many troubles in that place I came from."

He said, "I don't care what you do when you go back there. You just sit there in your room and chant Hare Kṛṣṇa, but stay there."

I said, '"How can I go traveling alone in the mountains? No strong association. Nobody will go with me. Too dangerous."

He said, "Then you go alone. You should be very careful of this so-called strong association." Contradicting again and again everything I said.

One time, "There's nothing to eat, Śrīla Prabhupāda!"

He said, "Then eat meat if you have to."

I said, "But what about my consciousness?"

He said, "Damn your consciousness. You have to preach." He just bewildered me. Unbending. He wanted it done. That's all. "Make my books. Distribute my books. Preach. That's all. Don't come back here crawling on the floor, wanting to sit in front of me and wave your fingers." I was typing his books, listening to his latest words in my ears, completely happy.

He wants these things. He's very insistent. And because I would probably get all lost in sentimentality, I don't think I would have been able to tolerate Prabhupāda's disappearance. Even to this day I cannot stand to see a picture of Prabhupāda's disappearance. I cannot stand to hear descriptions of Prabhupāda disappearing. I don't watch Yadubara's movie because of this, and he doesn't like that, but I just can't stand it. I don't know. I'm too sentimental. I can't stand it. Prabhupāda knew me perfectly; he dealt with me in a completely unique way just to circumvent that sentimentality and make me attached to his instructions. Prabhupāda dealt with each and every one of us so perfectly. Every single devotee. So uniquely. No one can say they have a complete picture of

Śrīla Prabhupāda. You can't even know one small feature, because in each and every circumstance, how Prabhupāda dealt with everybody was so unique and marvelous—just like Kṛṣṇa. You cannot know Kṛṣṇa fully. His glories are unlimited. You can see in Prabhupāda's dealings how he's manifesting more and more of his energies, his *śaktis,* making devotees do things that are inconceivable all over the world. Inconceivable things.

I'll never forget what Satsvarūpa Mahārāja once wrote in his *Back to Godhead* editorial on charisma. A police captain in New York City said, "Do you know why this New York Ratha-yātrā is a success? Because the Swamijī wanted it so. Because he wanted it." Everybody can understand Prabhupāda's potencies, how Prabhupāda is forcing us to just push on more and more.

Gradually, gradually, as the years go on, I understand the *vāṇī* is Śrīla Prabhupāda. I'm somewhat more satisfied, although I'm sure if I had the opportunity I would still be diving at his lotus feet and saying, "Take me with you." But we have this responsibility, regardless of our feelings of separation in ISKCON. In all circumstances, just keep on, keep on printing, keep on distributing, keep on building, and keep on working together, just so we can massage the transcendental body of Śrīla Prabhupāda all together. Each one of us is taking a portion of his body and massaging it so that he'll be satisfied and comfortable. Somebody is massaging Śrīla Prabhupāda in this way, somebody in that way, but as long as it's all pleasing Śrīla Prabhupāda, that should be our whole pleasure.

—*Harikeśa Swami*

19

REALIZATIONS

I'd like to analyze an important *śloka* from the *Śrīmad-Bhāgavatam,* First Canto, which I've studied carefully and in which I've found some interesting implications. This verse is in the Fifth Chapter, text 11:

tad-vāg-visargo janatāgha-viplavo
yasmin prati-ślokam abaddhavaty api
nāmāny anantasya yaśo 'nkitāni yac
śṛṇvanti gāyanti gṛṇanti sādhavaḥ

Translation: "On the other hand, that literature which is full of descriptions of the transcendental glories of the name, fame, forms, pastimes, etc., of the unlimited Supreme Lord is a different creation, full of transcendental words directed toward bringing about a revolution in the impious lives of this world's misdirected civilization. Such transcendental literatures, even though imperfectly composed, are heard, sung and accepted by purified men who are thoroughly honest."

This verse contains some very interesting points. One is that this literature being described is meant to bring about a revolution. If we historically analyze the *Bhāgavatam,* it was compiled by Śrīla Vyāsadeva five thousand years ago, and it was compiled for the sake of bringing about a revolution in the world.

Since the time of Śrīla Vyāsadeva's writing this, we cannot find a revolution created by this literature until this present revolution of the Kṛṣṇa consciousness movement, which is directed towards bringing about a revolution in the impious lives of this world's misdirected civilization. That means that the *Śrīmad-Bhāgavatam* was compiled for the purpose of this Kṛṣṇa consciousness movement. The revolution being described in this verse is a world revolution, so there's no doubt that this cannot but be applied to the present Kṛṣṇa consciousness movement.

Now there's another very interesting point here. It says "such transcendental literatures, even though imperfectly composed . . ." we all know, especially those of us who have read and relished Śrīla Prabhupāda's original *Bhāgavatams* written in Vṛndāvana and published in Delhi, that they were imperfectly composed. The indication I take from this verse is that this is a prediction of Śrīla Prabhupāda's appearance and the spreading of the Kṛṣṇa consciousness movement to create a revolution to change the misdirected civilization that presently exists.

Previously, Prabhupāda has been described as *śaktyāveśa-avatāra,* and we find that generally *avatāras* are predicted and described in the revealed scriptures. Here we find a genuine confirmation that Śrīla Prabhupāda is the *śaktyāveśa-avatāra* of Lord Kṛṣṇa who was deputed by the Lord to accomplish the purpose described in this verse—to create a worldwide revolution in the misdirected lives of an impious civilization. Therefore, by analyzing and understanding this verse, we can get great inspiration and become very enthusiastic to help this revolution.

Of course, before I became a devotee I was also a revolutionary. Many of us were, although of a different type, of course, but that revolutionary spirit is properly channeled in this Kṛṣṇa consciousness movement. Śrīla Prabhupāda is the greatest revolutionary; he actually knows how to transform the world into what it should be. A revolutionary generally is a person who has a vision of utopia, or a vision of a better way in which the world can go on, so he tries, using his ideologies and rhetoric, to enlist support. Some revolutions are violent and some are nonviolent, but generally they all fail, either quickly or in the long run, due to the people's imperfect notion of reality and their false goals of ideology. This revolution has the greatest revolutionary as its leader; he has a very clear vision of the world situation, a clear ideology which is taken directly from the Supreme Lord Himself.

Arjuna understood when Kṛṣṇa spoke to him on the battlefield that, by Kṛṣṇa's arrangement, the outcome of the battle was already decided. Arjuna was to win and the opposing side was to be completely vanquished. Therefore we can understand from this scriptural evidence that this revolution is to take place, that the misdirected civilization is to be redirected and established according to the Lord's plan in a Kṛṣṇa conscious civilization. Of course, we also know this from Lord Caitanya's teachings, but now we can also know that it is found within the pages of the *Śrīmad-Bhāgavatam* and that Śrīla Prabhupāda's appearance is also predicted there. It can give us even more enthusiasm, more strength, more conviction that we will be successful in our revolutionary efforts. The people of the world will either have to accept the Kṛṣṇa consciousness movement and redirect their impious lives or else be left behind. Of course, everyone will benefit. Every living entity who comes in touch with this movement, who comes in touch with the chanting, is being benefited and transformed.

On the battlefield of Kurukṣetra, because Kṛṣṇa was present, the persons who would not accept Kṛṣṇa and His devotees were weeded out, and Kṛṣṇa and His devotees were established. The same thing is now taking place and success is certain. We simply have to apply whatever intelligence and abilities Kṛṣṇa has given us in our respective fields by working cooperatively.

It is a great battle. We may not always see it clearly, just as Arjuna, in the chaos of the battle, may not have been able to clearly see the outcome. But because he was confident of Kṛṣṇa's plan, having heard it from Kṛṣṇa Himself, he had no fear. He was completely absorbed in His service, confident that in the end he and his brothers would be successful. The *Śrīmad-Bhāgavatam* is, after all, the literary incarnation of Kṛṣṇa, so we know straight from Kṛṣṇa's mouth that we are to be successful in our endeavor. All we require is conviction and complete dedication in whatever service Kṛṣṇa has given us. It may look like chaos sometimes. Sometimes it appeared that the Pāṇḍavas were losing. There were setbacks, but because it was Kṛṣṇa's plan, success was certain and ultimately victory was achieved. We can also be confident of the total victory of the Kṛṣṇa consciousness movement.

—*Jagadīśa Goswami*

20

In Hawaii, one woman disciple went in to see Śrīla Prabhupāda and brought her one-year-old daughter with her. The temple president introduced her, telling how they were trying to arrange that this woman could earn money for her needs without unduly straining the temple's finances.

The woman said that she heard there was a job picking guavas available on the island. Prabhupāda said no, a woman with a child should not take such strenuous labor. When she said that as an alternative she could distribute his books, Prabhupāda smiled and approved, "Yes, do that."

While this talk was going on, the woman's young child began to play with papers on Prabhupāda's desk.

"No," said Prabhupāda, shaking his finger at the child.

The woman picked up her child and placed her beside her, but the little girl crawled forward and started to touch Prabhupāda's feet.

"No!" the mother called out, and she began to drag her child away, but Prabhupāda said, "My papers she should not touch, but my feet, that is all right. You must learn how to instruct the child properly."

Knowing that her time in the *darśana* was soon up, the mother tried to introduce a philosophical question to get some spiritual benefit from the rare opportunity of talking to Śrīla Prabhupāda. She asked, "How do you become free from fear?" Prabhupāda replied by giving the example of Prahlāda Mahārāja. For him, Prabhupāda said, he saw everything as coming from Kṛṣṇa, whether it was good or bad, whereas for the demon, there was only fear.

Prabhupāda then drank water and held the cup out to the small child. By now, however, the child was getting tired and cranky. She refused the water and threw herself on the ground, hitting her head in a temper tantrum. Before she actually began to cry, Prabhupāda interrupted her and said, "Look!" pointing to the floor. "You have broken the floor!" The child immediately got up, stopped crying, and looked at the floor. Then Prabhupāda gestured that they should leave.

21

LITTLE DROPS *of* NECTAR

In September 1976, Prabhupāda was sitting in Vṛndāvana. Two of his *sannyāsī* disciples came before him. Prabhupāda spoke to them individually, giving different instructions.

To one he said, "You are a *sannyāsī.* Why are you spending such long time here? You have a bus, and you must travel. *Sannyāsa* means that now you have to preach all over the world. So why you should be thinking of becoming temple president here? Actually a *sannyāsī* should not stay in any place for more than three days at a time. When the wheels stop turning, then preaching is stopped also. Still, the temple is *nirguṇa,* so you may stay, but not for more than three days. That is allowed, but only if you have business there." In this way, Prabhupāda encouraged one of his men to immediately go out and preach, and he admonished him for staying too long in one place.

As soon as he had finished speaking in that way, Prabhupāda turned to the other *sannyāsī* and told him, "Now you must never leave Vṛndāvana unless I say so. You should stay here and do the management." All the devotees present laughed. It seemed wonderful how Prabhupāda had just given two completely contradictory statements, and yet everyone accepted them as truth.

When Prabhupāda was attending the Kumbha-melā in Prayāg in 1977, a few devotees from England arrived with a special gift. They had brought *rasagullās* that had been offered the previous day to the Rādhā-Kṛṣṇa Deities in London.

"Not even the Queen of England," said Prabhupāda, "could enjoy a *rasagullā* made in England while sitting at the Kumbha-melā. This is the first time that anyone has been able to do this." Prabhupāda was alluding to the fact that in India, from the time of British occupation, things that were "made in London" were considered the best. Anything made in London was the best and the most expensive. Certainly *rasagullās* were available all over India, but the fact that one was made in London and immediately exported to Prabhupāda in his tent at Kumbha-melā was a symbol of the wonder and wealth of the Kṛṣṇa consciousness movement.

Prabhupāda's servant, Hari Śauri related to Prabhupāda that his grandmother had advised Hari Śauri's mother to abort the child who was to be born of her. The mother refused, so he was born. After hearing this, Śrīla Prabhupāda brought it up in different conversations. "Now I understand," he said, "the advantage of a birth in India. People here could not even dream of such a thing." Prabhupāda explained how people are taking the great risk of becoming murderers simply due to the sex urge. "All the women in the West," he said, "are encouraged by their parents to become prostitutes and capture some rich man while they are still young."

22

In 1974, at ISKCON Dallas *gurukula*, one of the teachers introduced a new learning contest for the children. He called it "Kṛṣṇa Bowl," modeled after a television program called "General Electric College Bowl." "College Bowl" was a contest that tested the wits of the brightest college students, so Kṛṣṇa Bowl was a contest to see which students had the best memory for incidents in the *Kṛṣṇa* book. The competing *gurukula* students would sit at desks facing the assembly of children and teachers, and a tense competition ensued. The questions tended to be extremely intricate, and the first student who knew the answer had to press an electric buzzer. Whoever buzzed first got to answer.

The games caused great excitement among the children and sometimes caused tears and tantrums for the losers of the game. Some of the adult devotees in Dallas wondered if maybe the whole Kṛṣṇa Bowl was just so much mental speculation. One of the teachers in favor of the game wrote to Prabhupāda for approval.

Prabhupāda replied as follows:

"I beg to acknowledge receipt of your letter regarding the Krsna Bowl game, and it should be stopped immediately. This thing will be a taxation on the brain of the young children. Why are you inventing? Why are you not satisfied? You are all only inventing and spoiling money. You teach the children perfectly Sanskrit and English instead of spoiling time and money. The children cannot pronounce correctly the Sanskrit. But then read it correctly. That is wanted first. They must pronounce nicely Sanskrit and English. The English is no difficulty. If you can do this, then your education is all right."

Another letter from Śrīla Prabhupāda soon followed, sent to one of the GBC representatives. "I received one letter from *gurukula* regarding the Kṛṣṇa Bowl contest," wrote Prabhupāda, "and I want you to know that nothing new should be added. Whatever I've introduced should remain. Nothing new should be added. New things means that their brain is not clear. Carefully manage things that I have established."

23

Jagadguru dāsa Brahmacārī and another *brahmacārī* journeyed to Māyāpur three weeks before the annual festival in hopes of getting a private *darśana* with Śrīla Prabhupāda. They had been preaching in North Africa and were carrying a $12,000 check from a man who asked that it be personally given to Śrīla Prabhupāda.

While being massaged by Hari Śauri, Prabhupāda received Jagadguru on the roof of the Māyāpur building. Prabhupāda asked where the devotees were coming from, and they proudly answered that they were coming from North Africa.

"Oh, North Africa," said Prabhupāda, and he seemed impressed.

When the *brahmacārīs* gave Prabhupāda the donation, he remarked that this was successful preaching. The people must have been pleased, he said, otherwise they would not have given such an amount of money. He then asked Jagadguru if he liked India. When he replied, "Yes, Śrīla Prabhupāda," Prabhupāda was pleased and asked him to stay in India.

As a member of ISKCON Africa, Jagadguru was working under Brahmānanda Swami, the GBC for that continent. Jagadguru was Brahmānanda Swami's only *saṅkīrtana* collector, and Brahmānanda had asked him to request of Śrīla Prabhupāda that the $12,000 be used to pay ISKCON Africa's BBT debt.

"Can this money go to the credit of our debt?" Jagadguru asked.

"No," said Śrīla Prabhupāda. Anticipating Brahmānanda Swami's displeasure, Jagadguru tried to explain about the

BBT debt. Again Prabhupāda said, "No." Jagadguru tried a third time to explain, but again Prabhupāda said, "No!"

Prabhupāda put out his hand and slapped it with his other hand. "My Guru Mahārāja always kept us in debt," he said. "If we simply pay their BBT debt, they will become lazy. As for Brahmānanda Swami," said Prabhupāda, "we will not hang him, but he will work for this debt."

Prabhupāda then told a story of how Bhaktisiddhānta Sarasvatī Ṭhākura used to build a temple or create a big project and put the whole Gaudiya Math into debt. *Sannyāsīs, brahmacārīs,* and all members would enthusiastically go out and collect money, and Guru Mahārāja would simply start another program so that the Gaudiya Math would remain in debt. "In this way," said Prabhupāda, "he always kept us in debt and always working and always busy."

24

ŚRĪLA PRABHUPĀDA SAID

On Women

"Here in this spot, New Vrindaban, the woman's business will be taking care of the children, cooking, cleansing, and churning butter. And those who have got the knowledge of typing can help in typing also. That's all. This for women. No other hard work. And for men, hard work, field work, taking care of the cows, or the animals, going to collect wood, constructing the buildings, and in this way cooperate. Girls who are here, they should learn to prepare nice *prasādam,* so that the boys, they can get their *prasādam* timely. This is duty. And they must be given timely breakfast, lunch, *prasādam.* They will work hard. And the churning business is for the girls. That will keep your health very nice. Mother

Yaśodā, the mother of Kṛṣṇa, just see how exalted she was. Materially, she was rich also. She had many maidservants. Still, she took pleasure in churning."

—*Lecture at New Vrindaban*

Pālikā-devī dāsī inquired from Prabhupāda about the meaning of marriage in Kṛṣṇa consciousness. Prabhupāda looked at her and said, "There's no such thing as marriage in Kṛṣṇa consciousness. Everyone is wife to Kṛṣṇa; everyone is female to Kṛṣṇa. Kṛṣṇa is the masculine. So there is no such thing as marriage."

"I have no objection to marriage, but to bless it by a fire sacrifice, I am thinking that if they don't stay together then it is not good. But if they can remain together for one year, then there can be fire sacrifice. But changing three times in a month husband and wife, that is not good."

—*Letter of September 2, 1975*

Prabhupāda sometimes quoted the poet Tulasī dāsa about four things that can be beaten. One can beat a drum, or a dog, or a woman, or a *śūdra.* One time when Prabhupāda mentioned this, he laughed and turned to his disciple Nara-Nārāyaṇa. "Nara-Nārāyaṇa understands this principle very well," said Prabhupāda, and the other devotees also laughed. But then Prabhupāda turned seriously to Nara-Nārāyaṇa and said, "But don't do it. These are not ordinary women. These are devotees."

One time a devotee told Prabhupāda a famous story about Mīrabāi. According to this story, Mīrabāi wanted to meet Jīva Gosvāmī, but Jīva Gosvāmī sent back a message, "I am a *sannyāsī* and you are a woman, so I cannot meet you." Then, according to the story, Mīrabāi sent another message to Jīva Gosvāmī, saying, "I thought that Lord Kṛṣṇa was the only male in Vṛndāvana and that all others were female." When

Jīva Gosvāmī heard this reply, he supposedly agreed to meet her. When Prabhupāda heard this story he said that this may not be true, because in our line the *sannyāsīs* do not refuse to meet women.

On one of his visits to Boston, Prabhupāda was introduced to a young Indian woman who had joined the temple. She had been married to a man who was not at all interested in Kṛṣṇa consciousness and who had mistreated her in many ways. With his permission, she had left him and was now living with the other devotees. Prabhupāda approved of this but then said, "You have got only one defect."

The girl asked, "Oh, what is it?"

Prabhupāda said, "You have no husband. Woman without a husband, that is not good. You must get a husband, and then you will be perfect. When a woman follows her husband, then she is perfect."

25

ŚRĪLA PRABHUPĀDA TELLS A STORY

Śrīla Prabhupāda told a funny story to illustrate a serious point about the teachings of Śaṅkarācārya. Śaṅkarācārya is accepted by the Vaiṣṇava *sampradāya* as an incarnation of Lord Śiva, and therefore Śaṅkara is exalted. But Śaṅkara's deceptive teachings of the Māyāvādī philosophy were intended for a particular time and place and were not intended to be perpetuated as eternal *dharma,* as is done by his so-called Māyāvādī philosophers. To illustrate the foolishness of the imitative followers of Śaṅkara, Prabhupāda told a story about a doctor and his apprentice.

There was a famous veterinarian who traveled to many farms and had good success in curing the illnesses of animals.

The veterinarian also had an assistant who accompanied him, but this apprentice had an envious and ambitious desire to replace his master and to prematurely become a master veterinarian himself. On one occasion the veterinarian was called to a farm where he discovered a valuable horse whose neck was greatly swollen. The veterinarian opened the mouth of the horse, examined inside, and then asked the apprentice to hand him his work bag. Taking out his hammer, the veterinarian proceeded to smash at the horse's neck. Very soon after this unusual action, the horse's swelling subsided, and the farmer thankfully praised and paid the veterinarian for his work.

Almost immediately after this incident, the apprentice deserted the doctor and decided to become a veterinarian himself. Word soon reached the master veterinarian that his apprentice was running around presenting himself as a genuine veterinarian, but was causing havoc wherever he went. The report was that the so-called veterinarian was actually killing animals whenever he attempted to treat them. Finally, the master veterinarian caught up with his rascal apprentice and challenged him, "What do you think you're doing? I hear that you are imitating my practice, but as a result you are killing animals wherever you go."

"But I am only doing what I saw you do," protested the apprentice. The apprentice then explained that he was just doing what he had seen his master do on their last visit. Whenever he went to see an ailing animal, he would smash on that animal with a hammer, but unfortunately he did not get good results.

"You fool!" said the veterinarian. "What you saw was a very special case. That horse had swallowed a watermelon, so I had to break the watermelon by hitting him from the outside. That was not a practice to be repeated in every case."

In this way, Prabhupāda illustrated how the Māyāvādī followers of Śaṅkara should be scorned and beaten just as the apprentice was by the veterinarian.

26

PRABHUPĀDA TELLS SHORT STORIES

A disciple asked Śrīla Prabhupāda how it was that favored disciples who were once close to Śrīla Prabhupāda could fall down and leave their Kṛṣṇa conscious practices. Prabhupāda replied that physical closeness or intimacy does not matter. He gave the example that the king may be sitting on the throne and a mosquito may be sitting on the lap of the king, but that doesn't mean the mosquito is favored by the king. Rather, that mosquito may simply be causing a disturbance to the king. But because of our past conditioning, however, we associate physical closeness with intimacy. Service to the spiritual master is not restricted only to those who are physically close, and in fact, those who are physically close may even be creating a disturbance rather than helping.

Prabhupāda said that the people of India are ninety percent Kṛṣṇa conscious; they just need a proper leader. To illustrate this he said that a dead elephant and a live elephant are both worth a great deal of money. An elephant is valuable even when dead, because it has good tusks, hide, and so on. Similarly, India's Vedic civilization is so supremely wonderful that even if it is practically dead, it is very valuable.

Prabhupāda explained how the English schemed to break India into Hindustan and Pakistan. Their tactic was similar to that of a cat who advised two monkeys who were fighting over a cake. The cat said, "Let me cut it in half. We will weigh two sides on the scale." The cat cut the cake in half and then said, "Oh, this one side is too heavy." To even out the two pieces, the cat said that he would have to bite off one piece. So he ate a piece of the cake and then put the two pieces back on the scale. Then he said, "Oh, now the other side is too heavy. Let me bite this one." In this way, the cat quickly ate the whole thing. Similarly, by this "even division" by Great Britain, India was finished.

A professor told Śrīla Prabhupāda that he regarded himself more as a *jñānī* than a *bhakta,* although he was attracted to *bhakti.* Prabhupāda replied, saying that an impersonalist philosopher is not actually a *jñānī* but a learner. Only when one realizes Kṛṣṇa, as described in the twenty-ninth verse of the Seventh Chapter of *Bhagavad-gītā,* does one become a *jñānī.* The real meaning of knowledge is the ability not for grammatical or sophisticated expression, but to actually know the truth. To illustrate this, Prabhupāda said that once in India, a monkey had come into a man's office and had thrown the papers everywhere and then left. When the English supervisor asked the clerk what had happened, the clerk could not speak sufficient English to explain how the monkey had caused chaos. He began to imitate the monkey, jumping and leaping around, making monkey noises and throwing the papers in the air. In this way, the supervisor quickly understood what had happened. So, Prabhupāda said, somehow or other we have to communicate Kṛṣṇa consciousness, and the important message will be understood.

27

PERSONAL

His Chanting

Like Prabhupāda's preaching, his chanting was constant. While talking in his room with professors in Toronto, Prabhupāda silently chanted the Hare Kṛṣṇa mantra in between their academic words.

When Prabhupāda encouraged his disciples to chant Hare Kṛṣṇa while sitting with them during a *prasādam* feast, one of the devotees replied, "But Swamijī, how can we chant and eat at the same time?"

"Chant in between bites," said Śrīla Prabhupāda.

We can hear Śrīla Prabhupāda's *japa* on a recording: he chants quickly and he said that sixteen rounds of *japa* could be done in one and a half to two hours. During an initiation lecture, he commented that it should take five or six minutes to chant a round, although he admitted that it might not be possible in the beginning.

When a devotee said that it was hard to chant and keep awake, Prabhupāda replied that they should then do as he does, as he walks in his room in the afternoon while chanting *japa*.

In the early morning, after completing his dictation of *Śrīmad-Bhāgavatam* translations at maybe 4 or 5 A.M., Śrīla Prabhupāda would sit back and chant *japa*. He did not chant very loudly, but from the other room one could sometimes hear, especially the words, "Rāma, Rāma." Then in the afternoon sometimes he would remark that he had a few extra rounds to chant, and he would move the counting beads. We took it that Prabhupāda's statements about his own chanting of prescribed rounds were for our benefit, but it was encouraging for our own regulative habit.

Often he would spontaneously utter the words "Hare Kṛṣṇa," or he would state *harer nāma harer nāma harer nāmaiva kevalam,* with great feeling and expression.

When in the course of a lecture Prabhupāda would say the words of the Hare Kṛṣṇa mantra, the whole audience of devotees would repeat it word for word in unison with him. He did not ask them to do this, but it was a spontaneous response. The devotees could not resist the chance to chant along with him. On airplanes he would often chant for long periods, silently or barely audibly moving his lips, and intently fingering the beads, sometimes shaking them within the bag. Or sometimes during morning walks, instead of talking he would chant, and everyone would eagerly join with him.

Prabhupāda's speaking *about* chanting was also another type of chanting. He recommended the chanting of Hare Kṛṣṇa, and sometimes he would become surcharged with emotion and his voice would rise in volume: "We are simply asking everyone, *'Please chant Hare Kṛṣṇa!'"* At times like that, when Śrīla Prabhupāda put all his energy into the request that everyone should chant, we could understand that the Hare Kṛṣṇa mantra was the summum bonum of life. Therefore, often in a lecture he would state it loudly, "Please chant Hare Kṛṣṇa!" And yet he would often follow this by saying that people were so unfortunate that they could not do this simple thing. (He recalled a cartoon where a man asked his wife, "Chant, chant, chant," and she replied, "Can't, can't, can't.")

Śrīla Prabhupāda's *japa* beads were brown *tulasī.* He asked that his saffron beadbag be changed and a clean one given to him regularly. He gave his servants the blissful service of changing his counter beads and transferring them to the new bag. He was certainly a master at chanting Hare Kṛṣṇa, and Prabhupāda's followers were always eager to take part with him in his pure, empowered activities of chanting Hare Kṛṣṇa and distributing it to others.

28

SERVICE IN SEPARATION

I do not think that separation from Śrīla Prabhupāda is possible at any moment, provided that we want to keep his association. He is ready and waiting. Any time we turn to him, he is there—there to guide us and help us in any way. Mainly he is there to give us instruction in service and to chastise us if we disobey. But we should never go away.

He always gives us the chance to leave him—if we want—if the chastisement is too heavy. But leaving him is the greatest loss, complete disaster. It is better to accept the chastisement and try to improve, difficult as it may seem, and win his favor again, rather than try to run and hide, avoiding or, still worse, trying to forget.

Of course, Śrīla Prabhupāda loves us even when he chastises us. In fact, his chastisement is proof that he loves us, that he cares for us, that he wants us to improve and become good devotees of Kṛṣṇa.

And if we follow his instructions, he is very pleased, very easily pleased, and he reciprocally blesses us, encouraging us and giving us further direction.

We should never become puffed up or complacent, however, thinking that because Śrīla Prabhupāda is reciprocating with us he is favoring us or that we are perfect. Far from it. Śrīla Prabhupāda is helping us out of his causeless mercy. We have no other qualification whatsoever. Our only qualification or hope is Śrīla Prabhupāda's causeless mercy. That's all. So if we become proud, thinking that we are special or Prabhupāda's favorite, Prabhupāda is not pleased. He may by his causeless mercy arrange some difficulty to humble us, so we come crawling back to his shelter.

Overall, Śrīla Prabhupāda is a perfect person. He is wonderful. As we approach him, he reciprocates. And he is very personal—even humorous at times—as well as very kind and compassionate. If we make mistakes, he forgives us. He is always ready to forgive and give us another chance to serve him. When we follow his instructions, he is pleased. He reciprocates by giving us more service.

My advice to everyone is—and this advice is directed more toward my mind than toward anyone else—always remember Śrīla Prabhupāda and never forget him. He is always there. He is our father, our best friend, and our very life itself."

—*Girirāja Swami*

29

Śrīla Prabhupāda always accepted food cooked by his sister Piśimā, even though he knew that the oil and spices she used made him sick. Because she was very devoted to Śrīla Prabhupāda, he ate her cooked offerings of food as if it were ordained by Kṛṣṇa.

But sometimes he would confide to others that he shouldn't eat what Piśimā cooked. One time in Māyāpur when Prabhupāda told his disciple Pālikā that he did not want to eat Piśimā's cooking, Pālikā tried to satisfy Prabhupāda by bringing him what he wanted.

When Pālikā brought in Prabhupāda's lunch and he saw that it was made up exclusively of offerings by Piśimā, he became angry.

"Why haven't you brought me what I want?"

"Piśimā was there," said Pālikā. "What could I do? She hid the *dāl*."

"All right," said Prabhupāda, "try tomorrow. I'll tell you what I want and you cook it."

But the next day it was the same thing. Piśimā was using chilies and spices, and Prabhupāda was actually beginning to get sick from them. Pālikā tried hiding the chilies, and

Piśimā hid Pālikā's vegetables. Soon there was no communication at all between the two women.

Prabhupāda's Bengali disciples Bhakti-cāru and Nitāi-cānd were brought in to make peace between Piśimā and Pālikā, but Piśimā wouldn't discuss a thing. She said that whatever she cooked was what Prabhupāda wanted. She had been cooking for him for seventy years and she knew what he wanted. There was no way in the world she was going to cook anything else.

The devotees told Prabhupāda what Piśimā said and he replied, "All right, let her cook something, but Pālikā should also cook some things that I can eat."

After that the two women cooked in separate places. Piśimā would make some preparations and put them on the plate, and Pālikā would also put her preparations on the plate. Then one day, Piśimā decided that Pālikā shouldn't cook at all. So Piśimā cooked everything. When Pālikā tried to enter the kitchen, Piśimā raised her spoon and shouted in Bengali until Pālikā retreated from the door.

That day when Pālikā took the plate up to Prabhupāda and he saw that everything had been cooked by Piśimā, he said, "What is this? I cannot eat this!" Prabhupāda then smashed his fist on the desk and repeated, "I cannot eat this! She knows I cannot eat this! I will become sick if I eat this!" Prabhupāda sat staring at his food for a few moments, while Pālikā stood fearfully in the corner. Then Prabhupāda said, "But it is Kṛṣṇa's mercy. Therefore I will eat it." Of course, Prabhupāda knew that all he had to do was ask, and twenty devotees would have rushed down to the kitchen and cooked him whatever he wanted. Yet he declared that Kṛṣṇa had given him Piśimā's *prasādam*, and so he should eat it. That night, however, after eating a full lunch, Prabhupāda became sick. For the next two days he did not take anything except hot milk and medicine.

30

One time when Prabhupāda was at Bhaktivedanta Manor, a Māyāvādī *sannyāsī* came to visit. Śrīla Prabhupāda received him graciously and they had some discussion. When the man departed, he deliberately left behind a big stack of his pamphlets. The pamphlets contained a little essay on the monistic doctrine that "all is one," defying the direct meaning of the Vedic scriptures and completely omitting Lord Kṛṣṇa as the Supreme Personality of Godhead.

The next afternoon, Prabhupāda met with the devotees as usual. His practice was to receive a very big plate of fruit and nuts, take some himself, and then ask a disciple to distribute the *mahā-prasādam* to all the devotees. On this particular day, Prabhupāda called for the pamphlets. The devotees were surprised—"Why is Prabhupāda calling for these pamphlets?" When they were brought in, Śrīla Prabhupāda said, "Distribute one to each of the devotees." The devotees were bewildered as the Māyāvādī pamphlets were distributed to one and all.

Then Prabhupāda said, "Everyone take a pamphlet, open it up, and put it in your hand." He took a few fruits from the plate, began eating them, and then indicated that the rest should be distributed. He said the devotees should use the pamphlets as plates.

One of the devotees mentioned later that Prabhupāda was practicing *yukta-vairāgya* by this simple act. He had found a useful purpose for the atheistic tracts, simultaneously ridiculing their author and yet engaging him in devotional service.

31

LITTLE DROPS *of* NECTAR

Once at a lecture in the temple room in Los Angeles in 1970, just after moving into the building, Śrīla Prabhupāda asked the assembled devotees, "Is anyone not chanting sixteen rounds?" Only one boy raised his hand. It was Bhakta dāsa. Prabhupāda said, "You are not finishing sixteen rounds?"

"Well, Śrīla Prabhupāda," he said, "I've been working until late at night and only sleeping four hours, so I haven't had time to finish."

Śrīla Prabhupāda replied strongly, "Then sleep only two hours, but you must finish sixteen rounds a day."

While staying in Sydney, Śrīla Prabhupāda held an initiation and sacrifice in the backyard. The devotees then brought Śrīla Prabhupāda the Deities' *mahā-prasādam.* He looked at the plate and picked out one *purī.* He smelled it, poked it with his fingers, and then tasted it. "This *purī* is the best *purī,*" he said. "It is perfect. Bring me the man who has cooked this *purī.*"

The devotees ran off and found the fortunate cook, Kūrma dāsa. They brought him before Prabhupāda, who said, "Thank you very much for following the rules and regulations. I can understand that to cook such a *purī* you are following all the rules nicely." Prabhupāda explained that that was the way to do things properly—to follow, to be strict.

"I don't like second-class things," he said. "I like first-class *purīs.*" Every day while in Sydney, Prabhupāda used to have Kūrma's first-class *purīs* and he liked them very much indeed.

"If I were to have a son, should I train him to do my work?" Bharadvāja asked Śrīla Prabhupāda.

At that time Bharadvāja was in charge of the FATE studio, making diorama sculptures of *kṛṣṇa-līlā*. He had also seen in India how children are taught their father's work at a very young age so that they become proficient.

Śrīla Prabhupāda replied, "You are not a potter. Tomorrow you may be called to worship the Deity."

In this way, Śrīla Prabhupāda taught us to be attached only to the order of the spiritual master, not to any concept of oneself as an artist or *pūjārī*.

32

LITTLE DROPS *of* NECTAR

Prabhupāda's disciple Nava-yogendra became startled when he first saw Prabhupāda in a burst of anger. Prabhupāda was angry when the boy who was appointed to guard his room wandered off. Prabhupāda had to ring his bell again and again, but the devotee did not appear. Nava-yogendra was in Prabhupāda's room at the time. Prabhupāda turned to him and said, "Go out and see where is this rascal! He is supposed to stay there, and he is not there. Whenever he comes, bring him in."

Later, when the boy returned, Nava-yogendra brought him in and he saw Prabhupāda become very angry. "Where were you?!" Prabhupāda shouted, and the devotee began shaking. "Why did you not stay outside? Rascal, you are not faithful. Why are you not performing your duty properly?" Nava-yogendra also started to shake, although he was not the object of the chastisement.

Prabhupāda went on for several minutes, reprimanding the absent-minded guard and accusing him of serious inattentiveness in service.

As soon as the devotee left the room, however, Prabhupāda resumed his conversation with Nava-yogendra in a completely normal way. There was no trace of anger on his face. Nava-yogendra was struck with wonder, and he concluded that Prabhupāda's anger was only for the devotee's rectification and did not arise in any way from uncontrolled senses.

"Śrīla Prabhupāda," Nava-yogendra asked, "how should we feel if you are angry with one of us?"

Śrīla Prabhupāda replied, "If the spiritual master is angry, you should be pleased. It means that he's paying attention to you." Prabhupāda went on to say that there are so many hundreds and thousands of people in the streets, but no one is looking after them. But if the spiritual master becomes angry with a particular disciple, that is his loving mercy on that person.

"Preaching in Africa seems to be a waste of time," said Prabhupāda's disciple, Gargamuni. Gargamuni wanted to convince Prabhupāda that his brother, Brahmānanda Swami, should come and join them in India. "Prabhupāda, what is Brahmānanda doing there? He could be here in India. I don't really think the people there can become Kṛṣṇa conscious because they're so backward."

"You are thinking that the Negroes cannot become actually Kṛṣṇa conscious," said Prabhupāda, "because you are in a different body. You are in a white body. This is your body prejudice. You are thinking like that. But from my point of view, I am seeing you as a white Negro."

Gargamuni soon came stumbling out of Prabhupāda's room, aware that he had just been devastated by his spiritual master. To the first person he met, he said, "Do you know what Prabhupāda just called me? He said I was a white Negro!"

33

PRABHUPĀDA SAID

On Christianity

"Regarding the Christian Trinity, I believe it is God, the Holy Ghost, and the Son. A person in Krsna consciousness accepts this by the name Visnu, Paramatma, and *jiva.* God is a person, the Holy Spirit or Supersoul is a person, and the living entity is also a person. Also Mary is the representation of the energy of God. Either as internal energy, Radharani, or as external energy, Durga, the energy of Godhead can be considered the mother of the living entities. There is no clash between the Bible and the *Vedas;* simply some people formulate their personal ideas and cause quarreling.

"Nobody can say the Bible is meant for the same class of men as the *Bhagavad-gita. Bhagavad-gita* is the ABC's of spiritual knowledge. Beyond that is the *Srimad-Bhagavatam.* How great *Srimad-Bhagavatam* is, nobody can imagine. And beyond that is *Caitanya-caritamrta.* But beginning from the Bible or Koran on up, the principle remains the same. Just like beginning from the pocket dictionary up to the international unabridged dictionary."

—Letter of April 19, 1968

"The articles that appeared in the Christian paper *Southern Cross* are very nice. I'm pleased how the Christian community is appreciating our movement. Actually we have no quarrel with them. We accept Lord Jesus Christ as the Son of God, and he was a great Vaisnava. Because he appeared in another country does not mean that we should not offer him respect. If we stick to our principles as I have given you, more and more of these priestly class will come to respect us and appreciate something of our philosophy. Therefore I stress so much the devotional rules and regulations."

—Letter of August 5, 1974

"Those who are preaching in Christ's name are nonsense because they do not follow even the simplest of his orders, 'Thou shalt not kill.' I have met with so many Christians, and when I ask them why Christians are killing, they cannot answer. The first principle of spiritual life is nonviolence. They will say killing in this matter means actually murder. But accepting even this argument, it means that the society in which Christ was preaching was composed of murderers. So what kind of men they were? And practically we see it is a fact, because they murdered Lord Jesus Christ. At any rate, there is nothing in the world that can compare with our movement, our chanting and dancing. Chant and dance, and when you get tired, take *prasadam*. That is our actual solid preaching all over the world."

—*Letter of August 3, 1973*

34

ŚRĪLA PRABHUPĀDA TELLS STORIES

Śrīla Prabhupāda used to tell stories from ancient India collections such as the *Hitopadeśa*, and he had memorized many *ślokas* from Cāṇakya Paṇḍita. Here's a selection of examples Prabhupāda most frequently used from these literatures.

viśvaso naiva kartavyaḥ, strīṣu rāja-kuleṣu ca

Never trust a woman or a politician.

*

mātṛvat para-dāreṣu, para-dravyeṣu loṣṭavat
ātmavat sarva-bhūteṣu, yaḥ paśyati sa paṇḍitaḥ

An educated person is one who sees people's property as garbage on the street, deals with others as he would like them to deal with him, and sees every woman except his wife as mother.

*

ṛṇa-śeṣo 'gni-śeṣaś ca, vyādhi-śeṣas tathaiva ca
punaś ca vardhate yasmāt, tasmāc cheṣaṁ ca kārayet

Fire, debts, and disease should be treated immediately.

*

The senses are like serpents that bite, and therefore even a learned man should not sit alone with a woman, not even his sister or mother.

*

ṛṇa-kartā pitā śatrur, mātā ca vyabhicāriṇī
bhāryā rūpavatī śatruḥ, putraḥ śatrur apaṇḍitaḥ

The following are enemies in one's home: one's son if he is a fool, one's servants who speak back to him, one's wife who is very beautiful, or one's wife who speaks harshly with him. If a man has these enemies in his home, he should leave home and take to a renounced life.

*

arṇy ākhyavat

Happy is the man who is not in debt and who does not have to leave home. (Śrīla Prabhupāda used to quote this to criticize the civilization that sends modern-day workers to commute great distances before they reach their place of occupation. A simple villager has the opulence of taking care of his business at home, with a little land, a cow, or some small trade.)

*

lālayet pañca-varṣāṇi, daśa-varṣāṇi tāḍayet
prāpte tu ṣoḍaśe varṣe, putram mitravad ācaret

Fondle a son until he is five years of age and then use the stick for another ten years. When he has attained the sixteenth year, however, treat him as a friend.

*

varam eko guṇī putro, na ca mūrkha-śatair api
ekaś candras tamo hanti, na ca tārā-gaṇair api

A single son endowed with good qualities is far better than a hundred sons devoid of them, for the moon, though one, dispels the darkness, which the stars, though numerous, cannot.

*

ādau-mātā guroḥ patnī, brāhmaṇī rāja-patnikā
dhenur dhātrī tathā pṛthvī, saptaitā mātaraḥ smṛtāḥ

These seven should be considered as mothers: the king's wife, the preceptor's wife, the friend's wife, your wife's mother, your own mother, the land, and the cow.

35

PERSONAL

His Indifference and Detachment

Prabhupāda was never indifferent or uninterested in anything connected with the Kṛṣṇa consciousness movement. If he sometimes wouldn't respond to a disciple's question, that was his gravity, instructing us by ignoring us.

He was indifferent to his own health. In his desire to spread Kṛṣṇa consciousness, he didn't rest as he should have for someone his age. He continued traveling because he could not be indifferent to the fallen souls and to his disciples. He had created by his preaching and traveling the worldwide Kṛṣṇa consciousness movement, and he had placed himself in the center as its upholder. He could not be indifferent. He said if a body is cut in the finger, the whole body suffers.

When ISKCON in Argentina was closed by the government, Prabhupāda worried and wrote in his Bhaktivedanta purports how he was worrying in the mood of Vasudeva: Vasudeva knew that his son Kṛṣṇa could not be harmed, but he was in the ecstatic mood of anxious protection.

Prabhupāda was detached from the bad names people used against Kṛṣṇa consciousness in newspaper accounts, mostly because he saw the bright side of it—the fact that the newspapers were mentioning Kṛṣṇa's name. He cared for many things, yet on Kṛṣṇa's behalf he was also indifferent. Although much money came in, Prabhupāda was not concerned to keep any of it. He said his author's royalties for writing so many books was to take two *capātīs* a day. He was detached from the Fisher mansion purchased in Detroit and from other mansions. He was indifferent towards any books being printed about himself. He wanted Kṛṣṇa glorified. He was also not very eager to meet big heads of state. When someone asked him, "Why don't you try to meet President Nixon and tell him these things?" Prabhupāda replied, "What good would it do?" He was prepared to meet with the Pope, but when their schedules did not coincide, he did not pursue it. He knew that posing for a picture with a head of state did not mean much.

He was certainly indifferent to women's charms. He saw his female disciples as daughters and granddaughters and he respected their service to him. He saw them as spirit souls, but did not meet with them much in comparison to the meetings he had with his men disciples. He was not interested in sitting with women or looking at them for enjoyment.

He was indifferent to any kind of invitations to take tours in different cities he visited. He didn't want to go somewhere to see special downtown centers or tourist places, shopping places, and he never went to cinemas or sports events. He did like nice parks where he could walk in the mornings, and he liked big meeting halls in the city if there was an audience there to hear him speak Kṛṣṇa consciousness. He was interested in buildings for possible purchase as temples. Although he visited alluring cities like New York, London, and Paris, he was not interested to see the libraries, palaces, museums, natural wonders such as caves or waterfalls, seasides, or mountain resorts. They held no attraction for him. He preferred a simple room with a low desk where he could speak to guests and be among devotees for the best furthering of Kṛṣṇa consciousness. If by his service he was thrust into some situation in the midst of opulence or distraction, however, he was indifferent to the situation, even though externally it was in opposition to his way of life.

Especially in the first years in America, Prabhupāda was indifferent to the fact that his hosts in Pennsylvania ate meat or that he was moving into the hell of the material world known as the Bowery. He was indifferent to the fact that his first disciples were very sinful before becoming devotees. In such situations, he accepted and tolerated and was detached even from the desire to be in the most spiritual surroundings of a holy place. He was indifferent to a place being holy or unholy, as long as he was able to preach.

He kept a simple diet and wasn't interested in special foods such as the special cooking which the Italians could offer, or the French, or the Americans. Even within the Indian diet, which was his preference, he was not interested in fancy things, but in simple rice, *dāl, capātis,* and *sabjī.*

He was indifferent to clothes and would not sport any bright scarves or colorful *cādars* or special shoes or coats or hats. His simple *sannyāsī* dress he kept constant. He liked bright clothes for the Deities and the opportunity to spend money to build wonderful buildings and new ways to spread Kṛṣṇa consciousness, such as through dioramas. He also liked and appreciated the best quality in book printing and color reproduction of the paintings. In these things, even in their worldly aspects, Śrīla Prabhupāda was a connoisseur, a keen appreciator of quality, and he asked his devotees to compete in the market for the best quality and price; they should get the best deal and the best product for use in Kṛṣṇa's service.

36

REALIZATIONS

The conditioned soul thinks in a way separate from Kṛṣṇa, but a pure devotee has no separate idea or separate understanding from Kṛṣṇa. He has one idea and one understanding, and that is Kṛṣṇa consciousness. Prabhupāda would quote, "One flag, one *śāstra,* and one work—service to Kṛṣṇa." He even designed the ISKCON flag, an oval lotus with petals with the word "ISKCON" in the center. The whole world should be under one flag, ISKCON. The whole world should be under one *śāstra, Bhagavad-gītā.* The one principle of work is to surrender to Kṛṣṇa. That's the ISKCON movement. There should be one mantra, Hare Kṛṣṇa mantra. Or let us say, two mantras, Hare Kṛṣṇa and Jaya Prabhupāda.

Prabhupāda's idea was never separate from Kṛṣṇa's. When each of us individually is not separate from Prabhupāda and Kṛṣṇa and ISKCON's idea, then the qualities of forgiveness, gentleness, magnanimity of heart in distributing Kṛṣṇa's love—these will all manifest automatically. They will come out of the devotee's non-separate mentality. My personal appeal is that for me to maintain that mood of one idea, I need everyone's help.

I cannot say that I need only Prabhupāda and no one else. For years after Prabhupāda passed away I was bewildered, and only recently am I feeling more hope. I was bewildered, feeling, "How could Prabhupāda have left me like that?" I was thinking like that. It may be offensive, but I don't know. I was thinking, "How could he have left me like that?" My feeling was not of anger but of a kind of disappointment, "Why would you leave me at this time?"

But now I understand that Prabhupāda has not left, because if I look at my Godbrothers I can find in every one of them a little bit of Prabhupāda. Individually, they have their own, individual personalities, but if I study them, I'll find in each one at least one of the qualities that I loved so much. In another devotee I'll find another of the qualities that I loved so much in Prabhupāda, and in another, another quality of Prabhupāda. Those Godbrothers are very, very dear to me; because they are very, very dear to Prabhupāda, then they must be very, very dear to me. If I claim that I love Prabhupāda and yet I say his disciples, my Godbrothers, have nothing of Prabhupāda, then what is my future in this world? Then I'm in a hopeless condition—hopeless, because my personal memory of Prabhupāda's activities is diminishing, diminishing. But within ISKCON, and within service in separation, and in the qualities of my Godbrothers, Prabhupāda is very much present.

—*Bhavānanda Goswami*

37

At Bhaktivedanta Manor in London in 1973, Śrīla Prabhupāda held a series of conversations with respectable guests. Some of them were priests. During one young priest's visit, several of Prabhupāda's disciples began to argue with him on the basis of the Bible. The debate was whether the Bible condoned meat-eating. One of the devotees cited a passage in Genesis indicating that man was meant to protect the animals and eat vegetable foodstuffs, but the priest countered this by making reference to a later passage in the Bible regarding the covenant of Noah, where God allowed His followers to eat meat. Another devotee brought up the example of Daniel in the Old Testament and made a claim that he was a vegetarian. The priest also countered this with other Biblical arguments. The conversation then turned to Greek and Hebrew translations, with the priest countering the devotees' arguments and they again stating new arguments from different places in the Bible. During this excited exchange, Śrīla Prabhupāda was mostly silent. He had brought up his main argument that the Bible recommends "Thou shalt not kill," and that Jesus was upholding this law, but once the conversation got into many different areas of Biblical scholarship, Prabhupāda did not take part. Of course, the priest was not convinced by any of the Biblical arguments presented by the devotees, and after some time he left.

Later in the evening, Prabhupāda called the devotees into his room. Commenting on the discussion with the priest, Prabhupāda said that he did not think it was a good idea that the devotees had discussed so much on the basis of the Bible. Giving serious instructions to his preacher-disciples, Prabhupāda said that in the future, they should stick to the *Bhagavad-gītā* and make their arguments on this basis.

Soon after, in Paris, Prabhupāda met with more Christians. He regularly raised the point before them that the Bible states, "Thou shalt not kill." On one occasion, a Christian guest referred to the Gospel of St. John and the phrase, "In the beginning was the Word, and the Word was God." Prabhupāda liked this and related it to the Vedic conclusion that everything is created by the will of the Supreme.

In a lecture Prabhupāda gave in Paris, he quoted that verse from St. John, "In the beginning was the Word," and gave a Kṛṣṇa conscious purport. Some Christians in the audience, however, argued with Prabhupāda's purport and interpretation of the Bible.

During this same Paris visit, Śrīla Prabhupāda asked his secretary to begin writing a commentary on the Bible from the Kṛṣṇa conscious point of view. Prabhupāda was interested in the results, but then he called off the project, saying that the Christians would never accept our statements about the Bible.

Prabhupāda wanted Christians to appreciate the principles of Kṛṣṇa consciousness, and he wanted them to know that we appreciated them, but too much Bible scholarship or speculation by the devotees was not appropriate.

38

Tamāla Kṛṣṇa Goswami was the first disciple in ISKCON to receive sannyāsa while he was a member of the GBC. Śrīla Prabhupāda awarded it to him in Jaipur in 1971, and the initial concept was that Tamāla Kṛṣṇa Goswami would renounce his managerial responsibilities and simply travel and preach. After a brief, successful tour in Gujarat, he returned to see Śrīla Prabhupāda in Bombay. Because his ex-wife was a devotee in Bombay, Tamāla Kṛṣṇa Goswami thought that he could not actually go in person to the temple, so he sent his assistant, while he himself waited at the train station. When Prabhupāda heard, however, that he was waiting at the train station, he sent a devotee to pick him up and bring him to him.

As soon as Tamāla Kṛṣṇa Goswami entered Śrīla Prabhupāda's room and began to bow before his spiritual master, Śrīla Prabhupāda said, "There is no difficulty in this regard."

Prabhupāda explained, "The temple is a neutral place where they come in any case, in any situation. So there is no wrong."

Prabhupāda was pleased that his *sannyāsī* disciple was strict in his vow, but he reassured him that there was no harm in being in the same temple as his ex-wife. The *sannyāsa* initiation had been very humbling to Tamāla Kṛṣṇa Goswami, and since he was no longer a leading manager, he took his seat near the rear of the room. Prabhupāda had been talking to a roomful of devotees, but now he asked that everyone leave the room. He then asked Tamāla Kṛṣṇa Goswami to privately give his report on the recent preaching. The fact that Prabhupāda had asked the others to leave was unusual and indicated his special feeling about the *sannyāsa* preaching.

Tamāla Kṛṣṇa Goswami reported that they had enrolled eight members in about seven days. They held a big *paṇḍāl* lecture program that five thousand people had attended, and the governor of Gujarat, Narasingha Narayan, had been the chief guest. Prabhupāda was pleased to see photographs of these events as well as the newspaper clippings. He leaned back, satisfied, and said, "Now I can retire without any anxiety. Kirtanānanda and Brahmānanda and yourself are all preaching nicely. Everything will go on."

"Śrīla Prabhupāda," said Tamāla Kṛṣṇa Goswami, "I think I have to go now, because I want to go ahead of you to Madras, so I can be there to receive you in your next program."

"Yes, go now."

After Tamāla Kṛṣṇa Goswami offered his obeisances, Prabhupāda got up from behind his desk and embraced his disciple. Resting his head on one shoulder and then on the other shoulder of his disciple, Prabhupāda then released him from his embrace and said, "Now take this *sannyāsa-mantra* in your heart. Go everywhere and preach."

39

LITTLE DROPS *of* NECTAR

Within a few months of taking *sannyāsa,* Tamāla Kṛṣṇa Goswami was drawn back into ISKCON management. Too much was happening and the demands were too great for Śrīla Prabhupāda to allow him to renounce the heavy duties of Indian management. At one point, however, it became, from Tamāla Kṛṣṇa Goswami's viewpoint, an overburden.

Prabhupāda was allowing Girirāja to return to America because he had jaundice, and Girirāja's replacement, Mohanānanda, had also decided to quit India because it was too difficult for him. As Tamāla Kṛṣṇa Goswami was GBC for India, all of the Indian management was on him, and at the same time he now had to personally manage Bombay. Prabhupāda also told him that the GBC should personally collect funds.

In great anxiety, Tamāla Kṛṣṇa Goswami went before Śrīla Prabhupāda and began to cry.

"Prabhupāda, it is hopeless," he said. "How can I do it? It's impossible. How can I do so many things?"

Prabhupāda sat back and said, "This is very good. You should pray to be entangled in Kṛṣṇa's service so that there is not a free moment for *māyā* to attack."

During the cornerstone-laying ceremony in Māyāpur, Girirāja went to see Śrīla Prabhupāda in his grass hut. Prabhupāda told him that during the time of the British Empire there were three states in India—Madras, Bombay, and Calcutta—and there was one governor in charge of each state. "Which state do you want?" asked Śrīla Prabhupāda. Girirāja had always followed his authorities and had never before made any important decisions. He had no idea which to decide, so he said, "Prabhupāda, I will do whatever you want me to do."

"No," said Prabhupāda. "I want you to decide."

Girirāja meditated on his choice for about a week, but still he couldn't decide. He hatched a plan, however, to trick Śrīla Prabhupāda into deciding for him.

"I was thinking of going to Bombay," said Girirāja.

Girirāja's idea was that by mentioning Bombay, Prabhupāda's face would make some expression that would show Girirāja what Śrīla Prabhupāda wanted him to do, but Prabhupāda didn't show any expression at all. He only said, "That's all right."

"But then again," said Girirāja, "I was also thinking of going back to Madras." As with his Bombay choice, Girirāja gave some feasible reasons why he should go to Madras. He waited to see if Prabhupāda would reveal himself, but again there was no expression. "Yes," said Prabhupāda, "that is all right."

Then Girirāja realized that it wasn't going to work.

"I was thinking of staying in Calcutta," said Girirāja, "because . . . " But again the same thing. Prabhupāda did not show even the slightest hint of any expression that would reveal what he wanted.

"That's all right," said Prabhupāda.

At this point, Girirāja felt ashamed of trying to trick his spiritual master, but he was also exhilarated because he could see that Prabhupāda was so great and perfect that he could not be tricked by his foolish disciple.

40

LITTLE DROPS *of* NECTAR

In India Prabhupāda proposed that the devotees set up a library in a separate building. It would house all of Prabhupāda's books as well as all the books of the great *ācāryas,* including the *Upaniṣads* and other Vedic literatures. He even said that Śaṅkara's works could be included, but not anything from modern popular swamis and political leaders who claim to be spiritual writers.

"They're all rascals," Prabhupāda said. "The *Vedas* instruct us that we should not even look at their faces."

"But doesn't Caitanya Mahāprabhu say that if one even reads Śaṅkara's books, he'll be doomed?" asked Hari Śauri.

Prabhupāda replied, "Not if he reads with proper understanding. We can read to know what is their philosophy."

During a short visit to Boston in 1971, Prabhupāda gave the devotees a gift for their altar.

Brahmānanda had asked Prabhupāda why he always applied his Vaiṣṇava *tilaka* by using water from an old jar.

Prabhupāda replied, "I will give it to you. It is Gaṅgā water and never decomposes."

Brahmānanda thankfully accepted the jar of water. "Thank you, Śrīla Prabhupāda. We will get a silver container for it."

"No," said Prabhupāda. "Put it on the altar as it is."

So the devotees placed the jar, which was clearly labeled "Maxwell House Coffee," on the altar alongside the Rādhā-Kṛṣṇa Deities and all the other standard paraphernalia. Sometimes visitors to the temple would ask about the significance of the Maxwell House jar on the worshipable altar, and the devotees would proudly and gladly explain that it was a gift from Śrīla Prabhupāda.

When Śrīla Prabhupāda began the worship of *śālagrāma-śilā* in Māyāpur, he did not give much instruction to the *pūjārīs*.

"Give some *tulasī*," he said, "and then you can give this water drip." He meant that the *śālagrāma* could receive a daily watering as does *tulasī* during the month of Vaiśākha. "*Śālagrāma-śilā* means mantra," said Prabhupāda. "Mantra, sleeping, mantra, sleeping, mantra, sleeping . . . " Prabhupāda started laughing. He explained that *śālagrāma-śilās* are worshiped not so much in the temple, but privately. A *brāhmaṇa* will do his *pūjā* and then put the *śilā* away in a box, and then again at a later time take Him out and do *pūjā,* and then put Him away in a box. "Mantra, sleeping," laughed Prabhupāda. "this is *śālagrāma* worship."

41

PRABHUPĀDA SAID

On Reading Prabhupāda's Books and Becoming Strong by Following the Spiritual Principles

"I think it is very obvious, and you have admitted, that the problem is you are not following the basic principles for our Society. The fact that you have not chanted your rounds for a long time is enough to make you without any spiritual strength."

—*Letter of May 26, 1975*

"You say you want to go to preach to the Mayavadi swamis, but if you go to those rascals they will convert you. You are not so strong that you can convince them and convert them from their foolishness. It is distinctly said in the *Bhagavad-gita* that the purpose of Vedic knowledge is to understand Krsna, *vedais ca sarvair aham eva vedyah* (Bg. 15.5). So we are presenting Krsna in so many ways, politically, socially, economically, philosophically, and religiously, etc. We are describing Him in seventy-five books of four hundred pages each. Better read these books thoroughly and be firmly convinced yourself before going to these demons for convincing them. If you are weak yourself while trying to convert them, you will be converted by them. Don't try any hard task before you are very strong. Chant sixteen rounds daily. Follow the rules and regulations and read our books. Don't become a very big preacher immediately."

—*Letter of May 20, 1975*

On Devotees and the Bodily Concept

"Why should you be sorry if someone says you are an Indian and he is an American, and that Indians are no good but Americans are good? Why be affected by bodily relationships? Śrī Caitanya Mahaprabhu has advised us—and as an older grown-up student you should know it—that we have to become humbler than a blade of grass and more tolerant than a tree. Then we can execute our service and chant Hare Krsna.

"If Indians are bad, then I am also bad, as I am an Indian. But they have accepted an Indian as their guru. So Indians are both bad and good according to the behavior. They accused you as bad because you are Indian, yet they have accepted a bad Indian as guru. Don't be afflicted by all these external features of our bodily relationship. Be steady in Krsna consciousness and do your duty, and you may be blessed by Sri Caitanya Mahaprabhu and Krsna and make your life successful. We are neither Indian nor American; our real identity is that we are all servants of Krsna."

—*Letter of February 7, 1974*

"You have asked what is the origin of the black race. This is not an important question. Why should you be curious about the temporary body? If I am very interested in knowing about my clothing that I am wearing only temporarily, it is not a very important thing. We have had many bodies, which we change like sets of clothes. To be very absorbed in the present body one has, whether it is black or white or yellow, is not a sign of a wise person or a Krsna conscious devotee. As to whether the personality of Kali was black (African), it may not have been so. After all, Krsna is black also, although His body is different, He is *sac-cid-ananda*. So our inquiry should be to the point of Krsna, not in reference to the so-called race or religion or nationality of this temporary miserable body."

—*Letter of May 1, 1974*

42

ŚRĪLA PRABHUPĀDA TELLS A STORY

As a young *brahmacārī* in a young ISKCON movement, Tamāla Kṛṣṇa asked Śrīla Prabhupāda, "What is it like in the spiritual word, in Kṛṣṇaloka?"

Prabhupāda replied, "There are no draft boards there." The devotees laughed at Prabhupāda's witty pertinence. Śrīla Prabhupāda then told a story about a Christian missionary preaching among coal miners. The missionary began a fire-and-brimstone speech by telling the miners that a sinful person would have to go to hell and could only be saved if he surrendered to Jesus Christ.

On hearing the name Jesus Christ, one of the miners asked, "What is his number?" Since everyone in the mining company was assigned a number, the miners could not imagine Jesus Christ being anyone other than a mine worker.

The missionary tried again, by describing the misery of hell.

"Hell," he said, "is very dark and damp."

The miners looked back at the missionary without concern. His description of hell sounded just like the mine, which they already knew. Then the missionary understood that he was preaching to people with a very limited conception of reality, so he would have to address their actual experience.

"And in hell," he said, "there are no newspapers!"

"Oh, horrible! Very frightening!" the miners exclaimed.

Śrīla Prabhupāda's joke made the devotees laugh, and they also appreciated that a preacher has to think carefully when addressing an audience and speak according to time, place, and circumstance. But personally, for Tamāla Kṛṣṇa and the other young men, it was also a great relief to think that there *was* a spiritual world where they would not be in anxiety about being drafted into the army.

43

PERSONAL

His Eyes

In *The Nectar of Devotion,* Rūpa Gosvāmī states that by the glance of great souls people can become liberated. So it was with Śrīla Prabhupāda.

Prabhupāda's glance functioned both as the thunderbolt and the rose. If a devotee went before Śrīla Prabhupāda and he was not entirely honest or open, or if he was trying to bluff his commitment to Kṛṣṇa, Śrīla Prabhupāda could penetrate through all this by a straight gaze into the devotee's eyes. Then the disciple would feel like a most foolish creature. He could not lie to Prabhupāda unless he became the most hard-hearted liar. One looked within himself and saw deficiency when faced with Prabhupāda's stern gaze.

Prabhupāda also expressed hurt in his eyes when a disciple disappointed him and when he saw the sufferings of the conditioned souls. His eyes became particularly expressive with spiritual emotions when he was telling a story or laughing or crying. As the poets say, the eyes are the "windows of the soul."

After visiting the Gītā-nāgarī farm, Prabhupāda later described how he saw a cow there with a very big udder. In describing the cow, Prabhupāda put his arms out to show the size, and he opened his eyes very wide in an almost childlike way. His listeners also became childlike, taking part in Śrīla Prabhupāda's wide-eyed appreciation.

There is a film of Śrīla Prabhupāda taking his disciples around to holy places in Vṛndāvana. He is seen telling pastimes of Kṛṣṇa, and his eyes are full of transcendental light; his eyes are full of spiritual play, love, and delight. Only a dead man can fail to see the bliss of Kṛṣṇa consciousness coming from Prabhupāda's eyes.

Everyone knew that pushing on Kṛṣṇa consciousness was great trouble for Prabhupāda—his travel, his anxiety, his hard work—and yet his glancing, smiling eyes showed that he was above the struggle.

From Prabhupāda's eyes one could get the impression that he was not actually a person of the world like everyone else. He was with Kṛṣṇa in the spiritual world. Looking into Prabhupāda's eyes gave one the impression that Prabhupāda was deeper than anyone else; he was guru. He knew and realized a depth we could not fathom, and he conveyed this through the language of the eyes.

People like to present themselves as better than they are. A person may speak religiously or speak many superlatives of himself or claim to be honest or sincere. Sometimes it can be detected by looking at people straight in the eyes whether they are actually afraid or dishonest. People therefore are often evasive and uncomfortable to look another person in the eye. Śrīla Prabhupāda could easily expose another's lack of Kṛṣṇa consciousness by looking at him. Yet when one looked into Prabhupāda's eyes, he could see only full Kṛṣṇa consciousness.

44

REALIZATIONS

My realization from my personal meetings with Śrīla Prabhupāda was that he related to me as I related to him. When I was humble, he was very merciful to me, but when I was proud, Prabhupāda smashed my pride.

When I first met Prabhupāda in the Calcutta temple in 1971, I went in and just sat down. He asked me who I was and if I had any questions. I said to him, 'Well, why not Buddhism?' I was a wise guy.

Prabhupāda answered, "What does a Buddhist believe?"

I tried to recall my college course, Philosophy 101. I said something about the eight-fold noble path and the four-fold. I kind of mumbled what I could about what the Buddha had said, but I was already defeated, because I couldn't even think what the Buddha had said.

The next time I met Prabhupāda was at the Māyāpur festival in 1972. After first meeting Prabhupāda, I'd begun chanting Hare Kṛṣṇa and I'd become a vegetarian. This time I wasn't so proud. I was thinking, "Actually, Prabhupāda may know the answers to all the secrets of life." I went in to see him with the mood that he was a perfect spiritual master. Although my surrender was only on a theoretical basis, I approached him submissively, the way it says in the *Bhagavad-gītā,* and I was also rendering service while I was staying in Māyāpur. Without knowing it, I was following the injunction of the *Gītā*. Therefore, naturally Prabhupāda reciprocated by rendering to me the Absolute Truth. Those conversations are all published in the book *Perfect Questions, Perfect Answers.* Prabhupāda was very, very merciful to me. He even said to me, "You are a very good boy."

The next time I saw Prabhupāda was again in Calcutta. By now I was much more respectful. When I went in to see him, he was drinking coconut juice. The first thing he did was give me some. I entered his room feeling myself very insignificant. Then Prabhupāda immediately gave me his own coconut juice to drink. It was just a little thing, but it really touched me.

Another time I met him in 1973 I was also feeling very insignificant. This was when Prabhupāda was in New York at the Brooklyn temple. He was walking from his quarters to the temple room and I was standing in the hallway packed with devotees. I was thinking, "I hope he doesn't even see me." When Prabhupāda walked by, we all offered obeisances. I kept my head all the way down, saying the prayers slowly to make sure that he would be past me by the time I would stand up, but what I didn't know was that Prabhupāda had stopped and was waiting for me. I slowly finished the prayers and sat up, and there was Prabhupāda right in front of me. He said, "Oh! You're here!" He put his arms around me and gave me a hug.

Another time, however, Prabhupāda smashed my false ego. He was on a walk in Denver and I joined him. Yadubara said, "Prabhupāda, here's that Peace Corps worker. He's here to see you again." On this occasion I was feeling very proud, thinking, "Yes, Prabhupāda will be very glad to see me." But Prabhupāda only said, "Oh." That was all he said.

One time I also met Prabhupāda in his room in New Orleans. On this occasion, I walked in insignificantly and sat in the back of the room. I didn't want Prabhupāda to see me. The room was full of devotees, including many leaders, so I hid in the back. But Prabhupāda saw me and he paused in the middle of his *darśana.* He said, "Come here." I moved up about a foot. Again he said, "No, come here." I inched forward a little more. Then Brahmānanda Swami turned and said, "Come here!" I wound up sitting right next to Prabhupāda, at his feet. He wanted me to sit there.

The time I was ready to get initiated, I was proud again. This was in 1976 and I was thinking, "Now Prabhupāda will be so pleased with me. This is wonderful." Prabhupāda did not personally perform the initiation ceremony. He was feeling ill, but he was sitting on the *vyāsāsana* and then was giving out cookies. I was not very far away from Prabhupāda, and I looked at him directly, thinking, "Now I'm here. I'm going to be initiated. Prabhupāda will be glad to see me." I looked right at Prabhupāda because before, he had recognized me in New Orleans and in the hallway at Henry Street in Brooklyn. I was thinking, "Now I will be recognized again." I was actually thinking like that. I can remember. When I looked straight at Śrīla Prabhupāda, he looked right through me. He didn't even see me. He looked directly through me. It was the most eerie feeling, Prabhupāda looking at me and not seeing me. It was the most severe chastisement he could give me for being proud.

So I am convinced that Prabhupāda related to me as I related to him. If I was humble, he was kind. When I was puffed up, he practically ignored me."

—*Brahmatīrtha dāsa Adhikārī*

45

In 1972 Ātreya Ṛṣi dāsa arranged for Bob Cohen (later Brahmatīrtha) and his wife to have a private *darśana* with Śrīla Prabhupāda. Bob Cohen's wife had been coming to the temple for several months, and she was determined that no one was going to make her chant Hare Kṛṣṇa. She only went to the temple because her husband went. The devotees would say, "Hare Kṛṣṇa, Barbara," and she would reply, "Hi."

It was only her and her husband and maybe eight or ten *sannyāsīs* in the room that day. Bob offered prostrated obeisances and Barbara only bowed her head. Śrīla Prabhupāda looked at her and said, "So you are interested in Kṛṣṇa consciousness?" She didn't understand a word he said. Everything had to be translated for her. Śrīla Prabhupāda spoke for maybe an hour, and Barbara was impressed by him, although she didn't know exactly why. She asked Prabhupāda a few questions, but was too new to really appreciate Kṛṣṇa consciousness at that time. Śrīla Prabhupāda was merciful to her. Later he passed out *rasagullās*. "Hold out your hand," he said to Barbara, and he placed a *rasagullā* in her hand.

Then it was time for him to leave. Bob Cohen was going to be driving Śrīla Prabhupāda to the airport and everyone else was leaving the room. Barbara lingered around the room until everyone was out, and then she turned to Prabhupāda, folded her hands, looked him right in the eye, and very deliberately said, "Hare Kṛṣṇa." With an expression of welcome, Prabhupāda replied, "*Jaya*!" Somehow, Barbara was sure that Śrīla Prabhupāda knew she had never willingly chanted Hare Kṛṣṇa before and that this was the first time she had really chanted. This knowing and personal reciprocation seemed very wonderful to her, and she at once became determined to try and become a devotee.

46

When Śrutakīrti was serving as Prabhupāda's personal servant, he often felt embarrassed by the tremendous demonstration of love which the devotees offered to Prabhupāda, whereas Śrutakīrti himself felt a lack of love. Especially in arrival scenes at the airport, dozens of devotees would be dancing around, chanting, crying, and falling down on the ground. It was an amazing sight of love for Śrīla Prabhupāda. On one of these occasions, while accompanying Śrīla Prabhupāda, Śrutakīrti began to feel very sorry for himself. He thought that all these devotees were dancing and chanting, and here he was, walking beside Śrīla Prabhupāda, but he had no feeling, no real love. This began to disturb his mind.

One day during the massage, Śrutakīrti expressed it to Prabhupāda.

"Śrīla Prabhupāda, all these devotees have such love for you. It makes me feel so bad. I have none of this love. When I am with you, I can see everyone dancing and chanting and crying, but I have so much association and yet I don't feel that this is there." He was hoping that Prabhupāda would say something or do something, but Prabhupāda said nothing. He went on massaging and finished. Then Prabhupāda went and bathed. After putting on his *tilaka* and chanting his *gāyatrī,* Prabhupāda called Śrutakīrti into the room.

"So, do you like serving me?" said Prabhupāda.

"Oh, yes, Prabhupāda," said Śrutakīrti. "I like serving you very much."

"Then," said Prabhupāda, "that is love. Everyone can do so many things . . . singing, dancing, jumping up and down, but you are actually doing something. Isn't this love?"

"I guess so, Śrīla Prabhupāda."

"So you just do your service," said Prabhupāda. "That is all that is necessary. That is what love means—to do service."

47

Viśāla dāsa wanted to find an astrologer in Vṛndāvana. Without consulting Śrīla Prabhupāda, he found one who was wearing *tilaka* and chanting Hare Kṛṣṇa. Viśāla wanted to get something he had seen other residents of Vṛndāvana wearing, a charm you wear around your neck that has on it all the mantras of the demigods. It was supposed to counteract all the bad influence of the planets. The astrologer sold him one of these neckpieces, and it all sounded very nice. He told Viśāla to dip it into the Yamunā and to have an *ārati* at twelve noon.

Soon after this, Brahmānanda Mahārāja noticed Viśāla's new ornament.

"Viśāla," said Brahmānanda Swami, "what's that you have around your neck?" When Viśāla told him, Brahmānanda Swami replied, "Prabhupāda says we don't have to add anything to this process." At these words Viśāla became disturbed. He thought that Brahmānanda Swami was right and he also felt embarrassed.

"Why are you wearing this?" Brahmānanda Swami demanded. Viśāla replied that he would like to talk to Prabhupāda and he asked if he could have an appointment.

When Viśāla went to see Prabhupāda, Śrīla Prabhupāda asked him how much he had paid the astrologer and what he had said. Viśāla said the astrologer had claimed the charm would ward off the ill effects of the planets.

"Kṛṣṇa consciousness is beyond astrology," said Prabhupāda. "If you surrender to Kṛṣṇa, with a slight kick Kṛṣṇa can annihilate 100,000 Rāhu planets." So Viśāla put aside his astrological neckpiece and just depended on Prabhupāda and Kṛṣṇa.

Soon after, a Godbrother showed Viśāla a letter he had received from Prabhupāda about the same subject matter: "Astrology will not save you at the time of death. My Guru Maharaja was a great astrologer and astronomer, but he gave it all up. It is meant for the *karmis*. We have no interest in such things."

48

LITTLE DROPS *of* NECTAR

Tamāla Kṛṣṇa Goswami explains the difficulties of serving at Māyāpur when it was in its beginning days. He and Jayapatāka Mahārāja had to go out themselves to different parts of India and get wagon loads of stone chips, steel, sand, and cement. Even before obtaining the materials, they first had to get government sanction, which was not easy. It was also difficult to get any wagons or trains since there was a shortage. Somehow or other, they managed to gather some materials, and they proudly sent Prabhupāda a photograph. These materials were so precious that the devotees would sleep on top of the stone chips and steel at night to protect them from thieves. Prabhupāda wrote back a letter saying, "What is the use of so many pictures? Where is the building?"

Prabhupāda gave some money to begin the construction, but he told them that they had to raise all the funds. "Why are you sitting there?" Prabhupāda wrote in another letter to Tamāla Kṛṣṇa Goswami. "Now go out and collect more money." Even when Prabhupāda donated money, the devotees knew he did not want to, and they felt bad for asking.

"You are all just like widows," Prabhupāda told them sarcastically. "Better you all go to Māyāpur and sit there, and I will earn the money and maintain you all."

One day in France, Bhagavān dāsa and other disciples walked into Prabhupāda's room and found Prabhupāda looking up meditatively at the chandeliers. "Look at the chandelier," he said. "You should make the universal model for the planetarium just like that. The planets are hanging just like crystals in the chandelier."

After serving for a while in India, Girirāja became restless. He approached Prabhupāda one day during his massage.

"Śrīla Prabhupāda," asked Girirāja, "I have been discussing with Śyāmasundara and Tamāla Kṛṣṇa Goswami, and I was thinking that maybe I should go back to the West and preach in colleges and universities to the professors and writers."

Prabhupāda replied, "A devotee may be massaging Kṛṣṇa's left leg, and then he may think, 'Now I will massage Kṛṣṇa's right leg.' Of course, that is also service to Kṛṣṇa. But Kṛṣṇa may feel that He wants more massaging on His left leg still."

"Well, if that's the case," said Girirāja obediently, "if you want me to stay in India, I will stay. That's why I was asking. I wanted to know what you want."

"Yes," said Prabhupāda. "India is our most important work right now."

49

ŚRĪLA PRABHUPĀDA TELLS SHORT STORIES

"Human life means somebody is being killed, so he should be immediately warned, thinking, worried, 'Oh, my turn is coming, let me go away.' There is one story in this connection. Not stories, these are facts.

"A hunter spread his net. Some little birds fell down from the nest, and they are crying, they are crying. So when the father and mother came, they saw their children in danger. 'They are caught by the net of the hunter.' So the mother immediately jumped over it to save the children, and she was also captured. Then the father saw, 'Now if I go to save them, I will be captured. Let me go away. Let me take *sannyāsa*. That's all.' That is intelligence. You cannot give protection to your family, your society."

—*Lecture of February 26, 1976*

"I beg to apologize on behalf of my student and I shall solicit the pleasure of your goodness to visit our temple regularly. One should not be angry and eat his meals on the floor just because someone has stolen his plate. This is a Bengali saying. The logic is that if one's plates are stolen by a thief, he does not become angry and decide not to purchase new plates and eat on the floor."

—*Letter of August 31, 1975*

50

PRABHUPĀDA'S PERSONAL STAMP ON ISKCON

Early in ISKCON history, two foolish disciples broke away from the movement and remarked, "This is not the society for Kṛṣṇa consciousness. It's the society for Prabhupāda consciousness." Another disciple replied, "What's wrong with Prabhupāda consciousness? The guru is the representative of Kṛṣṇa."

Prabhupāda created the name ISKCON as well as the phrase "Kṛṣṇa consciousness," which he coined from a translation of a verse by Rūpa Gosvāmī. He shaped the society in his own personal way. He sometimes said that he never demanded that his disciples wear *dhotīs,* and yet they did. They did because they wanted to follow Śrīla Prabhupāda. A member of the Brahma-Madhva-Gauḍīya *sampradāya* and a disciple of Bhaktisiddhānta Sarasvatī Ṭhākura, Prabhupāda wrote his purports after great *ācāryas* like Jīva Gosvāmī and Baladeva Vidyābhūṣaṇa. Yet he was an individual person. Thus his society, ISKCON, bears his personal stamp. His particular viewpoint, for example, on why his Godbrothers did not vigorously follow the order of Bhaktisiddhānta Sarasvatī Ṭhākura, and why they did not assist Prabhupāda when he began to actually spread the worldwide movement—this viewpoint of the history is adopted by Prabhupāda's followers.

He intended his personal stamp to last long into the future. He worked hard so that things would go on as he had set them up, even after his disappearance. He built temples to last for generations and he set up a school system, intending that it would last as he introduced it. He said that his books would provide the foundation of civilization for ten thousand years.

These statements by Prabhupāda do not exclude the possibility that other teachers may come and make great contributions, but neither should we overlook the fact that Śrīla Prabhupāda is the only founder-*ācārya* of ISKCON. A special flavor is found in the Bhaktivedanta purports, and its essence is savored while its teachings are followed by Prabhupāda's *paramparā* descendants. Specific personal experiences of Prabhupāda are found in his purports as he drew examples for his teachings. These are also a part of the accumulated knowledge which may be called *smṛti.*

"Do as I am doing," said Prabhupāda. It's not that he wanted a cult of personal worship of himself, but because he set the standard for his GBC leaders and others, he wanted his followers to do as he was doing. His intention was that his followers should work together to keep what he gave. He had received the blessings of Lord Caitanya Mahāprabhu, and he wanted that success to be carried out by his followers. He also gave his own example when he said that any one person can go and open a center as he had done, one man alone lecturing, cooking, playing the *mṛdaṅga,* etc. He also gave his own life as an example when he encouraged his disciples to go to foreign countries and endure difficulties. He encouraged them by saying he had done the same thing when he had come alone to America. Every devotee has to develop himself to become a spiritual person and Śrīla Prabhupāda is the best example of that.

The guru is a very personal teacher and one may differ from another. For example, Śrīla Prabhupāda translated *The Nectar of Devotion,* and yet in his personal demonstration of Kṛṣṇa consciousness, he excluded some of the injunctions in *The Nectar of Devotion,* saying that they were not practical according to time and place. Therefore Śrīla Prabhupāda's emphasis on what should be done and what should not be done is an expert selection by an expert *ācārya.* Prabhupāda's personal stress on priorities in preaching, such as book printing and distribution, appear not to be simply personal with Śrīla Prabhupāda, and yet they are done *his* way. Prabhupāda wanted that.

Śrīla Prabhupāda lived in a very deliberate way as an example, desiring that his followers should do as he did. He also said that his followers should expand beyond what he himself had done. Prabhupāda established that a very important aspect of preaching was to defeat the scientists' speculation that life comes from matter, but he left it to his Bhaktivedanta Institute scientist-disciples to expand on this instruction and to write books in which the scientists would be defeated in their own scientific terms. Prabhupāda encouraged his disciples to paint pictures of Kṛṣṇa and to become great artists, to build buildings for Kṛṣṇa and to become great architects and engineers, and all this was done personally under his jurisdiction.

Prabhupāda Nectar 4

āpane ācare keha, nā kare pracāra
pracāra karena keha, nā karena ācāra

'ācāra,' 'pracāra,'—nāmera karaha 'dui' kārya
tumi—sarva-guru, tumi jagatera ārya

Some behave very well but do not preach the cult of Kṛṣṇa consciousness, whereas others preach but do not behave properly. You simultaneously perform both duties in relation to the holy name by your personal behavior and by your preaching. Therefore you are the spiritual master of the entire world, for you are the most advanced devotee in the world.

Cc. *Antya-līlā,* 4.102–3

1

In 1972, when Śrīla Prabhupāda was residing at the home of Kartikeya Mahadevia in Bombay, an unusual incident occured one morning. Prabhupāda's secretary, Śyāmasundara dāsa, and servant, Śrutakīrti dāsa, had taken Prabhupāda to Chowpatti Beach for his morning walk. Śyāmasundara had driven them in Mr. Mahadevia's car, one of those black Ambassadors popular throughout India. When they were ready to return, Śyāmasundara found that he couldn't start the car engine. He fitted the key into the ignition, but the key wouldn't turn. Śyāmasundara tried jamming, cursing, and forcing the key until he became completely frustrated.

"It's not going to work, Śrīla Prabhupāda," he said. "I'll go get a taxi." He dashed out of the car, leaving Śrīla Prabhupāda chanting *japa* in the back seat with Śrutakīrti. After a few minutes, two Indian gentlemen in suits and ties approached the car, opened the front door, and got in. Śrutakīrti became alarmed, but Śrīla Prabhupāda began a friendly talk with them in Hindi. When the man put his key in the ignition, started the car, and drove off, Śrutakīrti finally understood what had happened. Śyāmasundara had led Śrīla Prabhupāda to the wrong car! When the real owners of the black Ambassador heard from Śrīla Prabhupāda his explanation, they were honored and insisted driving Prabhupāda back to Mr. Mahadevia's.

Śrutakīrti tried apologizing for what had happened, but one of the men turned and replied, "Oh, no, this is very nice opportunity for us to do some *sevā* for Swamijī."

Śrīla Prabhupāda then began to explain the basis of Kṛṣṇa consciousness and his worldwide mission, and the men listened attentively.

When they arrived at Mr. Mahadevia's building, Śrīla Prabhupāda invited the men up to take some *prasādam*.

"No, we have to go to the office, but thank you very much, Swamijī."

"Yes, thank you, Swamiji. Hare Kṛṣṇa!"

After the pleasant incident, Śrīla Prabhupāda remarked to his servant, "This is the difference between India and America. In America if we had gotten into someone's car, we would have been in great difficulty."

2

Usually Śrīla Prabhupāda accepted devotees for initiation based on the temple president's recommendation, but sometimes he personally interviewed devotees to see if they were fit. At least that seemed to be his intention in Los Angeles when he called Śubhānanda dāsa, Śrīnātha dāsa, and another devotee into his room in June of 1971 before awarding them their brahminical initiation.

"What is your conception of Kṛṣṇa?" Śrīla Prabhupāda asked, turning to Śubhānanda.

"He is the Supreme Personality of Godhead," Śubhānanda replied, and he enumerated Kṛṣṇa's six qualities—all strength, all beauty, all knowledge, all wealth, all fame, and all renunciation.

"Thank you," said Śrīla Prabhupāda.

He then turned to Śrīnātha and asked, "Who is Lord Caitanya?"

Śrīnātha replied confidently, "Lord Caitanya is the most munificent incarnation of Kṛṣṇa."

"No," said Prabhupāda. Śrīnātha was surprised. "Not incarnation," Prabhupāda said, "He is Kṛṣṇa Himself." At first Śrīnātha thought to defend himself, remembering how Prabhupāda used the word "incarnation" for Lord Caitanya in *Teachings of Lord Caitanya*, but then he realized that he should not argue with the spiritual master. Śrīla Prabhupāda was correcting and refining his improper understanding.

Then Śrīla Prabhupāda briefly explained that there is no difference between Lord Kṛṣṇa and Lord Caitanya.

"Have you read the *Bhāgavatam*?" Prabhupāda addressed all three of them, and they nodded yes.

"Have you read the chapter on incarnations and expansions?" Again they all nodded and said yes.

"Kṛṣṇa is the source of all incarnations and expansions," said Śubhānanda, and Prabhupāda again replied, "Thank you."

"All glories to you, Śrīla Prabhupāda!" they said upon leaving.

"Jaya," Prabhupāda replied.

Conferring among themselves, the devotees agreed that Śrīla Prabhupāda's requirements seemed very little. They had not been devotees very long, and they had been born and raised in the degraded Western culture. Yet it had been so simple. He had only asked, *"Do you know who Kṛṣṇa is? Who is Lord Caitanya? How are They different?"* It required no great learning or austerities, but faith that Kṛṣṇa is the Supreme Personality of Godhead and Lord Caitanya is Kṛṣṇa Himself.

3

In July 1976, when Śrīla Prabhupāda visited New Vrindaban, he was feeling ill. His secretary announced there would be no open meeting that night. It was raining, and Prabhupāda stayed in a little house they had provided. He sat in the living room on a couch while Pradyumna dāsa read to him from *Bhagavad-gītā As It Is*. A few other devotees were also in the room. Prabhupāda had his hand on his head and he was looking down. Pradyumna read for about an hour and Prabhupāda said nothing. Everyone present was painfully aware that Prabhupāda wasn't feeling well, and they all knew he was being very merciful just to sit with them for a while.

Prabhupāda's secretary finally said, "Thank you very much for your association, Śrīla Prabhupāda." This was an obvious hint for everyone to leave.

"All glories to Śrīla Prabhupāda," said another devotee, and everyone bowed down and prepared to leave.

"Any questions?" said Prabhupāda, and he lifted his head. Devotees happily sat back down and started asking Prabhupāda philosophical questions. One of the questions was about the coming of Kali-yuga.

"Go get the *Bhāgavatam*," said Śrīla Prabhupāda. Pradyumna began reading a list of the coming calamities of Kali-yuga. At every point, Śrīla Prabhupāda stopped him and gave an explanation. Within a few minutes Śrīla Prabhupāda was preaching dynamically and everyone forgot how sick he had been.

He spoke of how Vyāsadeva could see the future. Therefore he predicted that the standard of beauty would be long hair. In the course of the conversation, Śrīla Prabhupāda also praised living at New Vrindaban, the favorite topic of the New Vrindaban devotees. He said that in India, if people live on the banks of a sacred river like the Ganges, they will travel a long distance to go to a *tīrtha*, or place of pilgrimage. The Ganges River flows through Calcutta, he said, but the people of Calcutta will go all the way to Hardwar to bathe in the same Ganges. Prabhupāda assured the New Vrindaban devotees that their place was nondifferent from Vṛndāvana and that they had no need to go on any other pilgrimage.

"You are already living in a sacred place."

After the rainy-night *darśana*, Rādhānātha remarked, "Prabhupāda was saying so many wonderful things!"

4

Anyone who has heard Śrīla Prabhupāda knows that he quoted many Sanskrit verses while preaching, but sometimes *after* preaching, he would *murmur* a verse or a portion of a verse which might serve as a final comment, a footnote, or merely a sign that His Divine Grace was absorbed in a chain of Kṛṣṇa conscious thought. *Hṛṣīkeṇa hṛṣīkeśa-sevanam* . . . Śrīla Prabhupāda might be dealing with someone's personal problems, ISKCON management or whatever, and the quotation could be viewed as a reminder; whatever Śrīla Prabhupāda did or said, he was always mindful that he was acting as the servant of Kṛṣṇa and the *ācāryas* in Kṛṣṇa's disciplic chain.

Satsvarūpa dāsa Goswami recalls being present during one of Śrīla Prabhupāda's ecstatic Sanskrit murmurings. It was in Dallas in 1971 and Śrīla Prabhupāda had been reprimanding Satsvarūpa for different mistakes he had made in the management. They then left the room together to go look at the Deities of Rādhā-Kālachandjī, which were being prepared for installation. As they walked through the hall, Prabhupāda murmured *gṛheṣu gṛha-medīnām* . . . This was the verse he had lectured on in that morning's *Bhāgavatam* class, but by Prabhupāda's murmuring it like a little song, Satsvarūpa felt assured that Prabhupāda was completely pure and transcendental and that his anger was simply meant for his disciple's benefit.

Śrīla Prabhupāda also took genuine pleasure in quoting Sanskrit verses. Jayādvaita Swami recalls one time being with Prabhupāda in his room in Brooklyn when Prabhupāda quoted a verse by Rūpa Gosvāmī. It was a verse that Prabhupāda quoted often, but as he quoted it yet again, the devotees could see Prabhupāda was relishing a deep, fresh pleasure. To Śrīla Prabhupāda it seemed to be another opportunity to associate with Rūpa Gosvāmī and serve him by passing on his teachings to others.

Prabhupāda used to say, "I have already given the example several times . . . " Several! This phrase invariably introduced an example that devotees had heard so many times they had long ago lost count. But for Śrīla Prabhupāda there was no need to invent anything new. "The same example . . . " was still serviceable, still perfect, still worth quoting yet again.

5

Letters from Disciples

"I am beginning to understand that anything in connection with Srila Prabhupada is truly nectarean. It is his causeless mercy that I have finally found a preaching engagement I am really attached to—that is, telling other devotees about the glorious activities of our beloved spiritual master. Every word spoken and step taken by him is a source of pleasure for thousands of disciples around the world. It is Prabhupada alone who can turn wretched lives into something worthwhile. He accepts the most insignificant service as a great deal.

" . . . While engaged in talking about New Vrindaban during Prabhupada's massage yesterday I mentioned how we used to do cow *aratis*. At that point Prabhupada frowned. I asked if they were okay to do and he said no. I asked if there was anything special to do for the cows. He said keep them clean, brush them nicely, bathe them, and also you can polish their horns and hooves.

"Prabhupada also received your *sandesa* yesterday, and I put two on his plate last night at his request, along with pineapple and hot milk. He bit into one and said Kirtanananda Maharaja made first-class *sandesa*. He then said how *sandesa* and *rasagulla* are called Bengali sweets and how they are 'standard.' He has been criticizing L.A.'s making of concocted sweets—sweets with puffed rice, carob, powdered milk, food coloring, peanut butter in different combinations that he did not care for. He said, 'I have given you *sandesa, rasagulla,* and sweet balls. These are standard sweets and are very good. Why do they go to these different things?' So last night I made cheese and turned it into *sandesa* this morning. I gave him one of the *sandesa* you had made and one I had made with his lunch. He ate both. When he was finished, I asked him how the *sandesa* was. His face lit up and he said, 'Did you make them?' I told him what I had done and he said they were very good. I am really happy because they are one of his favorite sweets."

— Letter by Śrutakīrti dāsa to Kīrtanānanda Mahārāja, September 27, 1972

"Here in Madras we were seated in Srila Prabhupada's room and His Divine Grace had just made an inspiring plea for Krsna consciousness. Then a clean-cut European in his twenties exclaimed, 'Yes, and then we can become more loving and less angry.' His Divine Grace replied, 'What is wrong with getting angry?' The boy was startled and stammered, 'Well, uh, if we are angry, it is hard to have peace of mind.' Prabhupada interrupted and said, 'Anyway, that is some speculation. Even Krsna Himself gets angry. We are part and parcel of Krsna, and the fact is that Krsna spoke the *Bhagavad-gita* to make Arjuna angry. Arjuna was not angry when he should have been. The whole *Gita* was spoken just to make Arjuna angry so he would fight. Similarly lust. In the *Bhagavad-gita* Krsna says that *kama* according to *dharma*, I am that lust.'"

—Letter by Girirāja Swami to Uddhava dāsa January 21, 1971

6

ŚRĪLA PRABHUPĀDA SAID

On Farming

"So take more land and engage them in agriculture, plowing by the bulls instead of tractor. Bulls can be engaged in plowing and transporting—nice bullock carts village to village for preaching. Make the farm the center and go ten miles this side, ten miles that side, ten miles this side, etc., with four bullock carts. Sell books and preach and live peacefully at the farm. People used to engage the bull for this purpose. So there was no problem which ways to utilize them. First of all, this artificial way should be stopped, and the bulls should be engaged in plowing and transporting and smashing the grains—to avoid machinery, petrol, machine oil, by nature's way."

— *Letter of January 3, 1977*

"Regarding the New Orleans farm, do not make sugar. Just boil it and make molasses. You can eat the molasses instead of sugar. Just boil it and keep it until granule forms and then keep in a pot. Don't try to make sugar and sell it. That will simply increase botheration."

—*Letter of November, 20, 1975*

"Yes, if our householders cannot distribute books, then let them live on the farm communities. They can produce thread for cloth, spinning, and other activities. But they must do something, not sit idly, for an idle brain is the devil's workshop."

— *Letter of April 12, 1977*

"Our cows are happy, therefore they give plenty of milk. Vedic civilization gives protection to all living creatures, especially the cows, because they render such valuable service to the human society in the shape of milk, without which no one can become healthy and strong. In your country the dog is protected and the cow is killed. The dog is passing stool and urine in the street, and he is considered the best friend, and the cow is all-pure, stool, urine, and milk, but they are taken to the slaughterhouse and killed for food. What kind of civilization is this? Therefore you have to preach against all this nonsense."

— *Letter of December 7, 1975*

"You can visit our farm projects at New Vrindaban and the farm in Port Royal, Pennsylvania. They do everything very nicely and you can develop your farm on their model. That you are growing all your grains is very good. It is my ambition that all devotees remain self-independent by producing vegetables, grains, milk, fruits, flowers and by weaving their own cloth on handlooms. This simple life is very nice. Simple village life saves time for other engagements like chanting Hare Krsna *maha-mantra.*"

— *Letter of August 23, 1976*

"When I was in Frankfurt, round our place I was happy to see the farms and the cows. Unfortunately they will kill the cows. So if we organize a farm without killing any cows, that will be a great example in that country. Instead of killing cows, if we let them live, we will get so many nutritional foodstuffs filled with vitamins. I have seen in New Vrindaban how happily our devotees are living there with free air, fresh vegetables, and ample milk, and simple living cottage. What you want more? We should not neglect the upkeep of the body, and we should save time to chant Hare Krsna. This mission should be propagated. Save time and chant Hare Krsna."

—*Letter of September 7, 1974*

7

ŚRĪLA PRABHUPĀDA TELLS A STORY

One time in India, while Śrīla Prabhupāda was staying in Māyāpur, two of Śrīla Prabhupāda's Western-born *sannyāsīs* visited a temple and heard an odd comment from a *pūjārī*. While Śrīla Prabhupāda's men were taking *darśana* of the Deities, the *pūjārī* seemed to appreciate their reverence and demeanor.

"Continue to render devotional service," the *pūjārī brāhmaṇa* advised them, "and maybe in your next life you will be born as a *brāhmaṇa*."

The disciples later went to Śrīla Prabhupāda and told him of the incident. Prabhupāda smiled and told a story.

Once there was an old lady who lived in a remote village. One day the British district magistrate visited her town. This old lady had been entangled in a quarrel regarding possession of land, which some of her relatives were trying to take from her. Friends advised that she see the magistrate and present the matter to him for a settlement. When she did so, the magistrate immediately ruled in her favor and made sure the land was put in her name. Delighted, the old lady attempted to bless the magistrate.

"I bless you," she said, "that in your next life you will become a police constable."

In the old lady's mind, Śrīla Prabhupāda explained, the office of police constable was the highest thing she could imagine. "Similarly," said Śrīla Prabhupāda, "these caste *brāhmaṇas* do not know that pure devotional service is much higher than being born as a *brāhmaṇa*."

8

PERSONAL

His Changing His Ways and His Staying the Same

Some devotees have analyzed that during Śrīla Prabhupāda's years with ISKCON (1966–1977), he passed through three stages. A first phase was when Śrīla Prabhupāda was the only responsible preacher or devotee and everyone turned to him as the sole spiritual guide with no intermediary. This was the way Śrīla Prabhupāda appeared to the devotees in the first New York temple and in the temple in San Francisco. As "Swamijī" he was lenient, he always seemed to have plenty of time to talk with anyone, and he only gradually requested his disciples to follow the rules and regulations. He was trying to get a movement started after a year in America, during which time no one had come forward; so if disciples left him alone to clean his own apartment or shared his bathroom, he tolerated it. During this time his dress was also distinct in certain ways from later. He did not wear *kūrtas*, but a *cādar* over his bare chest, or he wore an inexpensive turtleneck jersey that had been supplied by his followers. He rode with them on the buses and subways and trains, and he didn't travel very widely, but stayed in each center for months at a time.

This changed during the period when the movement grew quickly. From 1969 all the way to 1975, Śrīla Prabhupāda, by his own empowered endeavors, became a world leader of a major religion. It was a time of tremendous exertion for him. He revitalized India with Kṛṣṇa conscious preaching, personally traveling widely there and managing the construction of major temples. He also regularly made worldwide tours. As he initiated hundreds and thousands of disciples, he was not quite so accessible to the individual disciples as he had been in the early days. Now, by his arrangement, his leaders, especially the temple presidents, *sannyāsīs*, and his GBC, handled more of the affairs, although the final decisions and the burden for everything always rested with him.

The third phase was his gradual withdrawal from the more intense participation in the management. In one sense, the second phase of his full participation in the expansion of ISKCON always continued, but it is true that Śrīla Prabhupāda began to allow his GBC representatives to take over more and more. At least that was his desire. He expressed that he wanted to spend more time writing. He began to stay longer in India, where he seemed to feel more at home, and when he did make yearly tours to America and the West, he didn't become much involved in the management of the temple, but lectured. Gradually his public lectures were also something he assigned as the responsibility of older disciples, while Prabhupāda preached more to the devotees, giving them training as he went quickly from temple to temple. Now he no longer had to be the pioneer of every new opening in Kṛṣṇa consciousness; his disciples ranged far and wide over the globe to open new places, based on Śrīla Prabhupāda's credibility and armed with his books.

Then in the last year he clearly changed his mood of activity and stayed almost entirely in India as his bodily activities diminished. More and more he moved into his very last, departure pastime. He gathered a few disciples near him for intimate, personal service and made arrangements for the continuation of the movement after his disappearance.

While some of these changes in Prabhupāda's behavior over the years are undeniable, Prabhupāda had many unchangeable qualities. As he said, "There was never a time when I forgot Kṛṣṇa." Prabhupāda also said that he was always the same, even from the first days of his arrival in America. The only difference was that Kṛṣṇa sent men and money, and with these, Prabhupāda transformed the Kṛṣṇa conscious preaching, although he personally stayed the same. Śrīla Prabhupāda said, "ISKCON may be big, but I am small." He was always the pure person, the empowered preacher, and the kind well-wisher manifested in different roles as Kṛṣṇa required. He did not become in any way affected or spoiled by his success.

Over the years, Śrīla Prabhupāda began to wear nicer *sannyāsī* clothes, to ride in nicer cars, travel on jets, he accepted millions of dollars on behalf of Kṛṣṇa; but he remained the same, pure servant and used everything for the Lord without any enjoying tendency. Whatever was appropriate and useful for His service, he accepted. He always wanted the whole world to become Kṛṣṇa conscious, and he was ready to work for it constantly. He was always very sweet and considerate, and he was always in direct touch with Kṛṣṇa. He always carried his *japa* beads in a bag and chanted on them, and he always wore *kaṇṭhī-mālā* around his neck and *tilaka* on his forehead. He always worked on translating transcendental literatures such as *Śrīmad-Bhāgavatam,* rising in the early morning and dictating his Bhaktivedanta purports.

He never changed his philosophy the way speculating scientists or Western philosophers or stylish culture heroes and businessmen adjust theirs with time in order to stay popular. He always gave out the same precious product, the philosophy of Lord Caitanya and Lord Kṛṣṇa, exactly as he received it from his spiritual master. George Harrison noted and appreciated this quality in Prabhupāda when he stated, "He was always just speaking about Kṛṣṇa and it was coincidental who happened to be there. Whenever you saw him, he would always be the same. It wasn't that one time he would tell you to chant the Hare Kṛṣṇa mantra then the next time say, 'Oh, no, I made a mistake.' He was always the same."

We followers of Prabhupāda may also carefully learn this art from his *līlā*—how to keep up with the times and adjust according to time, person, and place, and yet how to keep our original Kṛṣṇa conscious personality intact. Prabhupāda's deep, unchanging convictions are miraculous when one considers how he didn't change in coming to America. He never changed his basic dress or eating or regulated living, despite advice from "swamis" who told him to do so. Also miraculous was his ability to make dynamic adjustments, such as giving his disciples a *japa* quota they could actually perform and his allowing equal rights of initiation to women.

All glories to the steady course of Śrīla Prabhupāda's pastimes in this world! All glories to his fixed position, more dependable than the steady orbit of the sun in the sky! And all glories to his transcendental intelligence in preaching by which he changed his ways according to the indications of Kṛṣṇa for the best results in presenting Kṛṣṇa consciousness to the unwilling conditioned souls! May his Kṛṣṇa conscious movement continue to reflect these two strengths of change and endurance.

9

Soon after the grand opening of the Krishna-Balaram temple, Śrīla Prabhupāda allowed the Punjab National Bank to open a branch within a large room of the Krishna-Balaram guesthouse, near Prabhupāda's residence building. The bank managers and their friends gathered, as well as many devotees, and a ribbon-cutting ceremony was observed. The devotees also distributed *prasādam* sweets. On this occasion, Prabhupāda gave a public speech, comparing the bank manager to Kuvera, the treasurer of the demigods.

Prabhupāda told the story of how Dhruva Mahārāja had been killing the Yakṣas "like anything." Svāyambhuva Manu had advised Dhruva to stop the killing, and Dhruva had complied. Then Kuvera personally came and offered Dhruva a benediction. Although the treasurer of the demigods was offering any boon that Dhruva might desire, however, Dhruva Mahārāja said, "Please give me your blessings that I can always be engaged in the service of Kṛṣṇa." Prabhupāda then said humbly that this was the same benediction he would like to ask of the local Kuvera, the manager of the bank.

On this same occasion, Śrīla Prabhupāda told a story of a man who had heard that "money attracts money." This man went to the bank to a place where a clerk was engaged in counting money. The man took his own money and threw it on top of the pile of cash. He then stood there motionless, watching the money for a long time. Finally the clerk asked him, "Sir, what are you doing?"

"I have heard that money attracts money, so I have thrown my money on the pile. Now I am waiting for the whole cash to come to me."

"Yes, it is a fact," said the clerk, "that money attracts money. Now *my* money has attracted *your* money!"

10

In his lectures, Prabhupāda often derided the "horseless carriage" civilization where cars go *whoosh-whoosh* back and forth on the highways and often end in fatal accidents. He also personally experienced the dangers of riding in cars.

One time on the way to Māyāpur, with Gargamuni driving, the car hit a man who was repairing the road. The man was not much hurt, but as Prabhupāda's car slowed down, the villagers barricaded the road and surrounded the car. Soon a crowd of Bengalis were shouting angrily around the car. Śrīla Prabhupāda rolled down his window and spoke out loudly in Bengali. After a while, Prabhupāda turned to Gargamuni and said, "Give them ten rupees." The ten rupees only produced more yelling and threatening.

"Give them ten more rupees," said Prabhupāda. After Gargamuni did that, Śrīla Prabhupāda instructed, "Now we can go." The car inched forward, the crowd parted, and Prabhupāda's party continued on after the horrifying experience.

Śrīla Prabhupāda then began reprimanding Gargamuni for driving too fast.

Another time, in America, while on a morning walk, Prabhupāda gave the same instruction. Rādhā-vallabha dāsa was reminiscing about a time when he had been speeding ninety-five miles an hour in order to greet Śrīla Prabhupāda at the airport in New York. An angry state trooper had stopped him, Rādhā-vallabha said, but when the trooper saw that Rādhā-vallabha was a Hare Kṛṣṇa devotee and heard that he was on the way to see Prabhupāda, he let him go.

Śrīla Prabhupāda did not seem impressed or interested in his story. "Don't speed," he replied. "Don't take advantage."

"Well, we were going to pick you up at the airport," said Rādhā-vallabha, smiling.

"That's all right," he said, "don't speed."

A few years earlier, when a devotee was killed in a car crash because of negligence during an all-night drive, Śrīla Prabhupāda lamented at the loss of a Vaiṣṇava, a disciple named Jaya Gopāla. In a letter he wrote after that tragedy, Śrīla Prabhupāda said whatever gains had been made by speeding all night were lost beyond measure by the loss of a devotee.

11

LITTLE DROPS *of* NECTAR

In Vṛndāvana there are hot winds called *loo* that come from the Rajputan desert and can be deadly when breathed or when they enter a person's ear. When a strong *loo* comes, most Vṛndāvana residents stay indoors and shut their windows. One evening while Śrīla Prabhupāda was sitting outside on the roof of his Vṛndāvana residence, a *loo* began. First the atmosphere became very calm, as before a thunderstorm. Then came the hot winds. Prabhupāda's servant, Upendra, ran out, covering his own head and securing the papers on Śrīla Prabhupāda's little desk. Śrīla Prabhupāda was in the process of dictating *Śrīmad Bhāgavatam* and he didn't want to leave, although Upendra pleaded with him about the winds. Prabhupāda accepted a *cādar*, but remained while his servant periodically ran back and forth from the roof to the building to see if Śrīla Prabhupāda was all right or if he wanted anything. This was during a time when Śrīla Prabhupāda was feeling ill, yet he sat silently and attempted to continue his work with great determination, despite the deathly winds.

"What is that?" asked Śrīla Prabhupāda. He had just come onto the roof of the Māyāpur building when he noticed a brass *loṭā*. It was sitting next to a line of *tulasī* plants in pots. Śrīla Prabhupāda seemed disturbed by the sight, although to the group of devotees walking with him, the *loṭā* and the *tulasī* plant seemed perfectly normal.

"Is something wrong?" a devotee asked.

"Look in the stool room," Prabhupāda replied, "and see if there is a *loṭā* there." Someone ran into the stool room, came out, and said, "No, Śrīla Prabhupāda."

"Just see," said Śrīla Prabhupāda. "This is a great *aparādha* (offense)."

Devotees were amazed at Śrīla Prabhupāda's immediate detective work in surmising that someone had taken the stool room *loṭā* and used it to water the *tulasī* plants.

Sometimes Prabhupāda circumambulated the Krishna-Balaram temple chanting *japa* as part of his morning walk. On one such occasion he turned to the devotees accompanying him and said, "You are blind, but I am seeing."

No one knew exactly what he meant. Was it a philosophical statement?

After another circumambulation, Śrīla Prabhupāda repeated, "You are blind, but I am seeing." This time he pointed to light bulbs that were burning outside the temple, although the sun was fully risen.

12

Rādhānātha Swami recalls a 1976 visit Śrīla Prabhupāda made to the old farm quarters in New Vrindaban. Prabhupāda had lived in that primitive woodland setting for a month in 1968 when it was the entire New Vrindaban. Although he had frequently visited the growing New Vrindaban project, Prabhupāda had never gone back to the old farmhouse.

"If you can clean this place up, I will bring him up," said Kīrtanānanda Swami, but later he changed his mind. "We are not going to bring Prabhupāda up here. He'll say it looks like a jungle. It is not proper." Rādhānātha was disheartened to hear it, because he was the *pūjārī* of the Deity Rādhā-Vṛndāvananātha, who resided in the little temple farmhouse. He had been feeling it would be the perfection of his devotional service to Rādhā-Vṛndāvananātha if the pure devotee, Śrīla Prabhupāda, would come to associate with Him. He decided to at least bring a picture of Rādhā-Vṛndāvananātha for Śrīla Prabhupāda to see.

One day during Śrīla Prabhupāda's visit, Kīrtanānanda Swami introduced Rādhānātha to Śrīla Prabhupāda and told him he had been making Śrīla Prabhupāda's *sandeśa*.

"Very nice," Śrīla Prabhupāda replied. Rādhānātha then showed Prabhupāda an eight-by-ten picture of Rādhā-Vṛndāvananātha. Śrīla Prabhupāda looked at Them silently and meditatively for about a minute. Then he began glorifying Lord Kṛṣṇa. He said Kṛṣṇa in Vṛndāvana is the sweetest. When Kṛṣṇa stays in Mathurā, Dvārakā, that is city beauty, but when He is in the village of Vṛndāvana, His beauty is the sweetest. While saying this, Śrīla Prabhupāda continued to glance at the picture of Rādhā-Vṛndāvananātha. He then spoke of how Kṛṣṇa goes out to the pasturing ground with His buffalo horn and flute to herd the cows and play with His friends. Kṛṣṇa and His friends would get so absorbed in their play that mother Yaśodā would have to go out and get Kṛṣṇa to bring Him home.

"Where are these Deities?" Śrīla Prabhupāda asked Kīrtanānanda Swami.

"They are at the original farm," said Kīrtanānanda Swami, "the place you stayed many years ago."

"You can take me there to see Them?" asked Śrīla Prabhupāda.

"It is very difficult to go there," Kīrtanānanda Swami replied. "The road is very bad. It would be uncomfortable for you."

"You have a jeep?" Śrīla Prabhupāda suggested.

Seeing Śrīla Prabhupāda's persistence, Kīrtanānanda Swami said that they would make all arrangements for his going there.

When the *brahmacārīs* from the old farm heard the news, they were ecstatic. They tried their best to clean and make ready their backwoods temple and planned how to greet Śrīla Prabhupāda. Rādhānātha emphasized that Kīrtanānanda Swami said it was important that the recording of the "*Govindam*" prayers begin as soon as Prabhupāda walked through the doorway to the temple. Therefore, the tape recorder should be cued and placed strategically. A guard should stand down the road and another near the house to signal Prabhupāda's advance toward the temple. Rādhānātha, the *pūjārī*, would stay poised by the recorder, ready to press the button at the right instant.

Meanwhile, Śrīla Prabhupāda traveled three-quarters of the way to the farm by pickup truck but then decided to walk the last part as his daily morning walk. As he walked, all the "guards" went to join him. Passing a black cow, one of the devotees said, "That's the first cow of New Vrindaban, Śrīla Prabhupāda."

"Yes, I know Kāliya," Śrīla Prabhupāda replied. Finally he walked up to the temple and entered. Somehow, the other devotees were all detained outside and Śrīla Prabhupāda entered the temple room alone. He stood with palms folded, looking at the surprised Rādhānātha. A bit belatedly, Rādhānātha pushed the button, and "*Govindam*" began. They then opened the curtains, and Śrīla Prabhupāda stood to one side, looking at Rādhā-Vṛndāvananātha. He nodded his head approvingly to the Deities and then to the *pūjārī*. After a few moments, Prabhupāda went to the rear of the room and sat on the rustic-looking *vyāsāsana*. Sublimely and naturally, he began to give the morning *Śrīmad-Bhāgavatam* class.

13

ŚRĪLA PRABHUPĀDA SAID

On Restaurants

The other day His Divine Grace revealed in detail his plans for Hare Kṛṣṇa restaurants, which can be opened anywhere in the world. After his talk most recently, he told me to see that this information is disseminated to all the devotees. He described it as "the next phase of our movement." Please therefore make a newsletter of the information that follows for all-ISKCON distribution.

Our Kṛṣṇa conscious farms, like New Vrindaban, are producing much ghee. This ghee should be distributed at a fee to the different centers, and once restaurants begin opening, the ghee will be one of their prime materials. Other supplies such as vegetables, grains, etc., can be obtained locally.

The restaurants could be cafeteria-style. The food is kept out on counters and people approach in a line with a tray and take what they want. Prabhupāda proposed that there should be one charge and that if a person takes more than another person, he is not charged more—as much as you like for a certain fee. But there should be no waste. A person should take what he can eat. One devotee, hearing this, said, "Prabhupāda, I think people will be carrying *samosās* home in their pockets." "No," he said, "it is a business. Only what they can eat. But they don't get charged more for eating more, like in a hotel, where immediately there is a bill if you eat more."

We can also make home deliveries. Food is cooked fresh, and as it is taken, more fresh batches are put on the counter. Always fresh. There will be about twenty sweet preparations, and twenty salty preparations like *samosās* (made with potatoes, peas, cauliflower, white flour, and ghee) and *kacaurīs,* etc. The vegetable preps must be served hot. Everything should be so clean that not even a single fly should be seen. After the first batch of *prasādam* is made, it will be offered to Lord Caitanya with *ārati,* then the *prasādam* for the rest of the day will be considered offered. Smoking, of course, is prohibited in the restaurant. Tapes can play of our *kīrtanas*. The idea is that people who will not come to our temples will come and eat at our restaurants and will be eating *prasādam* and hearing. Also it will engage men, our devotees in varieties of pursuits—not that without engagement men should eat in our temples in the name of devotional service. Hare Kṛṣṇa Restaurant! The name, Śrīla Prabhupāda said, should also be fully registered so that others may not imitate.

Foods cooked in ghee, foods cooked in water, all the standard varieties will be there. Foods cooked in ghee are especially wonderful and healthful. People should come and be relaxed, eat, and talk relaxed. See how nice Kṛṣṇa consciousness is. There will be a small book and record store in the restaurant.

Devotees will do all the work in the restaurant. We can even import an expert Indian cook if necessary. At the end of the day everything must be thoroughly washed down and no leftovers. No *prasādam* will be given away free. At a certain hour, at the end of the day, the leftovers can be sold half price or some even given away. But the venture has to be an economically profitable business.

Start out the business small and train up men on one restaurant. Then you can expand gradually. You can give them nice drinks. *Masālā* milk, made with small quantities of ginger, saffron, pepper, and cinnamon can be served hot, and cold juices. No tea is served. Yogurt can be made from hot milk and, when drunk as whey, it is very good for digestion.

"It is very good idea for people to come to our vegetarian restaurant and take so many nice things, especially the *panir*, fried cheese, and *sandesa, kacauri, rasagulla, samosa*, and in this way forget their meat-eating. If you make a soup like fried *panir* with asafetida and ginger, this will replace lobster soup nonsense. Of course, we are not interested in giving them vegetarian food; we are wanting to give them *prasadam*. Then gradually they will become devotees."

— *Letter of November 9, 1975*

"I want that all householders be engaged in managing these restaurants."

—*Letter of July 20, 1975*

"Regarding the restaurant, you should not name it as you have suggested but 'Hare Krsna Restaurant.' That should be the name. In each restaurant there should be the picture of Lord Caitanya, and the food should be offered and distributed to the respected customers. There should also be a tape recorder playing the *sankirtana* in mild voice."

— *Letter of August 16, 1974*

14

PRABHUPĀDA TELLS A STORY

"I am just trying to explain that the purpose of a book must be known to the author, and he knows it better than others. There is an instructive story to show this. It is not only a story, it is a fact. In Calcutta a great dramatist, Mr. Rath, who was also a very well known government official, wrote a book, *Shah Jahan*. Shah Jahan means the emperor Shah Jahan. The title on the book is the name of the book's hero. So one of the friends of Mr. Rath inquired, 'In your book, *Shah Jahan*, the actual hero is Aurangzeb. Why have you given the book the title *Shah Jahan*?' He could not understand it.

"The author replied, 'My dear friend, the actual hero is Shah Jahan, not Aurangzeb.' Yet the Shah Jahan book is full of activities of Aurangzeb. But the fact is that Shah Jahan was the emperor. He had four or five sons, and when his wife died at an early age, he built her a memorial. Those who have gone to India, who have seen the Taj Mahal building, that was constructed in the memory of Shah Jahan's wife, Mumtaz, by Shah Jahan. He spent all his money constructing that building. It is one of the seven wonders of the world. Shah Jahan was a very affectionate father also. He did not chastise his sons much. He spent all of his money constructing for the memory of his wife. But when the sons grew up, the third son, Aurangzeb, came out very crooked and he made a plan how to usurp the empire. He killed his brothers, and he arrested his father, Shah Jahan. So this is the plot of the book *Shah Jahan*. But the author says that Aurangzeb is not the hero. The hero is Shah Jahan. Then he explained.

"Why? Because Shah Jahan was living, sitting in the Agra fort as a prisoner, and all the reactions of Aurangzeb's activities—the killing of his other sons, the usurping of the empire—all these things were beating on the heart of Shah Jahan. Therefore he was suffering and he is the hero.

"This is an example that the author of a book knows very well what is the purpose of that book. That is my statement. Similarly, these *Vedānta-sūtras* were compiled by Śrīla Vyāsadeva, or Kṛṣṇa's incarnation, or Kṛṣṇa Himself. So He knows what is the *Vedānta-sūtra*. Therefore, if you want to understand the *Vedānta-sūtra*, you must understand Kṛṣṇa. And Śrīla Vyāsadeva explains the *Vedānta-sūtra* in the *Śrīmad-Bhāgavatam*. Many rascals will comment in different ways, but the author of *Vedānta* personally wrote a commentary, *Śrīmad-Bhāgavatam*."

15

REALIZATIONS

Śrīla Prabhupāda had a way of speaking so gravely that even when he said something simple, his words had significance beyond their immediate, apparent meaning. I experienced this several times that I can remember.

For example, the second time I met him in Surat, India, I was following the devotees on a photographic assignment from *Asia Magazine*, so I entered his room to take more pictures. As I sat by his side, Prabhupāda suddenly turned to me and said, "So, are you going to become a devotee?" At that time, I still had a mustache and wore long hair. Although I was very attracted to him and Kṛṣṇa consciousness, I said, "I don't think so."

Prabhupāda said, "Then you have to leave."

I had gone to much trouble and expense to go to India from New York City, so I was completely flabbergasted by Prabhupāda's comment that I had to leave. I *didn't* leave, and he never said anything else about my having to leave. Therefore, I came to the conclusion that Prabhupāda was making comments that transcend time and were not necessarily meant for that particular moment. I took his comment to mean that if one is not a devotee, then he cannot stay in the association of devotees in the long run.

Another time a similar incident happened with Prabhupāda and myself, where he said something that seemed to be connected with the present, but also the future. It was at the installation of the Rādhā-Kṛṣṇa Deities in Paris in 1973. I was photographing the occasion, and a big *kīrtana* was going on. Just after the actual installation, I put down my camera and went to join the *kīrtana*. I was dancing for a few minutes and when I turned to dance in front of Prabhupāda, he motioned that I should come and speak to him. This was unusual because it was right in the midst of a loud *kīrtana* with many people. I went beside Prabhupāda and put my head very close. I heard him say, "You should never put down your camera." I immediately went to get my camera and start taking pictures. Naturally, I took his words as immediate instructions for the present, but as I thought about it, I realized that he meant it also for the future, that I shouldn't give up this work. I should never put down my camera.

—*Yadubara dāsa Adhikārī*

16

REALIZATIONS

One of the first times I was in Śrīla Prabhupāda's presence I saw him drink water from a *loṭā.* It was amazing because I had never seen anything done with such precision. It was a small thing, a tiny gesture, but there was something unique about it. I realized that anyone who could drink a glass of water like that was not an ordinary person. Later on, as I would have more association with Śrīla Prabhupāda, I would see that happening more and more. He would do something and just do it very carefully. Most people do ordinary things carelessly without thinking about them, yet somehow or other he always acted with full deliberation. It was, I guess, just a side effect of being Kṛṣṇa conscious.

Once when he was in Philadelphia I remember he called me into his room. He had a *gamchā* tied around his waist and he had just been given a massage. When I entered the room there were several things going on at the same time. Several GBC men were there and there was a whole discussion going on that was way over the realm of responsibility I had. I came into the room and offered my obeisances, and he turned to me and said he had received a certain amount of money. He wanted me to take the money, bring it to the bank, and send it in a wire transfer to a bank account of his in Los Angeles. It was an ordinary thing, but what really astounded me was how he stopped everything else, told me what he wanted me to do, and explained it to me very clearly. It was the clearest explanation of any activity I have ever received. He told me exactly how he wanted it to be done and made sure I understood what he wanted. He called his servant over to make sure it was properly entered into the books and in the course of making sure of the proper entry in the books he found an error. With great precision and deliberation, not hurried, yet in a short amount of time, he accomplished a whole lot, sent me off, and then resumed his conversation, all with the same kind of precision he exhibited in drinking water. This is one quality of Śrīla Prabhupāda's association. It becomes very difficult to describe because his Kṛṣṇa consciousness would become manifest in these very small, insignificant things, and yet while you were there, they were so expressive of the whole nature of the pure devotee.

—*Ravīndra-svarūpa dāsa Adhikārī*

17

During the 1966 days Umāpati dāsa and Hayagrīva dāsa stopped attending the temple for a while because they thought Śrīla Prabhupāda wasn't "liberal" enough in his attitude toward some of the well known Māyāvādī monks and toward the Buddhists. One day they were sitting around their Mott Street apartment discussing this, when Kīrtanānanda walked in. Seeing their mood, Kīrtanānanda began to bait them.

"I have decided to leave the Swami," Kīrtanānanda said, "because I don't like what is going on."

"That's just what *we've* been talking about!" said Umāpati.

"You fools, " said Kīrtanānanda. "Do you think I would ever leave the Swami? If there is a problem on your mind, then you have to go and see him."

"But he doesn't really speak English well enough," said Umāpati.

"No, that's not true," said Kīrtanānanda. "He will understand."

So Umāpati and Hayagrīva went to see Śrīla Prabhupāda to reveal their minds.

"Why haven't you been coming?" Śrīla Prabhupāda asked.

"We don't like all these things you've been saying," said Umāpati, "about the Buddhist and the Māyāvādī monk."

Śrīla Prabhupāda said that they should not have thought they could not ask him about their doubts. Then he explained, first about the Buddhists. Prabhupāda said that he had never said anything bad about Lord Buddha. "I always call him *Lord* Buddha," Prabhupāda said. "But the Buddhists say there is no soul, and God is never mentioned in the Buddhists' writings."

Then Prabhupāda explained about the Māyāvādī monk. "I say, and I have always said," said Prabhupāda, "that he is nothing but a crazy priest." Prabhupāda then exposed the monk's discrepancies. According to this Māyāvādī, one can worship Kālī and go to Kṛṣṇa. But, Prabhupāda said, this is a direct contradiction, because in the *Bhagavad-gītā* Kṛṣṇa says that if you worship the demigods you will go to the demigods, and if you worship Kṛṣṇa you will go to Kṛṣṇa. So the Māyāvādī is contradicting the *Bhagavad-gītā*. To say that one can worship Kālī and go to Kṛṣṇa is like saying you can buy a ticket to Chicago and go to California.

Then Prabhupāda told them the story how the Māyāvādī monk met his chief disciple, and when he touched his disciple on the head both guru and disciple felt electric shocks and fainted. Prabhupāda said they had read the *Bhagavad-gītā* where Arjuna saw the universal form, but where does it say anything about electric shock? According to the Māyāvādī monk, when he and his disciple woke up, the guru was crying. The disciple asked, "Why are you crying?" and the Māyāvādī monk replied, "I have given you all my power; now I have none left." Prabhupāda scoffed at this and said, "Is spiritual knowledge something like money, that if you give it away you don't have any left? No. That is not the nature of spiritual knowledge."

These explanations convinced Umāpati and Hayagrīva. They were satisfied because Prabhupāda had convinced them with logic and reason. Prabhupāda then invited them to take *prasādam* in the next room and they happily accepted his offer, grateful to be back in his camp.

18

The scene: Māyāpur Gaura-Pūrṇimā festival, 1976. Prabhupāda is seated in his room, talking with Prajāpati dāsa and his wife, who are leaders of a Kṛṣṇa conscious dance and theater group. They are showing Prabhupāda pictures of one of their performances in a temple.

"Why are their backs to the Deities?" Prabhupāda asked.

"Because Jayatīrtha said . . . "

"Jayatīrtha?" Śrīla Prabhupāda said it in a way that obviously rejected their reply. He then asked that whatever GBC men were nearby should come at once to his room. When the men had gathered, Śrīla Prabhupāda began lecturing to them on the point of not turning one's back to the Deity. "Rūpa Gosvāmī has said, 'Do not turn your back to the Deity,' but now they say someone has said it is all right." Prabhupāda looked around heavily to the devotees in the room. "This is the problem," he said. "We have so many big, big *ācāryas.*"

When a devotee began speaking and mentioned another one of Śrīla Prabhupāda's leading disciples, Prabhupāda immediately cut down, with a few words, both the devotee in the room and the person he had referred to. Then everyone was silent.

Finally a devotee asked, "Śrīla Prabhupāda, what about women dancers onstage?" Earlier that day, a group of young women from a Bengali village had been dancing and playing *mṛdaṅga* in the temple and some of the devotees had questioned whether it was proper to watch them.

Śrīla Prabhupāda replied that women should not appear onstage for dramatic performances. Men should play the women's roles. He said that in India it was done that way previously; women's parts were played by boys. Only later were women introduced in the women's roles. Prabhupāda said no respectable woman would do that, so they used prostitutes. Prabhupāda continued speaking, outlining the history of Bengali drama.

He then told the devotees about the time he had played in a drama about the life of Lord Caitanya. It had been directed by a prominent figure in Bengali theater. Prabhupāda described how when the play was finished, all the actors stood there but there was no applause. They looked out at the audience to see why there was no applause, and they saw that everyone was so moved by the story that they all had tears coming from their eyes.

"That's because you were in the play, Śrīla Prabhupāda" remarked a devotee.

Prabhupāda shook his head and made a typical wave of his hand, as if to dismiss the notion that the play was important because of him.

19

LITTLE DROPS *of* NECTAR

Śrīla Prabhupāda repeatedly instructed that in a Kṛṣṇa conscious marriage there is no divorce. This was based on the authority of Vedic injunctions, and he intended his own disciples to strictly follow the rule. One time, however, Śrīla Prabhupāda received a written request by a disciple for permission to divorce his wife and marry another. In his reply, Śrīla Prabhupāda somewhat reluctantly gave his permission. Śrīla Prabhupāda's servant at that time, Śrutakirti, was bewildered by Śrīla Prabhupāda's action in this case, and he waited for an opportunity to inquire. *Śrīla Prabhupāda can do anything he wants,* thought Śrutakīrti, *but I can't understand why he would do this.*

Finally, in the evening, while massaging Śrīla Prabhupāda in his bed, Śrutakirti asked, "Śrīla Prabhupāda, this devotee who is asking about the divorce?"

Śrīla Prabhupāda replied that he had told him he could do it.

"Yes, I know," said Śrutakīrti. "But I was wondering. You always say that divorce is against the Vedic society. There can never be any divorce."

Prabhupāda replied that in "your society" these things are accepted.

"But in Western society," said Śrutakīrti, "they also accept meat-eating and intoxication, so why aren't any of these things allowed?"

Śrīla Prabhupāda then replied that whether he gave permission or not, the disciple in question was going to get a divorce. Prabhupāda explained that if he had told his disciple no and the disciple had gone ahead and done it anyway, the offense would have been greater. Prabhupāda said that he had given permission since he knew the man was going to do it anyway. In this way, the offense was not so great.

Śrutakīrti immediately appreciated that Śrīla Prabhupāda knew just what to do in each individual case for the benefit of his disciple.

Śrīla Prabhupāda demonstrated that he wanted to deal with his disciples in sensitive and particular ways. This even applied to the case when a disciple would fall down or go away from devotional service. On one occasion when a prominent *sannyāsī* disciple fell down, Śrīla Prabhupāda became disturbed when he heard that his secretary had broadcast the news widely, in detail, of the *sannyāsī's* falldown.

"You may have made it impossible for him to come back," said Śrīla Prabhupāda. Prabhupāda explained that the event should have been a personal matter mostly between the spiritual master and the disciple, and perhaps a few others concerned could have been informed. Prabhupāda said if it had been treated in this way, then there was more chance that they could rectify the fallen soul and that he would come back and be accepted by the devotees. By the wide broadcasting of his misbehavior, however, the man's pride would not enable him to come back very easily. Thus Śrīla Prabhupāda showed another aspect of his training and his compassionate, transcendental personality.

20

Once Śrīla Prabhupāda came to London when he was quite sick. He was next scheduled to go to New Māyāpur, France. In anticipation of Śrīla Prabhupāda's visit, devotees had gathered in New Māyāpur from Germany, Switzerland, and other European countries. The Deities of Kṛṣṇa-Balarāma were to be installed, initiations were to take place, and for these events devotees had been laboring hard to prepare for Śrīla Prabhupāda's arrival. Bhagavān dāsa, as GBC man, had personally worked to get Prabhupāda's rooms ready, buying chandeliers in Paris, having a bed and tables made in Italy, having a new marble mantle made for the fireplace, putting up wallpaper, and so on.

Then the word came that Śrīla Prabhupāda wasn't coming, so Bhagavān got on the next plane to London.

When he met Śrīla Prabhupāda, Bhagavān told him that many devotees had come to see him in New Māyāpur. Śrīla Prabhupāda said, "I will dictate a message for them." Prabhupāda meant that he would do this instead of going personally.

After some more discussion, Bhagavān said, "It is *hot* there." Bhagavān thought that this would be appealing because of Prabhupāda's bad cold.

"Actually, they are having a drought there," said Bhagavān. "It hasn't rained in weeks." Prabhupāda appeared unmoved.

Finally Bhagavān said, "We have an elevator in Paris. You won't have to walk up the stairs."

Then Prabhupāda said to his secretary, "Oh, an elevator! We should get this in Bury Place too." Finally he said, "Your invitation is a reasonable proposal," and he agreed to go. Prabhupāda then turned to his secretary and said, "Bhagavān is the supreme controller."

21

ŚRĪLA PRABHUPĀDA SAID

On Polygamy in ISKCON

"This incident with one of our temple presidents is not good. He can't even maintain one wife. Just see how lusty he is. Now he'll dare to take another. Anyway, he cannot live in the temple. If he wants two wives he must live outside. He should maintain his family by working and giving fifty percent to the temple. He may not live off temple funds. Temple president is generally meant for *sannyasi,* but a *grhastha* may be if he is restrained. It is not good if he remains as president."

—*Letter of November 8, 1976*

"Regarding the question of second marriage, it cannot be done. Neither the law will allow it, neither we can encourage it. If they want to marry more than one wife, they must live outside our temples in their own arrangements. We have no objection if he does it, but it must be done outside the temple. It cannot be done inside the temple jurisdiction. Outside he can work, earn money, and if he wants he can maintain 16,000 wives. But he must go outside the society. Within the society only one marriage can be allowed.

"I thought these boys and girls will be married and be happy. But I see they are not satisfied. In the Western countries they are trained up in a different way—jumping from one to another. Another wife, another husband. This is the disease all over the world. Simply by agreement, then canceling, then another agreement.

"Everyone wants more than one wife, that is human nature. This means their mind is not being diverted by Krsna. Because they are not *madana-mohana,* they are *madana-dahana,* they are in the Cupid's fire . . .

"They must go outside the society to do it. And, the sort of marriage where they are not satisfied cannot be allowed. Nor can woman with child, strictly she cannot marry again."

—*Letter of September 7, 1975*

"Regarding your taking a second wife, you cannot do this. At least you cannot stay in our temple in Vrndavana. If you want to take a second wife, then you have to leave our Vrndavana temple. Whether you can maintain them and take some job and earn? Our temple cannot support you and your two wives. You will then want three, four, and more. Anyway, as an American it is illegal for you to do this. We are trying to minimize sex and you are trying to increase it. Please give up this idea."

—*Letter of July 13, 1975*

22

ŚRĪLA PRABHUPĀDA TELLS A STORY

Śrīla Prabhupāda told a story about an insensitive worshiper of the goddess Kālī. The "devotee" went to the temple and prayed to the goddess in a materialistic way, typical of a demigod worshiper. He asked for a material benediction. After his prayers and a perfunctory *pūjā*, he soon got the desired material result, but his *pūjā* included an obligation that when he got the result he would offer the goddess a sacrifice of a goat. After some days passed, the goddess in the temple spoke to the worshiper and asked him, "Where is the goat you promised?"

"It is very expensive," he said, "and I don't think I can afford to offer you a goat."

"All right," said the goddess, "but you have to offer something, so go and offer me at least a pig."

The worshiper went away, but neglected the goddess's request. Then on another occasion in the temple the goddess spoke to him again and said, "Where is the offering of the pig?"

This time the devotee again excused himself and said, "I am sorry, but I could not find any pigs anywhere. It is not so easy."

The goddess replied, "This is not very good. You have received your benediction and now you must give something in return. But just to make it easy for you, I request you at least to offer something that is available for you. So why don't you at least offer me a fly?"

"But goddess," said the worthless worshiper, "there are so many flies buzzing around you. Can't you just grab one yourself?"

Such is the attitude of materialistic demigod worshipers, whose hearts are completely devoid of a loving service mood.

23

PRABHUPĀDA TELLS SHORT STORIES

On a morning walk in Boston Śrīla Prabhupāda told of a funny expression used in India. He said that if you see a fat man in India, you sometimes say to him, "Where do you get your merchandise?" The idea is that to become so fat, the man must be obtaining good merchandise. As he said this, Śrīla Prabhupāda was accompanied only by a few disciples, walking down Allston Street near the old Boston storefront temple. Suddenly, a beer-bellied cab driver got out of his car just in front of the devotees. Śrīla Prabhupāda looked directly at the fat man and said, "Where do you get your merchandise?" The meaning of Prabhupāda's words went completely over the cabbie's head, and Prabhupāda continued walking and talking.

While speaking at Harvard University one time, Śrīla Prabhupāda told the students the story of how the Himalayan mountains once gave birth. When the word spread that the world-famous, huge Himalayan mountain range was going to produce offspring, hundreds of people began to gather in the foothills of the mountains. In anticipation, crowds waited, and finally they saw hundreds of rats running out from the Himalayan mountains! Śrīla Prabhupāda linked this strange story to the student population of Harvard. He said that it was expected that from the greatest university in America something wonderful would come out, but unless they became Kṛṣṇa conscious, they would be like the offspring of the Himalayan mountains.

" . . . If one has got their own philosophy, then let them preach their own philosophy. But do not do it in the name of the *Gita*. This is our protest to all the interpreters of the *Bhagavad-gita*. If they do not believe in God, Krsna, and they don't want to surrender to Him, then let them preach atheism. Everyone has got the right to do this, but why through the *Gita*? This is like the man who wants to smoke *ganja*, but he does not want to be caught. So he takes a friend's hand and smokes it in his hand, and then when the authorities come, he says, "Oh, I have not smoked *ganja*. See, my hands are clean!" The idea is that if one wants to preach the *Gita*, then he must preach it as it is, otherwise don't go through the *Gita*."

—*Letter of June 6, 1976*

According to a Bengali story told by Prabhupāda, a deaf man used to call his wife. She would reply, "I am coming," but the deaf man could not hear her. He used to think, "This woman is deaf." In actuality he was deaf, but he accused her of being deaf. Prabhupāda said this was similar to the condition of the mass of people who are actually "brainwashed" by material illusion and yet who accuse the Kṛṣṇa conscious persons of being brainwashed. In this connection, Prabhupāda stressed that only a Kṛṣṇa conscious person knew the science of the soul and of changing bodies, whereas other religionists had little or no idea of this. Yet they criticize from their position of blind faith.

24

PERSONAL

His Giving the Morning Śrīmad-Bhāgavatam *Class*

No matter what else he was doing, Śrīla Prabhupāda put it in his schedule, even when he was ill. Wherever he traveled, he lived with the devotees and joined them to give the morning class.

Here was the opportunity to watch his gestures and expressions as he spoke, absorbed in *Śrīmad-Bhāgavatam.* A dull student might think that Prabhupāda was saying the same things, using the same repertoire of verses, but Prabhupāda was always quoting the verses to prove different points in different contexts. He was always discovering new lights. He also said that repetition was necessary to learn. For most devotees in the later years, this was the one sure time to be with him in his personal form, to sit and hear. It was formal, and one might wish for other situations in which to ask personal questions and to have a reply just for oneself, yet the lectures were great mercy, and to the receptive student they were very personal. Devotees have testified how in a large audience, when Prabhupāda said, "Distribute books," they took it to heart and formed their lives on that order. Many have testified that they found Prabhupāda looked at them and spoke especially to them in his lecture, even though they knew he was speaking to everyone else as well.

This was the time for all to be with him. Each morning without fail he would begin, looking at the verse and speaking As if he was entering a sacred river, he immersed himself at once in *Śrīmad-Bhāgavatam.* He hardly ever chose another literature to speak from in the morning. What an example, that the *Śrīmad-Bhāgavatam* contains all else and is perfect for all our days!

He sat in one place in the traditional posture of the guru—legs crossed, sitting on the *vyāsāsana*—with spectacles, book in hand, microphone, gesturing and looking up. He was a hundred percent Vyāsadeva's representative, giving us the transcendental wisdom. Seeing Śrīla Prabhupāda's personal example even today by means of movies or tape recordings, all the devotees of the Kṛṣṇa consciousness movement may adopt the same procedures and do as he taught. Like him, we can precede the class by singing "Jaya Rādhā-Mādhava" with *karatālas.* Then we can recite *oṁ namo bhagavate vāsudevāya,* then the Sanskrit, synonyms, translation, purport. We have no need to invent something new. After he showed us hundreds and hundreds of times, how can we fail to grasp the instruction—that we should continue the morning tradition of sitting together and hearing and speaking?

A devotee once told Śrīla Prabhupāda that many disciples slept during classes and Śrīla Prabhupāda replied that he knew. He said his classes were for advanced students. Śrīla Prabhupāda gave untiringly as the loving instructor, but it was up to his disciples to benefit. I confess that I was one of those who sometimes slept in *Śrīmad-Bhāgavatam* class. Once I even asked Śrīla Prabhupāda what to do about my sad plight. At first he replied by making a joke. He said there is an atheistic joke in India, "*Śrīmad-Bhāgavatam* is a sure cure for insomnia." When Śrīla Prabhupāda said this, I laughed, but I didn't want it to be true of me. Sometimes when Prabhupāda found a devotee sleeping in his class, he would tell him to stand up and go to the rear. *Śrīmad-Bhāgavatam* class was for his advanced students, but he kept giving us chances to become more advanced.

Śrīla Prabhupāda spoke with rhetorical power and emotion, straight from his deep convictions. He had great oratorical skill, emphasizing his points with aesthetic effects, but none of it was done for show or with lack of realization, not like the *rāsa* dance talks of bogus *Bhāgavatam* reciters. Śrīla Prabhupāda *wrote Bhāgavatam* purports and he *lived* the life of the *Bhāgavatam*. He was also the *Bhāgavatam's ideal preacher*; when he spoke, the emotions were always right.

Śrīla Prabhupāda kindly gave all of those classes, and now, by tape recording, we hear them still, even as we wake in the morning, while taking *prasādam*, driving the car, flying in the plane, in sick bed or death bed; these matchless gifts continue in our ears, to cleanse our hearts and remind us that we are his *śiṣya*. We are followers of the *Śrīmad-Bhāgavatam*.

25

REALIZATIONS

For a while I was the headmaster of Vṛndāvana Gurukula when it was a fledgling *gurukula*. At that time, Śrīla Prabhupāda's Vṛndāvana friend, Bhagatjī, was often going in to see Prabhupāda. Bhagatjī was also like the sugar daddy of the *gurukula*; he was helping me out in different ways. When he used to go in and see Prabhupāda, I was thinking, "Well, maybe I can go in with him when he goes." So Bhagatjī used to let me tag along, go in, and just sit in Prabhupāda's room and hear the different talk. A lot of times it was in Hindi or Bengali, so I couldn't really understand much, but it was nice to just sit and be with Śrīla Prabhupāda.

Then I got a little puffed up, thinking, "This is great. Now I have this position. I can go in and see Śrīla Prabhupāda." With that contamination in my mind one night, I went in to see Śrīla Prabhupāda while he was sitting out in his garden speaking to a couple of Indian guests. As I entered, the Indian guests were sitting there and Prabhupāda said to me, "Go and get some *āsanas.*" I ran out and tried to get *āsanas,* but I realized, "I don't know where to go to get *āsanas.*" Then I was in a quandary. I didn't know what to do. I thought "Well, I guess I'll have to go and ask Prabhupāda." I went back in and said, "Śrīla Prabhupāda?" He said, "Yes?" "Where should I get the *āsanas?*" He said, "Go and see Hari Śauri. He will show you." Then I ran and found Hari Śauri. "Hari Śauri, Prabhupāda wants some *āsanas* for the guests. Can you give me some?" He said, "I don't think we have any." Then I said, "Oh no!" He said, "Let me look." Then he rummaged around in his closet and he came up with one crumpled-looking *āsana.* I thought "I've only got one *āsana.* What am I going to do?" Then I went back out and the guests were getting up to leave.

Prabhupāda said, "Get them some *prasādam.*" So I ran back and found Hari Śauri again. I said, "The guests are leaving. Prabhupāda wants me to give them some *prasādam.*" He said, "All right, here is some *prasādam.*" Then I came out and gave them each some *prasādam.* At this point I was thinking, "Well, at least I did one thing right." But I still have this one *āsana,* so I went back to the garden.

As I came in, Prabhupāda was talking to Bhagatjī and no one else was around. It looked like Bhagatjī was already sitting on something and Prabhupāda was sitting on his own raised seat. I stood there with the one *āsana,* and I didn't know what to do with it. I couldn't understand whether Prabhupāda meant for me to use the *āsana,* or Bhagatjī, or whether it was for the guests or what—I didn't know. I was completely bewildered. As I came in, Prabhupāda said, "I have several times asked you to get *āsanas.* What is the difficulty?"

I said, "Śrīla Prabhupāda, I could only get this one *āsana.*"

Prabhupāda replied by just saying, "Hmmm."

"Śrīla Prabhupāda?"

"What?"

"What should I do with the *āsana?*"

Prabhupāda said, "Take your one *āsana* and sit down on it!" Then he began to laugh. I felt like a complete fool as he began to laugh. Bhagatjī also started laughing, and I also started to laugh. I could understand at that point how I was so puffed up thinking I was a big personality that I could go in and see Śrīla Prabhupāda, but he had just revealed to me what a complete fool I was—an incompetent bungler. They were both laughing and I was also laughing. I couldn't even quite understand why I was laughing, but somehow or other, by his chastisement in making me look like a fool, I felt completely relieved, because I could understand my actual position. I was just an insignificant, foolish servant who couldn't do practically anything right. Somehow it was a great relief just to know that, so I sat down, and they went on talking.

—*Rūpa-vilāsa dāsa Adhikārī*

26

Śubhānanda tells of a personal interview he had in Vṛndāvana with Śrīla Prabhupāda when Prabhupāda gave him permission and blessings to write a book on Vedic psychology.

Puṣṭa Kṛṣṇa Swami introduced them. "This is Śubhānanda dāsa, and he is a writer for the BBT. He wants to speak with you about writing a book on Vedic psychology."

Prabhupāda asked Śubhānanda if he had studied psychology.

"No, Prabhupāda," Śubhānanda replied.

Prabhupāda then turned to his secretary and said, "How can he write a book on psychology?"

Śubhānanda felt somewhat heartbroken and tried to explain himself. He said to Prabhupāda that the kind of book he wanted to write would not be a comparative study, comparing Vedic psychology to modern mundane psychology, but he wanted to write about psychology based on the *Bhagavad-gītā* and the *Bhāgavatam.*

"Have you read all my books?" Śrīla Prabhupāda asked. "Have you read *Bhagavad-gītā?* Have you read *Śrīmad-Bhāgavatam?*"

"Yes," Śubhānanda replied.

"What is the psychology in these books?"

Śubhānanda replied that psychology is the study of the self. It comes from the word *psyche,* which means "soul." So in the *Bhagavad-gītā* it is described that we are not the body, but the self is the spirit soul. "If one identifies with the body," said Śubhānanda, "he's crazy!"

Prabhupāda widened his eyes, nodded his head, and turned to Puṣṭa Kṛṣṇa. "Very good, very good!"

Śubhānanda continued giving a little synopsis of what his proposed book would say, describing the dynamics between the senses, mind, intelligence, and false ego. All these things would be taken from Prabhupāda's books and arranged in a literary way to show that Vedic literature contains a very profound science of psychology.

Prabhupāda seemed to approve, but he asked further, "What is the goal?"

"The goal of the book, Prabhupāda?" Śubhānanda asked.

"No, the goal of life."

"To surrender to Kṛṣṇa," Śubhānanda replied.

"Why?" Prabhupāda demanded.

"Because He is the Supreme Personality of Godhead," Śubhānanda replied, "and we are His parts and parcels. It is our constitutional position to surrender to Him."

Prabhupāda nodded, "Yes."

"So that should be the goal of the book," asked Śubhānanda, "that Kṛṣṇa is the Supreme Personality of Godhead?"

Again Prabhupāda said, "Yes." He was then silent, and it appeared that nothing more was to be said. But Śubhānanda wanted to be sure that Prabhupāda actually wanted him to write the book, and not that he was only humoring an attached disciple.

"Prabhupāda," asked Śubhānanda, "do you really want me to do this book? Is it something you think would be important, and do you really want me to do it?"

Prabhupāda nodded yes. Then Śubhānanda asked Prabhupāda for his blessings so he could write the book.

"In some of your purports," said Śubhānanda, "you explain that one cannot write transcendental literature unless he is empowered by his spiritual master."

Prabhupāda waved his arm and said, "You're empowered." Śubhānanda had had a long, formal presentation in mind, but Śrīla Prabhupāda had suddenly answered all his questions. To Śubhānanda, Prabhupāda's gesture was on the one hand casual, yet it was very dramatic. He had moved his arm just as though it were a magic wand, and in one transcendental motion he said, "You're empowered." Śubhānanda wasn't sure whether to take it that Prabhupāda meant that he was already empowered or that he was now hereby empowering Śubhānanda on the spot. Either interpretation meant the same thing, and Śubhānanda felt confident and humble. He knew that he had no personal qualification to write unless Prabhupāda gave him the ability.

Overcome with joy, Śubhānanda stood before Prabhupāda with folded hands and prayed out loud to him. "Prabhupāda, I'm trying to advance in Kṛṣṇa consciousness and I'm feeling that I need your mercy. Please benedict me with Kṛṣṇa consciousness."

Prabhupāda replied, *"Teṣāṁ satata-yuktānāṁ bhajatāṁ prīti-pūrvakam.* If the devotee is sincere, Kṛṣṇa will bless." Śrīla Prabhupāda then reached for an orange on his desk and handed it to Śubhānanda, who left, his mind swimming in an ocean of transcendental happiness.

27

During a visit to the Dallas Gurukula, Prabhupāda heard from the devotees of a local schoolteacher who was becoming interested in Kṛṣṇa consciousness. The man was anxious to see Śrīla Prabhupāda and Prabhupāda agreed.

As soon as he met Śrīla Prabhupāda, the teacher began to pour out his heart about his personal difficulty. The man explained that in order to make extra money he was also driving a school bus. A few weeks ago, while driving his bus, he had run over and killed a young schoolchild. Now he was being brought to court in a legal case. As the man went on with his story, a few of the devotees present felt sorry that Prabhupāda had to hear all of it, but Prabhupāda seemed very interested and he began asking detailed questions.

"Had you come to a full stop?" Prabhupāda asked. The teacher explained that the accident occurred on Valentine's Day. One of the children had dropped his Valentine and it fell under the bus. The child had climbed under the bus to get it. The teacher told Śrīla Prabhupāda that he had looked both ways in his rearview mirror and didn't see any children. It had looked like all the children had crossed to the other side of the road. But when he started up the bus, the wheel went over the child.

Śrīla Prabhupāda asked the man if the company had insurance. After hearing the whole story and asking different questions, Prabhupāda said that it seemed the teacher had followed all the safety precautions and that definitely any court of law would hold him blameless. When he heard Śrīla Prabhupāda's decision, the teacher became relieved.

Then Śrīla Prabhupāda, who was sitting in a rocking chair, began to preach to the teacher and the few devotees present. The light blue curtains and clean white walls of the room became effulgent in the last rays of sunlight streaming through the windows. Śrīla Prabhupāda spoke of a recent news article about the scientist Werner von Braun. The famous scientist had recently stated publicly that after all his research, he had concluded that there must be a creator, a Supreme Being, and that all scientists should come together and by different methods establish His existence without a doubt.

"Bring that news article," Prabhupāda said, and as the article was read about the scientist who accepted God, Prabhupāda became enlivened and made further points. He explained that the whole universe is like a big machine and that there is no question of any machine operating without a controller. There had to be a personality operating it. God, therefore, is a scientific fact, and now a world-famous scientist was recognizing this.

"Prabhupāda, this is really wonderful," one of the devotees exclaimed.

Prabhupāda agreed and said that they were sending a set of his books to Werner von Braun.

"Prabhupāda, if he becomes a devotee . . . he is so famous. He is the one who made the V-2 rocket."

Prabhupāda corrected the devotees and said that he was not interested in Werner von Braun because he was famous. He said he was interested to preach to anyone who had come to the right point. Because the scientist had come to the right point of inquiry and was interested in God, Prabhupāda was interested to preach to him. "We don't care for any big, famous personalities," Prabhupāda said. After Prabhupāda had spoken for over an hour, one of the devotees again brought his attention to the visiting school teacher.

"Prabhupāda, this teacher got an award from his school for being the best teacher of that county."

"Yes," said Prabhupāda. "Kṛṣṇa will send the best." And turning to the teacher, he said, "You should help us here. You should come here and help us with the teaching."

28

While visiting Vṛndāvana before the Krishna-Balaram Mandir was built, Śrīla Prabhupāda used to sometimes stay in his original rooms at the Rādhā-Dāmodara temple. On one visit, Yamunā-devī dāsī asked if she could cook for him and Śrīla Prabhupāda agreed. While Yamunā was cooking *capātīs* in one half of the kitchen and Śrīla Prabhupāda was eating *prasādam* at the far end of the same room, Prabhupāda's servant, Śrutakīrti, entered the room to watch.

"So, you have taken *prasādam*?" Śrīla Prabhupāda asked.

"No," Śrutakīrti replied. "I just bathed."

"Yamunā, fix him a plate of *prasādam*," said Śrīla Prabhupāda.

"No," Śrutakīrti protested, "that's all right. I'll wait until you're finished, Śrīla Prabhupāda."

"No," said Prabhupāda. "Sit down and take *prasādam.*" So Śrutakīrti sat down and received a plate from Yamunā. Under Prabhupāda's direction, she continued making *capātīs* and serving both Prabhupāda and his servant.

"So today she has fixed your lunch," said Prabhupāda. "Now tomorrow you cook for her. This is the Vedic custom. Today she has done some service for you; now tomorrow you must serve her."

"Yes, Prabhupāda," said Śrutakīrti.

Looking through the latticework into the courtyard of Rūpa Gosvāmī's *samādhi,* Prabhupāda began to reminisce. He said that often he would sit here and take *prasādam* and look at the *samādhi* and *bhajana kuṭīr* of Rūpa Gosvāmī. He said he was hoping Rūpa Gosvāmī would give him facility to spread the Kṛṣṇa consciousness movement.

During the same period, a startling incident took place with a monkey. Śrīla Prabhupāda was lecturing to a group of people in his small room. One man had brought a bunch of bananas and placed them at Prabhupāda's feet. All of a sudden, a monkey ran into the room and grabbed for the bananas.

Prabhupāda also grabbed for the bananas and got most of them, while the monkey got one or two and ran out the other door.

The whole thing had happened very quickly, and Prabhupāda was also quick to use the incident for teaching Kṛṣṇa consciousness. "Just see how expert the monkey is," Prabhupāda explained. He said that every species of life has their expertise to get some food.

29

LITTLE DROPS *of* NECTAR

During 1977 while Śrīla Prabhupāda was staying in Vṛndāvana, Puṣkara dāsa was also there, working on a painting. Puṣkara's practice was to paint on the front balcony of a room in the guesthouse. For a long time he had worked on a rendition of Kṛṣṇa playing His flute with the cowherd boys making offerings to Him.

Finally, he got an appointment to see Śrīla Prabhupāda and show him the painting. Prabhupāda looked at it for thirty or forty seconds without saying anything. Puṣkara became worried. On previous occasions Prabhupāda had said that he was "expert" and had made other complimentary remarks.

Looking at Puṣkara, Śrīla Prabhupāda asked, "What is the idea?"

"Well, Kṛṣṇa is there . . . " Puṣkara was now getting nervous; he had already guessed Prabhupāda didn't like the painting. " . . . playing His flute by the Yamunā."

"Where is it in the book?" asked Prabhupāda. Puṣkara then realized he hadn't been thinking of anything in the books.

"Well, Prabhupāda," he said, "the pastimes are unlimited, aren't they?"

"Kṛṣṇa is unlimited," said Prabhupāda, "but you are limited. Stick to the book."

"Is it all right for publication?" asked Puṣkara. Prabhupāda didn't say no, but he didn't look very happy.

"Stop that man! Stop that man!" yelled Prabhupāda from the balcony of his residence in Vṛndāvana. A devotee came running and grabbed a man as he exited from the kitchen.

"See what he has!" called Prabhupāda. They picked up the man's *cādar* and found he was carrying a large bag of sugar he had stolen from the kitchen. Prabhupāda had seen it all from the balcony and had caught him.

"Today, just over a year since I first joined Śrīla Prabhupāda, I made my greatest blunder. In the morning, as usual, Śrīla Prabhupāda went up onto the roof and through his room to the back veranda in order to rest in the sunshine. I left him there, thinking if he needed anything he would ring the bell to call. The bell was just inside the room, but due to my dull brain, as I walked through the room I closed the door behind me and unconsciously slid the bolt.

"Sometime later a boy came running from the guesthouse and shouted, 'Śrīla Prabhupāda is trapped on the roof!' I immediately realized what I had done and ran upstairs. As I came into the room, Prabhupāda was waiting at the fly-screen door. When I slid the bolt to let him into the room from the roof, he simply said, 'You rascal! I have been here for almost an hour. You have so much dull brain from so much voracious eating and sleeping.' He was very angry, but he did not shout. There was no need. The offense was obvious and nonsensical. He had awakened and could not get through, neither could he reach the bell to ring me, and it was forty-five minutes before he could attract anyone's attention. Later on in the afternoon I came and apologized to Śrīla Prabhupāda for what I had done and he very kindly forgave me.

But again he warned me that I should be very careful and be more attentive in my service. Otherwise, I would cause great inconvenience to him."

30

LITTLE DROPS *of* NECTAR

Śrīla Prabhupāda displayed his tolerance and lenience in accepting the sometimes inexpert offerings of his disciples. He demonstrated this amply at the San Francisco Ratha-yātrā in 1970 by accepting some unusual clothing which the devotees had sewn for him. Bhavānanda had purchased imported silk, Nara-Nārāyaṇa had purchased pearl buttons and set them in gold, and Dīnadayādri and Citralekhā had worked very meticulously on sewing Prabhupāda a western-style cowboy shirt. The shirt had sewn pockets with pearl buttons on them. The *dhotī* was supposed to complete a matching set, along with a "Prabhupāda hat" made for the occasion. When Prabhupāda put on the *dhotī*, the cloth was so wide that the *dhotī* dragged on the ground. (This can be seen in a series of photos of Prabhupāda at the 1970 Ratha-yātrā.) The cowboy shirt had its own unusual appearance, and as for the hat, it was too small and stuck up on the top of his head. Prabhupāda tolerantly accepted and wore the clothes offered by his American boys and girls.

While Śrīla Prabhupāda was speaking in his room, his disciple, Rukmiṇī devī dāsī, who is left-handed, was busily writing notes on Prabhupāda's talk. The left-handed phenomenon seemed strange to Prabhupāda and he finally commented on it.

"You write like Gargamuni," said Prabhupāda, "backwards and topsy-turvy." Prabhupāda then said that he had once seen a man in Calcutta who played harmonium with his elbows, *karatālas* with his knees, and *mṛdaṅga* with his feet. Prabhupāda seemed to think that the "backwards and topsy-turvy" writing was in a similar category.

31

ŚRĪLA PRABHUPĀDA SAID

On Sannyāsa

"The preaching in Poland is the first consideration. Vrndavana is being managed somehow. . . . Now the most important work is that side in the Communist countries. If you can do something there, it is more than if you come here. Our business is to glorify Krsna as Lord of Vrndavana and to popularize Lord Caitanya Mahaprabhu's Hare Krsna movement. I was a resident of Vrndavana, but at the age of seventy I tried to preach Krsna consciousness a little bit, and now this institution has come out. So, I think it is more profitable to preach about the master of Vrndavana, Krsna, outside of Vrndavana. A devotee of Krsna can create Vrndavana everywhere by preaching the glories of Krsna.

"There are many *sahajiyas* who imitate Rupa Gosvami not to go out of Vrndavana. But Caitanya Mahaprabhu always remained outside Vrndavana for preaching purposes, although He is the master of Vrndavana personally. I have no objection to your coming to Vrndavana, but as you have accepted the *sannyasa* order, it is more important to preach about Vrndavana rather than come to Vrndavana."

—*Letter of November 18, 1976*

"The purpose of *sannyasa* is that now one has no hindrance for preaching work. The purpose is to increase preaching. So if one takes *sannyasa* and does not increase preaching, there is no value. So you take this opportunity seriously by preaching and inspire others to also preach. Then there will be no question of thinking of other things. This will all vanish."

—*Letter of August 21, 1975*

"So far your question that the women sew clothes for the *sannyasis'* Deities, it is not possible. *Sannyasis* may have no connection with women."

—*Letter of January 13, 1976*

"Regarding taking *sannyasa,* this mentality that either I will have sex life or I will take *sannyasa,* this is not proper. *Sannyasa* means that one is finished with material life. So you have gotten married, and you are in family life. So you should remain there. You thought that by getting married you will expand your service. So you should do that. Actually all my disciples are *sannyasis* because they have surrendered everything in the service of Kṛṣṇa."

—*Letter of November 21, 1975*

"That you cannot stay anywhere very long due to the rules of your visa is a blessing in disguise. It is very good for a *sannyasi.* Narada Muni was similarly cursed by Daksa that he could not stay anywhere very long, and this only increases preaching. So you also increase your preaching and be more merciful to a greater number of persons."

—*Letter of January 24, 1976*

"Regarding returning to your own village, a *sannyasi* is not supposed to go back to his own village."

—*Letter of September 21, 1975*

"The spirit soul is equal in either a man or a woman. For one who is actually engaged in the service of Krsna, there is no such distinction as man or woman. In the *Bhagavad-gita,* sixth chapter, first verse, it is stated, *anasritah karma-phalam karyam karma karoti yah/ sa sannyasi ca yogi ca na niragnir na cakriyah.* Anyone acting for Krsna, he is a *sannyasi* or *sannyasini.* It is also stated: *striyo vaisyas tatha sudras te pi yanti param gatim.* So spiritually everyone is equal. But materially a woman cannot be given *sannyasa,* but you should not be bothered because you are certainly on the spiritual platform."

—*Letter of February 4, 1976*

"Regarding your wanting to leave your family and take *sannyasa,* what is your family? You live aside from your wife, and you have no children, so you are already *sannyasa.* Anyway, we can consider later on. First we have to push this movement. That is most important."

—*Letter of July 29, 1975*

"I think that B. should follow the example of Rupa Gosvami. Rupa Gosvami took *sannyasa* and gave fifty percent in charity, twenty-five percent for family use, and he kept twenty-five percent for emergencies. Krsna wants to see that their life is sacrificed, but also accumulation of money should be given to Krsna. Life to Krsna and money to wife is not a good decision."

—*Letter of February 21, 1976*

"If you feel *maya* attractive, then live an honest life as a householder and contribute to our movement. As a family man you can join Svarupa Damodara and help with the Bhaktivedanta Institute. Caitanya Mahaprabhu says it doesn't matter whether one is a *sannyasi, grhastha, brahmana,* or *sudra.* You have intelligence. Study more and more. If you think you should be married, then do that and assist Bhaktivedanta Institute by giving service. My request is that you don't become an ordinary foolish man. Keep Krsna consciousness in any condition of life. That is success."

—*Letter of October 29, 1976*

32

PRABHUPĀDA TELLS A STORY

In a lecture on August 5, 1972, in San Diego, Prabhupāda was explaining how foolish people demand to see God. But no one can see God unless he has the qualification of faithfulness. It is not a frivolous thing that one can simply ask or challenge, "Can you show me God?" Rather, one must be serious and eager to actually see God. Hearing submissively about God, one may develop the desire to see Him.

"There is a story in this connection. It is very instructive. Try to hear. One professional reciter was reciting about *Bhāgavata,* describing that Kṛṣṇa, being highly decorated with all jewels, is sent for tending the cows in the forest. There was a thief at that meeting, and when he heard about Kṛṣṇa, he thought, 'Why not go to Vṛndāvana and plan to catch this boy in the forest with so many valuable jewels? I can go there and catch the child and take all the jewels.' That was the thief's intention. He was serious, thinking, 'I must find out that boy. Then in one night I will become a millionaire.' He went there to Vṛndāvana. His qualification was, 'I must see Kṛṣṇa. I must see Kṛṣṇa.' That anxiety, that eagerness, made it possible that in Vṛndāvana he saw Kṛṣṇa. He saw Kṛṣṇa in the same way he was informed by the *Bhāgavata* reader. Then he thought, 'Oh, You are such a nice boy, Kṛṣṇa.' He began to flatter. He thought that flattering, 'Yes, I will take all the jewels.' But then he proposed his real business to Kṛṣṇa. 'I may take some of Your ornaments? You are so rich.'

"'No, no,' said Kṛṣṇa. 'My mother will be angry. I cannot do it.' Kṛṣṇa was only a child. So he became more and more eager for Kṛṣṇa, and then by Kṛṣṇa's association he had already become purified. At last Kṛṣṇa said, 'All right, you can take.' But then the man became a devotee, because by His association, some way or other, we should come in contact with Kṛṣṇa. Some way or other, then we will become purified."

33

PRABHUPĀDA TELLS SHORT STORIES

"There is a very instructive story, and it is a historical fact. The Muslim emperor Akhbar once inquired from his minister, 'How long does one remain in lusty desires?'

"The minister replied, 'Up to the last point of death.'

"Akhbar did not believe it, and he said, 'No, no, how can you say that?'

"'All right,' said the minister. 'I shall reply in time.'

"So one day, all of a sudden, the minister approached the emperor and said, 'You be immediately ready to come with me with your young daughter.' Akhbar knew that his minister was very intelligent and that there must be some purpose. He went with him, and the minister took him to a person who was going to die. The minister then asked Akhbar, 'Kindly study the man who is about to die, on his face.'

"So Akhbar noticed that as he and his young daughter were entering, the dying man was looking to the face of the young girl. In this way, Akhbar understood, 'Yes, what he said is true. Up to the last point of death the desire is there to see the face of a young girl.'

"This is called *duṣpūreṇa*—it is never fulfilled. This attraction of man and woman and family life continues."

Once there was a monkey who was jumping around in the forest when he saw a big tree that was half cut through with a plug wedged in it. The system of the wood cutters was that they would sometimes half cut through a big tree, leave it for the day, and then come back and cut the rest of it the next day. In the meantime, to preserve their cut, they would put a plug there. This monkey became very curious about the half-cut tree and he managed to push out the plug. The big tree suddenly joined and cut off his tail. The moral: mind your own business.

34

PERSONAL

Meticulous

Prabhupāda was meticulous. He put on his Vaiṣṇava *tilaka* that way, artistically and methodically performing each function. He used his pen that way also. He took it out of his pen box, used it, and then returned it to the box on his desk. Prabhupāda warned his servants never to touch anything or move anything on his desk.

His book writing was also like that. His standard was that each and every word out of tens of thousands of words from thousands of verses must have its own synonym. Prabhupāda had a limited time for writing the *Bhāgavatam* every day, yet he never diminished his standard that each word get its own synonym. Then he always gave the English translation, and then a purport. Whenever he saw the editors or publishers failing in this meticulous standard, he became very upset.

In general, he demanded his disciples be very careful in all their activities. Deity worship, for example, he only gradually introduced because of its meticulous demands. When a devotee who was worshiping the Deity inquired how to obtain *bhāva,* or ecstatic attachment to the Lord, Prabhupāda replied by stressing a meticulous following of the rules and regulations: the devotees should be punctual, clean, and give the Deity nice dresses and food.

Śrīla Prabhupāda was particularly meticulous in handling finance for Kṛṣṇa, especially in India. He personally looked into the accounting and saw down to the single rupee how his managers spent money.

His Self-Sacrifice to Give Kṛṣṇa Consciousness to Others

Śrīla Prabhupāda always stressed that Kṛṣṇa consciousness should be given to others and that one should sacrifice his own activities to do that. Prabhupāda spent his own energies lecturing on an elementary level again and again, but he was enthusiastic to do this. He didn't just sit in one place and think of Kṛṣṇa, but he dedicated himself, always traveling, giving his all.

Sometimes even his main work of writing was put aside in order to travel in India to carry out the instruction of his spiritual master. As for the writings themselves, they were aimed as welfare work to help others. Thus he produced the *Bhāgavatam* to help people in Kṛṣṇa consciousness, to provide his followers and other readers with sufficient scripture, because by reading, their lives would become perfect.

This was the special nature of Prabhupāda's Kṛṣṇa consciousness, that all of his activities were aimed at distributing it. Thus he would always give time to his own devotees and answer their questions and guide them.

If one claimed to be a devotee, Prabhupāda could size him up to see whether he had any of Prabhupāda's spirit—to give his life to Kṛṣṇa consciousness. Since no one could measure up to Prabhupāda's commitment, he could cut down in a no-nonsense way any person's pretension of spiritual stature. Yet although Prabhupāda had the power to do this, he was always humble about himself and his own contribution. He said, for example, that he was fallen, that he was not a great scholar, that he was just trying to carry out the order of his Guru Mahārāja, that he had no good qualities of his own. However, Kṛṣṇa says of a person like Prabhupāda that he is the dearmost servant who will ever be. Prabhupāda also encouraged whatever little spark of self-sacrifice he found in others.

Sometimes when a person is very intensely involved in his own cause or a cause for which he is working, he may have to sacrifice very personal and lovable qualities. Yet although Prabhupāda was fully intent in the campaign to spread and organize Kṛṣṇa consciousness, he was always full of lovable personal qualities. He appeared to be simple, spontaneous, and of course, highly spiritual to whomever he met as he extended Kṛṣṇa consciousness to them according to their capacity to receive it.

35

REALIZATIONS

There is a devotee in Vṛndāvana named Viśāla who is sometimes a source of comic relief because he has some humorous character traits. One time I saw how Viśāla became like a little boy in front of Śrīla Prabhupāda and pleased him.

On one particular day, Prabhupāda was having *darśana* with a room full of Indians. Viśāla suddenly walked in along with his wife. Although Prabhupāda was preaching, Viśāla entered with such a commotion that Prabhupāda's conversation came to a halt. Some of the people in the room looked at Viśāla as a source of disturbance, but Viśāla went ahead and paid his full obeisances to Prabhupāda in a very loud voice: *nama oṁ viṣṇu-pādāya kṛṣṇa-preṣṭhāya bhūtale śrīmate bhaktivedānta-svamin iti nāmine.*

As Viśāla became the focus of the room's attention, I was thinking, "Boy, this guy is really something!" Then Viśāla sat up and walked right up to Prabhupāda's table. He was carrying a little wicker basket covered with a cloth, and he placed this in front of Prabhupāda, pulled the cover off, and said to Prabhupāda, "My wife made some simply wonderfuls for a simply wonderful spiritual master!" Viśāla said it with a total, big smile, and Śrīla Prabhupāda also smiled back in a complete way.

Then I began to think, "Now *that* is the kind of thing I would like to do in front of Prabhupāda one of these days. I would like to be able to be so unattached, so uninhibited, just once to go in front of Prabhupāda and be able to glorify him. If I could only say something praiseworthy of Prabhupāda." Because usually there was a big debate in my mind going back and forth. I would think I will go ahead and say this to Prabhupāda, but then I would think no, that's not worthy enough. Then I would think well, what about this? And then I would think no, that's not good enough. I usually ended up not saying anything. There would be a long silence. Then whatever opportunity I had to praise Prabhupāda—which is the disciple's duty—would slip through my fingers. Yet Viśāla had come in and he just did it in a fling, unabashed.

When Prabhupāda smiled, the whole roomful of people felt relieved. At first, when Viśāla had come in, everything had become quiet and heavy because he had interrupted. Now, because Prabhupāda was pleased, everyone else was pleased.

Then Viśāla did another fascinating thing. He turned around and faced the entire room, reached into the little shoulder bag he was wearing, and pulled out some *Back to Godhead* magazines. He started preaching about Prabhupāda and Prabhupāda's books and *Back to Godhead,* and he just went ahead and distributed them to all the people in the room. The thing was done so nicely that he had the whole room completely charmed and friendly. Prabhupāda just sat back, and you could see that Prabhupāda was pleased with him. Viśāla went on glorifying Prabhupāda's books and told how professors in the West had reviewed the books. Many of the Indians in the room didn't even speak enough English to follow all of what Viśāla was saying, but because of his mood, everyone became relaxed.

Then to end the whole thing, Viśāla did something else that really blew my mind. He turned to Śrīla Prabhupāda and said, "Śrīla Prabhupāda, my beloved spiritual master, I have read all of your books except for one. I haven't read the *Madhya-līlā,* Volume Three." At that time, the *Madhya-līlā* had just come out, and the only person in Vṛndāvana with a copy was Prabhupāda because a copy had just been sent to him from the West. After a silent pause, Viśāla said, "Śrīla Prabhupāda, may I borrow your copy?" The devotees in the room were stunned at this boldness, but Prabhupāda simply called Nava-yogendra forward and said, "Give him the *Madhya-līlā,* Volume Three." Viśāla, very pleased, took the book and exited after a wonderful exchange with Prabhupāda.

—Kuṇḍalī dāsa Adhikārī

A devotee took me to see Śrīla Prabhupāda—it was in Los Angeles in 1968—and I went into his room. When I first saw him I thought, *I should be nice to this old man and say something nice.* The first thing I asked him was, "How are you feeling, sir?" Śrīla Prabhupāda immediately pointed to his Deities. He said, "With Rādhā and Kṛṣṇa here, how could anyone not be well?" I didn't understand what he was speaking about or what the Deities were. I just sat there and then he started talking to me. After receiving his *darśana,* I had become very impressed. I had some money in my pocket and I thought I would like to give him an offering, so I took out the money, about a hundred dollars, and I gave it to Prabhupāda. He embraced me and touched my head, and at that moment I felt that I had found my true father.

When I left Prabhupāda's room I kept walking down a long road, and all I could think about was how I was going to stay with Prabhupāda. I had no conception at all of what Kṛṣṇa consciousness was or devotional service, but Prabhupāda was such a wonderful person that by visiting him for an hour, my heart was totally captivated.

—Dīnanātha dāsa Adhikārī

When I first met Prabhupāda I was eight years old. The first time he said something to me personally was on a morning walk on Venice Beach. I ran up to Prabhupāda and said, "Prabhupāda, I have found these shells. What should I do with them?" Śrīla Prabhupāda looked at me. He put his cane in the sand, and he said, "Put them down and wash your hands." It was just a little instruction, but I felt so happy that Prabhupāda told me to put down the shells and wash my hands. I immediately ran back to the water, put the shells down, and washed my hands. Then I came back and followed Prabhupāda.

It wasn't so much the things that Prabhupāda did, it was Prabhupāda himself that made them wonderful. Just to be next to him was not only an honor, but it was a pleasure. You wanted to be near him, to hold his feet, to hear from him. You wanted to see him. Just like at *kīrtana,* the devotees would crowd around Prabhupāda and there would be bodyguards to clear a way for him. The wonderful thing was the *way* that he did everything."

—*Raghunātha dāsa*

36

REALIZATIONS

One time in Hyderabad Śrīla Prabhupāda revealed the essence of our relationship with him. We were walking east about a mile from the main road as the sun rose in our faces. Suddenly, a car came forward driven by some young ruffians. I was next to Śrīla Prabhupāda on his right side and Mahāṁsa was walking on his left side—like bodyguards. The car didn't slow down, but kept approaching us. I became so angry that I ran out in front of Prabhupāda, right in front of the car, and I put up my hands and yelled "Stop!" My mood was as if to say, "You better run over me first if you come any closer!" I was shaking all over because the car almost did run me over. It was driven by two Indian teenagers. They stopped just in front of me. Prabhupāda then came up beside me. He looked happy and was smiling. He said, "Very good, Mūrti. You laid down your life for me." Then he walked around the car and kept walking down the road. I took it that this was a sign of our relationship.

Prabhupāda's opinion of me and other devotees like me who were not his intimate *sannyāsī* disciples, was like the relationship of a general to his soldiers. He always related to us in a military mood—very strict and cordial. We never felt that we could be on familiar terms with Śrīla Prabhupāda in terms of conversation or in activities, as did some of the other devotees, like Gurudāsa and others that we knew. For some reason, many in our generation of devotees related to Prabhupāda in that way, that he was the master, the great general, and we were the privates. He lived that relationship and so did we.

—*Mūrti dāsa*

My first personal encounter with Śrīla Prabhupāda was in Switzerland. Prabhupāda was meeting a very famous person, and he was in his room along with Guru Gaurāṅga and Bhagavān and Yogeśvara. I was cooking for Prabhupāda, so when he came out we rushed to the door to see him. As Śrīla Prabhupāda and the others went by, they were almost facing the kitchen door. When they saw us there, Yogeśvara stopped the party and said, "Śrīla Prabhupāda, this is a very famous—world famous—fashion model, blah, blah, blah . . ." As he went on talking it was so embarrassing for me to have to listen. I wanted to tell Śrīla Prabhupāda, "It's not true, I'm a devotee now. Don't listen to him." I was looking at Prabhupāda like I was saying, "Help!" Prabhupāda looked at me straight in the eyes, and then Yogeśvara stopped. Then Yogeśvara rephrased the whole thing again. I felt like I was sinking into the ground. I had the feeling that I had disappeared from the surface of the globe, and when I came back to my consciousness, Prabhupāda was still there looking at me. Yogeśvara was finishing off his little speech. Prabhupāda then gave me a beautiful smile, like a little five-year-old, a mischievous, brilliant smile. It was just unbelievable, like the whole sun is in your room. He looked at me with a glint in his eyes and said, "Chant Hare Kṛṣṇa." I said, "Yes, Prabhupāda," and I fell flat on the ground. Prabhupāda continued walking.

When he told me to chant Hare Kṛṣṇa then, I felt that this was the instruction I had been waiting for all my life. I was very satisfied, and I knew for sure that Kṛṣṇa consciousness was for me. He confirmed the importance of chanting Hare Kṛṣṇa, but it was also for me specifically. I became convinced that this was my way to please Śrīla Prabhupāda."

—*Śatarūpā-devī dāsī*

37

Prabhupāda's activities in the unusual and sometimes stressful situation of airplane travel constitute a special *līlā*. Sometimes the devotees accompanying Prabhupāda felt acute discomfort in having to see their spiritual master in such an inconvenienced setting. For example, it was Śrīla Prabhupāda's habit to eat alone, but on planes this was not possible. Of course, he was sitting on the same, equal level with his disciples and with nondevotees. Usually, after finishing eating, he told his disciples to share the remnants among themselves. Sometimes the devotees felt that such eating in Prabhupāda's presence was perhaps offensive, but Prabhupāda always insisted that they should honor the *prasādam* after he did. He was concerned to see that the devotees were nicely taken care of. Sometimes passengers in the opposite seats would observe the devotees eating and notice that they were eating leftovers from their master's plate. These situations had their nice features in that the devotees were forced, by Prabhupāda's presence, to stay in transcendental consciousness and not be affected by the mundane opinions of the *karmīs*.

On one occasion when Śrīla Prabhupāda was flying from Venezuela, the only food he had with him was puffed rice wrapped up in aluminum foil. When his servant told Śrīla Prabhupāda that this was all they had and asked whether Prabhupāda wanted to take something from the plane kitchen, Prabhupāda replied, "No, we have our *prasādam*. That's all right."

Prabhupāda's servant unwrapped the aluminum foil and sat it on the little table before Prabhupāda. Śrīla Prabhupāda ate about half of the puffed rice and then handed it over to the two disciples beside him. Just as the devotees were about to share the remnants, a stewardess walked down the aisle, looked at the scene with Prabhupāda, stuck her hand into the puffed rice, took a handful, and ate it. "This is very good," she said innocently. "What is it?"

Prabhupāda's servant replied, "It is puffed rice."

Prabhupāda looked up at the stewardess and was smiling at her. She smiled back at Prabhupāda, saying, "This is very good."

"I'm glad you like it," said Prabhupāda's servant.

"Are you having anything else to eat?" the stewardess asked.

"Well, we are vegetarians," said Śrutakīrti. "Unless there is some fruit or something, we won't take."

"Oh, I'll go up to first-class and get you a basket of fruit," she said. The stewardess was back in a few moments with a basket of fruit along with knives and glasses. She asked if there was anything further she could get.

"Prabhupāda, would you like some milk?" asked Śrutakīrti.

"Yes," said Prabhupāda, "*hot* milk." Usually it was not an easy thing to get a cup of hot milk from the airplane crew, but on this occasion, the stewardess was very willing. She went forward and soon returned with hot milk. Everything had happened spontaneously, starting from the moment the stewardess took a bit of *prasādam* from Prabhupāda's plate. Devotees in the temple used to run and dive to get Prabhupāda's *mahā-prasādam,* but this stewardess had just spontaneously grabbed a handful and eaten it, and then she had become inspired to render service to Śrīla Prabhupāda.

"That was really something," remarked Śrutakīrti after the stewardess had left.

"It's natural," said Śrīla Prabhupāda. "Women have a motherly tendency to be like this."

On another flight, coming from Japan to Hawaii, Śrīla Prabhupāda wanted to have another exchange with a stewardess. Śrīla Prabhupāda was reading in a magazine about women's liberation. With this in mind, he turned to the devotee sitting beside him and said, "Call the stewardess over. Tell her if she wants to be liberated, she should shave her head like us. Then she will be liberated."

The devotee with Prabhupāda couldn't believe that he really meant it.

"Go ahead," insisted Prabhupāda. "Call her over and cut a joke. Tell her to shave her head."

Prabhupāda seemed quite serious about his request and repeated it, but the devotee with him refused to do it.

38

Śrīla Prabhupāda could do something very unusual, yet he would do it as if it were perfectly normal. Such was the case when he decided to bathe in a washroom at the airport in Bangkok. He had been flying several hours and was taking a two-hour stop-over in the transit area before heading on for another several hours' flight. It was very early in the morning, and the airport was not crowded. While waiting, Śrīla Prabhupāda decided he wanted to bathe, so he asked his servant to get him fresh clothes and his bathing paraphernalia. To accomplish this, the servant had to first locate their luggage, which was being changed from one airplane to another. When his servant managed to do that, he and Śrīla Prabhupāda went to the men's room.

This particular airport had no shower facility, but Śrīla Prabhupāda wanted to use whatever they had. He walked up to the small sink and said he would bathe there. The local attendant was with them in the bathroom, and when he saw what Prabhupāda was about to do, he became upset. Prabhupāda proceeded coolly. Using his *loṭā,* he obtained water from the faucet and, covering the lower portion of his body with a *gamchā,* began washing with soap. The attendant didn't directly confront them, but he became increasingly upset, mumbling to himself as Śrīla Prabhupāda spilled water all over the floor. When Prabhupāda finished, his servant handed him a towel, and he dried off. Then he put on his fresh clothing.

Only as they started to leave did the attendant come forward. He approached Śrīla Prabhupāda and began speaking in the Thai language. They couldn't understand his words, but he was obviously angry.

"Just go away," said Śrīla Prabhupāda's servant, and he thought, *You're lucky you're getting to wipe up* this *water.*

"I think he's a little upset," said Śrīla Prabhupāda's servant.

Prabhupāda laughed and said, "I had to bathe. I was feeling very tired."

39

Prabhupāda's sister Piśimā was a great favorite of his and also of his disciples as they witnessed her devotion to Śrīla Prabhupāda and his transcendental relationship with her.

The devotees first heard of her when she sent Śrīla Prabhupāda some *papadums* in the mail in 1967. When Prabhupāda said these things had been sent by his sister, the devotees became curious and asked more about her.

"Yes," said Śrīla Prabhupāda, "she always attacks me."

The devotees were shocked and asked, "What do you mean, Śrīla Prabhupāda?"

Prabhupāda laughed heartily and said, "She attacks me with her tears. Sometimes when she sees me, she cries. That is a woman's weapon." When they asked more, Prabhupāda told a little more about Piśimā.

He said that when he was a young boy, he used to beat her once a day. When she got married, he once went to her house and was beating her there, but their mother told him, "You don't have to beat her now because she has a husband. If she does something wrong, her husband can beat her." Prabhupāda objected and said, "No, this is my relationship with my sister. I must be strict with her."

One day in Vṛndāvana, Prabhupāda entered the sewing room where his female disciples were working. His sister had been there, distributing sweets to the girls, but she had momentarily gone off to the bathroom.

"Where is the fat one?" asked Prabhupāda.

"The fat one?" asked one of his disciples.

"My sister, where is she?"

"Oh, she stepped out to the ladies' room, Śrīla Prabhupāda."

"When she comes back," said Śrīla Prabhupāda, "tell her I want to see her."

By intimate dealings like this, devotees enjoyed associating with Prabhupāda and Piśimā.

One time in Māyāpur, the lights went out and Prabhupāda called over his *sannyāsī* disciple Pañcadraviḍa Swami.

"Please take my sister downstairs," Prabhupāda requested. On Prabhupāda's order, Pañcadraviḍa led Piśimā downstairs, appreciating the relationship of Prabhupāda and his sister.

Sometimes Prabhupāda would mock his sister in his disciples' presence. She could not understand the language, but enjoyed the attention from her wonderful brother.

"Look at her," said Prabhupāda, "how fat she is." When the devotees started laughing, Piśimā looked up and started laughing also. "Do you know any person who is fat without eating?" Prabhupāda asked.

"No, Prabhupāda," a disciple replied. "I don't think that is possible."

"Yes," Prabhupāda laughed, "but she tells me she is eating very little, yet she keeps on gaining weight. But I know she is eating."

Sometimes devotees working on Prabhupāda's personal staff were bewildered how to deal with her. One servant complained to Prabhupāda that Piśimā was sleeping in the servants' quarters and the men couldn't use the room. Although they had spoken to her, she would not listen. Prabhupāda said that he would tell her that she cannot do that. Even after talking with Prabhupāda, however, she was determined and continued to loiter around the servants' quarters, just in order to be near to Prabhupāda.

When the devotees tried to explain to Piśimā that her cooking was not good for Prabhupāda's digestion, she replied that if he wanted to, Prabhupāda could eat nails and digest them.

One night at a *paṇḍāl* attended by tens of thousands of people, Piśimā joined in the ecstasy of worshiping Prabhupāda. Indians were rushing to the stage to touch Prabhupāda's feet. Piśimā herself went up, touched Prabhupāda's feet, and then returned to the audience and touched many persons. She began to go back and forth, touching Prabhupāda's feet and then touching persons in the audience. Prabhupāda stopped her angrily. "Tell her to sit down!" Śrīla Prabhupāda ordered. "Stop this!" Piśimā realized that she had made a blunder, and so she went home and returned the next day with a big feast for Prabhupāda.

40

LITTLE DROPS *of* NECTAR

"Prabhupāda, when there is a choice to make in the service of Kṛṣṇa and you don't know whether to do this or that, how do you choose?"

"There is no choice," Prabhupāda replied. "You simply do what Kṛṣṇa gives you." Raṇacora dāsa was trying to understand whether he should go back to Manchester, England. He had been there twice to open a preaching center, but for different reasons he had had to come back. Now he was asking Prabhupāda for his permission and blessing to make another attempt.

"I was wondering whether I should go to Manchester to preach," Raṇacora asked directly. "Perhaps you can tell me what to do."

Prabhupāda answered while walking toward the window. "How many times has a center been opened in Manchester?"

Raṇacora replied that it had been tried twice.

"This time if you go," said Śrīla Prabhupāda, "it must not close."

Prabhupāda looked away, and Raṇacora took this to mean the meeting should end. He made his obeisances at the door, but just before leaving, he asked another question.

"Prabhupāda, is there any special instruction, special service, you can give me?"

Prabhupāda looked at him and said, "Simply preach, that is all. Simply preach."

When the tape recorder at 26 Second Avenue broke, it was Umāpati dāsa's responsibility to fix it. One time a fuse had blown and Umāpati needed thirty-five cents to get a new one. Meeting Śrīla Prabhupāda in the courtyard of the building he asked for the money.

"The student shouldn't ask the spiritual master for money," said Prabhupāda.

Umāpati didn't know what to do or say. He didn't have any money, and he wanted to fix the tape recorder. Despite Prabhupāda's instructions, Umāpati repeated that he didn't have the money.

Prabhupāda also repeated that the student should not ask the spiritual master for money. Finally, Prabhupāda gave him the thirty-five cents, but only after making sure that he understood very well that a disciple should not ask the spiritual master for money.

While Jagaddhātrī-devī dāsī was receiving her *gāyatrī-mantra* instructions from Prabhupāda, she asked him when the mantra should be chanted. Prabhupāda replied, "morning, noon, and night." Then she asked, "Śrīla Prabhupāda, how am I going to remember you and surrender to you for the rest of my life?" Prabhupāda smiled and replied that if she chanted sixteen rounds a day and followed the four principles she would remember him and surrender to him. Prabhupāda was then quiet for a few seconds and added, "Don't forget to feed me."

41

ŚRĪLA PRABHUPĀDA SAID

On Challenges and Outside Influences on ISKCON

"Regarding the two men who have come to us from Gaudiya Math, for the time being we should try not to give shelter to such persons unless they are tested."

—*Letter of December 4, 1976*

"Why Nitai should be attending lectures outside our temple? If he is not satisfied with the standard of lectures in our temple, then he should be permitted to give some lectures himself, but this habit of going outside to hear others should be stopped immediately. I am writing one letter to Nitai, a copy of this is enclosed for your reference."

—Letter of July 14, 1976

"I have received reports that you have been developing the habit of going outside the temple to hear lectures by others outside like Nrsimhavallabha. Also, I have heard now that some of the Indian devotees are doing likewise.

"Strictly nobody should go outside to hear lectures by others. If you are not satisfied by the caliber of the classes of the Krishna-Balaram Mandir, then you should give another class. But you cannot go outside for hearing others' lectures. Kindly stop this habit immediately."

—Letter of July 14, 1976

"Do not let your mind be disturbed by so many things. Our movement is for chanting Hare Krsna. One can be happy under any condition. *Samah duhkha-sukham dhiram.* Krsna consciousness does not depend on any external arragement. You should not go outside the shelter of this ISKCON. Just try to be happy by chanting Hare Krsna and follow the regulative principles."

—Letter of February 15, 1976

"I am actually authority accepted by authority. In the *Caitanya-caritamrta* it is said, *krsna-sakti vina nahe tara pravartana.* So now the Hare Krsna movement is world known, and learned scholars, etc., give plaudits to me as Professor Judah has. So why am I not authority? Nobody says Bon Swami has done it, or Vivekananda, or any other Swami. There are so many *yogis* and swamis coming, but nobody is giving credit to them, they are giving credit to me. So why am I not authority? If Krsna accepts me as authority, then who can deny it? . . . On the whole, if his motive is to suppress me and that is why he has come here, how can we receive him? He has already given one professor a wrong impression. He may be treated as a guest. If he comes to our center, give him *prasadam,* honor him as an elder Vaisnava, but he cannot speak or lecture. If he wants to lecture, you can tell him there is already another speaker scheduled. That's all."

—*Letter of June 4, 1975*

42

ŚRĪLA PRABHUPĀDA TELLS SHORT STORIES

"If you simply understand Kṛṣṇa thoroughly, then you are liberated. *Janma karma ca me divyam.* They question, 'If Kṛṣṇa is God, why is mother Yaśodā binding Him?' But they do not know that that is pleasure. There are many instances . . .

"I will cite one instance. There was a big prime minister in England, Gladstone, Queen Victoria's prime minister. Someone came to see him and the servant informed him that the prime minister is busy, so you wait. The man was waiting and an hour passed and still there was no message. Finally he opened the door because he wanted to see what the prime minister was doing. He saw then that the prime minister had become a horse and his grandchild was driving him. That is enjoyment. He is the prime minister, but he has become the horse of his grandson. This is the position with Kṛṣṇa."

"Yes, you cannot want something unless you derive some pleasure from it. Just like the devotees' theater performance in Ahmedabad. They showed how the butcher was killing animals and he was attracted to that killing. I have also seen this myself in Calcutta. I was passing through, and one hotel man was cutting the throat of a chicken. After being cut, the chicken was jumping and the man was laughing. He was taking pleasure in this. For me it was horrible, but he was taking very nice pleasure in it. The half-cut chicken was jumping, and the man's son was crying. The man was asking his son, 'Why are you crying?' So it is a question of different qualities. One is attracted and one finds it something that is detracted. The attractiveness is called mellow, *rāsa*, taste."

"There is a Bengali proverb that one girl was to dance on a stage. So in Indian civilization, the women, they cover their heads in front of their superiors. But this girl was to go on stage. So why should she put on her veil in this case? Where is the opportunity to appear as a household wife on stage? So the saying is, 'You have come to dance, so why put on the veil?' Similarly, Arjuna was chastised, 'You have come to fight, and now you are becoming very unviolent.' This is all nonsense. You have to do your duties in proper place. That is Āryan."

"There is a story about one man, a cook, who bought a nice new pair of shoes. But all morning long he was in the kitchen cooking, so he couldn't use his shoes. Similarly, all afternoon he was cooking. So what did he do? At night when he went to sleep he wore the shoes. So these shoes (which the devotees had sent Prabhupāda in the mail) are so nice, but I don't know when I shall be able to wear them. So when taking rest at night I shall wear them."

"The scientists admit their ignorance. They are simply bluffing. Another bluff is the Mars-going expedition. The business is going on in Arizona, that's all. After a few years they will present some stones and say, 'Now we went to Mars. There is no possibility of living there. Take this stone and sand and be satisfied for your millions of dollars that you have spent.'

" . . . There is a song in Bengal that formerly anything European, *sāhab*, that is good. So one person was selling meat, the flesh of a dog. No one takes the flesh of a dog, at least in India, but he said, 'This is not ordinary. This was the dog, that was killed by a viceroy. It is *that* dog. So because the viceroy killed it, it has become a nice dog and you can eat it.' The scientists are like that. Anything they say is to be accepted."

43

PERSONAL

His Method of Teaching

Prabhupāda taught from an elementary level of Kṛṣṇa consciousness up to the highest point of the philosophy, and this he did in his books, his talks, and his actions.

He was strongly against people taking Kṛṣṇa consciousness cheaply, such as the *prākṛta-sahajiyās* do. Therefore, he repeatedly stressed that one must first understand, "I am not this body." As a compassionate teacher, Prabhupāda gave people as much Kṛṣṇa consciousness as they could assimilate and as was best for their advancement. But his writings ranged the gamut from the preliminary teachings of the *Bhagavad-gītā* all the way to the *Caitanya-caritāmṛta* and the intimate *līlā* of Kṛṣṇa and the *gopīs*.

Furthermore, since Śrīla Prabhupāda was preaching in the twentieth century, he had to confront the heavy forces of atheism represented by Darwinism, Marxism, and Freudism. He wrote and spoke to establish God's existence, the need for God in human society *(varṇāśrama-dharma)*, and to defeat the scientific theory that life comes from matter. This defense of Kṛṣṇa consciousness did not consist of very easily accepted lessons. Kṛṣṇa consciousness had to be presented with logic and by boldly attacking the opposition.

Because Prabhupāda was representing the Vaiṣṇava *sampradāya* from Lord Caitanya, he continually opposed the Māyāvādī philosophy. Lord Caitanya Himself always spoke on the basis of the *Vedānta-sūtra,* establishing the Absolute Truth as the Supreme Person whenever He met with leading scholars. Lord Caitanya 's talks about Rādhā and Kṛṣṇa were reserved for a few people such as Rāmānanda Rāya and Svarūpa Dāmodara. Śrīla Prabhupāda followed this *paramparā* of Lord Caitanya by constantly giving arguments against Māyāvādism and by stressing the chanting of Hare Kṛṣṇa.

Revealing the higher aspects of Kṛṣṇa consciousness was a matter of time, person, and place. Śrīla Prabhupāda gave the highest nectar, the Vṛndāvana-līlā of Kṛṣṇa, in a way fresher than ever. Rūpa Gosvāmī, in a prayer to Lord Caitanya, praised the Lord for giving the highest truth more freely than anyone had given before. That is also true of Śrīla Prabhupāda's magnanimous gift. Without discrimination, Śrīla Prabhupāda presented the *Kṛṣṇa* book in 1969, explained in the form of a summary study so it would not be misunderstood. He also guided his devotee artists to paint pictures of Rādhā and Kṛṣṇa as the very first paintings in ISKCON, along with pictures of Kṛṣṇa and the eight principal *gopīs,* the *rāsa* dance, and Rādhā and Kṛṣṇa on a swing. In the *Caitanya-caritāmṛta,* Kṛṣṇadāsa Kavirāja states that at first he hesitated to tell the most confidential *līlā* of Lord Caitanya, but then he went ahead and wrote, after he considered that the foolish people would not be able to understand and would neglect the confidential knowledge, whereas the sincere devotees would appreciate. Similarly, Śrīla Prabhupāda went ahead and presented *Kṛṣṇa* book even though it is the Tenth Canto and the most confidential part of *Śrīmad-Bhāgavatam.* Soon after this, Prabhupāda presented *The Nectar of Devotion,* in which Kṛṣṇa is repeatedly described as the most attractive youth, as the transcendental lover of Rādhārāṇī.

As soon as Śrīla Prabhupāda's followers became even the slightest bit advanced, Prabhupāda brought them to a standard of worshiping Rādhā-Kṛṣṇa in the temple. Then he introduced the disciples to dressing, feeding, bathing, and putting to rest Their Lordships Rādhā and Kṛṣṇa. As a teacher, he trained them just as his spiritual master had taught: "Don't try to see Kṛṣṇa, but act in such a way that Kṛṣṇa can see you." By unalloyed service in the Kṛṣṇa consciousness movement, by preaching, by taking the trouble to elevate the masses of people, by working when necessary with materialistic persons, a devotee would *earn* the right to understand more and more about Kṛṣṇa.

Śrīla Prabhupāda was the topmost *paramahaṁsa sannyāsī*, yet he appeared in humble saffron. He restrained himself from displays of ecstatic tears, although it was sometimes not possible to entirely restrain them. He showed the ideal behavior and balance in life that cannot be imitated but only strived for and followed. *Avadhūta*, or antisocial behavior, was not Prabhupāda's mission, but rather he appeared as the perfect Vaiṣṇava for all to follow in ISKCON, the saintly teacher and ecstatic devotee. He was a fighter, preacher, a relisher of Kṛṣṇa's pastimes in Vṛndāvana and Māyāpur, as well as a relisher of the continued pastimes of Lord Caitanya in the Kṛṣṇa consciousness movement in Bombay, London, New York, Moscow, and in many other places.

When one thinks of the many qualities of Prabhupāda, that thinking itself brings one to the highest nectarean spiritual platform. Hearing of Rādhā-Kṛṣṇa *from* Śrīla Prabhupāda or hearing about Arjuna *from* Śrīla Prabhupāda is the best way to enter the confidential knowledge of Kṛṣṇa consciousness. No one was a higher teacher or better realized knower of *śāstra,* or a more compassionate worker among the people of this age.

44

REALIZATIONS

I went to one *darśana* with Prabhupāda. Prabhupāda was sitting in a very casual pose with one leg stretched out and the other propped up. His hand was resting by his side, and although he was leaning back, his head was erect.

When Prabhupāda asked for questions, I knew I had to ask him a question. I thought I would ask something that meant a lot to me, something that was troubling me. I asked Prabhupāda, "How does one become humble, and how does one stay humble?" I had the tendency when I was distributing the most books in the temple to become proud. I wanted to know what to do. Prabhupāda looked at me and then looked over at Harikeśa Mahārāja and said, "Tell him what I told them in Chicago." Harikeśa Swami said that there was one *saṅkīrtana* girl in Chicago who had asked Prabhupāda a similar question, and Prabhupāda had replied that she should be like a lion in the chase but a lamb at home.

While I was absorbing this reply, I was looking at Prabhupāda and he was looking back at me. Then suddenly a great surge came from Śrīla Prabhupāda and he said, almost yelling, "Be aggressive for Kṛṣṇa, then it is successful. There are two things: First, if I am aggressive, I should be aggressive in my service for Kṛṣṇa. And second, I should be aggressive also in trying to get Kṛṣṇa's mercy. So both ways—aggressive to preach and aggressive to get the mercy." I had asked Prabhupāda how to become humble, but he said the opposite thing. Yet now I have found out that it is by aggression that I am factually the humblest, because to be aggressive you have to surrender. Within those few words Prabhupāda had actually given me the essence of Kṛṣṇa consciousness."

—*Kṛṣṇa Gopāla dāsa*

Bhūmi-devī dāsī and I were distributing books at the airport when Śrīla Prabhupāda was departing. We had managed to get into the departure lounge. No other devotees were there except Prabhupāda, Jayādvaita, and Śrutakīrti. We were in ecstasy, Bhūmi and I, because here was Śrīla Prabhupāda, but he didn't know we were there. We knew that he was there, and we told the people, "See this gentleman? He's the one who wrote this book. He translated these books." People began to look at the books and look over at Prabhupāda. We distributed many books in the half hour Prabhupāda was there. Then Jayādvaita told Prabhupāda that we were there distributing his books. Prabhupāda looked at us. He had a big smile and was nodding his head. He was very pleased and of course, this was a source of great encouragement for us. We didn't want any personal *darśana;* we just wanted Prabhupāda to know that we were distributing his books.

I remember I used to look at the *saṅkīrtana* board in the temple and they used to write slogans like "We have to make Prabhupāda the most famous man in the world." I used to think, "Yes, that's what we have to do." That used to impress me very much and that's why I wanted to do *saṅkīrtana* so much, because we have to make Prabhupāda the most famous person in the world.

Another time, we were again distributing books at the airport when Prabhupāda was leaving. This was in 1976, in New York, after the Ratha-yātrā, when Śrīla Prabhupāda was feeling sick. He was about to leave. I was distributing at BOAC Airlines in *karmī* clothes. We just wanted to see Prabhupāda and it wasn't my intention to be obvious and stand in front of him, but when I was in the middle of distributing a book to a man, Prabhupāda happened to pass right by me. I was so nervous, I said, "Oh, my God. I didn't mean to do that!" As Prabhupāda passed he saw his book and stopped a little bit. Then he looked, and Tamāla Kṛṣṇa Goswami said, "That's Sunīta, Prabhupāda. She distributes your books."

Prabhupāda said *"Acchā,"* and he turned around and looked at me. "Very nice," he said. He then raised his hands, giving his blessings. That was another source of great encouragement for us. We really didn't want anything else from him, just that he knew we were distributing his books.

—*Sunīta-devī dāsī*

45

REALIZATIONS

In Māyāpur in February of 1977, when Prabhupāda first started to get really sick, we were taking turns sitting in his bedroom with him. He was just lying in his bed, so one person would always have to be there. I had a shift of about one hour a day where I would sit next to Prabhupāda's bed. If he coughed you would have to make sure he had his spittoon there and a handkerchief to wipe his face, or you would help him with his blanket or give him water, or help him go to the bathroom, things like that. Prabhupāda was so sick that he was sometimes moaning and he could not sleep because he would be coughing so much. Sometimes he would fall off to sleep for an hour or so.

I had been sitting there for quite a while. It was dark and Prabhupāda was sleeping. Then all of a sudden, he opened his eyes and said "Have you ever been to Allahabad?"

I said, "No, Śrīla Prabhupāda."

Prabhupāda went, "Hmmm." After that he went back to rest. I was amazed how out of nowhere, he had opened his eyes and asked me that. Then after another while he was resting, and he opened his eyes and said, "Is the model of the new building here yet?"

I said, "Yes, Śrīla Prabhupāda. Surabhi Swami brought it. It is just outside the window."

Prabhupāda said, "Ahh . . ." Then he began to rest again. And so it went. He would sleep for some time, then suddenly open his eyes and ask a very specific question, then go back to sleep again. I could see that he wasn't like us. When we sleep, we just go completely unconscious. Even while moaning and coughing, sleeping, Śrīla Prabhupāda was meditating on preaching.

—*Rādhā-vallabha dāsa*

Śrīla Prabhupāda's quarters in Hawaii took up the top floor and faced the front of the temple. His servants also had one bedroom. One day while Śrīla Prabhupāda was there, I was standing and talking with Kuśa. We were redoing Prabhupāda's *vyāsāsana* and talking about the best type of glue to use to put on jewels. I was going on and on about how when I was in New Dvārakā we used a certain kind of glue. All of a sudden, someone came over and said, "Do you know that Śrīla Prabhupāda is standing by the open window, listening to everything you are saying?" We looked up and immediately paid our obeisances. I felt so embarrassed. He was just watching us the whole time.

Later, I reflected on that experience and I realized that if we just remember Prabhupāda, he is always with us. We can carry on whole conversations as if Prabhupāda is standing there listening, and our dealings and everything should be conducted just as if Prabhupāda were here. He *is* with us. As much as you love him, that's how much he is present in the heart of the disciple.

—*Sangītā-devī dāsī*

46

PRABHUPĀDA'S PRASĀDAM

Pālikā-devī dāsī regularly cooked for Śrīla Prabhupāda and she recalls his favorite preparations.

"A first favorite for Prabhupāda was always *kacaurīs,* especially *urad dāl kacaurīs.* In sweets he liked *sandeśa* and *rasagullās*. Also, he liked a good, hot *jallebī.* With every meal there had to be a bitter vegetable made with *karela* (bitter melon) or *nīm* leaves. He liked *nīm baigan* very much, a preparation mentioned in the *Caitanya-caritāmrta*. Prabhupāda loved *urad dāl,* and he taught me to make it with fennel, ginger, and asafetida—all these must be in the *chaunce*. Actually, Śrīla Prabhupāda enjoyed a wide variety of foods.

"Once, for weeks he would have *kitchrī* daily with vegetables in it and lots of ghee, and hot *purīs* and *baigan bhāgī* (deep fried eggplant). That and nothing else. I would put the *kitchrī* in his big rice bowl and sometimes he would ask for seconds. If Śrīla Prabhupāda was hungry in the evening, he would take different things according to his taste—many times a ghee vegetable and *purīs* with hot milk. I would generally use *miśrī* (sugar candy or rock candy) rather than sugar. Sometimes he wanted milk only or a tangerine. Often he would have *murī* (puffed rice) with peanuts and milk. I remember a few times he would request me to leave a dish or two of *sandeśa* on the bookshelf in case he became hungry while translating in the night. But always, except once or twice, however the *sandeśa* would be there in the morning. Also, for months Śrīla Prabhupāda had me prepare *baḍas* and coconut chutney for breakfast and *dahī-baḍas* for lunch. He liked these preparations and he remarked on them often. He had yogurt with his lunch every day. As time passed, it became a rule that whenever there was *kitchri,* there must be *kadhi.*"

Mādrī dāsī, who also cooked for Prabhupāda, recalls the time she watched Prabhupāda eating in Surat.

"One day, he finished his lunch and they gave him a whole banana. Prabhupāda started to peel the banana, but I never saw anyone peel a banana like he did. He didn't touch it at all with his left hand. He picked it up in his right hand and started to peel it with his teeth, pulling the strips down with his teeth and then picking out the white part in the center. Then, pulling the white part away, he let the whole banana skin drop from his teeth. He did all this without touching it with his left hand."

Anirdeśavapur dāsa used to cook for Prabhupāda in Māyāpur and he noted Prabhupāda's particular taste for golden raisins.

"We gave Prabhupāda different kinds of dried fruit. He liked golden raisins from China. Aside from these golden raisins, of course, there are the regular black raisins, and also the common golden raisins from the West. In the West they take black raisins and put sulphur in them to turn them golden. Once, a devotee who knew about natural foods would not allow us to get the golden ones, because he said they had sulphur dioxide in them and were unnatural and not good. They gave Prabhupāda the black raisins. Prabhupāda looked at them, but he wasn't very happy. He said, 'These look like little black flies. You don't have the gold ones?'"

47

POTOMAC ISKCON, JULY 1976

It was evening, and Śrīla Prabhupāda had been sitting at the poolside until dark. Just as he was leaving to walk toward the house, two disciples, Praghoṣa and Subuddhi Rāya, ran up to meet him.

"These are some of the boys who are distributing books at the airport, Prabhupāda," said Hari Śauri.

The boys had thrown themselves on the ground and were uttering obeisances, while Śrīla Prabhupāda greeted them heartily: "*Jaya*!"

As the devotees stood up, Prabhupāda asked them, "You are coming back so late?"

"Yes, Prabhupāda!"

"So, what was your score?" asked Prabhupāda.

"Between Vaiseṣika and I," said Praghoṣa, "we did 130 books."

Prabhupāda raised his hands and said "Jaya! Victory!" He then began to walk slowly toward the house, and Praghoṣa began telling Prabhupāda about *saṅkīrtana* at the airport.

"Śrīla Prabhupāda, I met one boy today who gave eighty dollars."

Prabhupāda stopped and looked at Praghoṣa. "*Acchā*! How many books you gave him?'

"Nine books."

Śrīla Prabhupāda smiled, looked at Hari Śauri, and said, "Quite a nice profit."

As they continued walking, Praghoṣa related that this boy was a soldier, so Praghoṣa told him about Arjuna, who was also a soldier and a family man, and who rendered pure devotional service to Kṛṣṇa.

"I explained to him, Śrīla Prabhupāda, how you told us."

By now Śrīla Prabhupāda was at the door of his house. A devotee took off Prabhupāda's shoes.

"Do you want to come in?" Prabhupāda asked Praghoṣa and Subuddhī Rāya.

"Yes, Śrīla Prabhupāda. Of course!"

Inside, they sat on the rug as Śrīla Prabhupāda sat on the couch. Only a small light illuminated the room.

"So how are they liking the books?" asked Prabhupāda.

Praghoṣa then told about a soldier from North Carolina who said that there were nine soldiers in his base who met every Wednesday night and read *Bhagavad-gītā* together.

"Our *Bhagavad-gītā*?" Prabhupāda asked innocently.

"Yes, Śrīla Prabhupāda. *Your Gītā*."

"Just see," said Prabhupāda.

When Hari Śauri explained that Praghoṣa had been working for years with Tripurāri, Prabhupāda asked about Tripurāri's well-being. He also asked about Dhṛṣṭadyumna and said that he was a very good devotee. When Praghoṣa said that he was connected with the New York temple, Śrīla Prabhupāda asked if they were distributing *prasādam* there. He specifically asked if they were selling *kacaurīs*. Śrīla Prabhupāda asked about Bali Mardan, who had left the movement for years and had just returned. Prabhupāda suggested that Bali Mardan cook *kacaurīs* because "he makes the best."

Turning to Subuddhī Rāya, Prabhupāda asked where he was from.

"I was working in India with Gargamuni Swami," said Subuddhī Rāya. "It was nice, but there wasn't much time for reading."

Prabhupāda replied, "Anyway, they are working hard," and he didn't seem to want to hear the criticism.

After a few moments, Prabhupāda asked that the devotees be given *prasādam*. His cook gave them cups of mango ice cream.

Taking the ice cream outside, Praghoṣa and Subuddhī Rāya sat down by the temple and *looked* at the ice cream in ecstasy, trying to remember the whole experience and Prabhupāda's reciprocation with them.

48

ŚRĪLA PRABHUPĀDA SAID

On Cheating

"Unknowing, by some bad habit, if you have done something wrong that is excused. But if you intentionally do wrong thinking, 'I am a devotee, Kṛṣṇa will excuse me,' then you are a rascal. That is cheating Kṛṣṇa. Cheating Kṛṣṇa is to be punished. You cannot cheat Kṛṣṇa. But if by accident knowingly or unknowingly, you have done something which is not good, that is excused."

"Why are we always being cheated, Śrīla Prabhupāda?" This question was asked by Dhanañjaya, a co-manager of Vṛndāvana ISKCON, during a morning walk.

Śrīla Prabhupāda's reply was fiery: "Because you want to cheat Kṛṣṇa. When you stop wanting to cheat Kṛṣṇa, then you will stop being cheated."

One time in Bhubhaneswar, a few GBC men were discussing with Śrīla Prabhupāda whether it was wise to publish certain confidential information that might then be utilized by the movement's enemies. Śrīla Prabhupāda said that confidential information should not be disclosed. He quoted Cāṇakya Paṇḍita, who said that one should not disclose his plans lest they be disrupted. Prabhupāda said that when one is dealing with cunning people, he should also be cunning, or else they will take advantage.

In 1968, when Śrīla Prabhupāda was seeing Śivānanda, the first devotee to go to Europe, off, Prabhupāda warned him to be careful. "I was an old Calcutta boy," said Prabhupāda. "When I came to New York, I never got cheated."

One afternoon, when Prabhupāda's cook brought him his *prasādam*, Prabhupāda did not like the look of the potatoes.

"Why are they pinkish?" he asked.

"I don't know, Śrīla Prabhupāda," the girl replied.

"They are rotten," said Śrīla Prabhupāda. "They put them in cold storage and they are rotten. Everyone is cheating. The whole world is cheating. This material world is rotten."

Later in the afternoon Śrīla Prabhupāda talked further with the devotees about the rotten potatoes and how it was an indication of the material world's cheating.

Śrīla Prabhupāda was anxious when he discovered how the devotees were being cheated in different ways by the contractors in the construction of the Krishna-Balaram temple. One morning Prabhupāda was examining the outside of the building, where there was an unusual mixture of patterns. Prabhupāda decided that the stone patterns were another form of cheating.

"They have given you rejected stone and made this arrangement," said Prabhupāda.

One of the devotees argued, "But Prabhupāda, actually it is a pattern. They had to turn here in the wall, so they made a different pattern."

Prabhupāda said the explanation was nonsense and that it was not a pattern. The contractors had given them rejected stone and charged them for good stone.

The devotee, however, persisted in his explanation: "But Prabhupāda, it is a pattern. Actually it's a pattern."

"Yes, it is a pattern," said Prabhupāda. "It is a clown's pattern and you are a fool for thinking it is a pattern."

During a Sunday feast in Hyderabad, Prabhupāda asked for a sample of the *prasādam* being served to the life members. When the *prasādam* was brought, Prabhupāda said it was terrible and he was infuriated. Prabhupāda asked his disciple in charge, Mahāṁsa Swami, about the cook. Mahāṁsa explained that the man was hired, but was a *brāhmaṇa* cook, and he even wore a thread.

Prabhupāda only became more angry and began to criticize Mahāṁsa.

"But Prabhupāda," said Mahāṁsa, "he's chanting Hare Kṛṣṇa."

Prabhupāda was so convinced that the so-called *brāhmaṇa* chanter was bogus that he fired the cook on the spot.

One of the devotees distributing books to libraries in India informed Prabhupāda that a professor in Aligarh was willing to donate his *Bhāgavatams* to Prabhupāda. Prabhupāda wanted these books for his translation work because they contained different commentaries from the *ācāryas*. Prabhaviṣṇu was sent to get the books with the understanding that the books would be given free.

When he arrived at the man's house, however, the man said that the books were worth 3,000 rupees and that he wanted to become a life member in exchange. Prabhaviṣṇu replied that he would have to ask his authorities, but he supposed it would be all right. He then took the books back to Vṛndāvana and gave them to Śrīla Prabhupāda.

Prabhupāda said the books were only worth a thousand rupees. He said that the man could pay the balance if he wanted to become a life member. Prabhaviṣṇu then wrote back to the man and informed him of this. The man never paid further, but Prabhupāda kept the books.

49

LITTLE DROPS *of* NECTAR

During one visit in Los Angeles, Śrīla Prabhupāda became quite ill. The devotees suggested that he should not come down for the class and that someone else could give it.

"I have to go," said Śrīla Prabhupāda, "because if I do not go, then they will all use it as an excuse not to go when they are sick."

The devotees then volunteered to carry Prabhupāda down the stairs, but he insisted on walking, saying that if they carried him it would be an embarrassment.

However, Prabhupāda's throat was so congested that he did not give the class that morning. He sat on the *vyāsāsana* and attended, just for the sake of his disciples.

When Prabhupāda was very ill in Vṛndāvana, his servant Śrutakīrti used to lie down directly under Prabhupāda's cot, just to be ready if Prabhupāda needed him during the night. Prabhupāda would spread his sleeping net over his bed and Śrutakīrti would extend it to the floor, where he lay "like a dog." One night, however, Śrīla Prabhupāda got up and tried walking without calling for his servant. Because he had so little strength, Prabhupāda fell after a few steps.

"Prabhupāda, what are you doing?" Śrutakīrti jumped up. "Why didn't you call me?"

Prabhupāda replied that he thought he could make it on his own. "I didn't want to disturb you because you are resting."

Śrutakīrti protested that he was there just for that reason —to help Prabhupāda.

Prabhupāda replied that he thought he had the strength, but now he saw that he did not.

When Śilāvatī-devī dāsī introduced a new improvement in the Deity worship, she wanted to make sure that Prabhupāda noticed it, and she hoped he would praise her. While bringing in the Deities' plates onto the altar, she started thinking how it wasn't very nice that everyone should see the plates before they were offered to the Deities. She decided to make a cover for the plates. She prepared a silk cover and planned to use it for the first time on a Sunday afternoon when Prabhupāda was present. According to the schedule, the offering was made just before Prabhupāda's lecture.

When Śilāvatī went onto the altar with the plate and its new cover, however, she noticed that Prabhupāda was not looking. He was looking straight ahead into the room that was crowded with people. Prabhupāda's *vyāsāsana* was adjacent to the platform on which the Jagannātha deities stood. The deities were covered by a curtain that was pulled by hand and went around them like a shower curtain. Śilāvatī was sorry that Prabhupāda was not noticing her new cover, but she went ahead anyway, picked up the cloth from the plate, and began to walk with the curtain, closing it before the deities.

Before she could close the curtain, Prabhupāda leaned towards the microphone and said loudly, "You have gone to all the trouble to make that cover so that no one will see the offering, and yet you have taken the cover off before you have closed the curtain. This is the action of a fool."

50

CHASTISEMENTS

Māyāpur

Starting on a walk from the temple in Māyāpur, Prabhupāda pointed to some plants and asked what they were.

"They are only weeds," replied one of his disciple-managers. "They have no value."

"Everything has a value," said Prabhupāda, "but you don't know it. You don't know how to utilize it, but everything has value."

Another time, walking by the kitchen near the ladies' bathroom, Prabhupāda noticed a bad odor. He turned to the *sannyāsī* disciples walking beside him. "Why is no one complaining?" Prabhupāda objected. "This is such a bad smell. Why are none of you complaining?" Prabhupāda explained that they should immediately complain when there was some sign of the mode of ignorance. The devotees were supposed to be developing at least the mode of *sattva-guṇa,* so when they come in contact with the lower mode, the *tamo-guṇa,* they should make a complaint.

Commenting on Śrīla Prabhupāda's mood in Māyāpur, Bhavānanda Goswami said if a water tap on the land was dripping only once every three hours, then Śrīla Prabhupāda would come at exactly the time it dripped, see it, and say, "Just see, Kṛṣṇa's energy is being wasted." Prabhupāda was especially vigilant within the Māyāpur building. When he found that the *brahmacārīs* did not keep their rooms clean enough, he said, "*Brahmacārī* means dirty." He said the building was meant for guests, and if the devotees were not keeping it clean enough, then they should move out.

Ānakadundubhi dāsa was in charge of cleaning Prabhupāda's room. He knew that Prabhupāda would not tolerate a single grain of dust and would call him back to clean it. One day, after Ānakadundubhi tried his best to keep things perfectly clean, Prabhupāda called him back.

"Śrīla Prabhupāda, something has displeased you?"

"You don't know how to put these sheets straight?" asked Prabhupāda. Prabhupāda's *darśana* room had mattresses covered with white sheets on the floor, but Prabhupāda did not like it if even a single sheet had improper creases in it.

"You have not put these sheets on properly. Did you change them?"

"Yes, Śrīla Prabhupāda. They're fresh."

"Then put them on right," Śrīla Prabhupāda said, and he had several devotees work out the creases and tuck the sheets in properly.

Śrīla Prabhupāda was also strict with the Bengalis in Māyāpur. One day, on the road in front of the temple, a man walked up to Prabhupāda and said that he wanted to give his son to the *gurukula* Prabhupāda said, yes, he should bring him. "I also want to join," said the man. Prabhupāda said yes, but the man would have to come every day for a month. At night he could sleep in his own place. Prabhupāda said the temple would give him *prasādam* and he could work, but at night he would have to go back to his own place.

"I live in Vāmana Pukura and it is far away."

Prabhupāda said it was not so far. The man could walk or take a *ricksha*.

"I don't have so much money," said the man.

Śrila Prabhupāda looked at the man sternly and said, "No conditions!"

Prabhupāda
Nectar 5

Prabhupāda told me that if I simply study the character of Lord Caitanya in *Caitanya-caritāmṛta*—even apart from His being the Supreme Personality of Godhead—just by studying Him as a Vaiṣṇava, I will become perfect. So in the same way, I feel that if people study Prabhupāda, apart from what his inner identity might be—which we don't even know—if they study him just as a Vaiṣṇava or as a great *ācārya* or as a great personality, they will benefit.

—*Girirāja Swami*

1

LITTLE DROPS *of* NECTAR

Śrīla Prabhupāda was always expert in the way he dealt with people. Once his Indian disciple, Haridāsa, walked into Śrīla Prabhupāda's room, put his beads on Prabhupāda's desk, and told Prabhupāda he was leaving. Prabhupāda asked him what the difficulty was. Haridāsa explained that although they were struggling so hard to raise money and make life members, no one wanted to join. It was just too difficult to continue. Prabhupāda said, "Be patient, be patient." He said that when the new building opened up, people would line up to become life members. Then Haridāsa said that he could not work with the foreign disciples. Prabhupāda explained that when you milk a cow, you should expect to get kicked sometimes. He told Haridāsa that the foreigners were doing so much service and that their kicks must be tolerated because we want the milk. In this way, Haridāsa was pacified and he renewed his determination and enthusiasm.

When Prabhupāda first arrived in San Francisco in 1967, Mukunda dāsa had a beard. The beard was very full, but it was not very long, and Mukunda kept it trimmed. Shortly after his arrival, Prabhupāda said, "You look just like a sage." This left Mukunda feeling satisfied, and he did not think it necessary to shave his beard or his hair. Later, however, as more and more disciples shaved their heads, Mukunda felt unsure of himself. One day he approached Prabhupāda. "Prabhupāda," he said, "do you like this?" and he gestured to his beard. Prabhupāda stroked his own clean face and said, "I like this." Then he smiled. Mukunda understood that the beard was not in order and he shaved it off the next day.

Prabhupāda visited Philadelphia in 1975. At that time the temple was located in the Germantown section of the city. The devotees all crowded together on the front porch to greet Prabhupāda. They stood closely together in two rows. When Prabhupāda arrived, the devotees began throwing flowers, and Prabhupāda walked slowly toward the crowd, carrying a cane.

Suddenly a little six-year-old girl named Sarina bolted loose from the devotees and ran up to Śrila Prabhupāda. "Śrila Prabhupāda," she called, "I have a question! I have a question!" She said she had trouble making garlands. She said when she put a flower on the garland, she then got mixed up and didn't know which flower to put on next. Prabhupāda looked down at her and then took a very beautiful, opulent garland from around his neck and placed it on the little girl! "You look at this garland and you will learn," he said.

Once in India, a mailman brought a letter addressed to Prabhupāda which required a signature upon delivery. Tejās dāsa told the mailman that he would sign on Prabhupāda's behalf, but the mailman said that he could not allow this. Tejās told the mailman that he was Prabhupāda's secretary and that he could sign, but the mailman was adamant. Then Tejās said that he would take the letter to Prabhupāda and return with the signed carbon copy. Again the mailman refused, saying he would not know if Prabhupāda had actually signed it. Tejās then told the man that Prabhupāda was a great saint and that he was very busy, and again he asked the mailman to give him the letter. The mailman refused. Finally Tejās went to Prabhupāda and explained the situation. Prabhupāda agreed to see the man and Tejās then showed him into Prabhupada's room. The man was there for ten minutes, and when he came out, he was smiling broadly. "I have seen Swamiji," he said.

2

In the summer of 1971, Indradyumna dāsa accompanied Śrīla Prabhupāda on his flight to London, where he was to attend the Ratha-yātrā festival. On the flight, a film was shown—an old silent film of Charlie Chaplin.

When the film began, Indradyumna dāsa began reading the *Bhagavad-gītā,* but he noticed that Śrīla Prabhupāda, who was sitting two seats away, was watching the film and chuckling. Indradyumna felt a little confused, since he knew devotees were not supposed to watch movies, but seeing Prabhupāda's appreciation of the film, he stopped reading and laughed along with Prabhupāda and his servant at Charlie Chaplin's humor.

When the film was over, Indradyumna met Pradyumna dāsa at the back of the plane and asked why Śrīla Prabhupāda was laughing during the film. Pradyumna said he would go and ask Prabhupāda. He soon returned smiling and said, "Prabhupāda said that Kṛṣṇa is the original source of everything, and since Charlie Chaplin's humor was original, he could appreciate Kṛṣṇa there." Indradyumna returned to his seat, appreciating how Śrīla Prabhupāda saw Kṛṣṇa everywhere.

As the plane landed in London, Indradyumna was looking forward to seeing the devotees and hearing Prabhupāda's arrival address at the Bury Place temple, but the airline had misplaced Prabhupāda's suitcase and Indradyumna was asked to wait behind in case it showed up. Disappointed, Indradyumna was left alone as the other devotees performed *kīrtana* while escorting Prabhupāda to his car.

Indradyumna waited for two hours before the suitcase was finally located. He then took a taxi to the temple, but to his great dismay, he found the ceremonies over and the devotees finishing up a feast in honor of Prabhupāda's arrival. Indradyumna asked the devotees where Śrīla Prabhupāda's room was and was told it was four flights up the stairs.

Upon reaching the fourth floor, Indradyumna knocked on Prabhupāda's door and then entered the room, dragging the big suitcase behind him. Suddenly he noticed Śrīla Prabhupāda standing there watching him. Embarrassed for having walked in on Prabhupāda, Indradyumna fell to the floor, offering his humble obeisances. Suddenly he felt a firm slap on his back and he heard Śrīla Prabhupāda say something to him. When he arose, Śrīla Prabhupāda had gone back into the adjoining quarters. Still feeling Prabhupāda's strong slap, he turned to Nanda-kumāra, who stood there with wide open eyes and a big smile on his face.

Indradyumna then asked what Prabhupāda had said. "Prabhupāda said," Nanda-kumara replied, "that in this material world everything is very difficult, but when you go back to Godhead, everything will be very easy."

3

PRABHUPĀDA TELLS SHORT STORIES

"We have become first class imitator," Prabhupāda told the devotees during a *Bhāgavatam* class in Vṛndāvana in 1976. Then he told a story.

It was 1914. World War I was in progress and the high court judges in Calcutta were on their tiffin hour.

"Mr. Mukerjee," an English judge, said to Ashutosa Mukerjee, "now the Germans are coming. What are you going to do?"

"We shall offer our respects to them and invite them to do as they will," replied Mr. Mukerjee. The answer startled the Englishman.

"Why do I say that? You have simply taught us how to be slaves."

Prabhupāda then explained how before Gandhi, the people of India thought that to have an advanced civilization, they had to imitate the English fashion. "But we should not make that a fashion," Prabhupāda said. "Guru is not a fashion. Who requires guru? *Tasmād gurum prapadyeta jijñāsuḥ śreya uttamam*—he requires a guru. *Jijñāsa. Athatho brahma-jijñasa*—that is human life. One who is interested in inquiring about the Brahman requires a guru. One who has no business for understanding Brahman, but simply to make a fashion that 'I have a guru'—that is useless. It has no value. One must be inquisitive to understand this spiritual science. He requires a guru. *Jijñāsa* means inquisitive."

Śrīla Prabhupāda was on a morning walk in Tehran when he heard a lamb crying.

"Why the lamb is crying? They do not give the lamb something to eat?" Prabhupāda asked. A devotee then made a guess.

"No, I always hear this sound somewhere. They keep the lambs for killing."

Prabhupāda then explained that such killing meant that the people were living like animals, and he told a story.

A lamb was once drinking water from the side of a lake. Across the water was a tiger. The tiger challenged the lamb: "Why are you muddying the lake?" The lamb replied that he was not muddying the lake, but the tiger quarreled with the lamb and then killed it. Prabhupāda then said that people in animal consciousness look for faults in others and create quarrels in order to kill. Then he quoted an English proverb: "Give the dog a bad name and hang it." In this way Prabhupāda criticized material consciousness.

Prabhupāda once told a story to illustrate the *kṣatriya* spirit. Jasovanta Singh was commanding general under Emperor Aurangzeb. In a battle, Jasovanta Singh met defeat, so he returned home to his palace. But the palace gate was closed. He sent a message to his queen informing her that he had returned home and asking why she had closed the gate. Upon hearing the message, the queen replied, "Who has returned home? Jasovanta Singh? No, no, it cannot be he. Jasovanta Singh would not return home after being defeated. He would either conquer or give up his life. The person at the door must be a pretender." So saying, she refused to open the door.

4

PRABHUPĀDA SAID

On Tulasī *Worship*

"Please, please be merciful to us and send us specific personal instructions so that we may adequately serve the feet of Srimati Tulasi-devi!

We beg to remain your humble servants eternally.

Vidya-devi dasi and servants to
Srimati Tulasi-devi, Los Angeles

Questions:

1. Is each *tulasi* a separate *jīva* soul or an expansion of one pure devotee?

2. Where does her spirit soul go when she leaves this body?

3. May we place jewelry in her soil or just moon stones?

4. When *tulasi* is being cared for by householders in their homes, must two *aratis* still be offered?

5. When *tulasi* is being cared for by householders in their homes, may they use her leaves and *manjaris* on thier home offerings or should they take them to the temple?

6. When *tulasi* is being offered *arati* by the householders, must she have a ghee lamp?

7. Is it offensive to turn the baby *tulasis* back into the soil when they appear?

8. There are even questions concerning *tulasi's aratis*. We have always offered her incense, ghee lamp, and a flower. Is this correct?

9. In the manual, it states that *tulasi* should not be pruned. Does this mean trimming the branches which no longer have leaves or life fluids flowing through them?

10. We were told you once spoke the "four regulative principles of *tulasi* care" which will keep her from getting sick: (a) keep her moist; (b) keep her clean; (c) give her morning sunlight (at least); (d) give her two *aratis* a day. Is this bona-fide?

11. May *tulasi* be made into a tea after she has been offered?

12. May devotees carve *tulasi* wood for Deity paraphernalia?

13. When *tulasi* leaves her body and the body is too soft for carving beads, how should she be used? Should a small fire sacrifice be performed?

14. We have a letter from you requesting that no sprays be used on Tulasi-devi. May we use a spray of buttermilk and whole wheat flour dissolved in water which coats her leaves to keep spider mites from causing *tulasi* to leave her body?

15. Does *tulasi* sleep? Should she be left undisturbed after nightfall?

16. Is it permissible to use scissors to cut her *manjaris*, and when transplanting, to use knives to loosen her from her pot?

17. Is it an offense to step on or across her shadow (or the shadow of any pure devotee)?

18. For two years we have been waiting permission to use the following two prayers plus translations and a translation of the already existing prayer. Please tell us if these are bona fide:

om govinda-vallabham devim
bhakta-caitanya-karinim
snapayami jagad-dhatrim
hari-bhakti-pradayinim

"Now I am bathing the mother of the universe, the bestower of Krsna bhakti, the enlivener of the living force of the devotees and the dear one of Govinda."

cayanodbhava-duhkham ca
yad hrdi tava vartate
tat ksamasva jagan-matah
vrnda-devi namo stu te

"O mother of the universe, please forgive whatever misery exists in your heart caused by the cutting of your leaves. O Vrnda-devi, let me offer my obeisances unto you."

om tulasy amrta-janmasi
sada tvam kesava-priya
kesavartham cinomi tvam
barada bhava sobhane

"O Tulasi, you are born from netar and always dear to Lord Kesava. Now, for the service of Krsna, I am picking your leaves, O one who is shining brightly."

"My dear Vidya dasi,

Please accept my blessings. I am in due receipt of your letter dated September 27, 1976.

If it is not possible for Tulasi to survive the winters when planted in the ground, then a suitable house should be provided for her. Even in the Canadian temples, which are in a much colder climate, they are keeping Tulasi nicely. Why should there be so much difficulty in Los Angeles, which has such a nice climate? Just do everything very carefully. Tulasi flourishes where there is love and devotion.

In answer to your questions: (1) Tulasi is one devotee who appears wherever there is devotion to Kṛṣṇa. (2) Tulasi's body is spiritual. (3) Yes, jewelry is all right. (4) If possible. (5) Tulasi leaves should be offered to the Deity. (6) If possible. (7) Yes. (8) Yes. (9) You may cut the dead branches, but what is the necessity? (10) I never said that. (11) No. (12) Yes. (13) Use the wood for beads as far as possible, the balance may be placed within the earth. (14) I said no chemical sprays. (15) Undisturbed means what? (16) Use common sense and if you have none then consult with others. (17) No. (18) Don't try to introduce something new. The most important thing is the love and devotion.

Hoping this meets you in good health.

Your ever well-wisher,
A.C. Bhaktivendanta Swami"

5

Whenever Prabhupāda visited the New York temple, the devotees there would perform a play. Once the devotees performed "The Kidnapping of Rukmiṇī" and Prabhupada enjoyed the performance. He laughed when an envious prince, played by Nayanābhirāma dāsa, saw Rukmiṇī and said he was going to faint. And when Balarāma cut off Rukmī's beard, Prabhupāda said, "Oh, now he is more than dead." When the play was over, Prabhupāda said that seeing the drama was better than reading the book.

On another occasion Prabhupāda asked the New York devotees to stage a performance of the *Rāmāyaṇa*. The devotees had no time to memorize lines, so they arranged to have a narrator read the lines from offstage. The actors stood in a line and performed *mudrās* while a devotee played a guitar.

After the performance, Prabhupāda called for Nayanābhirāma dāsa and complimented him and the other actors for their good performance. He then suggested some ways the play could be improved. He said that in India, different people read the lines offstage according to the different roles the actors play. Prabhupāda said he liked that style and he asked the devotees to practice it more. Nayanābhirāma asked if it was all right to include guitar music rather than sitar. Prabhupāda said a guitar played expertly is better than a sitar played poorly.

Śrīla Prabhupāda's airport arrivals were always ecstatic events, with the devotees performing *kīrtana* and dancing (unless prevented from doing so by the airport authorities).

Whenever Prabhupāda arrived in New York, Nayanābhirāma dāsa would always be ready at the airport with some fruit which he would offer to Prabhupāda and then distribute to the devotees. When Prabhupāda arrived in New York in April, 1969, Prabhupāda himself danced along with the devotees, and the ecstatic *kīrtana* attracted a large crowd of spectators.

After his visit to the New York temple, Prabhupāda was to fly to Buffalo. On the day of his departure, the devotees accompanied Prabhupāda to the airport, but this time the airport authorities stopped their *kīrtana*. The devotees then began chanting *japa* on their beads. Again Nayanābhirāma offered Prabhupāda fruit and he began distributing the remnants to the nondevotees in the airport. Prabhupāda then surprised Nayanābhirāma by calling him back. He told his disciple to distribute his *prasādam* to the devotees first. "Charity begins at home," he said.

6

LITTLE DROPS *of* NECTAR

Prabhupāda's Humility

Once in India, a young Indian *sannyāsī* disciple of another guru came to visit Prabhupāda. After hearing Prabhupāda the young *sannyāsī* said he had one request. Prabhupāda asked him what it was. He humbly requested Prabhupāda to kindly finish translating all twelve cantos. Prabhupāda answered, "You just give me your blessings so that I can finish the translating." Although the *sannyāsī* could have been Prabhupāda's son, out of his humility, Prabhupāda begged him for his blessings.

Once in Hyderabad, the devotees hired a cook. When Prabhupāda found out about it, he became very angry. He said that they had hired a common sweeper who had disguised himself as a *brāhmaṇa* so that he could make some money, and that the food had been cooked in such bad consciousness that it had contaminated the innocent farmers who had eaten it. Then Prabhupāda looked at his disciples and said, "Why didn't you ask me to cook?" He said he would have cooked for them, and all the devotees felt ashamed.

While Girirāja Swami and Brahmānanda were with Prabhupāda in India, Prabhupāda told them how he then had to travel to America to flatter some of his leading disciples there in order to get money from them for building his projects in India. Brahmānanda and Girirāja Swami were surprised to realize how Prabhupāda had to humble himself to engage his disciples in devotional service.

Once, sometime after being chastised by Śrīla Prabhupāda, Śatadhanya dāsa went to the roof and found Prabhupāda by himself. Śatadhanya immediately paid his *daṇḍavats* and he told Prabhupāda that he felt Prabhupāda had blessed him when he chastised him earlier that day. Prabhupāda smiled. Śatadhanya said that his experience of being chastised was just like the story Prabhupāda told of how he was chastised by Śrīla Bhaktisiddhānta Sarasvatī. Again Prabhupāda smiled. Then Śatadhanya said, "But I feel great anxiety." With great humility, Prabhupāda said, "I didn't mean anything by that. Please don't feel that way. I didn't mean to upset you." Śatadhanya then felt very bad, and Prabhupāda said it was proper for a disciple to feel anxiety in relating to his spiritual master.

On a summer evening in Vṛndāvana in 1977, Tamāla Kṛṣṇa Goswami told Prabhupāda how much he appreciated Prabhupāda's books. Prabhupāda then began to cry. "I am only a child," he said, "but I have tried to please my Guru Mahārāja." He then said that he did not write the books, but that they were written by Kṛṣṇa and his Guru Mahārāja. Later he reprimanded Upendra for leaving some cabinet doors open. Then he told Upendra that although he chastised him very severely, he was actually praying to Kṛṣṇa, "I cannot deliver them. You do."

7

PRABHUPĀDA TELLS SHORT STORIES

Prabhupāda would often tell the story of "half a hen."

A man once owned a hen. Although he valued the hen for the eggs it laid, he did not like having to pay to feed it. The foolish man therefore decided to cut the hen in half and keep only the half that laid eggs. In this way, Prabhupāda would point out how errors arise from insufficient knowledge.

Prabhupāda once told the story of Gopāla Bhan and the *bakula* flowers. *Bakula* flowers are small, white, star-shaped flowers which are edible and can be cooked as a vegetable. Gopāla Bhan was once making a garland of such flowers when a friend approached him and asked him what he was doing. "I am making a garland for Lord Kṛṣṇa," Gopāla said. "You mean to say that Lord Kṛṣṇa will come and take that garland from your hand?" asked Gopāla's friend. "Yes," Gopāla said, "and if He doesn't, I shall cook it and eat it."

Śrīla Prabhupāda in Moscow

On different occasions Prabhupāda would speak of the quality of life in Russia. Prabhupāda once spoke of his visit with Professor Kotovsky in Moscow. After finishing his conversation with the professor, Prabhupāda asked him to call a taxi. Professor Kotovsky apologized and said that it would be impossible to get a taxi. Professor Kotovsky then personally accompanied Prabhupāda to the door and showed him a shortcut back to his hotel. Prabhupāda explained that from this incident, he could understand that the people of Russia were unhappy. He said that in no other city in the world had he seen so many people walking in the street.

Prabhupāda then related how on his entering the Soviet Union, customs agents discovered a *Bhagavad-gītā* among Prabhupāda's possessions. Immediately a customs agent called the police. Prabhupāda thought he would be arrested, but by Kṛṣṇa's grace the policeman did not consider the book dangerous and they let him go. Prabhupāda said that the people of Russia are always under suspicion and that it is a poor, fearful, and wretched country because they deny the authority of God.

8

PRABHUPĀDA SAID

On College Preaching

"If you can draft some educated men to help us, that will be your valuable contribution. We want the mass of men to support us, but we want the class of men to preach for us. If you can induce some intelligent students in the universities and colleges to take up this preaching work, that is as good as yourself converting hundreds of common men, because two or three good men, if you can catch hold of them, they can do the work of many other men, less intelligent."

—*Letter of December 27, 1972*

"In this way, try to recruit some men from the student class for joining us as future leaders of our Society. If we go on expanding and there are no qualified men to lead, then everything will be spoiled eventually."

—*Letter of January 5, 1973*

"The students cannot be overestimated as our best prospect."

—*Letter of November 12, 1970*

On Preaching

You cannot expect favorable situation. It is not possible. When I came to America, I never expected any favorable situation. I wrote that poetry in disappointment, that, "Who will accept this?" That is the position. By Kṛṣṇa's grace, gradually it will become a favorable situation, but don't expect any favorable situation. You have to handle the unfavorable situation and make a favorable situation for preaching. That is preaching."

—*Room conversation, August 10, 1976*

Prabhupāda once saw a picture of Balavanta preaching into a microphone during a political campaign. Behind him sat the mayor and another candidate. Balavanta wore a suit and tie, *tilaka*, and *tulasī* beads. His *śikhā* was trimmed, and his hair was grown out. Around his neck he wore his bead-bag, and he was fingering his beads as he spoke. When Prabhupāda saw the picture, he said that this is what we want, to preach in American dress. He said we should be known as American Kṛṣṇas.

One time Girirāja Swami went to Prabhupāda and asked, "Suppose in the course of time, by my gradual advancement in Kṛṣṇa consciousness, suppose I become expert at everything? Suppose I become the perfect preacher and at the same time become the perfect manager. Then what should I do?" Prabhupāda said, "You should preach."

9

REALIZATIONS

Prabhupāda's Humility

Just before the start of the Ratha-yātrā parade, Śrīla Prabhupāda was driven right up to where the carts were poised to roll. Right in the middle of the filthy, filthy street, Chicago's big State Street, he got down and paid his obeisances to Lord Jagannātha. What humility! Since then I have never hesitated to pay obeisances if the occasion called no matter how dirty the street. Again, example is better than precept.

—*Sureśvara dāsa*

The Force of His Preaching

In 1976 in Delhi, Prabhupāda was doing a *paṇḍāl,* and he stayed in the home of a rich Indian gentleman. They called a big press conference, and many Westernized, so-called hip young Indian reporters were there, both men and women. They had come to see the *sādhu*. They asked many questions.

Prabhupāda spoke so forcefully, he shook their hearts. He shattered their hearts by his speaking. Although they came in trying to be sophisticated young Indians, Prabhupāda shattered their hearts by his preaching. They became frightened. They gave up all their sophistication and simply began to treat him with great reverence, like the *sādhu* or spiritual master. Even in their fallen condition, when Prabhupāda began speaking so forcefully, they became very frightened of continuing with their sophisticated attitude. They became very humble and submissive and simply began to treat him as a spiritual master. Prabhupāda was so powerful that any cultured person, anyone who was a little pious immediately became fearful of acting impiously or in an arrogant way in his presence.

—*Hṛdayānanda Goswami*

My story is from Chicago in 1975. I had been with the library party for about a year and we had been traveling nonstop doing book distribution in colleges and libraries. In July of 1975, Prabhupāda was in Chicago and we had the opportunity to have his *darśana*. My friend, Apūrva, was cooking for Prabhupāda. He asked if I could cook a preparation for Prabhupāda. I was very eager to volunteer. I made *sandeśa* for Prabhupāda. Then they put that on Prabhupāda's plate, and I got to take in the plate. I'm sure he didn't recognize me. I was just a *brahmacārī* coming in, offering him *prasādam*. Prabhupāda ate some of the *sandeśa*. Like every cook, the next day I asked Apūrva if Prabhupāda made any comments. Apūrva said, "Yes, Prabhupāda said, 'Why are so many men staying back from book distribution to cook for me?'" From this I realized that my relationship with Prabhupāda was not based on serving his *vapuḥ* form, but on distributing his books.

—*Kalakaṇṭha dāsa*

I had the realization that Kṛṣṇa is spreading Kṛṣṇa consciousness all over the world just to glorify Śrīla Prabhupāda. We are doing so little actually, but by Kṛṣṇa's grace, that little effort is producing such big results. Why? My realization is that it is only because Kṛṣṇa wants to glorify Śrīla Prabhupāda, His pure devotee. He is making everything so wonderful and so successful. Kṛṣṇa is even making us wonderful, us *mlecchas* and *yavanas*, just to glorify Śrīla Prabhupāda.

And why is Kṛṣṇa acting only to glorify Śrīla Prabhupāda? Because Śrīla Prabhupāda had no desire other than to glorify Kṛṣṇa. Reciprocally, at least in terms of the Kṛṣṇa consciousness movement in this material world (earth), Kṛṣṇa has no desire other than to glorify Śrīla Prabhupāda—and why?—because Śrīla Prabhupāda had no desire other than to glorify Śrī Kṛṣṇa."

—*Girirāja Swami, letter to Satsvarūpa dāsa Goswami, August 20, 1985*

10

LITTLE DROPS *of* NECTAR

Prabhupāda is Considerate

Prabhupāda once arrived in New York and as usual, hundreds of devotees had gathered at the temple to meet him. As Prabhupāda stepped out of his car, the devotees exploded in a tumultuous *kīrtana.* As he walked to the doorway of the 55th Street temple, hundreds of devotees followed close behind, chanting Hare Kṛṣṇa and "*Jaya* Prabhupāda."

A young mother carrying her baby followed immediately behind Prabhupāda as he passed through the glass doors that led to the temple's lobby. The lobby was also filled with ecstatic, chanting devotees. Seeing the young mother behind him, Prabhupāda stopped and held the glass door open for her. Even with hundreds of people worshiping him, Prabhupāda took the time to show proper etiquette to someone else.

Once Himavatī dāsī was serving as Prabhupāda's cook. One day she made eggplant *sabjī* for Prabhupāda. Prabhupāda tasted the *sabjī,* but didn't eat any more of it. After Prabhupāda had finished his meal, Himavatī distributed his remnants to the devotees, but the eggplant *sabjī* was too salty for anyone to eat. The next day, Himavatī made the same preparation, only this time she used the right amount of salt. Prabhupāda's only comment was, "Yesterday it was a little salty," and in this way he showed his consideration of his disciple's feelings.

Prabhupāda visited Geneva in 1974, and Līlāvatī dāsī arrived there to type for him, but she had contracted hepatitis and soon had to go into the hospital. Three days after his arrival, Prabhupāda called for the temple president, Guru Gaurāṅga, and asked him where Līlāvatī was. He was told that she was in the hospital. Prabhupāda then asked if anyone had gone to see her and Guru Gaurāṅga explained that everyone had been so busy that no one had thought to go. "We shall go see Līlāvatī. Make all preparation," Prabhupāda said.

Guru Gaurāṅga immediately set about readying the car and the devotees, and he made arrangements for *prasādam.* When everything was ready, he told Prabhupāda. Prabhupāda said, "Very good," and told them all to go see Līlāvatī. Prabhupāda himself stayed behind, but almost everyone else in the temple went to see Līlāvatī, who became very much enlivened by the care and concern which Prabhupāda had shown her.

11

LITTLE DROPS *of* NECTAR

Prabhupāda is a Powerful Preacher

Śrīla Prabhupāda possessed unlimited power to preach. Once in India, Prabhupāda was so ill he could hardly talk above a whisper, yet he possessed such spiritual potency that even big government leaders and members of Parliament were completely transformed by his preaching. One such politician went to see Prabhupāda. He was filled with doubts as to whether Kṛṣṇa even existed. After hearing Śrīla Prabhupāda speak, however, he became a stalwart defender of ISKCON and boldly stood up for ISKCON to the press and other politicians.

On one occasion in Melbourne, Prabhupāda was talking about how just by chanting Kṛṣṇa's holy name, anyone can be reformed and brought to perfection. He spoke of how bad a condition the world was in, but that simply by chanting, everything could be rectified. In a very serious and sober way, Prabhupāda said, "I think we can do it." In this way he impressed the devotees with the depth of his faith and realization.

Prabhupāda was once considering traveling to different places to preach and he wanted to know what his disciples thought of his plans. Rūpānuga wanted Prabhupāda to stay in the United States. Another devotee expressed his opinion, and then Prabhupāda asked Dayānanda what he thought. "Well, Prabhupāda," Dayānanda said, "I don't know what your desire is." Like an arrow, Prabhupāda answered back, "My desire is to spread this *saṅkīrtana* movement all over the world."

12

ŚRĪLA PRABHUPĀDA TELLS A STORY

A simple village man once wanted to serve the greatest person. He approached the mayor of his town and asked to be given some work. While serving the mayor, the village man noticed him giving tax money to a visitor. He asked who the visitor was, and the mayor told him he was a representative of the governor. "Is the governor greater than you?" "Oh, yes, he is greater than me," the mayor said. "Then I want to serve him," said the village man. The mayor appreciated the man's honesty and recommended him to the governor.

The village man served the governor for some time. Then one day a visitor arrived accompanied by a troop of horsemen. The governor welcomed the visitor graciously and treated him with all respect. When he had a chance, the village man asked the governor who the visitor was. "He is the king's viceroy," said the governor. "And who is the king?" the man asked. "He is the ruler of the whole land," said the governor. "He is very great." "Is he greater than you?" the man asked. "Oh, yes, I am just his servant." "Then I would like to serve him." The village man was talented, so to please the king, the governor sent the village man to him.

The man served the king for some months. Then one day, the king told him to ready the chariot. A great sage had arrived in the kingdom and the king wanted the sage's advice on how to rule.

The village man watched as the king approached the saintly person and offered respect. The king then sat and listened to the sage discourse for some time. Then, as the king was preparing to return to his palace, the village man approached the sage and asked if he were the greatest person. The sage said no, he was only a menial servant. "So please tell me, who is the greatest person?" "To find the greatest person, you must go to the temple of Nārāyaṇa," the sage told him. Without a moment's delay the man set off walking.

It was evening when he arrived and the temple doors were closed. The man knocked on the door for a long time. Finally a temple priest came and told him to go home and return the next day.

Not having any place to go, the man lay down by the gate and went to sleep. Before sunrise, some *brāhmaṇas* from a nearby village passed the temple and saw the man sleeping. They noticed that covering the man's body was one of the Deity's *cādars*. "He is a thief!" they said. In anger they woke the man and asked him where he got the *cādar*. The man was mystified and told them he did not know where the *cādar* had come from. The *brāhmaṇas* then tried to open the temple door and discovered it was locked. They then realized that Lord Nārāyaṇa Himself had placed the *cādar* over His servant to keep him warm while he slept. The *brāhmaṇas* asked the man where he came from and he told them his story. The man was then accepted into the temple and trained to serve the Deity. In this way the man came to serve the greatest person.

13

PRABHUPĀDA SAID

Prescriptions for Ailments

While living as a *brahmacārī* in Santa Fe, New Mexico, Toṣaṇa Kṛṣṇa dāsa developed a very bad headache. The headache continued day and night for over a month. Toṣaṇa Kṛṣṇa saw three different doctors, but not one of them could stop his headache. Finally, Toṣaṇa Kṛṣṇa wrote to Prabhupāda asking for advice. Prabhupāda answered him as follows:

"Regarding your headaches, your bowels are not clear. This is the cause of the problem. So you should take more milk and fruits, and eat less wheats and rice. If sandalwood oil is available, you try to massage on your shaved head. Let me know how this trouble is improving. A *brahmacari* should not have any complaint of bodily disease."

—*Letter dated February 17, 1969*

Toṣaṇa Kṛṣṇa followed Prabhupāda's remedy, and within four days the headache went away.

Madhusūdana dāsa once had trouble with acne and Prabhupāda asked him what was wrong. "Well," said Madhusūdana, "I'm growing up and a lot of kids get acne on their faces. It's pimples." Prabhupāda told him to put a little *tilaka* on each pimple. Madhusūdana did, and the remedy seemed to work, but because Madhusūdana thought the *tilaka* made his face appear ghastly, he stopped the treatment. When Prabhupāda saw him next, he asked why he was no longer using the *tilaka*. Madhusūdana explained why. Prabhupāda then told him to mix boric acid powder and olive oil in a spoon and heat it over the fire. The result is a skin-colored cream similar to the kinds sold in drug stores and effective for controlling acne.

Girirāja Swami once had a very bad case of boils. They were so bad that Girirāja Swami could only lie in bed listening to a tape of Prabhupāda singing the *"Govindam"* prayers. Prabhupāda came to his room to see how he was doing and recommended a cure made from camphor and other ingredients. Prabhupāda later commented to his secretary, Śrutakīrti dāsa, that like Śrutakīrti, Girirāja Swami liked sweets too much. He advised that Girirāja Swami go on a sugarless diet.

Pālikā dāsī was once very ill, and although doctors had prescribed mudpacks from the Yamunā and other remedies, she remained in a critical condition. A devotee described to Prabhupāda Pālikā dāsī's symptoms. Prabhupāda said she should take *caraṇāmṛta* and that two women devotees should alternate chanting Hare Kṛṣṇa right next to Pālikā all day and night. Pālikā dāsī was cured by this treatment.

Once, Satyabhāmā dāsī was sick and asked Prabhupāda if she should go to the doctor. Prabhupāda said yes, since we do not know very much about this body, if we are sick, we have to go to the doctor. He also said that if the doctor wants to learn about spiritual life, he has to come to us.

14

Yamunā dāsī was not sure of how Śrīla Prabhupāda wanted the Deity of Śrīmatī Rādhārāṇī to appear. Often Rādhārāṇī's right hand is raised with the palm facing outward, and Her left hand is at Her side holding a lotus flower. In Māyāpur at Śrīla Bhaktisiddhānta Sarasvatī's temple, however, Rādhārāṇī's arms are bent and Her hands are at the same height. "Should She be like that?" Yamunā dāsī asked Prabhupāda.

"No," said Śrīla Prabhupāda, "She should stand like *this*," and Prabhupāda struck a pose. He raised his right hand and cupped his palm, and he bent his left arm and held the palm downward. He then turned his head and tilted it slightly. To Yamunā dāsī, Prabhupāda appeared to be in a classic and very graceful pose of Śrīmatī Rādhārāṇī dancing. Then Prabhupāda said, "If Rādhārāṇī were to stop dancing, the whole business would be finished." He then explained that in Vṛndāvana, Rādhārāṇī never stops dancing, and that of all Her superexcellent qualities, Rādhārāṇī's cooking and Her dancing are particularly outstanding. Prabhupāda said that no one can excel Rādhārāṇī in Her ability to please Kṛṣṇa by cooking and that She cooks for Him eternally without ever making the same preparation twice. In this way, Prabhupāda explained, She keeps Kṛṣṇa under Her control. Then he said that even above Her cooking skill is Her dancing skill. Therefore, Prabhupāda said, in the Krishna-Balaram Mandir in Vṛndāvana, Śrīmatī Rādhārāṇī will be dancing. Later he said, "Rādhārāṇī is the color of *sindura* powder and *hinglu* powder mixed with milk."

15

Before becoming a devotee, Śacīnandana dāsa had been associating with the German devotees for several weeks, but he had not actually resolved to join. He had certain doubts and a resistance to becoming a devotee. He therefore decided to put all of his doubts into one question, which he thought of as a kind of test to prove that Śrīla Prabhupāda was his spiritual master. He got the chance to ask his question when Prabhupāda visited London in 1972.

"Why did Kṛṣṇa create *māyā,* which is only good for keeping us bound in birth and death?" Śacīnandana asked. Śrīla Prabhupāda did not hear the question, and his secretary asked Śacīnandana to repeat it. Śacīnandana did, and suddenly Prabhupāda shouted, "Not Kṛṣṇa created *māyā*! you created *māyā*!" Prabhupāda went on to explain how the living entity is guilty of separating himself from God. Śacīnandana was deeply shocked. He felt as if he was personally to blame for forgetting Kṛṣṇa and that Prabhupāda had cut through his own *māyā.* A few days later, he resolved to surrender to Kṛṣṇa and become a serious devotee.

The devotees met with some difficulties in their preaching in Japan and a Madras newspaper picked up the story and reported on ISKCON's troubles there. Then during their Janmāṣṭamī celebration, some members of the Gaudiya Math made an announcement about ISKCON's troubles in Japan. A life member told Prabhupāda what was being said by his Godbrothers and the members of the Gaudiya Math. Prabhupāda then spoke very strongly about how ISKCON was at least doing something.

Later, on a morning walk in Nelore, Śrīla Prabhupāda's disciples mentioned how some disciples of Prabhupāda's Godbrothers had said that if Lord Caitanya wanted Kṛṣṇa consciousness to be spread all over the world, He would have done it Himself. Prabhupāda lifted his cane above his head and said that Lord Caitanya had left the work to him. Prabhupāda spoke with unquestioning and undeviating conviction. He gave the example of how Kṛṣṇa let Arjuna fight for Him instead of killing everyone Himself. He said that Lord Caitanya had left it for him so that he could get the credit.

16

PRABHUPĀDA TELLS SHORT STORIES

During a class in Los Angeles, Prabhupāda commented on a cinema sign that he had seen. The movie title was, *Is There Sex After Death?*

Śrīla Prabhupāda: Because material life means sex, they are seeking sex after death. This is plain acceptance of materialistic life. They are inquiring, "Is there sex after death?" because if there is sex after death, then they are not fearful of death.

There is a story that one man was drinking. In India drinking is considered a great sin, so his friend advised him, "Because you are drinking, you will go to hell!" He replied, "Oh, my father also drinks." So his friend said, "Then your father will also go to hell!" And he replied, "Oh, my brother also drinks." "Then he will also go to hell!"

In this way he continued to say my father, my brother, my sister, my this, my that, and his friend was replying, "Yes, they will also go to hell." Then the man said, "Oh, then hell is like heaven! Because if we are all drinking here and we can drink there, what is the hell? That is heaven!"

Similarly, this sign is like that. If sex is there after death, then materialists think that is not death, that is life.

Actually, they have got sex after death, because they will get another body. Now they are having sex as human beings in very nice apartments or in the street, on the beach, as they like. In the next life also, as cats and dogs, they will have sex life. Sex life is not denied because the next life is there.

Prabhupāda would sometimes tell a joke which criticized the mentality of Indians who blindly copied Westerners.

There was once an Indian man who came to America knowing only three English words: yes, no, and "vedy good!" One day a policeman who was investigating the theft of a car questioned the proud immigrant. The policeman said to the man, "Did you steal the car?" "Yes!" "Are you going to give it back?" "No!" "So then we are going to throw you in jail!" "Vedy good!"

17

PRABHUPĀDA SAID

Question: How many other people are there on the planet who have made as much spiritual progress as you have?

Śrīla Prabhupāda: Some, but not many. But there are a few. There are no statistics in my possession. What is the use of taking statistics of how many are there? Why don't you become one of them? Why are you wasting your time in that way? These are not very intellectual questions. You just try to become enlightened. What is the use of knowing who is enlightened or not? You try to be enlightened, that's all.

When you are going somewhere, purchasing the plane ticket, do you ask, "How many tickets have you sold?" Huh? What is the use? You just purchase your ticket and get on the airplane and go.

Don't waste your valuable time in that way. If you are serious, just purchase your ticket and get on the airplane. That's all. All right. Chant Hare Kṛṣṇa.

Question: If we are on the street collecting money and we are thinking, "Oh, I am a very good collector; I am collecting so nicely," is that all right?

Śrīla Prabhupāda: Yes, yes. You are a very good collector for Kṛṣṇa.

Question: But if we—

Śrīla Prabhupāda: Yes, yes, you should be proud. You should feel proud, "I am working for Kṛṣṇa very nicely." We don't reject anything, even this pride. Yes. "I am greater servant of Kṛṣṇa. Yes, I am proud." That kind of pride is nice. Yes?

Question: This might be a stupid question, but—

Śrīla Prabhupāda: Well, we are all stupids. So questions must be stupid because we are stupids. He says, "I have heard in the street." We have to hear everything from Kṛṣṇa, then it is perfect.

Question: Well, sometimes I feel what they call *cakras*. I feel clear light over here and I feel something swirling over here that they call the house of the upper lotus. Is this my imagination or are these things real?

Śrīla Prabhupāda: Yes, it is imagination. If you just open your skull, you will find no lotus there. It is your imagination, that's all. These imaginations are prescribed for persons who are too much absorbed in the bodily concept of life. "Here is a lotus, here is a nonsense, here is an ocean of bliss. You have to find out." It is just to make him concentrate. Just like a naughty boy, to make him stop doing nonsense, "Please sit down here. Stop all this." Our proposition, "I am not this body." Even if there is lotus, what I have to do with this lotus? My first proposition is: "I am not this body."

18

REALIZATIONS

Prabhupāda never showed any odd moment that was not in his character. The more we realize it, the more we benefit.

I was with Prabhupāda in Toronto. He was preaching to some professors and then the devotees brought in a big, opulent plate of *prasādam* for him. Prabhupāda looked at it and almost under his breath he said, "I have no teeth, and I have no appetite."

Śrīla Prabhupāda could not take the *prasādam* due to his condition, yet he was fully tasting the mellows of Kṛṣṇa consciousness. Despite the inconvenience, he was preaching. He did not say, "I cannot eat so I'm going to lie down. A nurse and a doctor should be there, and I'll just worry." Under his breath, Prabhupāda may say, "I cannot eat," but he's preaching to the professors.

—*Satsvarūpa dāsa Goswami*

Prabhupāda's qualities are so real that a person can develop great respect for him just by seeing his picture and hearing his lectures.

When I joined the movement, my parents were extremely upset. My father had a very big position in the civil government and we used to chant near the parliament building where he worked. Victoria is a very small town, and to be a man of importance and to have your son out in the streets in bed sheets was very difficult, so my parents opposed. I used to send them *Back to Godhead* magazines, however, and just by looking at the magazines, they both developed a great respect for Śrīla Prabhupāda. When Prabhupāda became sick, they showed real concern and asked, "How's Prabhupāda?" Just by seeing Prabhupāda's picture and reading his articles, they came to realize that he was a very saintly person. Prabhupāda was such a saint that anyone who would be exposed to him—even if they were at first inimical—would actually develop some faith that he was at least a great man.

—*Bahūdak dāsa*

Trivikrama Swami had been serving in the Far East for four years and he wanted to return to America to preach. He approached Prabhupāda in Māyāpur and told him of his desire, but Prabhupāda only said, "I have so many preachers in America." Trivikrama took this as a sign that Prabhupāda wanted him to remain in the Far East and he began approaching people to help him open a center in Korea. Then Gopāla Kṛṣṇa, the GBC for India, came to him and said, "Prabhupāda wants you to stay and help manage Māyāpur." Trivikrama Swami told Gopāla Kṛṣṇa that he already had his ticket and that he was not going to stay.

The next day, Trivikrama Swami visited Prabhupāda in his room and Gopāla Kṛṣṇa was there. "Prabhupāda, Trivikrama Swami said he's not going to stay in Māyāpur like you wanted," Gopāla Kṛṣṇa said. Prabhupāda then asked Trivikrama why, and Trivikrama began offering excuses. After hearing his excuses, Prabhupāda told him that although our philosophy was "plain living, high thinking," Trivikrama Swami was addicted to the cities, so wouldn't agree to stay in the country. Trivikrama Swami then made another excuse and Prabhupāda again chastised him. He said that as a *sannyāsī,* Trivikrama Swami had given up everything but his whim. Then Trivikrama offered another excuse. He said that although he had been a *sannyāsī* for five years, he had not had a chance to preach in English. Trivikrama Swami asked how he could preach in Bengal since he didn't speak Bengali. "Oh," Prabhupāda said, "you've been a *sannyāsī* for five years and you haven't had a chance to preach? So what makes you think you know how to preach?" Trivikrama Swami then realized that without Prabhupāda's mercy, he would not know how to preach. He then surrendered and felt spiritual strength.

19

While working with Prabhupāda in India, Tamāla Kṛṣṇa Goswami had many opportunities to see how Prabhupāda conducted himself while interacting with the material world. Prabhupāda was the first preacher of Kṛṣṇa consciousness in the modern age to travel around the world engaging the material energy in Kṛṣṇa's service. Śrīla Bhaktisiddhānta Sarasvatī said that only a Vaiṣṇava is ideally suited to ride in cars and to use large buildings for spreading Kṛṣṇa consciousness, and Śrīla Prabhupāda set a perfect example of using such things without attachment. Prabhupāda wanted the Vaiṣṇavas to be appreciated, and in his own sweet and innocent way, he was proud of the material facility which came to him for spreading Kṛṣṇa consciousness.

Śrīla Prabhupāda would sometimes speak with great pride over the fact that as an author, publisher, and businessman, he had received $50,000 credit with the Dai Nippon printing company of Japan after making a down payment of only $5,000. He also expressed transcendental pride in his Bank of America credit card, which enabled him to withdraw $100 from banks and other businesses simply by showing the card.

Prabhupāda was also proud of his "green card" which allowed him to remain in the United States for as long as he wanted.

Prabhupāda would sometimes show his Bank of America credit card and his "green card" to life members in India. He took pride in these preaching facilities, which he received on the merit of his good character and his established position.

20

PRABHUPĀDA TELLS A STORY

Dealing with Indians

Prabhupāda was once speaking to his disciples about bogus *yogīs*. He named four prominent Māyāvādī gurus and noted that each one of them was a Bengali. He said that they had ruined the whole world with their philosophy, but that there was another Bengali who would destroy them. The devotees began to laugh and Prabhupāda told a story.

An ax was talking to a tree. "I will cut you down," said the tree. "No, you cannot do that," said the tree. "But I am very sharp," the ax answered. "You cannot do anything unless I first give you one of my branches for a handle," the tree said. Then Prabhupāda began to laugh. He asked his disciples if they understood, but no one did, so Prabhupāda gave an explanation. He said that although they were very intelligent American boys and girls, they could not cut down the Bengalis. He said that only if another Bengali helped them could they defeat the rascal Bengalis.

On another occasion, Prabhupāda told his Indian listeners not to be like those Indians who are quick to say, "I know Kṛṣṇa, I know Kṛṣṇa." Then he told a story.

There was once a man who every day brought water to the temple of Lord Jagannātha. The man used to think, "I don't need to see Lord Jagannātha. I come here every day, so I can see Him anytime I want. Let the others see Him." Day after day went by, but the man never went to see Lord Jagannātha. Finally the man died without once seeing the Lord. Prabhupāda then instructed his Indian audience to learn from his disciples how to serve Kṛṣṇa.

Once some of the Indian guests of the London temple formed a club of their own and they would hold programs in the Bury Place temple and present gifts to the Deities. A lady who was a member of the club once complained to Prabhupāda about some of the club members' dealings with her. Prabhupāda became angry. He called Prabhaviṣṇu Swami, the temple president, and severely reprimanded him for allowing the club to exist. He told Prabhaviṣṇu Swami that the club must be disbanded at once, and he stressed that only the most qualified devotees should be allowed to speak in the temple.

21

PRABHUPĀDA TELLS SHORT STORIES

Prabhupāda once told a story showing how Vedic education satisfies. Three hundred years ago, there lived a very staunch but very poor *brāhmuṇa* in Krishnanagar near Māyāpur. The king, Rāja Kṛṣṇacandra, heard of the learned *brāhmaṇa,* and he went to visit him. "*Brāhmaṇa,*" the king said, "can I help you in any way?" "No, I don't require any help from you," the *brāhmaṇa* answered. "But I can see you are so poverty-stricken," the king said. "No," said the *brāhmaṇa,* "I am not poverty-stricken. My students beg some rice, which my wife boils, and here is a tamarind tree, so I take some leaves and boil them. I am not poverty-stricken." Prabhupāda then explained that one who knows Brahman is satisfied, *brahma-bhūtaḥ prasannātmā.* He said that a *brāhmaṇa* is satisfied with whatever comes to him, and he said that formerly, this independence from material desire was very much valued. Modern education, however, kills this independence. Prabhupāda said that high technology means that people must depend upon machines for their livelihood, so they suffer.

Prabhupāda once told a story about word jugglery. Long, long ago, a student appeared for his big examination. One of the questions was about the reign of Hardwar Bastha. The student did not remember anything about this person, but to pass his time, he began to manufacture words. "Hardwar Bastha was a dobendi lactilized by the plactony of tinda." In this way the student filled up the whole paper. The examiner saw that the boy had simply manufactured words, but understanding that this required a little intelligence, he gave the boy a passing mark. In a similar way, many books are published that are manufactured only out of nonsense, but because it takes a little intelligence to juggle words, those books are considered valuable.

22

PRABHUPĀDA SAID

On Eating

"You should not eat the whole thing. You should eat half. And one fourth you shall fill up with water, and one fourth you should leave vacant so that there may be ventilation, your digestion will be easily done. This is Āyur Vedic law. Even if you think that you can eat so much, you should not voluntarily eat so much. You should eat half, and one fourth you should fill up with water, and one fourth you should keep vacant for air ventilation. Then there will be no disease. It is hygienic principle. As soon as you eat more than what you can digest, you become diseased."

—*Conversation, August 26, 1973*

Prabhupāda once asked Hari Śauri dāsa about his health. Hari Śauri said he had been cutting down on his eating. "In Australia you are reducing?" Prabhupāda asked. "If there is hunger, you should eat." Hari Śauri then told Prabhupāda how he had read in the Seventh Canto that if someone is serious about spiritual life, he will eat only once a day. Prabhupāda's mood then changed. "Oh, that is good. Yes, by not eating one becomes weak but does not die. One dies by eating. By not eating one does not die. Like me—I am not eating, but I am not dying."

Once in Hyderabad, Prabhupāda and some of his disciples visited the home of a wealthy gentleman from Gujarat. While there, the devotees were served sumptuous *prasādam*, which they relished enthusiastically. In the middle of the meal, Prabhupāda said, "This is how *prasādam* should be, so good that even if you're not hungry, you'll eat it. Not that even if you're hungry, you can't eat it."

Once in Madras, Harikeśa Swami and Śravaṇānanda dāsa made *capātīs* for Prabhupāda. As a *capātī* would come off the fire, Harikeśa Swami would rush from the kitchen to Śrīla Prabhupāda. The first time he did this, Prabhupāda rejected the *capātī,* saying it was not hot. Harikeśa Swami and Śravaṇānanda then rushed back to the kitchen to heat up another *capātī.* Harikeśa Swami took the *capātī* off the fire, again ran the short distance to Prabhupāda's room, and dropped the *capātī* on Prabhupāda's plate. Prabhupāda asked what was wrong with them that they couldn't bring it hot. Once more the devotees ran to the kitchen. Just as the *capātī* puffed up on the fire, Harikeśa Swami sprinted to Prabhupāda's room and put the *capātī* on his plate. Prabhupāda pulled the *capātī* apart, and as he did, some steam escaped into the air. "Yes," Prabhupāda said, "this is *capātī. Capātī* means hot."

On Prasādam and Health

"In Miami there are so many mangoes and coconuts. I am enjoying the dobs from Florida. The orange ones especially are very nice. I am taking one each day. From the green mangoes you can make pickles. Cut them into pieces with skin intact, and sprinkle with salt and tumeric. Dry them well in the sunshine and put into mustard oil. They will keep for years and you can enjoy with eating. They are nice and soft and good for digestion. If no vegetable is available, you can eat them with *puris,* similarly with pickled chilies. When mango pickles and chili pickles are combined, it is very tasteful. The Miami temple sounds to be very nice with bathing place and peacocks, just like Vrndavana. Krsna will supply you everything, don't worry. Just work sincerely."

—Letter of July 8, 1976

"If a man works, then he can digest stones."

Prabhupāda once said that he who cannot sleep immediately upon resting and who passes stool immediately after eating will soon be called by Yamarāja. But if he passes stool before eating and urine after, a physician cannot earn a living from him.

Prabhupāda once asked about the health of the New Vrindaban community's horse. A disciple said the horse was sick. Prabhupāda told the devotee to feed the horse chickpeas. He said chickpeas are very good for horses and make them strong.

23

LITTLE DROPS *of* NECTAR

Pictures of Māyāpur

Every year in Māyāpur, the devotees cut sugarcane, press it and cook down the juice and press it into *gur*. One year, the sugarcane was stacked outside the kitchen near the *gṛhastha-āśrama*. Many of the boys and girls from the *gurukula* would come and take pieces of sugarcane, chew them, and spit the pulp here and there. On one occasion, these spittings had been swept into a pile and left near the stack of unoffered sugarcane. Prabhupāda saw the pile of spittings and he began chastising the devotees, most of whom were Bengalis. He told them that although they called themselves Hindus, they had come to the temple just to go to hell. He asked them what had become of their culture that they would leave spittings near Kṛṣṇa's *bhoga*.

As Prabhupāda chastised the devotees, a two-year-old toddler came walking by eating a piece of sugarcane. Seeing this, a sixty-year-old Bengali devotee grabbed the sugarcane from the child's hand and chastised the child, who immediately began to cry. Prabhupāda said, *"Ustāḍī bocā:* although your eyes were blind, you are now the coach."

In Māyāpur, dacoits would attack the temple. They would take some explosive, roll it into a ball along with scraps of iron, and wrap it up with jute twine. The completed bomb was the size of a baseball and could remove a limb or kill someone.

One night while Prabhupāda was staying in the Māyāpur temple, the dacoits attacked, throwing many homemade bombs. No one was hurt, but the next day Prabhupāda wanted a report. Jayapatāka Swami told Prabhupāda that some shrapnel had been left by the bombs, and he explained the situation. Prabhupāda told him to get some guns and he told a story about Nārada Muni.

Nārada Muni once had a cobra as his disciple. After the snake became Nārada's disciple, he gave up his dangerous habits. Knowing this, the village children would harass him with sticks. The snake became distraught. Nārada asked the snake what was wrong and the cobra explained his difficulty. Nārada then told the snake that whenever the children came to harass him, he should expand his hood and raise his head up as if prepared to strike. He said the sight of this would scare the children away. Prabhupāda then instructed Jayapatāka Swami to take guns and frequently fire them into the air to scare off the dacoits.

The devotees acquired two guns and they divided themselves up into crews to stand guard at night. Sometimes Prabhupāda would be up late at night translating, and he would go out with a flashlight to inspect the guards. One time Prabhupāda shined his flashlight into Śatadhanya Swami's face. Śatadhanya Swami had been eating *capātīs* with *gur*. Prabhupāda asked him what he was doing and Śatadhanya Swami explained that he had gone out all day and that the devotees had saved him something to eat. Prabhupāda told him to be alert.

Later that night, Śatadhanya Swami was patrolling with his flashlight. He somehow sensed that there was someone hiding under a stairway. He crouched down and shined his flashlight under the steps and there was Prabhupāda. "Prabhupāda!" Śatadhanya Swami exclaimed, and offered his obeisances. "I was just checking on you," Prabhupāda said.

24

LITTLE DROPS *of* NECTAR

Prabhupāda Doesn't Waste Anything

Śrīla Prabhupāda was once walking with some disciples when he stopped and pointed to a willow tree. "Take twigs," he said. After Aravinda dāsa removed three or four twigs from the tree, Prabhupāda raised his hand and said not to take more than necessary. The devotees realized he did not want to cause unnecessary harm to the tree.

In Los Angeles in 1972, Prabhupāda went on two morning walks wearing an oversized *dhotī* that the devotees had offered to him. The *dhotī* was twice as long as it should be and almost twice as wide. Prabhupāda had wrapped this *dhotī* around himself and rolled it up so that it formed a very large bundle around his stomach. When the devotees saw him in it, everyone—including Prabhupāda—laughed.

When Ātreya Ṛṣi asked Prabhupāda if he could get a pair of scissors and cut the *dhotī* to the proper size, Prabhupāda became upset. "Cut, cut, cut," he said. "Everything you want to cut." He then explained that although his Western boys were very wonderful, they had no concept about wasting Kṛṣṇa's energy. He then began to complain of how the New York temple had been repainted two, three, four times.

Prabhupāda looked at Ātreya Ṛṣi with a pained expression on his face, and Ātreya Ṛṣi felt Prabhupāda was imploring him to help stop the waste.

Navīna Kṛṣṇa dāsa was a *gṛhastha* with many family responsibilities. He once asked Prabhupāda how it would be possible for him to think of Kṛṣṇa twenty-four hours a day, since he had so many family duties.

Prabhupāda looked at Navīna Kṛṣṇa dāsa and asked if he had twenty-four hours in a day. Navīna Kṛṣṇa said yes. Prabhupāda then said that out of those twenty-four hours, he worked eight or ten hours, spent six or seven hours sleeping, and used two hours for eating. This left five or six hours free. Navīna Kṛṣṇa dāsa agreed that this was a true picture of his schedule. Prabhupāda then asked him if he was using all of that extra time to serve Kṛṣṇa. Navīna Kṛṣṇa dāsa couldn't reply. Prabhupāda then said that if he used all his time in Kṛṣṇa's service, then Kṛṣṇa would show him how to serve Him more. On hearing this, Navīna Kṛṣṇa dāsa became very enlivened.

25

ŚRĪLA PRABHUPĀDA TELLS A STORY

Before coming to America, Prabhupāda was a family man. One day his servant began to cry out in what seemed to be great discomfort, "Oh, I am dying! I am dying!"

Prabhupāda immediately called an ambulance and went with the man to the hospital.

In the hospital, several doctors examined the servant and concluded that he required an immediate operation. Prabhupāda asked why, and the doctors gave a technical answer. Then a senior physician came and said they would wait until morning to operate. Prabhupāda returned home. His wife then told him that a neighbor's wife had come and told her that the servant was only drunk. "No," Prabhupāda replied, "the doctors said this is a serious case. He needs an operation."

The next morning the servant came home. When Prabhupāda asked him why he had returned, the man replied that he was all right and did not need an operation.

After telling this story to his disciples, Prabhupāda explained how demoniac doctors simply want to operate. He recounted how whenever one goes to a doctor in America, they immediately require you to give blood. Then they give you an injection. He said that sometimes in India doctors inject only water and then charge a fee. The doctor will ask, "Which do you want, a bottle of medicine or an injection?" The patient will ask for whichever is better, and the doctor will then give the patient an injection of water and charge five rupees. In this way, Prabhupāda illustrated how human civilization is a society of cheaters and the cheated.

26

PRABHUPĀDA SAID

All Services Accepted

"Please continue your very good service, and do not feel any feeling of uselessness. It is true that Krsna has given some the opportunity to serve Him by nice writing, some by good business ability, some by nice cooking, and so on, but these various services are all accepted equally by Krsna. On the transcendental plane, one service is as good as another. There is no question of higher or lower. We are very tiny, and so we cannot really do very much. Simply we can engage our time and energy, and that is all Krsna sees. He sees this boy or girl is spending his time in My service and He is pleased. I hope you are both well."

—Letter to Haṁsadūta dāsa and Himavatī-devī dāsī, March 3, 1968

"So there is no question that one activity is more important than another or that Deity worship is more important than *sankirtana*. But one individual may be able to perform one activity more satisfactorily than another, so to him that activity will be more important. But in general we cannot say that any of the nine processes is more important than the others, except that if hearing, chanting, and remembering are there, that is the most vital consideration for the general class of men in this age. Service to the Deities, as you are asking me, begins whenever you remember Them and offer all your services by remembering Them at the same time. All activities, words, everything should be offered as service to the Deities, and this offering with remembering will gradually increase as you practice it."

—Letter of June 16, 1976

"Don't think that if one is engaged in the Deity worship, and if one is engaged in the gardening work there is a distinction. No. The one who is working as a gardener, he is as good as the one who is dressing the Deity. Because it is the absolute plane, there is no difference between them, just like in the material world if one is working as a manager and another is working as a menial servant, there is a difference of pay, or a difference of service. No, in the spiritual world there is no such thing. In the spiritual world even a small ant is serving Kṛṣṇa. If by chance there is an ant and a flower is thrown onto the lotus feet of Kṛṣṇa, and if the ant kisses the lotus feet of Kṛṣṇa, he is as good as the *pūjārī*. This is the spiritual world."

—Lecture on Śrīmad-Bhāgavatam *6.1.1*

27

SERVICE IN SEPARATION

Śrīla Prabhupāda was a wonderful person and everyone who met him immediately fell in love with him. The entire city of Bombay is completely infused and permeated by Śrīla Prabhupāda's personal presence. Wherever we go, we meet people who say they had met Śrīla Prabhupāda—They heard him lecture or they met him on a walk or perhaps they met him at a friend's house. Invariably they were very impressed with Śrīla Prabhupāda and feel they have some relationship with him. Actually our entire preaching in Bombay is simply encouraging the relationships so many people had with Śrīla Prabhupāda. Wherever we go people welcome us and say, "You are disciples of Swami Bhaktivedanta?" It seems that his significance is being recognized more and more since his disappearance. While we develop our own individual identities as devotees of Kṛṣṇa and as preachers, still people tend to see us as Swami Bhaktivedanta's disciples. Unlike other famous gurus who are known in name only, with Prabhupāda they also know his philosophy. They know that he was preaching *bhakti*, surrender to Kṛṣṇa. They know that he was condemning everything else besides surrender to Kṛṣṇa. They know he was preaching the regulative principles. And many of them are understanding his preaching about *Bhagavad-gītā As It Is*.

—*Girirāja Swami*

The spiritual master is not limited by any material barriers. Śrīla Prabhupāda would sometimes laugh and say, "I have captured them, I have not bribed them." He is giving us love so deep that it is completely boundless—love that can even manifest through tape recorders, records—wherever there is a tiny bit of reciprocation, he is instantly present and giving himself fully to that person. That is the power of the pure devotee. By Kṛṣṇa's grace he can be completely present in his voice. You can feel perfectly situated hearing his voice and doing devotional service. It is not impersonal either. No one is as aware of my activities as is Prabhupāda; no one is giving such instructions as Prabhupāda is on his tapes. He is explaining what devotional service is, what the result of performing devotional service is, and he is directly speaking to me.

—*Satya-nārāyāṇa dāsa*

I never could go right up to Prabhupāda and say something—but now I feel that I can do it. Prabhupāda is always in the temple room and nobody is going to say that Prabhupāda is taking rest or that I can't go up to his room because he is writing, etc. He is more accessible now. The whole idea is that Prabhupāda made a house in which the whole world can live—with him. While Prabhupāda was on the planet, it seemed he wasn't accessible because you had to come to see him at a particular time and a particular place—you had to cut through the whole material world to get through that door to sit down with Prabhupāda. But now it isn't like that. For example, in Vṛndāvana you can go at any time of the day to his house and sit and chant. Prabhupāda is sitting on the *vyāsāsana*.

It seems being Prabhupāda conscious is much easier now. Whatever happens to you, you can always remember the sort of things that happened to him. You can always talk about Prabhupāda and you can always see something that Prabhupāda did and relate to it. For example, when you go to buy groceries you can immediately remember how Prabhupāda would keep receipts and only spend a couple of dollars a day for vegetables. Whatever you do, it seems like he is a lot more accessible.

—*Viśvaretā dāsa*

28

When Prabhupāda visited New Vrindaban, in addition to his philosophical lectures, he gave many practical instructions about farm life and about daily life in Kṛṣṇa consciousness. Sometimes these were just impromptu suggestions, but they were very important. Paramānanda dāsa would note these instructions down as important for anyone living on a Kṛṣṇa conscious farm.

When Prabhupāda visited New Vrindaban in 1969, the devotees had four cows. They asked Prabhupāda to name them, and he instructed them to name each of the cows Surabhi. After a short time, the devotees again approached Prabhupāda and asked him how they could speak about the different cows, since they all had the same name. Prabhupāda said they could call the cows Surabhi 1, Surabhi 2, Surabhi 3, and Surabhi 4. After some time, however, the devotees developed the habit of thinking of the cows simply as One, Two, Three, and Four, and the devotees felt dissatisfied. By this time Prabhupāda had left New Vrindaban, but in their letters to him, the devotees would repeatedly ask Prabhupāda to name the cows. In his answers, Prabhupāda would usually ignore the question of naming the cows, but after some time, he named the cows Śukla, Kāliya, Dutya, and Satya. After that, the devotees made up their own names.

Many of Prabhupāda's instructions emphasized not wasting Kṛṣṇa's energy. These instructions were particularly applicable to the self-sufficient life on the farm. Paramānanda noticed that Prabhupāda was conscious of even the smallest details of daily life and he didn't like to see anything wasted. He would make notes on old scraps of paper and even write letters on the backs of old sheets of paper.

Once, Paramānanda was cutting down some thorny brush that was growing in a pasture at New Vrindaban. The devotees had a disdainful attitude toward these weeds and considered them very impious living entities. The cows would often get into the weeds and the thorns would scratch their udders.

Prabhupāda saw Paramānanda cutting down the thorny bushes with an ax. "What are you going to do with them?" Prabhupāda asked. "You're going to use that in the fire?"

Prabhupāda's question had a profound effect upon Paramānanda, who became conscious of the importance of never wasting anything or treating anything whimsically.

29

LITTLE DROPS *of* NECTAR

Once in London, Trivikrama dāsa was giving Prabhupāda a massage, and Prabhupāda asked him if he was getting enough to eat. At that time, the devotees in London would eat only one meal a day. Trivikrama said yes, and Prabhupāda asked him how many *capātīs* he ate each day. Trivikrama told him four. Prabhupāda said that wasn't very many, and Trivikrama replied by saying he could probably eat more, but that was all he was given. Beginning that night, Prabhupāda arranged for the devotees to be served a second meal in the evening.

Prabhupāda was always very concerned that his devotees maintain their health. One time he expressed this concern to one of his spiritual daughters who was pregnant, and he gave her advice about health.

When Prabhupāda was in Philadelphia, Sarveśvarī dāsī would cook for him. Once, when she went into Prabhupāda's room to remove his plate, she noticed that there was a full cup of milk left. Prabhupāda told her she should drink it. He said she should drink as much milk as possible while she was pregnant and nursing and in this way her baby would be very happy, healthy, and peaceful. Sarveśvarī dāsī said she would drink the milk and she took his plate away.

As Sarveśvarī carried Prabhupāda's plate down the stairs, Brahmānanda passed her and spotted the milk. "Give me that milk!" he said. But Sarveśvarī said she couldn't because Prabhupāda had told her to drink it. Brahmānanda then conceded that she needed it more than he.

Prabhupāda once asked Nandarāṇī dāsī if her children ate *dāl* and *capātīs* every day. At that time the children were aged one and two. Nandarāṇī said yes, and Prabhupāda approved. He said that if children ate *dāl* and *capātīs* from the time they were young, they would always be healthy. He said the *dāl* should be very hot and that she should soak the *capātī* until it was very soft, and then the children could eat it. He said she could mix rice in the *dāl* as well. Prabhupāda said that *urad dāl* is the best, then mung, then lentils, but that soybeans are not needed.

Spiritual Life in the Material World

Jagattāriṇī dāsī was first introduced to Prabhupāda as a professional actress from Australia. Prabhupāda asked that she play the role of Śacīdevī in a play that Hayagrīva was producing. Śrīla Prabhupāda then began to speak of his own theater experience. He mentioned how when he was a boy, his uncle ran a theater company and had allowed him to play Advaita Ācārya in a play about Lord Caitanya. Prabhupāda said that the play brought tears to the eyes of the audience.

In the course of his conversation, Prabhupāda mentioned the theatrical term "green room." This had a profound effect upon Jagattāriṇī dāsī. In the English theater tradition, actors would formally and properly receive members of the aristocracy in the "green room." Jagattāriṇī was amazed that Pra bhupāda, whose life as a holy man from India seemed so removed from Western culture, was so knowledgeable of Western ways and so socially sophisticated.

Hari-vilāsa dāsa once accompanied Prabhupāda on a morning walk in downtown Paris. While walking along the bustling city streets, Prabhupāda stopped suddenly and stood silently for thirty seconds. Then he said, "This is such a nice breeze, just like Vṛndāvana." Hari-vilāsa then realized that Prabhupāda's senses and consciousness were completely transcendental to the material world.

30

PRABHUPĀDA TELLS SHORT STORIES

"There is a Bengali verse, 'What is there that a goat will not eat and a madman will not say?'" Prabhupāda then told a story to show how mad the modern civilization had become.

The Indian government once wanted a painting of a war scene depicting a child being killed in front of its mother. Government workers asked many artists to paint pictures showing how the mother's face would look upon seeing her child killed. The winning painting showed the mother covering her eyes with her arm. Prabhupāda explained that anyone who can bear to see a child being killed is an uncivilized, merciless demon. He said that the scientists are all madmen who will kill their own children and even eat the corpses. In this way he spoke of how demoniac the materialistic culture had become.

Prabhupāda once told a story about Prahlāda Mahārāja and his father, Hiraṇyakaśipu. Because Prahlāda was his son, Hiraṇyakaśipu felt some affection for him. One day,

Hiraṇyakaśipu asked Prahlāda, "My dear son, what have you learned from your teacher? Tell me the best things. Kindly let me know." Prahlāda Mahārāja answered, "I have learned *śravaṇaṁ kīrtanaṁ viṣṇoḥ/ smaraṇaṁ pāda-sevanam/ arcanaṁ vandanaṁ dāsyaṁ/ sakhyam ātma-nivedanam.*"

Prabhupāda then explained how we are hearing and chanting about so many things other than Viṣṇu. Prabhupāda said that in every country, millions of different types of magazines are being sold. He related how patients with diabetes have formed a society and have published a magazine. For two dollars a year, a person can receive information on how to protect himself from diabetes. Prabhupāda said that in America, two dollars is nothing, yet the diabetic society is collecting millions of dollars with their magazine. That sort of hearing and chanting is not needed. Prabhupāda said that because we are followers of Prahlāda Mahārāja, we are not interested in all these magazines.

31

PRABHUPĀDA SAID

On Sannyāsa

Prabhupāda once spoke with his servant Hari Śauri about disciples who fall away from their vows. He said he was simply trying to engage everyone—fools, rascals, thieves, anyone—to spread Kṛṣṇa consciousness. He said that if a disciple could not maintain himself as a *sannyāsī*, then he should change his *āśrama*, but he should not live as a hypocrite.

Hari Śauri asked about one *sannyāsī* who had performed much service but who had recently fallen down. Prabhupāda said he could either take up his service again or become a *gṛhastha*. Hari Śauri then mentioned the story from the *Caitanya-caritāmṛta* about Choṭa Haridāsa, and said that it would seem very difficult for a fallen *sannyāsī* to regain the mercy of Lord Caitanya. Prabhupāda said that such a *sannyāsī* is called a *vāntāsi*, one who eats his own vomit. Prabhupāda then said if the spiritual master continues to accept his fallen disciple, then Kṛṣṇa would accept him also, and that in time he could again take *sannyāsa*. Prabhupāda mentioned how he had allowed two of his fallen *sannyāsī* disciples to become *gṛhasthas* rather than send them away. But he said it was a shameful position. Prabhupāda said that his own Godbrothers and every *sannyāsī* in India criticized him for holding *brāhmaṇa* and *sannyāsa* initiations in the West, for installing Deities there, and for allowing women to live in the temples. He then said that for all of that, he was expanding Kṛṣṇa consciousness, and for all of their strictness, the others were doing nothing.

"Regarding your questions how to offer respects to *sannyasis*, every *sannyasi*, even if you see a Mayavadi *sannyasi*, offer him your respects—there will be no harm. As you have observed we shall follow Lord Caitanya's instruction that we give all due respects to others regarding their position, but there is no need of always associating with each of them. Even if one is Vaisnava, but not of good character, we can give him the Vaisnava respect, but we cannot associate with him."

—Letter of April 30, 1970

On Preaching to Fools

Brahmānanda: He says that in the *Bhāgavatam*, because the knowledge contradicts the mundane scientific knowledge, people who had some faith in Kṛṣṇa become discouraged and turn away from Kṛṣṇa.

Śrīla Prabhupāda: Let him go away. Don't care for him. Let all the fools go away. There is a Bengali proverb. Instead of maintaining some bad cows, let the cowshed be vacant. We shall prefer the cowshed be vacant, no cow, than keeping all bad cows who do not give milk and get disturbed.

Devotee: In our temple—

Śrīla Prabhupāda: We are giving a *chance*, but we don't want bad cows. We haven't got to agree with *their* views. They must agree with *our* views. Then they can live. Otherwise, let them go away. This is our position.

About Scientists

When Prabhupāda visited New Vrindaban in 1969, he used to sit on the hillside by a small table under a persimmon tree. He used to look into the valley at the forests. One time he said that Kṛṣṇa had created all the trees with their leaves. Then he imitated someone making something with his hands and said that the scientists make one leaf after great endeavor, but that Kṛṣṇa has made so many leaves. He said that the scientists can only imitate what Kṛṣṇa does with the trees in the fall. He also said that on Kṛṣṇa's order, all the leaves fall, and that the scientists can use their atom bombs to make the leaves fall, but they cannot create.

Prabhupāda: Kṛṣṇa says so long as we live we suffer—*janma-mṛtyu-jarā-vyādhi*—and they are making plans for enjoying. He says the real business is suffering and these rascals are still planning, just like Rāvaṇa, who constructed a staircase to go to the heavenly planets. All places are suffering, but we have to preach among such rascals. . . . We have to deal with them, talk with them, and we have to preach among them. Lunatic asylum treatment . . . Our treatment is genuine. If they take it, they will be cured. But because they are all lunatics it is very difficult to induce them to take the treatment. Otherwise this is the correct remedy but they won't take this because they are lunatics . . . They are making their own plans following these demons—scientists, philosophers, Darwin, Freud. Fraud. Humbug education . . . How are these things going on as science? . . . These rascals do not know that they are themselves bound up, and yet they are giving theory. The whole world is surrounded by all these rascals. We have to devise the means, "Please come here and take a little mercy. Sit down. Read a book." We have to work for that. Don't become angry by this lunatic asylum; otherwise the preaching will be finished.

On Dreams

"So far your dreams are concerned, it is very nice that you are thinking about Krsna consciousness even while sleeping. Krsna is so nice that we want to remember Him even more than twenty-four hours daily. Regarding instructions from the spiritual master, there is no need of taking instructions spoken in a dream while the spiritual master is still present. Lord Jagannatha is very kind, and He can also appear in the mind in His own form, so why not in your dream?"

—Letter of February 19, 1970

While receiving his midday massage, Śrīla Prabhupāda once told his servant, Hari Śauri, that on the previous evening he dreamt the temple courtyard was flooded to the top of the steps and he was thinking, "Oh, one more inch and everything will be spoiled." Hari Śauri then asked Śrīla Prabhupāda about dreams. Prabhupāda explained that they are impressions stored within the mind and may be coming from previous lifetimes. He said that although the objects in dreams are real, the dreams themselves are illusory. He then gave an example. Picking up a bottle of oil, Prabhupāda said that although the bottle of oil and his bed were both real objects, if he put the bottle under the pillow, then such an act would have no meaning. "The pillow and the oil are real," he said, "but *I* am crazy."

"I once had a dream like this: that we would have a moving temple on the water, going from town to town. So you are making that dream come true. Thank you very much. Do it nicely and maybe I will come and join you also."

—*Letter of August 31, 1971*

32

LITTLE DROPS *of* NECTAR

Śrīla Prabhupāda was extremely tolerant of physical discomforts. One morning while Prabhupāda was staying in his quarters at the Rādhā-Dāmodara temple, the devotee who was making Prabhupāda's bed found one of Prabhupāda's back teeth under the pillow. It had fallen right out and Prabhupāda had placed it under the pillow without telling anyone.

Soon afterwards, he contracted a bad infection in his leg. One of his toes had been cut and had become infected. The infection spread and Prabhupāda's leg became red and swollen to the middle of his calf. Prabhupāda had a poultice made of *nīm* leaves, turmeric, and mustard oil, and he made a bandage of banana leaves. The infection finally began to subside after five days. Although it must have been very painful, Prabhupāda never complained, nor did he reduce his preaching. In public he hardly even limped so that no one knew he was suffering.

In May of 1977, Śrīla Prabhupāda traveled to Hrishikesh to regain his health. His party included Tamāla Kṛṣṇa Goswami, Trivikrama Swami, and Pramāṇa Swami, who accompanied him across the Ganges by motor launch to Svarga Ashram. (Svarga Ashram was a guesthouse owned by a Mr. D. P. Mandelia, and it was said to be the finest in Hrishikesh.) Upon arrival, Prabhupāda asked the devotees to buy him some *kacaurīs* and *jallebīs*, and he ate them with great relish. Then he asked for Ganges water to be drawn from the center of the river and brought to him.

There was some delay in getting earthen water jugs, so Tamāla Kṛṣṇa Goswami took a Thermos bottle, dove into the river, swam to the center, and then returned to Prabhupāda with a full bottle of water.

Prabhupāda was taking his massage, but when Tamāla Kṛṣṇa Goswami arrived dripping wet with the Thermos bottle, Prabhupāda immediately drank the cool, clear Ganges water. Immediately he belched. He said that such belching indicated that his stomach had accepted the water. Prabhupāda then had the devotees fill buckets with Ganges water and set them in the sun to heat for his bath.

Several days later Caitya-guru dāsa arrived from Chandigarh with a box of nice fruits—mangoes, cherries, plums, apples and lichees. When Prabhupāda saw the lichees he immediately wanted to taste some. He said that as a little boy, his father always kept lichees hanging on the wall and he would ask for them.

On arriving once in Māyāpur, Prabhupāda entered his quarters, leaned back in his seat, and relaxed with his legs on his desk. He then drank from his water glass. "Ah, Māyāpur water," he said. He then related how Māyāpur is the spiritual kingdom and that living and dying in Māyāpur is the same. He said that if you live in Māyāpur, then you are living in the spiritual world, and that if you die in Māyāpur, then you go back to the spiritual world.

33

Prabhupāda once visited the ISKCON temple in Vṛndāvana when the temple was having financial difficulties and he ordered some cuts in the budget. He cut the amount of rupees the devotees were to spend on the Deities' garlands, and he said that the deity of himself, that of Bhaktisiddhānta Sarasvatī Ṭhākura, and those of the two *gopīs* should not be offered garlands at all. The devotees followed Prabhupāda's instructions, but they continued to offer opulent garlands to Prabhupāda himself while he was staying at the temple. For two days, when Prabhupāda entered the temple room in the morning, the devotees gave him a beautiful, opulent garland, and they would give him a second garland when he sat down on his *vyāsāsana*. The devotees would offer small, stringlike garlands to the Deities on the altar.

On the third day, Prabhupāda entered the temple room and the devotees garlanded him as usual. Then Prabhupāda sat down on his *vyāsāsana*, but when the devotee approached him with a big garland, he became angry. "Why are you giving these to me?" he yelled. "They should be given to the Deities."

For the next few days the devotees gave the Deities very opulent garlands and they gave Prabhupāda a thin garland. Prabhupāda then complained that the devotees were spending too much on garlands, so they cut down on all garlands. Then Prabhupāda appeared pleased. In this way the devotees came to understand that when the spiritual master asks for water, they should give him water.

34

PRABHUPĀDA TELLS SHORT STORIES

As a young man, Śrīla Prabhupāda once traveled through the Howrah train station. There he saw a person who was traveling with some half-burned pieces of wood to use as fuel. Prabhupāda could understand the man's mentality. "This is my possession. I have saved this." Regardless of how insignificant our possessions may be, everyone is thinking, "This is mine." Prabhupāda said that this is everyone's material disease.

In Vṛndāvana in June 1977, Prabhupāda spoke of how decadent human life had become. He related how the grandmother of one of his disciples advised the mother to kill her son. Then Prabhupāda told how the wife of one of his Godbrothers was an adulteress. The woman's son found out and threatened to tell his father, whereupon the mother poisoned the boy. When the father learned that his wife had poisoned their son, he committed suicide. Prabhupāda concluded by saying in this age that there is no culture, no God consciousness, no religion, and no standard of behavior. He said the only hope for Western civilization is to chant Hare Kṛṣṇa.

While in New York in 1966, Prabhupāda told a story about finding happiness. A man once told his friend that sugarcane tastes nice and sweet when you chew it up. The friend did not know what sugarcane was, so he asked the man. He was told that it was "just like a bamboo log." The foolish friend then began to chew different kinds of bamboo sticks, but he could never taste the sweetness. Similarly, Prabhupāda explained, materialists are trying to find happiness and pleasure by enjoying the material body, but they find no real happiness or pleasure. The temporary experience of material happiness is like a little spark of lightning in the night sky, whereas real happiness is like the sun which blazes in the sky and illuminates everything.

35

PRABHUPĀDA SAID

On Prasādam

Upon arriving at the Bhaktivedanta Manor, Prabhupāda asked, "Where is Revatīnandana Swami?" Revatīnandana Swami came out of the kitchen. "I'm in the kitchen, Prabhupāda, cooking," he said. "I'm a kitchen *swami.*"

"Ah," Prabhupāda answered, "that's Rādhārāṇī's department." Then Śrīla Prabhupāda said that Kṛṣṇa would leave Rādhārāṇī if He were not so attached to Her cooking.

"Regarding offering food: the custom is to offer the foodstuff first to the spiritual master; we cannot offer anything directly. The spiritual master accepts the offering on behalf of his disciple, and offers the same to Krsna. After Krsna's eating, the spiritual master eats it, and then the devotees take it as *maha-prasada.* This is the system. Everything is offered to the spiritual master first, with the prayer, *'nama om visnu-padaya. . . .'*

"If, in the cooking process, food falls on the floor, if it is raw and can be washed nicely, then it can be offered. But if it is prepared and cannot be washed, then it is not to be offered, but can be eaten rather than wasted."

—Letter of February 15, 1968

"Regarding the lollipops, there is nothing wrong. It is something attractive and I can understand, an introduction of friendship. What is the wrong? It is sugar, so it can be offered to the Deity. Just like here we can offer sweets purchased in the marketplace. It is stated in the *sastras* that if you pay something for it, it is purified even if there is some fault in it."

—Letter of November 2, 1974

"Concerning the use of sour cream in the temple, it should be stopped immediately. Nothing should be offered to the Deities which is purchased in stores. Things produced by the *karmis* should not be offered to Radha-Krsna. Ice cream, if you can prepare, is OK, but not otherwise. Now, you have such a big stock of this sour cream, so sell the stock at any cost. Who is the rascal who has purchased without permission?"

—Letter of April 6, 1976

"Regarding your questions, you may not be so advanced that you will take the *karmi* remnants as *prasada*. The *karmis* should not be given so much that there is waste. You can give them a little, and then if they like you can give them more. This system should be introduced everywhere. I have seen myself that so much *prasada* is being left. This is not good. Regarding the attitude for taking *prasada*, if you think it is something palatable, so let me take more and more, then that is sense gratification. But, still it is *prasādam* so it will act. *Prasada* is transcendental, but one should not take too much. *Sannyasis* may take the *maha-prasada* but not to overeat. Caitanya Mahaprabhu was taking, but on principle He was avoiding."

—Letter of August 4, 1975

36

REALIZATIONS

Toṣaṇa Kṛṣṇa once designed some brochures and posters advertising the devotees' traveling rock opera. He wanted to show the materials to Prabhupāda so that he could converse with his spiritual master.

Toṣaṇa Kṛṣṇa approached Prabhupāda with the advertising materials. Included was a poster showing the Vaikuṇṭha planets and Kṛṣṇaloka, as depicted on the cover of *Śrīmad-Bhāgavatam*. In an effort to flatter Prabhupāda, Toṣaṇa Kṛṣṇa told him that the cover was actually Prabhupāda's idea. Prabhupāda looked at Toṣaṇa Kṛṣṇa and said, "Why my idea? This is coming from *śāstra*." Then Prabhupāda asked, "Are you chanting your rounds?" Toṣaṇa Kṛṣṇa said yes, but he felt some disappointment. It took him several years to realize that Prabhupāda could not be distracted from his duty as spiritual master or from his concern for the spiritual life of his disciples.

In Dallas, Garuḍa hoped to hear Prabhupāda give the *Bhāgavatam* class. Before class Prabhupāda chanted Hare Kṛṣṇa. On this occasion, Śrīla Prabhupāda kept chanting and chanting Hare Kṛṣṇa from the *vyāsāsana*. Instead of giving the class, Prabhupāda kept chanting and chanting on and on. Garuḍa then realized that the sole purpose of Prabhupāda's mission was to spread the chanting of Hare Kṛṣṇa. He realized that the chanting permeated Prabhupāda's whole life, and that the only reason Prabhupāda traveled was for the chanting of Hare Kṛṣṇa.

Prabhupāda used his time perfectly in Kṛṣṇa's service. He had a specific time for everything—for receiving his mail, for getting up, for eating, for talking, for receiving guests. He did not waste a second.

In Los Angeles, Prabhupāda would give his disciple, Aniruddha dāsa, letters and packages to mail. Once, after getting into the car, Prabhupāda noticed that his letters had not been posted. He had Aniruddha stop the car at the mailbox so as not to miss the pickup time. The packages had to be the proper weight—just under the next rate level. By organizing his daily affairs so carefully, Prabhupāda could maximize the amount of work he could perform in Kṛṣṇa's service.

37

On different occasions of Prabhupāda's touring in Europe, Guru Gaurāṅga dāsa got the opportunity firsthand to see Prabhupāda's expertise in preaching according to time and place.

In 1972, after his arrival at the Orly airport in Paris, Śrīla Prabhupāda held a press conference. Guru Gaurāṅga acted as translator. One reporter was interested in Śrīla Prabhupāda's personal life before he became the leader of the Kṛṣṇa consciousness movement. Prabhupāda went along with the line of questioning and explained how he had given up his family and had accepted the *sannyāsa* order. Then the reporter asked how many children Prabhupāda had. At that point, Prabhupāda just looked at him and said, "Thousands." the man widened his eyes and began writing in his pad as if he had just gotten a sensational story. "And all of them I have had without my wife," Prabhupāda said. Then he said that many of his children were sitting there with him in the room. When he said that, the devotees shouted, "*Haribol!*" The reporter looked sheepish, as he began to understand what Prabhupāda meant.

In 1974, when Śrīla Prabhupāda traveled to Geneva, Guru Gaurāṅga was temple president, and he got a chance to see Prabhupāda even more closely. Guru Gaurāṅga had arranged for Prabhupāda to speak at the World Health Organization. Half an hour before Prabhupāda was to speak, Guru Gaurāṅga showed Prabhupāda a copy of a journal published by the WHO. The journal described the organization's birth control programs, and when Prabhupāda saw their pictures and read what they did, he became angry. He asked Guru Gaurāṅga why he had arranged a program there.

Guru Gaurāṅga explained that it was a very influential forum.

"They do not care what I say," Prabhupāda replied. "Whatever I say they will simply print my picture and they will say, 'Bhaktivedanta Swami at the WHO,' and they will publish it in such a way that it looks like I'm supporting these activities."

Prabhupāda then asked various devotees in the room whether or not they thought he should go to the program. The devotees expressed their opinions, and then Prabhupāda asked Guru Gaurāṅga if they could hold a *kīrtana* at the program.

"They can't stop us once we start, Śrīla Prabhupāda," Guru Gaurāṅga answered. Finally Prabhupāda just said, "Let's go."

In his talk, Prabhupāda said that only dogs and cats could create overpopulation, but that first-class human beings could not. He then smashed the World Health Organization's scientific birth control program, and at the end of the program, many Indians crowded around him, praising him and expressing their appreciation.

38

LITTLE DROPS *of* NECTAR

Prabhupāda visited San Francisco in July of 1974. After his arrival, the devotees accompanied Prabhupāda to his apartment near the temple. Prabhupāda sat in a rocking chair, and his leading disciples sat at his lotus feet. Prabhupāda began speaking about a song by Bhaktivinoda Ṭhākura in which Bhaktivinoda says he simply wants to be the dog of the Vaiṣṇavas. These words entered Hṛdayānanda Goswami's heart and he felt a deep desire to serve Śrīla Prabhupāda. As Prabhupāda spoke, Hṛdayānanda Goswami's desire to serve became even more intense. In his mind he began praying to Kṛṣṇa to allow him to do some service for Śrīla Prabhupāda. Śrīla Prabhupāda then handed Hṛdayānanda Goswami a pile of checks and said, "Write down the numbers of these checks." Prabhupāda then handed him his pen and a sheet of paper. Hṛdayānanda Goswami became ecstatic and realized that his prayer had been answered. He wrote down the numbers, trying very hard to do it properly. Then the meeting ended and Prabhupāda left the room.

Once, Prabhupāda visited Australia. As he walked into the Sydney temple, Jagattāriṇī dāsī ran ahead to remove his shoes and picture from the *vyāsāsana*. Upon seeing Prabhupāda, she immediately began to cry. Prabhupāda asked the temple president who she was and he was told she was Bhūrijana's wife. Prabhupāda then asked if she had been fighting with her husband. Jagattāriṇī dāsī lied and said no. "Good," Prabhupāda said. "Husband and wife should never fight." He then told a story of how Gandhi once threw his wife out of the house, but later allowed her to return. He explained that even if a husband and wife were fighting, that should not be taken seriously. He compared such fights to clouds which thunder but do not produce rain.

During the Kumbha-melā in 1977, Prabhupāda said that he wanted to bathe in the Triveṇī, but that he did not want to go into the crowd. He requested the devotees to go at the auspicious hour and return with water so that he could bathe with it the following day. Two devotees managed to reach the Triveṇī and return with a bucket of water.

The next morning, Prabhupāda gave a *darśana*. Everyone wanted to know how his bath had been. Prabhupāda thought for a moment and said it was like any bath in any water from the tap. He went on to explain that even though many millions of people go to the Triveṇī during Kumbha-melā to take their auspicious bath, any service that anyone does anywhere in the world for the pleasure of Kṛṣṇa is more auspicious.

39

LITTLE DROPS *of* NECTAR

Don't Sleep in Class

In 1974, when Garuḍa dāsa was a new *bhakta,* he had a tendency to fall asleep during *Śrīmad-Bhāgavatam* class. He went with the devotees to India for the Māyāpur festival, and while in Vṛndāvana, he got a chance to hear Prabhupāda give *Bhāgavatam* class.

During his lecture Śrīla Prabhupāda appeared to look in Garuḍa's direction. He pointed, and said, "What is he doing?" Garuḍa thought his devotional life was about to come to an end. Prabhupāda again asked what he was doing and he instructed the devotees to tell him to leave. Some devotees started walking over to where Garuḍa was sitting. Garuḍa thought he was really going to get it, but the devotees suddenly stopped and told the devotee sitting in front of him to leave the assembly. Never again did Garuḍa fall asleep in *Bhāgavatam* class.

While Prabhupāda was traveling in India in 1971, one of his *sannyāsī* servants, Devānanda Mahārāja, had difficulty staying awake in class. Even when Devānanda Swami would sit as straight as a *yogī,* he would still close his eyes. In the middle of class Prabhupāda would then say, "Don't come here to class and sleep. Go away and sleep twenty-four hours a day, but don't come and fall asleep in front of me."

On another occasion, Prabhupāda again noticed devotees sleeping during *Bhāgavatam* class. He became annoyed and asked the devotees, "Why this sleeping phenomenon? Why are you all sleeping? Is it because you don't get enough sleep at night?" The devotees attempted to respond.

"It's because we're going to bed late," someone said. "It's because we're eating too much at night," said someone else. Śrīla Prabhupāda made a sour face, shook his head, and said that even if they slept fourteen hours a night, they would still sleep in class. He said their excuses were no answers, and that they would only stay awake when they had the conviction that their work in Kṛṣṇa consciousness was so important that they had no time to sleep. Prabhupāda spoke so forcefully that everyone's attention became riveted.

40

PRABHUPĀDA TELLS SHORT STORIES

In Māyāpur in 1974, Prabhupāda told two stories to show how acts of charity should be performed in knowledge, not in ignorance.

A boy was raised by his aunt, who treated him very liberally. Through bad association, the boy became a thief, yet the aunt encouraged him, "Oh, it is a very good business. You are bringing so many things without much labor." In time the boy became a murderer. He was captured and sentenced to be hanged. When asked what was his last wish, the man said he wished to speak to his aunt. The aunt was crying and crying. When she leaned forward to hear what her nephew wanted her to hear, the man bit off her ear. He then rebuked his aunt, saying that if she had chastised him for being a thief instead of showing him kind affection, he would not be hanged and she would not be lamenting.

Prabhupāda then related how he once had a neighbor whose daughter-in-law was one day beating her child. Prabhupāda sent his servant to find out what was the cause. The servant returned and explained that the small boy's brother had typhoid fever. The sick boy told his young brother that he was very hungry and he asked him to bring him a *paratha*. The little boy was sympathetic and brought the *paratha* to his brother. When the sick boy ate it, however, the *paratha* aggravated his disease. When the mother found out, she punished the boy for endangering his brother's life. Therefore, charity given in ignorance results only in suffering.

41

PRABHUPĀDA SAID

On Deity Worship

"Yes, at least once daily the Deity's clothes must be changed, in the morning. If the Deities are small, as They appear to be from the photograph, then They can be laid down in a bed at night. And They can be given nightgowns to wear before taking rest. That is nice. If there is time and facility, then these things can be implemented. So far as bathing is concerned, it requires two hands and one tongue. In your left hand be ringing a bell and simultaneously with your right hand pour water. Chant Hare Krsna, *Cintamani, Govinda jaya jaya*, etc., like that.

"So far as touching the Deity, this is possible only in a big temple with big Deities, but not in a small temple. In big temples like Jagannatha Puri, the devotees circumambulate and sometimes touch the lotus feet of the Lord, but in a small temple that is not possible. If you need help in caring for Tulasi-devi, you can write Govinda dasi in Hawaii for instruction.

"Deity worship can be learned by children at not less than ten years. Before that they can assist. They can learn how to bow down, how to dance and chant, how to make garlands, clean *arati* utensils, etc. In this way they can be engaged. These are also different parts of Deity worship."

—Letter of May 1, 1971

"The photos of my *murti* are very nice. The *murti* of the spiritual master should be treated as good as the Deity. *Saksad-dharitvena samasta-sastrair, uktas tatha bhavyata eva sadbhih/ kintu prabhor yah priya eva tasya.* The guru should be treated as good as God. This is stated in all the *sastras*. The difference is that God is master-God and guru is servant-God. So the installation ceremony for such a *murti* should be similar to that done for other Deities. All temples can have this deity if they like. But temples which have only Panca-tattva painting worship should not be given this deity.

"You should make a *murti* of Srila Bhaktisiddhanta Sarasvati and then we may be worshiped together as is now being done in our Krishna-Balaram temple. They should be placed with Gaura-Nitai—Guru-Gauranga."

—*Letter of January 29, 1976*

"The schedule to be followed in worshiping the Deity is as follows. Morning *arati* may be performed at 4:30 until 5:00 A.M. Then immediately following, the Deity room should be washed clean and the dirty utensils removed. Then everyone can chant before the Deity until 6:30. The Deity should then be bathed and dressed and fresh flowers put. It should not take longer than one hour to bathe and dress the Deity if one actually knows how it is done. But it may take longer, so you may offer the *bhoga* at 8:00. The idea of bathing the Deity after offering *bhoga* is not correct. So please follow this schedule as I have advised."

—*Letter of December 26, 1971*

"Regarding your question on how to carry your Deities to different places with you, you should of course always carry Them personally, if at all possible, in a small box or cabinet for that purpose. Then when you come to another temple you may place Them on the altar with the other Deities. That is nice."

—*Letter of June 21, 1970*

"Regarding your question about taking Gaura-Nitai Deities with you on traveling *kirtana*, this is not so important. When Caitanya Mahaprabhu was touring India, He did not bring His Deity with Him. But if you can make proper arrangements then you may take Them, but if you say you have no *brahmanas*, then I think for the time being you may postpone this program."

—*Letter of February 14, 1973*

42

REALIZATIONS

Pratyatoṣa dāsa was an expert sound technician, and from the time he first joined Kṛṣṇa consciousness, he thought of traveling with Śrīla Prabhupāda and recording his talks and lectures.

In 1972, Pratyatoṣa went to see Śrīla Prabhupāda at New Vrindaban and he brought his tape recorder. While there, he was asked to go to Prabhupāda's cabin and record Śrīla Prabhupāda reciting from the *Bhagavad-gītā* and *Śrīmad-Bhāgavatam*. Pratyatoṣa entered Prabhupāda's room and began setting up his tape recorder. As he worked, Pratyatoṣa explained to Prabhupāda his idea of traveling with him. Prabhupāda put his head back and waited for a few seconds, and finally told Pratyatoṣa it was a good proposal and that he would think about it.

Śrīla Prabhupāda then chanted several chapters of the *Bhagavad-gītā* and Pratyatoṣa recorded him. After Prabhupāda finished the reading, Pratyatoṣa again asked about traveling with him. Prabhupāda then said it was very expensive to travel and that he already had many devotees traveling in his party. He said he did not think the temples could afford it.

Pratyatoṣa had volunteered his services, and Prabhupāda rejected his proposal. Yet Pratyatoṣa felt completely satisfied. Śrīla Prabhupāda had been pleased by his proposal and had given it serious consideration. Pratyatoṣa had never felt so wonderful after having had a proposal rejected.

Prabhupāda is nondifferent from his books. I had the idea that an author and his books were separate; I tended to think an author had his literary life as well as his private life. But whether Prabhupāda was alone in his room or with one or two people, he was always just speaking from his books, just as he did when lecturing in public. The book *bhāgavata* and the person *bhāgavata* are the same, and realizing this made me very much inspired to study the philosophy.

—Cāru dāsa

Śrīla Prabhupāda never wanted to be late for any preaching engagement. He used to say that Bhaktivinoda Ṭhākura would arrive at the train station hours early just so that he would not miss the train. Prabhupāda himself always preferred to be early.

Once in Japan, Śrīla Prabhupāda had an appointment with executives of the Dai Nippon printing company. He did not wish to be late, so he dressed quickly and then chanted his *gāyatrī* while walking to the car. Although he was very strict about matters of *sādhana*, he was willing to forego certain rules in order to spread Kṛṣṇa consciousness.

Whatever Prabhupāda did was great. He is the first person whose eating of *dāl* and *capātīs* has made thousands of people all over the world eat *dāl* and *capātīs*. Whatever a great man does, other people will follow. A lot of people ate *dāl* and *capātīs* in India before Prabhupāda, but it didn't make anybody else do it.

—Tamāla Kṛṣṇa Goswami

43

LITTLE DROPS *OF* NECTAR

On Giving Mercy

In Calcutta in 1971, Yamunā dāsī was bringing Prabhupāda his lunch. Prabhupāda asked her if she was teaching the girls how to cook. At that point, Kauśalya dāsī, who was outside the room, spoke up and said that Yamunā was actually not teaching them to cook. Prabhupāda then looked at Yamunā dāsī and in a very serious tone told her that if she did not distribute her knowledge, she would become envious. Yamunā then understood that whatever she learned from Prabhupāda she should share with others, including knowledge of cooking.

Once Prabhupāda was leaving Paris. The devotees accompanied him to the airport and sat with him in the departure lounge, waiting with him until the time he could board the airplane. At one point, Prabhupāda took off his flower garland and instructed the devotees to distribute it to nondevotees. Hari-vilāsa dāsa got up and began handing out flowers. Hari-vilāsa was struck by Prabhupāda's magnanimous nature; Prabhupāda was not only engaging them in service, but also teaching them how to preach. He realized that Prabhupāda wanted his devotees to use every minute to spread Kṛṣṇa consciousness to the conditioned living entities.

Prabhupāda watched them distributing the flowers and he seemed very pleased. When they returned to their seats beside Prabhupāda, he expressed his pleasure that they had done this, and they too became pleased.

Paṅkajanābha dāsa was nervous when he received *brāhmaṇa* initiation. A devotee had shown Paṅkajanābha how to count the different *gāyatrī-mantras* on his fingers, but the method which he showed him was not correct. When Paṅkajanābha went in to receive *gāyatrī*, Prabhupāda demonstrated the correct method of counting, but because Paṅkajanābha was nervous, he could not hear Śrīla Prabhupāda's instructions, so he repeatedly used the wrong method of counting the mantras. "You cannot be initiated." Prabhupāda finally said. "Your memory is too short. Call my servant."

Paṅkajanābha stood up and got the servant. When the servant came in, Paṅkajanābha told him he was too nervous. Prabhupāda then told Paṅkajanābha to go outside and practice. He later returned and counted the mantras correctly.

From the time the devotees first moved into the Berkeley temple, the neighbors caused trouble. The people living across the street from the temple made a large sign blaspheming the Hare Kṛṣṇas and hung it on the front of their house.

When Prabhupāda came to Berkeley for Ratha-yātrā, the devotees became anxious. They tried to take Prabhupāda down another street so that he would not see the sign, but road construction and a detour forced the devotees to take Prabhupāda past the house. To keep Prabhupāda from seeing the sign, the devotees began pointing to the opposite side of the street. "Prabhupāda," they said, "look at the trees, aren't they nice? Do you see the temple?" Then Prabhupāda happened to turn and he noticed the sign. He said it was nice, and that this was the only house in America with Kṛṣṇa's name on the front.

44

In November of 1976, Purīdāsa dāsa visited Prabhupāda in Vṛndāvana. Purīdāsa had come from Paris and he had brought with him the new French translation of *Kṛṣṇa* book.

Purīdāsa felt nervous as he entered Prabhupāda's room and paid his obeisances. Śrīla Prabhupāda was speaking with a student from America at the time. Prabhupāda and Purīdāsa exchanged a few words, then Purīdāsa said that he had brought the new French *Kṛṣṇa* book. "Ah," Śrīla Prabhupāda said, "this is what I like," and he began to look at the new book. As he looked at the pages, his face lit up and he held the book up for everyone in the room to see. He then turned to the student from America and said how boys and girls in every country of the world are taking seriously to Kṛṣṇa consciousness. "Chant, dance, feast, and philosophy—this is Kṛṣṇa consciousness," Prabhupāda told the boy, and he again began looking at the new book.

In the summer of 1974, Prabhupāda traveled to Paris to install Śrī Śrī Rādhā-Paris-īśvara. The Deities were very large and required several men to carry Them into the temple room. Prabhupāda was pleased by how nicely the temple had been decorated. During the *abhiṣeka*, Śrīla Prabhupāda stopped for a moment to look at Śrīmatī Rādhārāṇī's face. There was a spot of paint on Her face. Prabhupāda took some yogurt on his fingertip and with great care and devotion, began to massage the spot on Her face. He did this for some time, and the devotees could understand that Prabhupāda was in full awareness that this Deity was Rādhārāṇī Herself. In this way he demonstrated complete absorption in the worship of the Deity.

45

PRABHUPĀDA TELLS SHORT STORIES

In 1977, the construction of the Bombay temple was going slowly. On several occasions Surabhi Swami told Prabhupāda that the marble contractors would be arriving in fifteen days. Śrīla Prabhupāda then told a story about a professional witness who worked in the court system. This witness would repeatedly be called upon for various testimonies, and for this he would receive a fee. When being sworn in, the witness would always testify that his age was sixty years. One day, the judge pointed out that for years the man had been claiming to be sixty years old. The witness replied that a man should not change his word of honor. In the same way, Prabhupāda concluded, Surabhi Swami would not change his word of honor.

On a visit to Tehran in 1976, Prabhupāda told a story. Lord Śiva and his consort Pārvatī were once passing through a town disguised as ordinary people. On their way, they passed a beggar in the street. "This poor man is begging, so why don't you give him something," Pārvatī said to Lord Śiva. "Even if I give, he will not be able to enjoy. He is so unfortunate," Lord Śiva answered. But Pārvatī again requested him to give the beggar something, so Lord Śiva consented. "Take this," Lord Śiva said to the man, and he gave him a watermelon containing a great treasure of gold and jewels. On receiving the watermelon, the beggar thought, "What shall I do with this?" And he sold the watermelon to a man for only a few cents. Prabhupāda then explained how we are as unfortunate as the beggar. Kṛṣṇa is giving perfect knowledge, but like the beggar, we are not taking advantage.

46

LITTLE DROPS *of* NECTAR

Prabhupāda is Always Right

While visiting Los Angeles in 1971, Prabhupāda took a walk through a park. After walking for some time, Prabhupāda and the devotees came upon a section of the park that was fenced in. The gate was open, but a sign said, "Unauthorized Do Not Enter." Prabhupāda began walking toward the gate. Karandhara told Prabhupāda that he should not pass through the gate. Three times he told Prabhupāda it was unauthorized. Finally, Prabhupāda stopped, looked at Karandhara and said, "*Mahājano yena gataḥ sa panthāḥ*: 'One should follow in the path of the *mahājanas*.'" He then proceeded through the gate. Prabhupāda chose the path that led directly to their car and thus saved a long walk back the way they had come.

Once some devotees acquired a special mechanical device for lifting the top of the *ratha* cart. The devotees assured Prabhupāda that Nara-Nārāyaṇa dāsa could assemble the mechanism, but Prabhupāda said they should form a committee and consult together rather than have just one man take on the work. He said it should not be that only one man understood and that everyone else did not know what he was doing.

When the devotees told Nara-Nārāyaṇa what Prabhupāda had said, Nara-Nārāyaṇa felt bad, thinking that Prabhupāda doubted him. But then the devotees sat down and had their meeting. They soon realized that neither Nara-Nārāyaṇa nor anyone else among them had the ability to construct the complex device. Nara-Nārāyaṇa then resolved to always consult others before beginning a project.

Once, in Hyderabad, Prabhupāda stayed in a room with a slanting roof. He asked his servant, Hari Śauri, to put a picture of Śrīla Bhaktisiddhānta Sarasvatī on top of the *almirā*. But because the roof slanted, Hari Śauri could not figure out a way to hang the picture. Prabhupāda said it took a little intelligence, and then he related a story.

Christopher Columbus and a companion were sitting at the table. "Actually, your going to America was not anything special," said the gentleman. "You didn't plan to go there, it was an accident. Anybody could have done it, but you just happened to be the first." Columbus then put an egg on the table and said, "Make this egg stand on its end." The man tried and tried but he could not balance the egg. Finally, he gave up in desperation. Columbus then took the egg and tapped the big end until it became flat. Then he stood the egg on its end. "Well," the man said, "you didn't say I could break the egg." "It takes a little intelligence," answered Columbus.

After telling this story, Prabhupāda then tilted the picture so that it was resting on the wall in the opposite way from that of a conventional picture. In this way he was able to slip the picture between the *almirā* and the slanting roof.

47

LITTLE DROPS *of* NECTAR

In Bombay, Śrīla Prabhupāda was visited by a follower of Rama-Krishna who claimed that Rama-Krishna was an incarnation of God. The man explained how Rama-Krishna had saved a drunkard. Prabhupāda asked if this fact made Rama-Krishna an incarnation of God. Prabhupāda said that he had converted thousands of drunkards—"Not only drunkards, Western drunkards," he said. "Therefore I am much bigger incarnation than him."

Prabhupāda visited Gorakhpur in 1971 and while there he had an intimate exchange with his disciples.

When asked how a devotee should decide between various services to offer to Kṛṣṇa, Prabhupāda told the disciple to inquire from his spiritual master. The disciple expressed a doubt, thinking that his questions might seem foolish. "No, don't speculate." Prabhupāda said, "You should immediately ask your spiritual master."

"Then I would be asking you questions all day long and you'd have no time to do anything else," the disciple said.

"No," Prabhupāda said, "you are welcome, you are welcome."

In London in 1969, Trivikrama dāsa was giving Prabhupāda a massage. Prabhupāda was preaching about how Kṛṣṇa has form. Prabhupāda turned and put his arms on Trivikrama's shoulders and said, "Just as Trivikrama has form, Kṛṣṇa also has form."

Prabhupāda once stayed in a small room that had a ceiling which was higher in the middle than it was around the walls. Prabhupāda liked the room very much. He said it reminded him of his room at the Rādhā-Dāmodara temple. "To me, this is sense gratification," he said.

In Māyāpur in 1976, Śrīla Prabhupāda held an evening *darśana* for his devotees. Someone brought in sweets and Prabhupāda's servant put them away. Prabhupāda asked the servant why he didn't serve the *prasādam*. The servant replied that there were too many devotees in the room and that he would pass out the *prasādam* as everyone was leaving. Prabhupāda quickly answered, "They will never leave," and the devotees all shouted, "*Jaya* Śrīla Prabhupāda!"

Prabhupāda's room that the devotees of the Santa Fe temple offered to him was almost bare, and his bed was only a mattress on the floor. One evening, as Prabhupāda sat on his mattress, his disciple Toṣaṇa Kṛṣṇa dāsa noticed a small insect walking across the floor. The bug approached Prabhupāda's mattress and Toṣaṇa Kṛṣṇa wanted to shoo it away, but Prabhupāda said it was all right. The bug climbed up on the mattress and walked up to Prabhupāda. Prabhupāda smiled and bounced the bug off the mattress and back onto the floor. Again the insect crawled to the mattress and climbed up to where Prabhupāda was sitting and again Prabhupāda bounced it back onto the floor. "We should have sprayed," said Toṣaṇa Kṛṣṇa. "No, no," said Prabhupāda, "you can just keep it clean."

48

PRABHUPĀDA SAID

From a Handwritten Diary:

What is Krishna Consciousness?

1. Krishna consciousness means clear consciousness.
2. Material existence means hazy consciousness.
3. Identifying the body as self is hazy consciousness.
4. One has to understand himself first before making progress in Krishna consciousness.
5. Constitutional position of a living entity is being eternal servant of Krishna, or God.
6. God or Krishna means the Supreme Person and the supreme cause of all causes.
7. Forgetfulness of the eternal relationship to God, or Krishna, is the beginning of hazy consciousness.
8. To revive the original clear consciousness of the living entities the Vedic literatures are there.
9. The Vedic literatures are as follows:
   a. The four *Vedas*.
   b. The *Upanishads* numbering at least 108.
   c. The Vedanta philosophy.
   d. The 18 *Puranas*.
   e. The *Ramayana* (original Valmiki).
   f. The *Mahabharata*.
   g. And any book following the tenets.
10. The *Bhagavad-gita* is part of the *Mahabharata*.
11. The original Veda is *Atharva-veda*, later on divided into four for divisional understanding.

12. *Mahabharata* is called the fifth Veda and is meant for less intelligent class of men who love history more than philosophy.
13. *Bhagavad-gita* being part of *Mahabharata* is the essence of all Vedic knowledge for less intelligent class of men in this Age.
14. B.G. is called the Bible of the Hindus, but actually it is the Bible for the human race.
15. In the B.G. the following subject matter has been discussed:

a. What is a living being.
b. He is not the body but spirit soul.
c. The spirit soul is encaged in material body.
d. The body is subjected to birth, death, old age, and diseases.
e. The spirit soul is eternal, never takes birth or dies but he exists even after the annihilation of the material body.
f. The living entity is transmigrating from one body to another.
g. He can however stop this transmigration process and attain eternal blissful life of knowledge by Krishna consciousness.

16. What is God.

a. God is individual person. He is chief of all other persons of different parts namely the demigods, the human beings, animals and the birds, insects, trees, and aquatics.
b. All these living entities are sons of God and therefore they are all servants of God.

How to Open a Center

1. At least three devotees will form a party to open a center.
2. They will go on the streets to perform *kirtana* twice in a day—morning and evening.

3. Will hold classes thrice a week where classes will be taken, B.G. etc., preceded and followed by *kirtana*.
4. On every Sunday there must be a love feast festival.
5. As the members increase, the *sankirtana* party for street increases and the strength for selling BTG and other books.

49

LITTLE DROPS *of* NECTAR

Prabhupāda Was Precise

Śrīla Prabhupāda was very precise in his use of words and in his presentation of Kṛṣṇa consciousness. Once one of his *sannyāsī* disciples was giving a lecture in Prabhupāda's presence and he was explaining the absolute nature of the holy name. "Kṛṣṇa is in His name," the disciple said. Then Prabhupāda interrupted him. "Oh, He is in His name? Where in His name is He?" His disciple fell silent. "Kṛṣṇa is not *in* His name," Prabhupāda explained, "Kṛṣṇa *is* His name."

Prabhupāda held an initiation in Geneva in 1974. Puṣṭa Kṛṣṇa Swami performed the fire sacrifice and Prabhupāda presided over the *yajña* from his *vyāsāsana*.

The devotees had covered the sacrificial area with cloths of different kinds. One of the cloths that was used was a *hari-nāma cādar*. Puṣṭa Kṛṣṇa Swami sat on a cushion with his foot on the *cādar*.

Prabhupāda looked down and said, "What is that?" Puṣṭa Kṛṣṇa said, "What is what, Prabhupāda?" Prabhupāda said, "What mantra is that?" Puṣṭa Kṛṣṇa Swami said it was the Hare Kṛṣṇa *mahā-mantra*. Prabhupāda said that it was not the Hare Kṛṣṇa mantra. Puṣṭa Kṛṣṇa Swami said yes, it was the Hare Kṛṣṇa mantra. He said that it was printed in English letters that had been stylized to look like *devanāgarī* script, but that it was actually the Hare Kṛṣṇa mantra.

Prabhupāda looked down and was silent for a few moments, then he said, "If that is the Hare Kṛṣṇa mantra, why have you put your foot on the holy name?" Puṣṭa Kṛṣṇa Swami moved his foot.

Once Śrīla Prabhupāda held a preaching program at the Pārtha-sārathi temple in Madras. In that temple there is a *mūrti* of Kṛṣṇa on the Battlefield of Kurukṣetra. The *mūrti* wears a little mustache. After the program, Śrīla Prabhupāda went to the home of a Mr. Mahesuri, who asked Prabhupāda how it was that Kṛṣṇa was wearing a mustache. Prabhupāda explained that this was bogus. He said that Kṛṣṇa is *nava-yauvanam,* ever-youthful, and never has a mustache. Then Prabhupāda took his finger and began very gently touching the area above his lip. He began searching for a word to describe Kṛṣṇa's upper lip. One of his disciples said, "Like peach fuzz, Prabhupāda?" indicating the very soft hair that grows on a young boy's lip as he reaches puberty. Prabhupāda said yes.

A senior devotee once advised that BTG editors should specialize in different areas of material knowledge, like psychology, economics, and politics, and write articles about these topics for BTG.

Jayādvaita Swami reported the idea to Prabhupāda and Jayādvaita Swami added that he did not like the idea. He said he felt that the devotees who write for BTG should simply read Prabhupāda's books. Prabhupāda agreed that this was the right idea. He said the other idea was useless.

On another occasion, Jayādvaita Swami approached Prabhupāda with the First Canto of *Śrīmad-Bhāgavatam* which he had re-edited. Jayādvaita Swami read several translations which he had changed. Prabhupāda asked him to explain what it was he had done. Jayādvaita Swami said he had revised the text to bring it closer to what Prabhupāda originally said. "Closer to what *I* have said?" Prabhupāda said, "Then it is all right."

On yet another occasion, Jayādvaita Swami was traveling with Prabhupāda. As they waited to board their Pan Am jet, Jayādvaita Swami noticed that the plane had a name—the *Clipper Intrepid*. He told Prabhupāda that this was a suitable name because Prabhupāda was such an intrepid preacher. Prabhupāda then asked Jayādvaita Swami what the word *"intrepid"* meant. Jayādvaita Swami told him. Prabhupāda then thought for a moment and asked how it was spelled. Jayādvaita Swami spelled the word, and reasoned that Prabhupāda thought it was a good word and that he might have a use for it sometime.

50

SERVICE IN SEPARATION

"The spiritual master is present wherever his sincere disciple is trying to serve his instructions. This is possible by the mercy of Krsna. In your attempts to serve me and in all your sincere devotional sentiments I am with you as my Guru Maharaja is with me. Remember this always."

—Letter of December 1, 1973

"You write to say, 'I really miss Swamiji and my Godbrothers' association so much.' But I may remind you that I am always with you. And so wherever I am, and you are there, all your Godbrothers are there. Please remember always the humble teachings you have received from me, and that will make you always associated with me and with your Godbrothers."

—Letter of August 24, 1968

"To feel separation from the spiritual master or Krsna is very good position. That means one who is in pure love with Krsna and His representative, spiritual master, he thinks always of them. And this thinking process is Krsna consciousness. If we can think always of Krsna even in separation, that is Krsna consciousness. And in the absolute platform, there is no difference of separation and meeting. The separation is also meeting, rather in separation one relishes the loving relationship more tasty. So don't be disappointed that you are separated from me, I am also thinking of you how you are making progress there."

—*Letter of October 21, 1968*

VOLUME ONE NOTES

1. Aniruddha dāsa, interview. The distinction is between a preference as seen as one's whim or opinion and the higher principle of doing what is best in devotional service. It had become best for Swamijī to accept the more honorable title, "Prabhupāda." "Swamijī" was a nice name for our innocent beginning days, but it was more fit that the founder-*ācārya* of the most important movement in the world be known by his more glorious and accurate name, as the master at whose feet the other masters sit.

2. Nandarāṇī-devī-dāsī, interview. Umāpati dāsa, interview. Prabhupāda gave many strong warnings that such tearful emotions should never be imitated or induced; we should not cry like the *sahajiyās,* whose tears wash away all scriptural injunctions. Real crying is described in *The Nectar of Devotion:* "In other words, one should learn how to cry for the Lord. One should learn this simple technique, and he should be very eager and actually cry to become engaged in some particular type of service. This is called *laulyam,* and such tears are the price for the highest perfection." (*NOD,* p. 83)

3. Nanda-kumāra dāsa, interview. Prabhupāda said that he had a tongue, but he did not say that he had an uncontrolled tongue. The Kṛṣṇa conscious *siddhānta* is that the tongue should be used in the service of Kṛṣṇa, *sevonmukhe hi jihvādau:* one cannot realize Kṛṣṇa or Kṛṣṇa's name with the blunt senses, but only when one purifies his consciousness by engaging in *bhakti-yoga,* beginning with the tongue. Prabhupāda describes this higher principle of renunciation in *The Nectar of Devotion.*

"Śrīla Rūpa Gosvāmī, then, recommends that one should not be attached to material sense enjoyment, but should accept everything enjoyable which is in relationship to Kṛṣṇa. For example, eating is necessary, and one wants some palatable dishes to satisfy his sense of taste. So in that case, for the satisfaction of Kṛṣṇa rather than for the satisfaction of the tongue, some palatable dishes may be prepared and offered to Kṛṣṇa. Then it is renunciation. Let the palatable dishes be prepared, but unless they are offered to Kṛṣṇa one should not accept them for eating. This vow of rejecting anything which is not offered to Kṛṣṇa is actually renunciation. And by such renunciation one is able to satisfy the demands of the senses."

4. Yadubara dāsa, interview.

5. Viśākhā-devī dāsī, interview. Śrīla Prabhupāda's reply was unexpected. Instead of telling why the moon gave taste, he replied, in effect, "Why don't you ask the moon yourself?" Another expert way of teaching. Once when a disciple asked too many detailed inquiries about the nature of life in the spiritual world, Śrīla Prabhupāda replied that when you will actually go to the spiritual world, then you can see these things for yourself. When a devotee asked why Lord Śiva appeared as Śaṅkarācārya, Prabhupāda replied, "You have no right to question Lord Śiva's activities." In this way, Prabhupāda detected dubious mentalities in the questioners. As the waterfall sometimes flows and sometimes does not, so the pure devotee may speak or be silent—or he may make an enigmatic reply. In any case, we learn from him.

6. The letter regarding leftover *prasādam* was by Prabhupāda to Kīrtirāja dāsa; the information about how a gentleman should eat was given by Jayapatāka Swami; the information about Prabhupāda's opinion on rice was from Pālikā-devī dāsī; the letter about apple cider was addressed to Rukmiṇī-devī dāsī.

7. Śatadhanya Swami, interview. Śatadhanya Swami was able to supply us with accurate Bengali because of his pro-

ficiency in the language. One time, when in the presence of Śrīla Prabhupāda and some guests, including Prabhupāda's Godbrother Kṛṣṇa dāsa Bābājī, Śatadhanya Swami was able to please Śrīla Prabhupāda by his use of Bengali. To one of the guests Śatadhanya Mahārāja said in Bengali, "Why don't you go now, because Guru Mahārāja needs some rest. He's not so well. You come back next Tuesday." Hearing Śatadhanya Mahārāja speak Bengali, Kṛṣṇa dāsa Bābājī, who was always laughing, almost rolled on the floor in uncontrollable laughter. He slapped Prabhupāda's back, and then Prabhupāda also began to laugh. Prabhupāda then turned to Kṛṣṇa dāsa Bābājī and said, "*Kubh bhāl bāṅglā jāne,*" which means, "He speaks very good Bengali." After this, Prabhupāda and his Godbrother continued laughing.

8. SDG.

9. Daiviśakti-devī dāsī, interview. If one thinks Prabhupāda's words are too cutting, he or she may consider the *Śrīmad-Bhāgavatam's* statements of Jaḍa Bharata, Nārada Muni, or Prahlāda Mahārāja wherein a similar estimation is made of family life. Household life and raising a family may also be taken up in a spirit of pure devotional service, but if a genuine *sādhu* such as Śrīla Prabhupāda, in a particular situation, calls a spade a spade, no one should be offended.

10. Rāmeśvara Swami, interview.

11. Interviews with Daiviśakti-devī dāsī, Rādhā-vallabha dāsa, Ānakadundubhi dāsa.

12. Satya-nārāyaṇa dāsa, interview. Satya-nārāyaṇa thinks that Prabhupāda praised Western medicine "just to shock me into the right consciousness." Prabhupāda's actual conviction was more like that stated in the *Bhāgavatam* by

Prahlāda Mahārāja: "Whatever remedies they accept, although perhaps temporarily beneficial, are certainly impermanent. For example, a father and mother cannot protect their child, a physician and medicine cannot relieve a suffering patient . . . (*Bhāg*. 7.9.19) Śrīla Prabhupāda writes in the purport to this verse, "Unless one is protected by the mercy of the Lord, no remedial measure can act effectively. One should consequently depend fully on the causeless mercy of the Lord. Although as a matter of routine duty one must, of course, accept other remedial measures, no one can protect one who is neglected by the Supreme Personality of Godhead."

13. The letters quoted were written by Prabhupāda to the following persons respectively: Madhusūdana dāsa (written by Prabhupāda's secretary on his behalf), Satyabhāmā-devī dāsī, Lalita-kumāra dāsa, and Satyabhāmā-devī dāsī again.

14. Vicitravīrya dāsa, interview.

15. SDG.

16. SDG, Śrutakīrti dāsa, and others, from interviews and memoirs.

17. Mahābuddhi dāsa, interview.

18. The plane incident is from Śrutakīrti dāsa; the *kīrtana* singer incident is from Bahūdak dāsa, and the Māyāpur cooking incident is from Pālikā-devī dāsī.

19. Nanda-kumāra dāsa, interview.

20. Hari Śauri dāsa, diary and tape recordings.

21. Rādhānātha Swami, interview.

22. The incident about the *mṛdaṅga* following the leader is from Viṣṇugadā dāsa, interview. The comment that the drum should not be louder than the voice was recalled by Abhirāma dāsa, who heard Prabhupāda say it in Calcutta. The sitar music incident is from Umāpati dāsa, interview.

Pālikā-devī dāsī also recalls that Prabhupāda did not like harmoniums played during the *kīrtana.* His comment was that it would "drag" the *kīrtana.* Prabhupāda used to say that his Guru Mahārāja, Bhaktisiddhānta Sarasvatī Ṭhākura, banged the *karatālas* together and would only have *karatālas* and *mṛdaṅga* played for *kīrtana.* The point is that artistic musicianship can sometimes be distracting from chanting the holy name.

23. Tejās dāsa, interview.

24. SDG.

25. Yadubara dāsa, interview.

26. Tejās dāsa, interview. It may seem contradictory to hear Prabhupāda stating that there is no danger in married life, when often his *Bhāgavatam* purports say the opposite. One can take it that in the *Bhāgavatam* he is describing the *gṛhamedhī* life, whereas Kṛṣṇa conscious *gṛhastha* life is without such dangers. On the other hand, Prabhupāda was sometimes very much in favor of a young man's resolve to take *sannyāsa.* This may bring up the whole question as to the importance of presenting separate anecdotes, as we are doing in *Prabhupāda Nectar* One may argue that unless we thoroughly know the background of each incident, we cannot know Prabhupāda's mind and intent. In this case, did he think that his disciple was not fit for *sannyāsa* at that time, or did he think he was too attached to his wife to attempt renunciation, or did Prabhupāda think that the man's wife was too attached and not ready, or that it was unnecessary for either husbands or

wife's preaching at that time? While there are answers to these questions, I do not think the anecdote as it stands is superficial. The points Prabhupāda makes to Tejās concur with the śāstric conclusion regarding the real meaning of *sannyāsa,* as stated in *Bhagavad-gītā* (5.1). Aside from that, we get a nice glimpse of Prabhupāda reciprocating with a disciple and carefully guiding him with emphasis on preaching as the real renunciation. Even if we research further into the particular background of each anecdote, when all is said and done, we still cannot know the mind of the *ācārya.* Even Kṛṣṇadāsa Kavirāja sometimes presents the pastimes of Lord Caitanya and Lord Nityānanda and concludes that no one can completely understand the grave meaning of these activities. Let us therefore appreciate and take edification from the accurate renditions of what Prabhupāda said and did, and in due course of time we may realize the meanings more and more.

27. Jagadīśa Goswami and Śatadhanya Swami, interviews.

28. Pañcadraviḍa Swami, interview.

29. Prabhupāda's maxims for book-printing are from Devāmṛta Swami, interview; the incident about ISKCON Press, SDG and Nara-Nārāyaṇa dāsa; letter about book distribution, to Śrutadeva dāsa; Prabhupāda's words to the book distributors, Sañjaya dāsa, interview.

30. SDG, memoir.

31. Śrīla Prabhupāda, from a lecture.

32. SDG.

33. Jayādvaita Swami, memoir.

34. Praghoṣa dāsa, interview.

35. Pañcadraviḍa Swami, interview.

36. The Hyderabad incident is from Śrutadeva dāsa, interview; the monorail incident is from Bhūrijana dāsa, interview; the Māyāpur incident is from Satya-nārāyaṇa dāsa, interview.

37. Prabhupāda on the gold standard, Girirāja Swami, interview; Prabhupāda proverb about money intelligence, Girirāja Swami, interview; fifty percent to the Book Fund, Tejās dāsa, interview; letter by Prabhupāda on *saṅkīrtana* to Haṁsadūta dāsa; Prabhupāda saying Kṛṣṇa will provide, Nanda-kiśora dāsa, interview; Prabhupāda on Ganeśa worship, letter to Bhakta dāsa; Prabhupāda on banking, from Rāmeśvara Swami, interview; Prabhupāda saying we have no problems, SDG, memoir.

38. The account about the airport in Australia is from Amogha dāsa, memoir; the story of the fever is from a lecture by Prabhupāda.

39. The story of the envious man is from a letter by Prabhupāda to Yamunā-devī dāsī, November 18, 1970; details of the story about the purchased car are from a letter by Prabhupāda to Puṣṭa Krsṇa dāsa, January 10, 1976.

40. The story about unnecessary change is from Rādhā-vallabha dāsa, interview; the story about the Taj plasterer is from Raṇacora dāsa, interview; the story about Hindi handwriting is from Bhumadeva dāsa, interview.

41. SDG.

42. Rāmeśvara Swami, interview.

43. SDG.

44. Śrutakīrti dāsa, interview.

45. Girirāja Swami, interview.

46. Girirāja Swami, interview.

47. SDG, Rāmeśvara Swami, Bhavānanda Goswami, interviews.

48. Letter to Revatīnandana dāsa, June 13, 1970.

49. SDG.

50. Letter to Bhavānanda Goswami; letter to Karandhara dāsa; testimonies by devotees from interviews.

VOLUME TWO NOTES

1. Girirāja Swami, Nava-yogendra dāsa, and Rohiṇī-nandana dāsa, interviews.

2. Nanda-kumāra dāsa, interview.

3. Nara-Nārāyaṇa dāsa, interview.

4. Ānakadundubhi dāsa, interview. This incident has a disastrous but instructive follow-up. Although Prabhupāda's warnings had pointed to the danger in his disciple's actions, the artist devotee wandered away from Prabhupāda's instructions and became the disciple of a Vṛndāvana *bābājī*.

5. The incident about Śrīla Prabhupāda's brother is from Nandarāṇī-devī dāsī. By depending on Kṛṣṇa, Prabhupāda not only got long life but everything materially and spiritually, which his family members could never get by all their endeavors in the material world. The incident with Mr. Pithi is from Pālikā-devī dāsī, interview. The third incident is from Subhaga dāsa, interview.

6. The first two items are from SDG, interview; Prabhupāda's statement that he has to "Stay and manage" is from Girirāja Swami, interview. The talk to ISKCON Press, SDG, memoirs; Prabhupāda in Māyāpur, Śatadhanya Mahārāja, interview; Prabhupāda on American Express, Girirāja Swami, interview; Abhirāma dāsa, interview; letter to Kīrtirāja dāsa, January 2, 1972.

7. Letter to Jadurāṇī, April 13, 1968; letter to Haṁsadūta, December 7, 1968.

8. SDG.

9. On the train in India, Mahāṁsa Swami, interview; reference to the verse *dravya-mūlyena* is also found in a letter dated October 10, 1968, to Brahmānanda Swami.

10. Jaya Mādhava dāsa, Raṇacora dāsa, Sākṣī-Gopāla dāsa, interviews.

11. Ānakadundubhi dāsa, interview. A reader may ask, "What is the point of this anecdote?" The "point" may be stated as follows: Śrīla Prabhupāda was so absorbed in appreciating the newly published volume of Kṛṣṇa's book that he both overlooked a discrepancy caused by his servant and he overlooked that the book now had a spot on it. It is a portrait of Prabhupāda in ecstatic concentration. By way of justifying this anecdote as well as others, I would like to state that the real "point" of the anecdote is its charm and the fact that it gives us a glimpse into Prabhupāda's life. Whatever allows us to be drawn closely into Prabhupāda's presence is itself worthwhile; the Vedic instruction is there blended into Prabhupāda's personal presentation of that instruction by his every act.

In researching through English literature to find precedents for books in the form of anecdotes, I found an interesting essay, "A Dissertation on Anecdotes," by Isaac D'Israeli, an eighteenth century author. His appreciation of the unique strength of anecdotes can be perfectly applied in the case of anecdotes about Prabhupāda. D'Israeli writes that while it is possible for anecdote writers to sometimes write of items too minute or trivial in describing a historic person, if the person is truly illuminating, anything is worthwhile. "For my part," he writes, "I shall be charmed that we have a good life of Homer, or Plato, or Horace, or Virgil, and their equals. It is in these cases that the minutest detail would not fail to interest me." (He states, however, that he is not interested in even the main important facts in the lives of persons who actually lack greatness.) In our case, writing of

Śrīla Prabhupāda, we are confident that he is of the greatest stature whether considered humanly or spiritually, so we should be confident that if we nicely tell any anecdote about Prabhupāda it will be worthwhile. I have already stated in the Preface to Volume One, however, that considerations of etiquette should be applied in describing the spiritual master. When I have gone ahead and told an anecdote that may possibly be misconstrued, I have tried to explain it more fully in these notes.

Before leaving D'Israeli's dissertation on anecdotes, I would like to share a few more of his quotes to help us more appreciate the gain in reading about Prabhupāda through the anecdotal medium. While these reflections by an eighteenth century literary gentleman were not intended exclusively for descriptions of the pure devotee of the Lord, we may happily engage them when thinking of anecdotes about Śrīla Prabhupāda.

"An intelligent reader frequently discovers (through anecdotes) *traits* which seem concealed. He does not perceive these faint touches in the broad canvas of the historian, but in those little portraits which have sometimes reached posterity. He acquires more knowledge of individuals by memoirs than by history. In history there is a majesty, which keeps us distant from great men; in memoirs, there is a familiarity which invites us to approach them. In histories, we appear only as one who joins the crowd to see them pass; in memoirs we are like concealed spies, who pause on every little circumstance, and note every little expression. A well chosen anecdote frequently reveals a character more happily than an elaborate delineation, as a glance of lightning will sometimes discover what has escaped us in a full light. We cannot therefore accumulate too great a number of such little facts. It is only the complaint of unreflected minds that we recollect too many anecdotes. Why is human knowledge imperfect but because it does not allow sufficient years to enable us to follow the infinity of nature? Human nature, like a vast machine, is not to be understood by looking on its superficies but by dwelling on its minute springs and little wheels. Let us no more be told that anecdotes are the little objects of a little mind."

12. Hṛdayānanda Goswami, interview.

13. Jananivāsa dāsa, memoirs; Amogha dāsa, memoirs.

14. SDG.

15. Maṇihara dāsa, interview; Tamāla Kṛṣṇa Goswami, diary.

16. SDG; letter to Jaduraṇī-devī dāsī, September 4, 1972.

17. Nara-Nārāyaṇa, interview; Bhārgava dāsa, interview.

18. Śrutakīrti dāsa, interview.

19. Śatadhanya Mahārāja, interview.

20. Dayānanda dāsa, interview; SDG.

21. Nṛsiṁhānanda dāsa, interview.

22. Prabhupāda in Delhi, Tejās dāsa, interview; gardener in England, Dhanañjaya dāsa, interview.

23. Visit to Rādhā-Govinda, Abhirāma dāsa, interview; *ricksha* bargaining, Śatadhanya Mahārāja, interview.

24. Letters on Deity worship, Himavatī-devī dāsī, December 26, 1971; Mukunda dāsa, January 1, 1974, Patita Uddhāraṇa dāsa, December 8, 1971; Kīrtika-devī dāsī, February 19, 1973; Pañcadraviḍa Swami, interview.

25. Yaśomatīnandana dāsa, interview; Nanda-kumāra, Nara-Nārāyaṇa, interviews.

26. Jadurāṇī-devī dāsī, interview; Harikeśa Swami, interview.

27. SDG.

28. Pañcadraviḍa Swami, interview.

29. Ibid.

30. Bharadvāja dāsa, interview.

31. Hṛdayānanda Goswami, interview.

32. Jagattāriṇī-devī dāsī, interview; Kulaśekhara dāsa, interview. We should not be like this neophyte Kṛṣṇa conscious *gṛhastha* and be puzzled by Prabhupāda's advice for the householders. In his memoir, the devotee states that he thought Prabhupāda didn't understand him, Prabhupāda understood perfectly. He also gave advice for the bona fide behavior of the *gṛhastha*. There are full instructions for the *gṛhastha* given in the Seventh Canto of *Śrīmad-Bhāgavatam,* and these few words spoken by Prabhupāda are among the scriptural directions for household life. We cannot say why Śrīla Prabhupāda chose to give exactly these instructions and only these instructions. First of all, however, the new householders should accept that Prabhupāda's instructions of *are* śāstric, and secondly, they should try to think why Prabhupāda has chosen to give these particular instructions. He did not arbitrarily select from the many scriptural instructions.

The particular instruction Śrīla Prabhupāda gave—that a householder should not just make an arrangement for his own sense gratification in eating but should share it with others first—stresses that the *gṛhastha-āśrama* is a renounced way of life. The young householder admitted that he wanted to hear from Prabhupāda about the intimate dealings of husband and wife, but Prabhupāda pointed out that that is not what *gṛhastha* life is about. According to the *varṇāśrama* system, the *gṛhastha* is actually the material provider of the whole society. A neophyte devotee may think that if he gets married, he can make a better arrangement for an independent life of eating and being comfortable, which he could not arrange so nicely as a *brahmacārī*. The particular instruction that Prabhupāda chose to give cuts this misconception to pieces. Rather than become a sense enjoyer once married, the *gṛhastha* is seen here as one who has to carry a burden for all human beings and even other living creatures. This is a picture of a householder not making arrangements for enjoyment, but getting up from his table and going out to provide for others before he takes his own meals. Whatever instruction Srīla Prabhupāda gave, however odd or puzzling it may have seemed in context, was certainly scriptural, and if one thinks about it carefully, he will see how the teaching applies perfectly to his own case. When acted upon, it will bring success.

In *Prabhupāda Nectar*, we see Prabhupāda giving particular instructions to particular persons. We may say that these instructions do not have to be universally applied, but at least in every case they are absolute instructions. It is a test of every sincere disciple whether he followed the instructions Prabhupāda gave him. We have already cited this point in connection with Prabhupāda's warnings to the devotee-artist who was developing *sahajiyā* symptoms. Reading anecdotes about Śrīla Prabhupāda's practical instructions, we can appreciate the particular instructions he gave different persons and we can imbibe the general instruction: that one should always respect, meditate on, and carry out the instructions he or she received from the spiritual master.

33. Amogha, interview.

34. Jagadguru Swami, interview.

35. Mahābuddhi dāsa, interview; Girirāja Swami, interview. Prabhupāda also described that his spiritual master was very strict in following the rule of not being alone with a woman. One time, one of Bhaktisiddhānta Sarasvatī's disciples, a Dr. Kapoor, accompanied by his very young wife, was seeing Bhaktisiddhānta Sarasvatī Ṭhākura. During the discussion, the young wife said to her husband's guru, "I would like to ask you something in private." Bhaktisiddhānta Sarasvatī replied, "I cannot see you in private. Whatever it is you can ask me here." Śrīla Prabhupāda commented that at the time, Bhaktisiddhānta Sarasvatī said this was old enough to be the young girl's great-grandfather, yet he strictly applied this rule to set an example. Bhaktisiddhānta Sarasvatī's great disciple, Śrīla Prabhupāda, did the same.

36. Letter to Bhakta dāsa, May 7, 1975; letter to Śukadeva dāsa, April 5, 1974; letter to Kṛṣṇa-nandinī-devī dāsī, April 8, 1975; letter to Govinda-devī dāsī, February 12, 1972; letter to Kṛṣṇa-vilāsinī-devī dāsī, June 3, 1975; letter to Gandharva dāsa, November 6, 1974; letter to Revatīnandana Swami, November 14, 1973.

37. Jayapatāka Swami, interview. The story wherein Gopāla Bhan outwitted the man who tried to pass stool in Gopāla's newly constructed house contains lessons that can be applied in higher matters. Prabhupāda used it to illustrate a cheating mentality of people who appear to say one thing but then secretly make conditions to make their main statement impossible to carry out. It is very difficult to pass stool without passing at least a drop of urine. Gopāla was giving the man permission with his speech, but the proposal was almost impossible. Moreover, Gopāla was ready to punish him if he failed to do the impossible. We should be careful that we

ourselves do not become duplicitous in our dealings with others, so that we ask of them things that are impossible to achieve.

Also, a devotee preaching in the world of shrewd materialists should be careful not to be cheated by the luring proposals of businessmen, politicians, and other sense enjoyers. By clear intelligence, if we can penetrate through such devious word jugglery, we shall be able to assert pure Kṛṣṇa consciousness and expose the cheating attempts of others.

It is one thing to be amused when hearing how Gopāla outsmarts the king and his friends, but it can also be a more serious matter when we are tested with difficult-to-solve life problems. In the *Śrīmad-Bhāgavatam,* we read how Bhīma and Lord Kṛṣṇa advised Arjuna to kill Aśvatthāmā, whereas Yudhiṣṭhira, Draupadī, and others advised Arjuna to spare Aśvatthāmā. It was impossible to satisfy the desires of all these exalted persons, but by Kṛṣṇa's grace, Arjuna was given a brilliant solution. There are similar cases of Vaiṣṇavas being given difficult or seemingly impossible tests, yet they were able to solve the contradiction. When a Vaiṣṇava, by his Kṛṣṇa conscious intelligence, eludes the traps of the materialists or defeats them with superior, Kṛṣṇa conscious logic, it is more than mere amusement it is a wonderful victory.

38. Jayapatāka Swami.

39. SDG.

40. Bharadvāja dāsa, interview.

41. Candanācārya dāsa, interview.

42. Tape recording, January 1, 1974; tape recording, 1977.

43. Tape recording, December 26, 1976; tape recording, January 15, 1977.

44. Letter to Ādi-keśava dāsa, January 2, 1975; letter to SDG, January 19, 1975; letter to Śukadeva dāsa, November 14, 1973; letter to Guru-kṛpa Swami, December 25, 1973.

45. Letter to Tejās dāsa, April 8, 1974; letter to Śama dāsa, September 12, 1974; letter to Trivikrama Swami, December 27, 1974; letter to Pañcadraviḍa Swami, January 4, 1975. Śrīla Prabhupāda stresses a similar point in a letter to Hṛdayānanda Goswami, dated June 4, 1974: "We want to firmly establish centers in South America," Śrīla Prabhupāda wrote. "I fully agree that the centers should be as far as possible manned by men who are native to the country; that will make our position even stronger, just as in the U.S.A. all you men and women have managed." The principle of the spiritual master assigning devotees to work in a certain land is known as *prabhu-datta-deśa*. It might seem that a foreign mission could be instigated quicker by importing men from countries like America, but in the long run, there is no avoiding the conclusion that the preaching in a country will seriously flourish only when its native members take to Kṛṣṇa consciousness and become leading preachers among their countrymen. Prabhupāda writes in the same letter to Hṛdayānanda Goswami, "Our progress is slow but sure. When walking down the street, we first place one foot down and when it is firm we take another step." When native devotees of all nations take responsibility for Kṛṣṇa consciousness and manage their own centers, then we have actualization of the statement by Prabhupāda that ISKCON is a spiritual United Nations. Thus the prediction of Bhaktivinoda Ṭhākura is realized, when all these devotees from around the world, who are seriously developing their *prabhu-datta-deśa*, gather

in Lord Caitanya's birthplace at Māyāpur and chant together, "Jaya Śacīnandana! Hare Kṛṣṇa! Hare Kṛṣṇa!"; letter to Girirāja dāsa Brahmacārī, February 4, 1975.

46. Amogha dāsa, Bhūrijana dāsa, interviews.

47. Govinda-devī dāsī, interview; lecture tape, February 29, 1976.

48. Hari Śauri dāsa, diary; Bhūrijana dāsa, interview; SDG.

49. SDG.

50. Hṛdayānanda Goswami, Bhavānanda Goswami, Mukunda Goswami, Yaśomatīnandana dāsa, Pālikā-devī dāsī, interviews.

VOLUME THREE NOTES

1. Surabhi Swami and Guṇārṇava dāsa, interview. There are many other examples of how Śrīla Prabhupāda was careful and frugal about spending money in India. He was concerned that his Western disciples were always getting cheated by the Indians. Even to this day those who were trained up by Prabhupāda in India practice this austerity of saving money in any way they can. In the West, especially in America, Srīla Prabhupāda did not attempt to introduce the same strictness in spending.

These differences in application bring up a larger issue—whether Prabhupāda's activities and teachings are all to be strictly followed. The answer is, "Yes." Even if on of Prabhupāda's instructions cannot be followed literally, we should never ignore its spirit. We should think how to apply it according to time and place. We are collecting many anecdotes of Prabhupāda's life not for mere reading entertainment, but for their instructive value. Neither are Prabhupāda's instructions applicable only to himself. Because Śrīla Prabhupāda was in essence always a teacher, therefore his *līlā* as a spiritual master is always filled with instruction. As Prabhupāda told us, "Do as I am doing." Although some of his activities are beyond imitation, nevertheless the main intent of this collection of stories—which we also think is the main intent of Prabhupāda's life—is to give perfect examples of Kṛṣṇa consciousness to be followed by aspiring devotees.

2. Hare Kṛṣṇa dāsa, interview. Hare Kṛṣṇa dāsa also relates that this incident gave him lasting impressions of Prabhupāda's qualities. If the temple management had not made so many mistakes, he realized, then there would have been no cause for Prabhupāda's becoming so angry in front of all the guests. Nevertheless, it also revealed that Prabhupāda

did not care as much about the audience as he did for Kṛṣṇa and Kṛṣṇa's pleasure. The devotees were able to see how Prabhupāda was actually aloof from public opinion. They would remember this in their preaching when comparing Prabhupāda to other gurus. They could understand better now that Śrīla Prabhupāda was completely different from swamis who became involved in various public causes and political controversies. Prabhupāda was beyond all that, completely renounced and detached. He was concerned only with pleasing Kṛṣṇa and spreading Kṛṣṇa consciousness.

3. Karandhara dāsa, interview.

4. Dhanurdhara Swami and Dvārakādhīśa dāsa, interviews. Hari Śauri dāsa, diary.

5. Letter to Vipini dāsa, December 19, 1974; Hari Śauri dāsa, diary, February 16, 1977; morning walk, Tehran, August 10, 1976; letter to Kṛṣṇa-kathā dāsa, November 22, 1974.

6. SDG. This story has obvious modern-day application. In 1966 Śrīla Prabhupāda was pleased when Rūpānuga and Satsvarūpa persisted in wearing Vaiṣṇava *tilaka* to their jobs with the New York City Department of Welfare. Bhaktivinoda Ṭhākura also desired that one day the high court judges may wear Vaiṣṇava *tilaka,* and this would be a symbol of the successful influence of Kṛṣṇa consciousness in the world. Even in job situations where wearing *tilaka* is not permissible, a devotee should try in different ways to remember Kṛṣṇa while at work. The story told by Prabhupāda about the man who insisted on wearing *tilaka* to his job may remain an inspiration to all devotees who go to places of employment controlled by the *karmīs.* Somehow or other, we must remain devotees.

7. SDG.

8. Balavanta dāsa Adhikārī, interview.

9. Pañcadraviḍa Swami, interview.

10. Hari Śauri dāsa, diary. Devotees were always happy to hear Prabhupāda smash the arguments of atheists and nondevotees. We also knew that this was the spirit of Prabhupāda's spiritual master, Bhaktisiddhānta Sarasvatī, who liked bold disciples who did not compromise. Prabhupāda set the perfect example, but on some occasions he also pointed out that in our own smashing of the nondevotees we cannot exactly imitate him, but we have to find the strongest method according to time and place. One time in New York City, Prabhupāda visited an Indian official in the U.N. The man was younger than Prabhupāda, and Prabhupāda sternly reprimanded him when the man spoke his concocted philosophies. After leaving the U.N., while driving in the car, one of the devotees praised Śrīla Prabhupāda and said, "Prabhupāda, you really chastised that man like anything." Prabhupāda replied, "Yes, but you cannot do that."

Prabhupāda thus explained further that the particular way he had dealt with this man (who was junior in age to him and who was an Indian countryman) would not have been the way that one of Prabhupāda's young American disciples could have dealt with him. The intelligent disciple learns how to follow the spiritual master in a way that will please him. We should not be like foolish Aśvatthāmā who thought he would please his guru Droṇa by presenting him with the dead bodies of Draupadī's sons.

11. The anecdote about the mosquitoes is from Guṇārṇava, interview; the anecdote from Bhubhaneswar is from Hari Śauri dāsa, diary, January 31, 1977.

12. Hari Śauri dāsa, diary.

13. Letters on health to Sudāmā dāsa, December 10, 1973; Madana-mohana dāsa, July 23, 1969; Kīrtanānanda Swami, February 14, 1969; Revatīnandana dāsa, January 16, 1975. On a morning walk in Denver, July 1, 1975, devotees inquired from Prabhupāda about fasting. They gave the example that one of Prabhupāda's disciples had taken to reading non-Kṛṣṇa conscious books on health and had gone on a thirty-day fast, which some of the devotees said was the reason his consciousness had changed and he had left Kṛṣṇa consciousness.

"If one can fast, that is *tapasya*," Prabhupāda said, "but it should not be artificial. Just like Raghunātha dāsa Gosvāmī. He was fasting, but he was not just fasting. People fast artificially and become weak and cannot work; that is not required. If you fast and at the same time you do not become weak, then that is recommended. And if after fasting you cannot do service, then what is the use of fasting? Raghunātha Gosvāmī was fasting, but he was thrice taking bath and offering obeisances hundreds of times. His regular activities were not stopped, and he was taking every alternate day a little quantity of butter. That's all. It is not possible to imitate him We have to work."

14. Morning walk, May 5, 1973, Los Angeles.

15. SDG; Govinda-devī dāsī, interview; SDG.

16. SDG.

17. Comments on Prabhupāda's use of language are from Hṛdayānanda Goswami, Jayādvaita Swami, Hari Śauri dāsa, Hayagriva dāsa, Śivānanda dāsa, and Rukmiṇī-devī dāsī.

18. Harikeśa Swami, lecture.

19. Jagadīśa Goswami, lecture.

20. Bhavātariṇī-devī dāsī, interview.

21. Hari Śauri dāsa, diary; Tamāla Kṛṣṇa Goswami, interview; Hari Śauri dāsa, diary. The incident where Śrīla Prabhupāda gives contradictory instructions to two different *sannyāsīs* points to the value of supplementary literature such as *Prabhupāda Nectar*. Śrīla Prabhupāda selected instructions from *The Nectar of Devotion* for our application in ISKCON, but he also deliberately omitted certain instructions from that book. The *ācārya*, while always guided by guru, *śāstra*, and *sādhu*, will also sometimes simplify and select. Such selection, when done by a neophyte, can become dangerous speculation. Therefore, when we can record reliable accounts of Prabhupāda's personal dealings, we have another permanent record to which to turn, which is not merely of value as simply a footnote of curiosity, but which can show us dynamically and specifically how Śrīla Prabhupāda chooses instructions from the *Vedas* according to time, person, and place.

The incident of Prabhupāda's receiving a *rasagullā* made in England while at the Kumbha-melā demonstrates Prabhupāda's satisfaction with the expansion of the Kṛṣṇa consciousness movement. Prabhupāda did not take ISKCON's growth as his personal doing, but he saw it as the grace of Lord Caitanya and Śrīla Bhaktisiddhānta Sarasvatī Ṭhākura. Of course, historically no one can deny that Śrīla Prabhupāda was the one chosen to spread Lord Caitanya's mission worldwide, but Prabhupāda was prideless in the matter. He would freely state how wonderful it was that Kṛṣṇa consciousness was spreading. On another occasion, Prabhupāda was sitting in his garden in Vṛndāvana, talking with a British disciple who said that he was a great-grandson of Lord Macauley, a leader during the British occupation of India. After talking with his disciple for some time, Prabhupāda remarked on the wonder of the Kṛṣṇa consciousness movement, that now a British descendent of Lord

Macauley was fanning his Indian guru. Prabhupāda would also quote the imperialistic slogan, "The sun never sets on the British empire" and apply it to his Kṛṣṇa consciousness movement. He said that practically no *karmī* industrialist could have as many branches as Śrīla Prabhupāda had branches of ISKCON. Even if he were to stay only three days in each one of his temples, he would not have time in the year to do it. Prabhupāda made such transcendental boasting usually to impress audiences and to make them aware that Kṛṣṇa consciousness was no trifle. After a visit by one Māyāvādī *yogī*, Prabhupāda remarked that by this *yogī's śakti* he is only able to maintain one apartment flat in Calcutta, whereas Śrīla Prabhupāda, by the *śakti* of Lord Kṛṣṇa, had branches all over the world.

22. "Kṛṣṇa Bowl" letter from Prabhupāda to Akṣobhya dāsa, March 9, 1974; letter to Rūpānuga dāsa, April 9, 1974. Śrīla Prabhupāda was particularly concerned that concoctions not be introduced with the children. When someone wrote to him complaining that a child had been beaten, Prabhupāda replied that whoever had done the beating should himself be beaten. One major deviation occurred when a devotee in the *gurukula* became interested in Montessori teaching methods and attempted to introduce them into the school. Prabhupāda squelched them as definitely as he squelched the Kṛṣṇa Bowl. In his letter stopping the Kṛṣṇa Bowl, Prabhupāda mentions that the devotee's brain is not "clear," and therefore he had invented these things. This indicates that if we keep ourselves clearheaded in Kṛṣṇa consciousness by always following the *paramparā* and observing the rules and regulations, these unnecessary outside ideas will not occur to us.

23. Jagadguru Swami, interview. According to Jagadguru Swami, on another occasion Prabhupāda said that he would take on his head the dust from the feet of whoever went to preach in North Africa. Dayānanda dāsa says that Śrīla

Prabhupāda said the same thing regarding devotees who would go and risk their lives to preach in the Mid-East Muslim countries.

24. New Vrindaban, lecture; Pālikā-devī dāsī, interview; Oṁkāra-devī dāsī, letter; Dīnadayādrī-devī dāsī, interview; Girirāja Swami, interview; Balavanta dāsa, interview. Regarding Prabhupāda's statement that devotee wives should not be beaten, he also mentioned on different occasions that the quarreling between husband and wife should not be taken so seriously. In America, he said, whenever there is a big quarrel, then immediately there is divorce. But in India the marriage vows are taken more seriously. Therefore, the inevitable differences between husband and wife never become the cause for breaking up families. In the Cāṇakya Paṇḍita *ślokas*, the quarrel between husband and wife is taken as one of the occurrences that makes a big noise but has no serious result. Prabhupāda also quoted the poet Tulasī dāsa, who had a bitter personal experience with his own wife, who was unfaithful. Nevertheless, one of Tulasī dāsa's sayings is that a woman may be a tiger, but she may also be a goddess of fortune. In the Indian villages a tiger's entrance into the home is the most frightening thing imaginable, and yet, says Tulasī dāsa, every foolish man is keeping a tigress in his home. The woman may be compared to a tigress because she sucks the husband's blood through draining his semen, which is made up of many drops of blood. The same tigress-woman, however, if she is Kṛṣṇa conscious, may be like the presence of Lakṣmī-devī within the *gṛhastha* household.

25. SDG.

26. The story of the king and the mosquito and the dead elephant story are from Girirāja Swami, interview; the story about the cat cutting the cake is from Puṣkara dāsa, interview; the story about *jñāna* and *bhakti* is from Hari Śauri

dāsa, diary. Another story Prabhupāda told is about how one has to be qualified by his consciousness to sit on the king's throne or on the spiritual master's *vyāsāsana*. A qualified person may sit on the elevated seat, and a dog might also sit there, but if a dog were sitting on the *vyāsāsana* and someone threw a bone before him, he would immediately jump off the elevated seat and go after the bone. Thus his real consciousness would be exposed by his activities.

27. SDG.

28. Girirāja Swami, interview.

29. Nandarāṇī-devī dāsī, interview.

30. Raghunātha Swami, interview.

31. Dāṇavīra dāsa, interview; Jayapatāka Swami, interview; Rukmiṇī-devī dāsī, interview.

32. Nava-yogendra Swami, interview; Brahmānanda Swami, lecture.

33. Letters to Śivānanda dāsa, April 19, 1968; Amogha dāsa, August 5, 1974; Bhakta dāsa, August 3, 1973.

34. SDG.

35. SDG.

36. Bhavānanda Goswami, interview.

37. SDG.

38. Tamāla Kṛṣṇa Goswami, interview.

39. Tamāla Kṛṣṇa Goswami, interview; Girirāja Swami, interview. There is a similar statement in a letter by Prabhupāda where he cautiously allows that non-Kṛṣṇa conscious or supplementary spiritual books may be read:

"Do you think you shall require all these books? Of course I have no objection of you keeping these as reference books, but we should always remember that we have to give more stress on our spiritual side than the scholastic side. But at the same time, if our books are presented in a scholarly way, that will be very nice. So you use the best part of discretion and do the needful.

" . . . But you need not become such a scholar. You require simply to understand our *śāstras, Bhagavad-gītā, Śrīmad-Bhāgavatam,* etc., and chant Hare Kṛṣṇa mantra as much as possible. The thing is if you give more stress on the scholarly line, other devotees will try to imitate you. Already your wife has expressed such intention, and as soon as we try to be scholars, our devotional line will be slackened. These points are to be kept in view always."

40. Hari Śauri dāsa, diary; Bālāi-devī dāsī and Jāhnavā-devī dāsī, interviews; SDG; Jananivāsa dāsa, interview.

41. Letters on reading Prabhupāda's books and becoming strong by following the spiritual principles to Gaura Gopāla dāsa, May 26, 1975; Caitya Guru dāsa, February 7, 1974; Mārkaṇḍeya Ṛṣi dāsa, May 1, 1974.

42. Tamāla Kṛṣṇa Goswami, interview; Bhūrijana dāsa, interview.

43. SDG.

44. Brahmatīrtha dāsa, interview.

45. Bhakti-devī dāsī, interview. This anecdote given by Brahmatīrtha dāsa's wife is a case where the devotee is aware that Śrīla Prabhupāda knew her mind even though she did not speak it. In writing Prabhupāda's biography in the *Śrīla Prabhupāda-līlāmṛta*, I followed the standard rules for biography and always refrained from attempting to read Śrīla Prabhupāda's mind. This is not only a matter of the science of biography writing, but it is also the Vaiṣṇava's attitude toward the spiritual master. *Vaiṣṇavera kriyā mudrā vijñeya na bhujaya:* "No one can know the mind of the pure devotee." But in reviewing interviews from devotees, we find again and again incidents where devotees have very strong impressions that Śrīla Prabhupāda knew what they were thinking. There are too many incidents like this to simply categorically reject them all. One can say that these are subjective impressions, but in the lives of devotees there sometimes are such strong impressions that they are significant in keeping a devotee fixed in Kṛṣṇa consciousness. Why should we deny that Prabhupāda had the potency to know the mind of his disciples? Therefore, from time to time we shall also present such anecdotes in this series.

46. Śrutakīrti dāsa, interview. Śrīla Prabhupāda used the expression "*daṇḍavat* devotee" to describe a devotee who made a profuse show of respect and worship of the spiritual master but did not follow it up with a real service attitude. Especially the pious Hindu will always bow down or offer *daṇḍavats* before the guru. If the service begins and ends with formal *daṇḍavats*, however, then Prabhupāda considered such a person not a very important devotee, but a "*daṇḍavat* devotee." On another occasion, I was present when a devotee felt moved to make a spontaneous expression of love in Prabhupāda's presence: "Prabhupāda, I am giving my whole life to you." Prabhupāda replied to this in a matter-of-fact way, saying, "That I already know." In other words, devotional service really begins when a disciple says, "Now I accept you

as my spiritual master. Please instruct me." To feel or state to the guru that you want to follow him completely is auspicious, but it must be accompanied by practical service.

47. Viśālinī-devī dāsī, interview; letter to Sanātana dāsa, June 3, 1975.

48. Tamāla Kṛṣṇa Goswami, interview; Bhagavān Goswami, interview; Girirāja Swami, interview.

49. Letter to Śrī Rameshji Mahalinga, August 31, 1975. Prabhupāda's version of the birds in the nest is different from that printed in the *Śrīmad-Bhāgavatam,* Eleventh Canto. There, the father bird, after seeing his children and his wife captured in the net of the hunter, simply laments in a stunned way, so the hunter catches him also. Prabhupāda's bird is more intelligent, and therefore he decided to "take *sannyāsa.*" The image of a bird taking *sannyāsa* is another unique Prabhupāda-ism. Prabhupāda felt free sometimes to use different stories in his own way. Sometimes devotees have pointed out what they think are contradictions in sequence in books like the *Kṛṣṇa* book. For example, Prabhupāda sometimes quoted Kṛṣṇa at a young age referring to *Bhagavad-gītā,* "As I have said in the *Bhagavad-gītā.*" Of course, there is no contradiction, since the *Bhagavad-gītā* is eternal and is presented again and again during different incarnations of the Lord. In any case, when Prabhupāda was questioned about his method in the *Kṛṣṇa* book, he replied, "Therefore I have called it summary study. Summary study means I can do what I want."

50. SDG

VOLUME FOUR NOTES

1. Śrutakīrti dāsa, interview. Śrīla Prabhupāda repeated a similar anecdote in his lectures about the time he and his disciples had walked across a farmer's field in Vṛndāvana. The farmer had come out with members of his family to meet Prabhupāda and to express that it was a great honor for him to have Śrīla Prabhupāda walking in his field. Prabhupāda compared this to the West, where there are signs, "Beware of Dog," and where a trespasser may be shot.

2. Śubhānanda dāsa and Śrīnātha dāsa, interviews.

3. Rādhānātha Swami, interview. We have yet to fully appreciate how much Prabhupāda sacrificed in overcoming the difficulties of illness and old age to distribute Kṛṣṇa consciousness up to his last breath. Prabhupāda cautioned many times in his books that one should neither become attached to the body nor bothered by bodily discomforts. He exemplified this. One usually doesn't think much in terms of Prabhupāda's different illnesses, except that they were transcendental. His first illness after he came to America was in 1967, when he endured something like a stroke or a heart attack. Later, Prabhupāda was diagnosed as a diabetic, yet he never took regular treatment for any of these diagnosed diseases.

One time in India, a disciple of Prabhupāda's was worried about his own jaundice. The disciple told Prabhupāda that he had different symptoms of jaundice such as yellow eyes, and that his stool was changing from brown to white. Prabhupāda at first dismissed the possibility that his student had jaundice, although he had the symptoms. Of himself he said sometimes the stool was one color and sometimes another, but these things were temporary and not noteworthy; one should go on with his Kṛṣṇa consciousness.

Similarly, even when Prabhupāda was diagnosed as having certain diseases, he never thought of himself, "I am a diabetic" or "I am a victim of heart attacks." He just continued his transcendental service. This is an instruction for all of us. Prabhupāda's glories cannot be imitated, yet we should also always put our service first and not identify ourselves as victims of various diseases. When there was too much talk of a particular disease or even its cure, Prabhupāda would point out that the real disease is the material body and the real cure is chanting Hare Kṛṣṇa. We often think, rightly, that Prabhupāda's diseases were not materially caused but had transcendental causes. We may note that not only were the causes transcendental, but Prabhupāda's response to his so-called diseases was entirely transcendental. He understood that illness came from Kṛṣṇa, and as far as possible he went on with his service, always staying on the transcendental platform. (In anecdote 49, Rāmeśvara Swami also describes how Śrīla Prabhupāda transcended his physical illnesses to deliver Kṛṣṇa consciousness.)

4. SDG

5. Letter by Śrutakīrti to Kīrtanānanda Swami, September 27, 1972; letter from Girirāja dāsa to Uddhava dāsa, January 21, 1971. This is the first time I have used exchanges of letters between devotees as entries in *Prabhupāda Nectar*. It shows us another wonderful way to glorify Prabhupāda. These letters are especially nectarean because they give us a direct flavor of Prabhupāda's association, as if he is present in the next room. We therefore request any devotees who have letters they wrote when Prabhupāda was present or who have letters they received from devotees traveling with Prabhupāda to please submit them for use in *Prabhupāda Nectar*.

6. Letter to Balavanta dāsa, January 3, 1977; letter to Jagadīśa dāsa, November 20, 1975; letter to Nityānanda dāsa, April 12, 1977; letter to Rūpānuga dāsa, December 7, 1975; letter to Tuṣṭa Kṛṣṇa dāsa, August 23, 1976; letter to Haṁsadūta dāsa, September 7, 1974.

7. Bhakti-cāru Swami, interview. Although the Hindu *pūjārī* naively blessed the devotees to become Hindu *brāhmaṇas* in their next life, he at least appreciated their reverence and devotion in the temple. Because he appreciated their behavior in his own way, he wanted to bless them and wish them well. Proper behavior by Prabhupāda's followers is a credit to Prabhupāda, to the Kṛṣṇa consciousness movement, and to the devotees. The credit to the devotees, however, has to be earned; it is not automatic. Prabhupāda writes in *The Nectar of Instruction,* "Indeed, whether the devotees come from a family of previous *ācāryas* or from an ordinary family, they should be treated equally. One should not think, 'Oh, here is an American *gosvāmī,*' and discriminate against him. Nor should one think, 'Here is a *nityānanda-vaṁśa-gosvāmī.*' . . . According to the statements of Śrīla Rūpa Gosvāmī in this verse, an American *gosvāmī* and a *gosvāmī* in a family of *ācāryas* are nondifferent." If we go at all to a temple or place of pilgrimage, it should be for our devotional service, and we should do it with humility and purity to properly represent Prabhupāda. Prabhupāda also said that wherever we go in the world, if we follow the rules and behave properly, people will worship the devotees. Even if the *brāhmaṇa* in the temple does not bless us, however, Prabhupāda and Kṛṣṇa will be pleased with our proper public behavior.

8. SDG.

9. Jayādvaita Swami, letter to Satsvarūpa dāsa Goswami. The story of Śrīla Prabhupāda at a bank-opening in Vṛndāvana shows his wonderful ability to preach according to time

and place. Prabhupāda once preached to an assembly of lawyers. He made the point that the chanting of Hare Kṛṣṇa would alleviate the suffering of all sinful people, but for such a claim, he said, there must be evidence, as in a court of law. And his evidence was in Narottama dāsa Ṭhākura's song of Jagāi and Mādhāi, two great sinners who had been saved by the Hare Kṛṣṇa movement five hundred years ago. Today, however, one could see practically how drunkards and illicit sex hunters had been made saintly by the Hare Kṛṣṇa movement.

10. Śrutakīrti dāsa, interview; Rādhā-vallabha dāsa, interview; SDG; Hṛdayānanda Goswami, interview; Pūrṇacandra-devī dāsī, interview.

Devotees have noted on various occasions how Prabhupāda displayed an extrasensory perception of events. Prabhupāda was in Florida with Hṛdayānanda Goswami, and they were driving behind a fruit truck. Prabhupāda pointed to it and said, "Oh, watermelons?" Hṛdayānanda Goswami explains, "We looked, but all we could see were Florida oranges. We said, 'No, Prabhupāda. Those are oranges.' A few minutes later, as we were passing that truck, behind the oranges we saw watermelons. They were hidden. Prabhupāda just laughed and said, 'Yes, there are the watermelons.'"

In Bhaktivedanta Manor one time Śrīla Prabhupāda complained of a dripping water faucet that disturbed him. The devotees searched and searched, but found nothing. Finally, they found the offending faucet. It was outside his room, down the hall, down a small block of stairs, down another small hall, and inside a closet in a place from which water was hardly ever taken. No one knew how he could possibly have heard it drip.

11. Sarvamaṅgala-devī dāsī, interview; Rādhā-vallabha dāsa, interview; Rūpa-vilāsa dāsa and Candrikā-devī dāsī, interview.

12. Rādhānātha Swami, interview. Prabhupāda showed more than once how he immediately felt quite at home in New Vrindaban, and the *Prabhupāda-līlāmṛta* describes this in telling of Prabhupāda's first visit there. Although he was accustomed to big cities, as soon as he came to a place like New Vrindaban or to the farm in Hyderabad, he was at ease and quite happy with such primitive living conditions. In India, Prabhupāda had also spent most of his early years in the cities: he grew up in Calcutta, had his business in Allahabad, and he traveled as a businessman. But his attraction to such simple forest settings is transcendental. He also told us that Kṛṣṇa is attracted to such a setting in the original Vṛndāvana. Prabhupāda always became enlivened at the prospects of *varnāśrama-dharma*, village life and cow protection when he came into these settings. It enlivened him to see the Kṛṣṇa conscious farm developed in a simple setting.

Rādhānātha Swami tells that on one occasion in New Vrindaban, Prabhupāda said the devotees should stay in New Vrindaban and be satisfied. It was the same thing Kīrtanānanda had been repeatedly telling the devotees. Now that Prabhupāda said it, it became a great confirmation for the devotees there. Prabhupāda was satisfied to stay at their farm community and they should follow that example.

13. SDG, letter, while serving as secretary to Śrīla Prabhupāda, June 18, 1974; letter to Tuṣṭa Kṛṣṇa dāsa, November 9, 1975; letter to Batu Gopāla dāsa, August 16, 1974.

14. Lecture, May 21, 1972, Los Angeles.

15. Yadubara dāsa, interview.

16. Ravīndra-svarūpa dāsa, interview. Yadubara relates a similar incident. One time, on the roof in Bombay, Prabhupāda agreed to watch a dance troupe of little girls, as arranged by a life member. During the performance, Yadubara

began filming. He noticed that Śrīla Prabhupāda almost continuously avoided looking at the dancers. By looking this way and that way, sometimes up and down, Prabhupāda displayed an uncanny ability to sit before the show and yet avoid watching it.

As with most instructions and rules, there are also exceptions to the injunction that one should not hear singing by women. In 1975 a devotee in the Los Angeles temple became disturbed about having to hear "a woman" singing the "*Govindam*" prayers at greeting of the Deities. He wrote to Śrīla Prabhupāda, quoting Śrīla Bhaktivinoda Ṭhākura's commentary on the thirteenth chapter of *Antya-līlā* of *Caitanya-caritāmṛta* regarding Lord Caitanya's hearing the *devī-dāsīs* singing in the temple. He also referred to Śrīla Prabhupāda's purport in the eighteenth chapter of the Sixth Canto, where it is stated that a *sannyāsī* or *brahmacārī* who sees the face or hears the voice of a woman and becomes attracted is committing a subtle falldown. "In light of this," wrote the devotee from Los Angeles, "many of the *brahmacārīs*, including myself, approached the temple president here in New Dvārakā to see if it would be possible that when the Deities are greeted in the morning, instead of listening to Gurudāsa Mahārāja's former wife singing the *Brahma-saṁhitā* prayers, we could listen to Your Divine Grace sing the "*Govindam*" prayers, rather than hear a woman sing. I am sure all the devotees would be enlivened to hear you instead of electric guitars, London symphonic orchestra, etc., etc."

Śrīla Prabhupāda replied in a letter of December 12, 1975, from Vṛndāvana ISKCON:

"No! You have made some discovery. All along you have been hearing the recording of Yamuna-devi and now you want to change. It is not ordinary singing. It is concert. Many people are singing, so it is not bad. Just like *sankirtana*. I approve of it. Here in Krishna-Balaram temple we are hearing the same recording every morning, so if it is good here, why not there?"

19. Śrutakīrti dāsa, interview; Rāmeśvara Swami, interview.

20. Bhagavān Goswami, interview. As Vyāsadeva is the only one to ultimately know the *Vedānta*, so Śrīla Prabhupāda best knows the nature and potency of his own books. For example, he has stated, "If a person reads only one line, his life will become perfect." Others may not know how this is true, but Prabhupāda, the author of the books, says this is true. We shall try to understand it.

21. Letter to Rūpānuga dāsa, November 8, 1976; letter to Bhagavān Goswami, September 7, 1975; letter to Narottamānanda dāsa, July 13, 1975.

22. Recounted from memory by SDG.

23. Rukmiṇī-devī dāsī, interview; letter to Girirāja Swami, June 6, 1976; Rāmeśvara Swami, interview.

24. SDG.

25. Rūpa-vilāsa dāsa and Candrikā-devī dāsī, interview.

26. Śubhānanda dāsa, interview. Śubhānanda further explains what it meant to him to be empowered by Prabhupāda:

"I never have interpreted Prabhupāda saying 'You are empowered' as meaning that from now on, Kṛṣṇa will speak directly through you and everything will be very easy. But I take it that if I work hard and I am sincere and I try to surrender to Kṛṣṇa and guru, and if I try to my service nicely, then Kṛṣṇa will empower me."

27. Rūpa-vilāsa dāsa and Candrikā-devī dāsī, interview. As Śrīla Prabhupāda predicted, the schoolteacher was acquitted from any legal implications in the bus accident. Unfortunately he did not take up Prabhupāda's invitation to teach in the *gurukula* system. Neither did Werner von Braun take to Kṛṣṇa consciousness. Prabhupāda writes in *The Nectar of Devotion*, "Kṛṣṇa can easily offer a person material happiness or even liberation, but He does not agree very easily to award a person engagement in His devotional service."

28. Śrutakīrti dāsa, interview. Despite Prabhupāda's request that Śrutakīrti cook for Yamunā, he never did. The spirit of Prabhupāda's request was one he repeated in different ways: devotees should render service to other devotees. Prabhupāda used to explain this while defining the word *prabhu*. He said that *prabhu* means "master." If we call a devotee *prabhu* but always try to accept service from him, then we are accepting service from your "master." If we call a devotee *prabhu*, that means we must also render service to him.

When compiling several versions of the same Prabhupāda incident, I usually try to blend them into one rendition. However, I would like to quote Pañcadraviḍa Swami's version of the thieving monkey, because he tells it with his own flavor:

"The room was very crowded. One guest had come in and offered Prabhupāda a big bunch of bananas. What we could not see was that behind the swinging doors near the entrance to the temple a monkey was watching. He was watching everything, and all of a sudden he entered the room and ran. The room was narrow. He ran the entire length of it, grabbed the bananas, and was running out with the whole bunch when someone yelled, 'Stop him!' The monkey was exhibiting nice broken-field running, dodging people, but Prabhupāda managed to grab most of the bananas. Prabhupāda was laughing, saying, 'See how they are so intelligent in eating and defending.'"

29. Puṣkara dāsa, interview; Rūpa-vilāsa dāsa and Candrikā-devī dāsī, interview; Hari Śauri dāsa, interview.

30. Citralekhā-devī dāsī, interview; Rukmiṇī-devī dāsī, interview. It is easy for the devotees to understand and relish how Prabhupāda accepted ill-fitting or even unsuitable gifts from his disciples and yet utilized them just so the disciples' devotional service could be accepted by Kṛṣṇa. Sometimes nondevotees, on seeing a photo of Śrīla Prabhupāda, or seeing him with nondevotional eyes, thought that Śrīla Prabhupāda was enjoying material opulence obtained from his disciples. Specifically, nondevotees have criticized Prabhupāda's wearing of several rings, or his "gold" watches. At one point, when Śrīla Prabhupāda wore two or three rings, one of them was an inexpensive high school ring a devotee had given to Prabhupāda, which he simply wore for a while in recognition of the gift. When mass market technology first produced digital watches, Śyāmasundara dāsa gave Prabhupāda one, and it was considered a fancy item. Actually the watch never worked. Prabhupāda carried it for a while in one of his cases and finally left it somewhere. His general system was to accept a gift, use it or at least carry it for some time, and then give it as a gift to one of his disciples. Even today, some fortunate disciples have in their possession various pieces of Śrīla Prabhupāda's jewelry or possessions. Sometimes Prabhupāda would give away the gifts so quickly that the donor became a little disappointed.

Bhūrijana dāsa, for example, gave Prabhupāda a heavy gold-plated I.D. bracelet when Prabhupāda visited Hong Kong. Not long after, Prabhupāda gave the bracelet to another disciple, Bhagavān Goswami, and Bhūrijana was at first disappointed. Finally he came to see it as another form of Prabhupāda's mercy on all of the devotees. Therefore, for one who did not understand Prabhupāda's renounced mood and his loving interactions with his disciples, the sight of Prabhupāda wearing several rings or gold ornaments was sometimes misunderstood. Although Prabhupāda was aware of the risk of this misunderstanding, for the most part he nevertheless accepted the various gifts because of the importance of accepting offerings as Kṛṣṇa's representative and then using them in Kṛṣṇa's service.

In a famous taped discussion in Philadelphia, a lady reporter challenged Prabhupāda about his being picked up at the airport in a modern, opulent automobile. Prabhupāda reprimanded her, explaining that according to the scriptures, as Kṛṣṇa's representative he should be treated as good as God. Therefore, the car used at the airport was not sufficient; it should have been a gold car. In this way, Prabhupāda teased the nondevotees with their own misconceptions.

Of course, it is impossible to escape the envious remarks of people who have no appreciation for the pure devotee. Prabhupāda did his best not to give them anything to criticize, but still they criticized. When in Paris, Prabhupāda lectured as usual from the *vyāsāsana* and radical students in the audience at La Salle Playel yelled at him, Prabhupāda decided that he would not sit on such *vyāsāsanas* in public, especially before audiences known to be Communist or radical. Nevertheless, the Vedic tradition requires that the guru be worshiped and held in high esteem. Just to suit the mentality of the rebels, Prabhupāda couldn't always "come down" to appease their envious satisfaction.

The incident where Prabhupāda compared left-handed writing to very unusual phenomena brings to mind the fact that Prabhupāda encountered much behavior in the West, even in the acts of his disciples, that was unusual and bizarre by his standards. The unclean habits of the *mlecchas* were always a source of amazement and transcendental disgust for Prabhupāda. He remarked how in India, even the poor man bathes at least once a day, if only from an open pump, and a civilized man bathes three times a day. Prabhupāda saw that in America bathing was a difficult job. When he first moved onto the Lower East Side, he saw that some of his students who lived in outside apartments had no bathing facilities of their own and used to visit friends, or would even visit Prabhupāda, just to get the use of a bath. As for eating, Prabhupāda often commented on the disgusting habit of Westerners, who eat a piece of meat that is "three hundred years old" and prepare it by boiling it in hot water and then throwing some salt on top. And when they eat, they do not wash their hands either before or after the meal, but simply wipe their hands on their pants. Prabhupāda attempted to reform all of these unclean habits in the persons who became his disciples. At least on one occasion, however, Prabhupāda said it was really hopeless for the Western devotees to fully come up to the brahminical standards since they were so long accustomed to their dirty habits. Prabhupāda cautioned his disciples, therefore, not to be proud of their so-called Western achievements as part of their upbringing in Western society.

The civilization where superhighways are as smooth as velvet, where instant communications are available over vast distances, and where there is so much money that they can throw it away was ultimately not something to be proud of. Rather, it was something to become detached from in favor of Vedic society. Fortunately, we have the perfect example of Śrīla Prabhupāda, who proved that one can certainly live in Western climates and in modern situations without having to abandon the essentials of Kṛṣṇa conscious brahminical life. He engaged all—those with the harmless oddities like left-handedness or the inability to perfectly pronounce Sanskrit, as well as those with heavier "oddities," such as the tendency toward change and quarrel—in Kṛṣṇa's service, and even celebrated the activities of his "dancing white elephants" before the native-born Hindus of India.

31. Letter to Gurudāsa, November 18, 1976; letter to Gurudāsa, August 21, 1975; letter to Jayatīrtha dāsa, January 13, 1976; letter to Nalinīkaṇṭa dāsa, November 21, 1975; letter to Pṛthu Putra Mahārāja, January 24, 1976; letter to Gauragovinda Swami, September 21, 1975; letter to Aditya-devī dāsī, February 4, 1976; letter to Haṁsadūta dāsa, July 29, 1975; letter to Rūpānuga dāsa, February 21, 1976. In this case, Rūpānuga was informing Prabhupāda of a devotee in the temple who had inherited $19,000, which he loaned to the temple. The arrangement was that the loan should be paid back because the man planned to take *sannyāsa* in five to ten years and wanted to keep aside some money for his wife's maintenance. Letter to Puṣṭa Kṛṣṇa dāsa, October 29, 1976.

32. Lecture of August 5, 1972, San Diego. In my own reading of Śrīla Prabhupāda's books, I don't recall such a detailed description of a thief who wanted to steal Kṛṣṇa's jewels in the forest. There are many, many literatures and sources from which we can obtain different incidents of *kṛṣṇa-līlā,* but for Prabhupāda's followers, the most authorized and relishable source is Śrīla Prabhupāda himself, especially his books, but also his lectures and speaking. A true follower of Prabhupāda does not like to hear *kṛṣṇa-līlā* from other sources. Therefore, I consider it very special to transcribe and print a story like this, told directly by Śrīla Prabhupāda, about Kṛṣṇa and a thief in Vṛndāvana.

33. Lecture in Vṛndāvana, December 10, 1975; story remembered by SDG. The story about the Akhbar and his minister has always been, for me, one of the heaviest stories I've heard from Śrīla Prabhupāda. Each time I hear it attentively, I become stunned. Only if we serve Kṛṣṇa and Śrīla Prabhupāda with all our body, mind, and words can we escape a last-minute reversion to material attachment. As we quoted Śrīla Prabhupāda earlier in this volume, unless we

are *madana-mohana*, or attracted to Kṛṣṇa (the attractor of Cupid), we will be *madana-dahana*, or in Cupid's fire, attracted to the young girl.

34. SDG.

35. Kuṇḍalī dāsa, interview; Dīnanātha dāsa, interview; Raghunātha dāsa, interview. Kuṇḍalī's reminiscence about Viśāla dāsa is perhaps a first of its kind in *Prabhupāda Nectar*. It is a memoir not of a devotee in his direct relationship with Prabhupāda, but of a devotee appreciating another devotee's relationship with Prabhupāda. It would be nice if more devotees came forward with such reminiscences to help us expand the genuine, essential stories for *Prabhupāda Nectar*. This is also in the *paramparā* tradition, just as in the *Caitanya-caritāmṛta* devotees give their reminiscences of other devotees in relation to Lord Caitanya. Kṛṣṇadāsa Kavirāja, for example, tells of the special relationship Raghunātha dāsa Gosvāmī had with Svarūpa Dāmodara and of how Lord Caitanya reciprocated with Raghunātha through Svarūpa Dāmodara. Some devotees are reticent to speak of their relationship with Prabhupāda, yet other devotees will be more willing to recall the memories and even to sometimes better appreciate Prabhupāda's features of mercy as displayed toward all his disciples.

36. Mūrti dāsa, interview; Śatarūpā-devī dāsī, interview. Sometimes devotees tend to be envious of other devotees' relationships with Śrīla Prabhupāda. Reading this memoir by Mūrti, however, makes us aware that any relationship with Prabhupāda sincerely felt with dedication is the topmost. As Mūrti describes his distant, formal relationship with Prabhupāda, it actually appears to be superior to one with more physical intimacy where sometimes reverence is abandoned. Yet when we read an intimate memoir by a servant like Śrutakīrti, we will feel that we are certainly

getting wonderfully close to Śrīla Prabhupāda. Therefore, all the varieties of relationships, as long as they are founded on service to Śrīla Prabhupāda, are equally important and pure, and hearing about them can increase our devotion to guru and Kṛṣṇa.

We see in the case of Śatarūpā, the world-famous fashion model who became a disciple of Prabhupāda, that Prabhupāda gave her the same Kṛṣṇa conscious program he gave everyone else: "Chant Hare Kṛṣṇa." In her case, it was what she was waiting for, and she required no special treatment. Śrīla Prabhupāda was always sensitive, however, and could accommodate guests with exaggerated conceptions of themselves due to some fame or high standing in the world. If one actually wanted to become a devotee, Prabhupāda's advice was to become humble, to serve like the other devotees according to one's capacity, and to "chant Hare Kṛṣṇa."

37. Śrutakīrti dāsa, interview. As we read the anecdote of the disciple who refused to "cut a joke" with the stewardess despite Prabhupāda's order, we become disappointed in that disciple. However, in a larger sense, each of us is sometimes tested whether we have enough conviction to carry out sometimes "far-out" instructions from Prabhupāda. In the early days of ISKCON at 26 Second Avenue, Prabhupāda was once giving beadbags to the devotees in his room. He explained that one should keep the beads in the beadbag or wear them around the neck. In either case, one could walk down the street and chant Hare Kṛṣṇa—"If you are not ashamed." With this remark, Prabhupāda showed that he was aware that Westerners taking to Kṛṣṇa consciousness had to muster up their courage to appear in public as devotees or to act on the devotional platform in the face of different resistance in the material world. Prabhupāda writes in the *Śrīmad-Bhāgavatam* (3.24.13), "The disciple should accept the words of his spiritual master without hesitation. Whatever the

father or the spiritual master orders should be taken without argument: 'Yes.' There should be no instance in which the disciple says, 'This is incorrect. I cannot carry it out.' When he says that, he is fallen." So what if a stewardess laughs at us or is displeased with us? So what if the whole material world does not like the fact that we have become devotees of Kṛṣṇa? The important thing is not what others may think of us, but that we please Śrīla Prabhupāda and that we never refuse to carry out his order.

38. Śrutakīrti dāsa, interview.

39. Mukunda Goswami, interview; Nandarāṇī-devī dāsī, interview; Mañjvalī-devī dāsī, interview; Pañcadraviḍa Swami, interview; Śrutakīrti dāsa, interview; Citralekhā-devī dāsī, interview.

40. Umāpati dāsa, interview; Raṇacora dāsa, interview; Jagaddhātrī-devī dāsī, interview. The incident over thirty-five cents gives us another indication of how Prabhupāda's movement started from ground zero. In this connection, Professor Diana Eck made an interesting remark at a meeting at Harvard University. After seeing the movie *Your Ever Well-Wisher* and talking with some of the devotees, she asked how the Kṛṣṇa consciousness movement was able to rise from such a state of material poverty to considerable worldwide wealth. She said that in the beginning, from what she had heard, it seemed Prabhupāda's disciples didn't have more than the forty rupees Prabhupāda brought to America when he first came from India. Here we see that a sincere disciple like Umāpati, although willing to give what he had, lacked even thirty-five cents. This picture of the early devotees, who were materially impoverished and spiritually ignorant, yet so willing and submissive, gives us an indication of what Prabhupāda meant when he said, "Those were happy days."

41. Letter to Jayapatāka Swami, December 4, 1976; letter to Gopāla Kṛṣṇa Swami, July 14, 1976; letter to Nitāi dāsa, July 14, 1976; letter to Kṛṣṇāṅgī-devī dāsī, February 15, 1976; letter to SDG, June 4, 1975. We have the personal example of Śrīla Prabhupāda himself, the supreme authority in ISKCON, as one who did not go outside his movement for spiritual nourishment. Śrīla Prabhupāda preferred to read his own books and to reside in the temples of the International Society for Krishna Consciousness. In a country with an outside group of devotees opposed to ISKCON, as in Hawaii, Prabhupāda always chose to stay in his own temple, ISKCON. Even if there were discrepancies in the standards, by staying in the temple he could make a strong move to correct them. Although for preaching purposes Prabhupāda sometimes stayed outside the temple, he was not in his own place, his own home, unless he was in one of his Kṛṣṇa conscious temples. This attitude of Prabhupāda's of feeling at home in the temple is something he wanted all his followers to accept. He saw the ISKCON temple as a place where there was nice, sufficient food, the best philosophy, the best association, family life if one desired, and most important of all, the fullest opportunity for eternal life, to return home, back to Godhead. Therefore when asked in an assembly how one could be free from karma and sins, Prabhupāda replied, "Come live with us." And in a letter to Rūpānuga, dated April 28, 1974, he wrote, "We shall be very careful about them and not mix with them. This is my instruction to you all. They cannot help us in our movement, but they are very competent to harm our natural progress. So we must be very careful about them."

42. Lecture, May 1976, Los Angeles; lecture, December 26, 1972, Bombay; lecture, May 12, 1976; letter to SDG, August 4, 1971; morning walk, July 12, 1976.

43. SDG.

44. Kṛṣṇa Gopāla dāsa, interview; Sunītā-devī dāsī, interview.

45. Rādhā-vallabha, interview; Sangītā-devī dāsī, interview.

46. Pālikā-devī dāsī, interview; Mādrī-devī dāsī, interview; Anirdeśavapur dāsa, interview.

47. Praghoṣa dāsa, interview. According to Praghoṣa, he met Prabhupāda a few days later when Prabhupāda went to the New York temple. There Praghoṣa entered a room full of devotees where Prabhupāda was giving *darśana,* and when Prabhupāda saw him, he said, "Ah," and recognized him from their previous meeting. After that *darśana,* Rāmeśvara Swami told Praghoṣa, "I saw the way Prabhupāda took notice when you came into the room. He was remembering you from Washington. He was remembering you as the devotee who was so happy to go out and distribute his books."

48. Morning walk, March 25, 1976, New Delhi; Dhanañjaya dāsa, interview; Rāmeśvara Swami, interview; Śivānanda dāsa, interview; Anaṅga-devī dāsī, interview; Śrīdhara Swami, interview; Prabhaviṣṇu Swami, interview; Rūpa-vilāsa dāsa and Candrikā-devī dāsī, interview; Prabhaviṣṇu Swami, interview.

49. Rāmeśvara Swami, interview; Śrutakīrti dāsa, interview; Śilāvatī-devī dāsī, interview.

50. Jananivāsa dāsa, interview; Ānakadundubhi dāsa, interview; Śatadhanya Swami, interview.

VOLUME FIVE NOTES

1. Girirāja Swami, Mukunda Goswami, Prabhupāda dāsa, Tejās dāsa, interviews.

2. Indradyumna Swami, interview. I had a similar experience with Prabhupāda while serving as his secretary. In 1973, Prabhupāda wanted to travel from Calcutta to London. I met with some delays and difficulties in getting the passports, so at the airport, I asked him if going to the spiritual world means arranging for passports and tickets. He said no, you simply go there immediately. Although travel in the material world may be difficult, going back to Godhead is simple and swift.

The first incident shows how Prabhupāda could see Kṛṣṇa everywhere. In the Tenth Chapter of the *Bhagavad-gītā*, Kṛṣṇa shows how anything great comes from Him, so of humorists, Kṛṣṇa is Charlie Chaplin.

Although we cannot imitate Prabhupāda, we may still appreciate his *līlā*. He was a pure devotee, and it is wonderful and endearing that he could drink a *7-UP* or laugh at a Charlie Chaplin movie. Although these activities may appear ordinary, Prabhupāda was always extraordinary.

3. Lecture in Vṛndāvana, September 30, 1976; lecture in Tehran, August 10, 1976; morning walk in London, September 3, 1973. This story reminds us that Prabhupāda has described the meat-eaters as being "envious" of the animals. Sometimes we are puzzled to think why Prabhupāda considered human beings to be envious of animals. Certainly they have no pity for the animals since they kill them, but *envious?*

From a linguistic point of view, some interesting research has been done on this matter by Draviḍa dāsa. He said that according to old usage, the word *envious* once meant "malicious." This meaning was common usage during the time Prabhupāda learned English. This usage is still listed in the dictionary, although it is not so much current. Even in the current usage, however, we see that the meat-eater does not allow the innocent animal to live in peace. He is therefore envious of the fact that the animals exist within God's graces, not disobeying the laws of nature, and he kills them out of malice or envy.

4. Devotees will probably always continue to inquire how they may increase or improve the performance of Deity worship and their other service activities. Prabhupāda gives some important guidelines here when he writes, "Don't try to introduce something new. The most important thing is the love and devotion." Not simply by adding more mantras and more paraphernalia do we increase the standard of devotion. At the same time, Prabhupāda gradually introduced more of the temple activities as time went by and he saw that the devotees were able to do it. As far as possible, we should try to gather Prabhupāda's authoritative instructions and follow them, such as this valuable collection of advice about *tulasī* worship.

Vidyā-devī dāsi was impelled by her devotion to *tulasī* to ask Prabhupāda many questions about her worship, but Prabhupāda, by his short replies, reminds us that even on a practical basis, *tulasī* is kept alive and well by the love and devotion of her worshipers. That is the main ingredient.

5. Nayanābhirāma dāsa, interview.

6. Nava-yogendra Swami, interview; Mūrti dāsa, interview; Girirāja Swami, interview; Śatadhanya dāsa, interview; Tamāla Kṛṣṇa Goswami, journal.

7. Dāmodara dāsa, interview; lecture in Stockholm, September 7, 1973. Śrīla Prabhupāda would use this story to illustrate the foolishness of accepting some points of the

Bhagavad-gītā while rejecting others. If you reject any part of the *Bhagavad-gītā,* then the whole thing becomes invalid. The *Gītā* is absolute and every part of it is true.

8. Letter to Bahulāśva dāsa, December 27, 1972; letter to Ravīndra-svarūpa dāsa, January 5, 1973; letter to Vāmanadeva dāsa, November 12, 1970; room conversation in Tehran, August 10, 1976; Gokularañjana dāsa, interview; Girirāja Swami, interview.

9. Sureśvara dāsa, interview; Hṛdayānanda Goswami, interview; Kalakanṭha dāsa, interview; Girirāja Swami, letter to SDG. The "Realizations" entries in *Prabhupāda Nectar* have met with good response from our readers. We like to hear about Prabhupāda from the different angles of vision of his many disciples. Another way to appreciate "Realizations" is to understand that no one devotee can see the total extent of Prabhupāda in all his moods and with all his instructions. It takes the combined realizations of all the devotees to approach the "complete Prabhupāda"—and even then we can know only a little bit. When an individual devotee tells his realization, we can understand that he is telling as much about himself as he is about Prabhupāda. That is not a reason to reject such realizations. The seed of devotional service planted within the heart of an individual disciple is also an expanded form of Prabhupāda, and all Prabhupādānugas like to hear expressions of genuine love and realization from those who carry Prabhupāda in their hearts. A similar example is given in *Caitanya-caritāmṛta.* Lord Caitanya became ecstatic on seeing a *brāhmaṇa* who showed symptoms of love of God. He surmised that this *brāhmaṇa* must have contacted Mādhavendra Purī in order to show such symptoms of love of God. Therefore, Lord Caitanya loved the associate of the great Mādhavendra Purī.

Similarly, we want to hear from and honor every genuine devotee of Prabhupāda, and we want to experience Prabhupāda coming through such living representatives.

10. Rājendranātha dāsa, interview; Rukmiṇī-devī dāsī, interview; Guru Gaurāṅga dāsa, interview.

11. Girirāja Swami, interview; Cāru dāsa, interview; Dayānanda dāsa, interview.

12. SDG.

13. Letter to Toṣaṇa Kṛṣṇa dāsa, February 17, 1969; Madhusūdana dāsa, interview; Girirāja Swami, interview; Viśākhā-devī dāsī, interview; Satyabhāmā-devī dāsī, interview.

14. Yamunā-devī dāsī, interview. Everything Prabhupāda did was for serving Kṛṣṇa. This shows Prabhupāda as a wonderful teacher who would actually take the pose of Rādhārāṇī without any tinge of *sahajiyā* imitation just to show his disciple how Rādhārāṇī looked, using his own transcendental form to strike the pose, and then speaking some realized appreciation of Śrīmatī Rādhārāṇī.

There are other examples of how Prabhupāda would use his transcendental form to strike different poses to instruct his disciples. An artist-devotee reports that Prabhupāda once put on an extra piece of cloth to demonstrate for the artist how the folds in Kṛṣṇa's *dhotī* looked. He then struck the *tribhaṅga* pose and showed how Kṛṣṇa plays His flute. Many devotees have seen Prabhupāda make different expressions while lecturing. For example, he might widen his eyes to look like Nṛsiṁhadeva. He would also use many gestures and *mudrās*.

Prabhupāda was also able to speak in an intimate way about Kṛṣṇa and His eternal associates, as shown in this memoir. It is interesting to note that Prabhupāda usually made very intimate disclosures only to answer practical questions on devotional service. He posed as Rādhārāṇī to show Yamunā how the Deity should be sculpted, and he posed as Kṛṣṇa to show the artist how to paint Him. It was not for some idle reason or to simulate *rasas* in an artificial way. Prabhupāda has said that when one needs to know something intimate about Kṛṣṇa, then only will Kṛṣṇa reveal that to the person. Similarly, if a devotee qualifies himself through service, then Prabhupāda will reveal to him in the course of his work more intimate pastimes.

15. Śacīnandana dāsa, interview; Śravaṇānanda dāsa, interview.

16. Lecture in Los Angeles, June 27, 1972; Cintāmaṇi-devī dāsī, interview.

17. Lecture in Los Angeles, December 16, 1968.

18. SDG, interview; Bahūdak dāsa, interview; Trivikrama Swami, interview.

19. Tamāla Kṛṣṇa Goswami, interview. Often it was to an Indian audience that Prabhupāda would make some transcendental boast about possessions like his Bank of America credit card or his "green card." One reason for this is that his countrymen were clamoring for these objects, but when they attain them, they misuse them. Therefore, Prabhupāda showed them that as he was a Vaiṣṇava, Kṛṣṇa was blessing him with these much desired items, but that he was not misusing them. Rather, he used them in Kṛṣṇa's service. In this way, even a Bank of America card, which in the hands of most is a symbol of material greed, can be used as an instrument to gain credit for Kṛṣṇa. Other "boastful" items included the following:

Prabhupāda would often quote the amount of money that was being spent each month by the individual temples. He would sometimes total up the monthly or daily cost of maintaining all of his temples in the world. Sometimes Prabhupāda's Godbrothers misunderstood and thought that Prabhupāda was affected by opulence, but the fact is that he always remained humble. He actually purified these different material facilities by using them in a pure way.

20. Bharadvāja dāsa, interview; Sthita-devī dāsī, interview; Prabhaviṣṇu Swami; interview.

21. Lecture in Los Angeles; morning walk in Los Angeles, April 24, 1973.

22. Room conversation in London, August 26, 1973; Hari Śauri dāsa, diary; Jagadīśa Goswami, interview; Śravaṇānanda dāsa, interview; letter to Balavanta dāsa, July 8, 1976; Puṣkara dāsa, interview; Hari Śauri dāsa, diary; Raṇadīra dāsa, interview.

23. Jayapatāka Swami, interview.

24. Yogeśvara dāsa, interview; Ātreya Ṛṣi dāsa, interview; Navīna Kṛṣṇa dāsa, interview.

25. Room conversation in Gorakhpur, February 14, 1971.

26. Letter to Haṁsadūta dāsa and Himavatī-devī dāsī, March 3, 1968; letter to Prajāpati dāsa, June 16, 1976; lecture in Hawaii, June 8, 1975.

27. Girirāja Swami, interview; Satya-nārāyaṇa dāsa, interview; Viśvaretā dāsa, interview.

28. Paramānanda dāsa, interview. Meditations about Prabhupāda in particular places are sweet, such as his visits over the years to New Vrindaban.

Devotees of different countries have asked that special sections be written about Prabhupāda that they might include in their one-volume biography describing Prabhupāda's *līlā* in their country. It would be a worthwhile endeavor for devotees of particular *yātrās* to research and interview devotees in their area to make such portraits. The obvious materials to collect are the recorded lectures and morning walks Prabhupāda gave while visiting that place, as well as any references he might make to that place in his books. Also, an enterprising devotee could try to find the guests that Prabhupāda met while visiting the temples, some of whom may still be available for interviews. And of course, the devotees who had the good fortune of seeing Prabhupāda and being with him should be interviewed. In gathering such materials, interesting themes and patterns will emerge that may not be obvious until one actually begins to look closely at Prabhupāda's visits to a particular *deśa.*

Different areas of the world brought out different aspects of Prabhupāda's rich transcendental personality. Naturally, he spoke about cow protection and simple living when he was at New Vrindaban, and naturally he spoke about children's education when visiting Dallas *gurukula.* One particular place which we have not covered in describing Prabhupāda's pastimes is Hyderabad, which is an important *yātrā* in Prabhupāda's activities. Prabhupāda developed an important city temple there, and he also began a farm development.

We hope that devotees in different regions will uncover some of the hidden pastimes of Śrīla Prabhupāda. We admit that our small staff is unable to travel to many places and interview as many people as we would like, and we invite others to help us gather the nectar.

29. Trivikrama Swami, interview; Sarveśvarī-devī dāsī, interview; Nandarāṇī-devī dāsī, interview; Jagattāriṇī-devī dāsī, interview; Hari-vilāsa dāsa, interview. The first three drops in this section show Prabhupāda as the kindly spiritual father making sure that his children get enough to eat and drink. This is Prabhupāda in the spirit of "Take more, take more," which he introduced at the storefront at 26 Second Avenue. The devotees in these stories—Trivikrama Swami, Sarveśvarī-devī dāsī, and Nandarāṇī-devī dāsī—seemed prepared to be as renounced as possible, to take a minimum number of *capātīs,* to go without milk if necessary, and to give the children whatever Prabhupāda ordered. The disciples were acting in the spirit of the student who does not ask for more food but waits for the spiritual master's order. When ordered in this way by Prabhupāda to take care of themselves and take sufficient *prasādam*, the devotees responded with an increased love for Śrīla Prabhupāda that went beyond the bounds of their pleasure at being able to eat more. It was not the granting of permission to eat, but the personal attention to their needs that made them remember these instructions as little drops of nectar.

30. Tamāla Kṛṣṇa Goswami, journal; lecture in Los Angeles, May 27, 1972. Prabhupāda criticized the fact that Westerners create magazines out of all kinds of nonsense philosophies, but the one magazine that Prabhupāda advocated was *Back to Godhead.* In New Vrindaban in 1969, Śrīla Prabhupāda said, "Produce a page only, *Back to Godhead*! That will bring revolution to the human society about understanding spiritual life. Don't produce this nonsense literature!" (*The Back to Godhead Handbook,* Foreword)

31. Hari Śauri dāsa, diary; letter to Jayapatāka dāsa, April 30, 1970; lecture, undated; Toṣaṇa Kṛṣṇa dāsa, interview; letter to Hlādinī-devī dāsī, February 19, 1970;

Hari Śauri dāsa, diary; letter to Abhirāma dāsa, August 31, 1971.

32. Yamunā-devī dāsī, interview; Tamāla Kṛṣṇa Goswami, diary; Jayapatāka Swami, interview.

33. Vipramukhya Swami, interview.

34. Tamāla Kṛṣṇa Goswami, diary; lecture in New York, September 1966; lecture in Māyāpur, October 6, 1972.

35. Bhaumadeva dāsa, interview; letter to Jadurāṇī-devī dāsī, February 15, 1968; letter to Jagadiśa Mahārāja, November 2, 1974; letter to Puru dāsa, April 6, 1976; letter to Vedavyāsa dāsa, August 4, 1975.

36. Toṣaṇa Kṛṣṇa dāsa, interview; Garuḍa dāsa, interview; Aniruddha dāsa, interview.

37. Guru Gaurāṅga dāsa, interview. This visit to the World Health Organization is similar to the incident when Prabhupāda went to the love-in on the Lower East Side in 1967. In both cases, Prabhupāda finally went ahead and attended the meeting, even though it was controversial. These are examples of Prabhupāda's boldness and his conviction that the Kṛṣṇa conscious message would purify any situation, even if apparently controversial or entangling. On the other hand, we can learn from this and other incidents that Prabhupāda was concerned not to attend programs where we might be indiscriminately lumped in. He approved when Brahmānanda refused to give an interview about Prabhupāda to a reporter who wanted to write about the various gurus. Even when Prabhupāda would attend a controversial program, he would not mix the Kṛṣṇa conscious philosophy along with the philosophy of his sponsors. Rather, he would use the spot for broadcasting pure Kṛṣṇa consciousness. Thus, he would dis-

tinguish himself from the nonsense perpetrated by a particular program, and yet take advantage of the opportunity to glorify Kṛṣṇa. Usually, whoever hosted Śrīla Prabhupāda was quite pleased and never thought that he had exploited them, since he was always straightforward about his intentions to broadcast Kṛṣṇa consciousness.

38. Hṛdayānanda Goswami, interview; Jagattāriṇī-devī dāsī, interview; Śuka Śravaṇa dāsa, interview.

39. Garuḍa dāsa, interview; Mādrī-devī dāsī, interview. Girirāja Swami, interview. Those of us who were guilty of falling asleep during Prabhupāda's classes will especially regret the habit now that Prabhupāda is no longer present. New devotees to the Kṛṣṇa consciousness movement who did not have the opportunity to hear from Prabhupāda and yet who hear so many stories of Prabhupāda's beauty and greatness may wonder how Prabhupāda's disciples could actually fall asleep in front of His Divine Grace. The problem persists: inattention during *japa*, while hearing class, or while reading Prabhupāda's books. Prabhupāda has explained the root cause, as described in the memoir by Girirāja Swami, "They will only stay awake when they have the conviction that their work in Kṛṣṇa consciousness is so important that they have no time to sleep." It is a matter of consciousness.

40. Lecture in Māyāpur, January 26, 1974. The *Bhagavad-gītā* describes charity in the different modes of nature. Charity that is given out of duty at the proper time and place and without desiring a reward is charity in the mode of goodness. Charity that is given begrudgingly by someone who is attached to fruitive results is charity in the mode of passion, and charity that is performed at the wrong place and time and that is given to the wrong person without proper respect is charity in the mode of ignorance. In his purports, Prabhu-

pāda says that charity given to a person engaged in spiritual activities for the purpose of spiritual perfection is especially recommended.

41. Letter to Lakṣmīmaṇi-devī dāsī, May 1, 1971; letter to Karandhara dāsa, January 29, 1976; letter to Jayapatāka Swami, December 26, 1971; letter to Tamāla Kṛṣṇa Goswami, June 21, 1970; letter to Rūpānuga dāsa, February 14, 1973.

42. Pratyatoṣa dāsa, interview; Cāru dāsa, interview; Tamāla Kṛṣṇa Goswami, interview.

43. Yamunā-devī dāsī, interview; Hari-vilāsa dāsa, interview; Paṅkajanābha dāsa, interview; Viśvaretā dāsa, interview.

44. Purīdāsa dāsa, interview; Madana-mohana-mohinī-devī dāsī, interview.

45. Tamāla Kṛṣṇa Goswami, diary; room conversation, Tehran, August 10, 1976.

46. Toṣaṇa Kṛṣṇa dāsa, interview; Nara-Nārāyaṇa dāsa, interview; Tejās dāsa, interview.

47. Tamāla Kṛṣṇa Goswami, diary; room conversation, Gorakhpur, 1971; Trivikrama Swami, interview; Raṇadīra dāsa, interview; Sura dāsa, interview; Toṣaṇa Kṛṣṇa dāsa, interview.

48. Śrīla Prabhupāda, diary.

49. Girirāja Swami, interview; Guru Gaurāṅga dāsa, interview; Śravaṇānanda dāsa, interview; Jayādvaita Swami, interview.

50. Letter to Bhakta Dan, December 1, 1973; letter to Śivānanda dāsa, August 24, 1968; letter to Kṛṣṇa dāsa, October 21, 1968.

Acknowledgments

I would like to thank the following disciples and friends who helped produce and print this book:

Baladeva Vidyābhūṣaṇa dāsa
Kaiśorī dāsī
Keśīhanta dāsa
Lallita-mañjarī dāsī
Lalitāmṛta dāsī
Madana-mohana dāsa
Mādhava dāsa
Prāṇadā dāsī

Special thanks to Abhaya dāsī, Lalita-mādhava dāsa, Gopī-mañjarī dāsī, Goloka dāsī and Praghoṣa dāsa for their kind donations to print this book.

His Divine Grace A. C. Bhaktivedanta Swami Prabhupāda lived in this world from 1896 to 1977. Born in Calcutta, India, he first met his spiritual master, Śrīla Bhaktisiddhānta Sarasvatī Gosvāmī, in 1922. At their first meeting he was asked to spread the Vedic knowledge all over the world, and during his many years as a married businessman, he often contemplated this order of his spiritual master. At the age of 63, he accepted the renounced order of life (*sannyāsa*) to help fulfill this mission. From his humble surroundings at the Rādhā-Dāmodara temple in Vṛndāvana, he began work on his life's masterpiece: a multivolume English translation of the eighteen-thousand-verse *Śrīmad-Bhāgavatam* complete with elaborate commentary.

In 1965, with 40 rupees in his pocket, he came by freighter from India to New York City. After almost a year of great difficulty and heroic perseverance, he established the International Society for Krishna Consciousness. In the twelve short years before he passed away, he had guided the Society and watched it grow to a worldwide society of more than one hundred *āśramas,* schools, temples, institutes, cultural centers, and farm communities.

In Śrīla Prabhupāda's own view, his most significant contribution is his books. Highly respected by scholars for their authority, depth, and clarity, they are used as textbooks in numerous college courses. His writings have been translated into over fifty languages. Despite his advanced age, Śrīla Prabhupāda circled the globe fourteen times on lecture tours that took him to six continents. Yet this vigorous schedule did not slow his prolific literary output. His writings constitute a veritable library of Vedic philosophy, religion, literature, and culture.

For more information about Śrīla Prabhupāda and his work, please visit www.harekrishna.com, or contact Bhaktivedanta Book Trust, P. O. Box 34074, Los Angeles, CA 90034, Phone: 1-310-837-5283, FAX: 1-310-837-1056.

Satsvarūpa dāsa Goswami is a Vaiṣṇava writer, poet, and artist. He was among the first young Americans to assist Śrīla Prabhupāda with his mission in the West and, as Śrīla Prabhupāda's intimate disciple, he served as personal secretary for many years. He is also the author of Śrīla Prabhupāda's authorized biography, *Śrīla Prabhupāda-līlāmṛta.* While traveling, lecturing on Kṛṣṇa consciousness, and instructing disciples worldwide, he has published many books including poems, memoirs, essays, novels, and studies based on the Vaiṣṇava scriptures. In recent years, his devotional life has evolved to include the creation of numerous paintings, drawings, and sculptures that lovingly capture and express the artist's absorption in the culture of Kṛṣṇa consciousness.

For more information about Satsvarūpa dāsa Goswami and his work, please visit Gītā-nagarī Press at www.gnpress.org or contact P. O. Box 445, La Crosse, Florida 32658, 1-877-295-8942.

Satsvarupa dasa Goswami is an American-born poet and artist. He [illegible] the [illegible] associated with [illegible] the [illegible] [illegible] of [illegible] [illegible] [illegible] for many years. He is also the authorized [illegible] biography [illegible]

While traveling [illegible] and [illegible] he has published many books including [illegible] essays, [illegible] and [illegible] based on [illegible] activities. In recent years, [illegible] has [illegible] includes the creation of [illegible] drawings and [illegible] that [illegible] capture and [illegible] as the [illegible] the [illegible] consciousness.

For more information about [illegible] and [illegible] his works, please [illegible] Press, [illegible] or contact [illegible] [illegible] Florida [illegible]

Other books by Satsvarūpa dāsa Goswami

Prabhupāda Meditations

Life with the Perfect Master
Prabhupāda Nectar
Calling Out to Śrīla Prabhupāda/Poems and Prayers
He Lives Forever
My Letters from Śrīla Prabhupāda (Volumes 1–3)
Prabhupāda Appreciation
Prabhupāda-līlā

Living with the Scriptures

Qualities of Śrī Kṛṣṇa
Saints and Sages of Ancient India
Cc. Āśraya
Living with the Scriptures
Niti-śāstra: Sayings of Cāṇakya
Spiritualized Dictionary
A Poor Man Read's the Bhāgavatam

Devotional Practices

Entering the Life of Prayer
Japa Reform Notebook
Vaiṣṇava Behavior/ 26 Qualities of a Devotee
Vaisnava Compassion

Devotional Practices (continued)

Begging for the Nectar of the Holy Name
Reading Reform
Truthfulness, The Last Leg of Religion

New Writings

Every Day, Just Write
When the Saints Come Marching In
Sanatorium (A Trilogy)

Devotional Writings

Shack Notes
Passing Places, Eternal Truths
Photo Preaching

Poetry

Can a White Man be a Haribol
From Matter to Spirit
Gentle Power
Given Time
Prose-poetry at Castlegregory, Ireland
Stowies
The Waves at Jagannātha Purī
The Worshipable Deity and Other Poems (1984)
Writing in Gratitude